DEMON DIARY

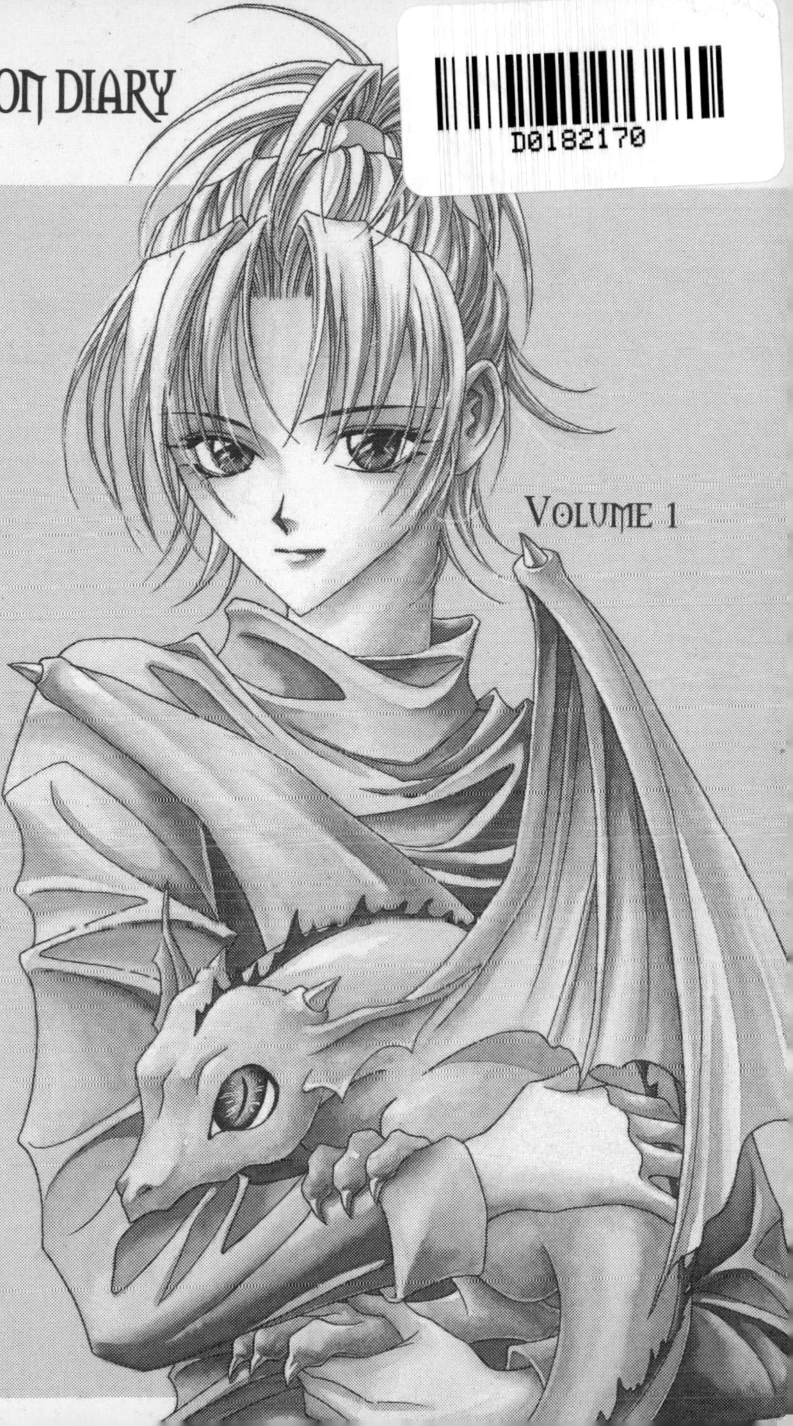

VOLUME 1

ALSO AVAILABLE FROM 🌀 TOKYOPOP®

MANGA

ANGELIC LAYER*
BABY BIRTH* (September 2003)
BATTLE ROYALE*
BRAIN POWERD* (June 2003)
BRIGADOON* (August 2003)
CARDCAPTOR SAKURA*
CARDCAPTOR SAKURA: MASTER OF THE CLOW*
CLAMP SCHOOL DETECTIVES*
CHOBITS*
CHRONICLES OF THE CURSED SWORD (July 2003)
CLOVER
CONFIDENTIAL CONFESSIONS* (July 2003)
CORRECTOR YUI
COWBOY BEBOP*
COWBOY BEBOP: SHOOTING STAR* (June 2003)
DEMON DIARY (May 2003)
DIGIMON
DRAGON HUNTER (June 2003)
DRAGON KNIGHTS*
DUKLYON: CLAMP SCHOOL DEFENDERS* (September 2003)
ERICA SAKURAZAWA* (May 2003)
ESCAFLOWNE* (July 2003)
FAKE*(May 2003)
FLCL* (September 2003)
FORBIDDEN DANCE* (August 2003)
GATE KEEPERS*
G-GUNDAM* (June 2003)
GRAVITATION* (June 2003)
GTO*
GUNDAM WING
GUNDAM WING: ENDLESS WALTZ*
GUNDAM: THE LAST OUTPOST*
HAPPY MANIA*
HARLEM BEAT
INITIAL D*
I.N.V.U.
ISLAND
JING: KING OF BANDITS* (June 2003)
JULINE
KARE KANO*
KINDAICHI CASE FILES* (June 2003)
KING OF HELL (June 2003)

KODOCHA*
LOVE HINA*
LUPIN III*
MAGIC KNIGHT RAYEARTH* (August 2003)
MAGIC KNIGHT RAYEARTH II* (COMING SOON)
MAN OF MANY FACES* (May 2003)
MARMALADE BOY*
MARS*
MIRACLE GIRLS
MIYUKI-CHAN IN WONDERLAND* (October 2003)
MONSTERS, INC.
NIEA_7* (August 2003)
PARADISE KISS*
PARASYTE
PEACH GIRL
PEACH GIRL: CHANGE OF HEART*
PET SHOP OF HORRORS* (June 2003)
PLANET LADDER
PLANETS* (October 2003)
PRIEST
RAGNAROK
RAVE MASTER*
REAL BOUT HIGH SCHOOL*
REALITY CHECK
REBIRTH
REBOUND*
SABER MARIONETTE J* (July 2003)
SAILOR MOON
SAINT TAIL
SAMURAI DEEPER KYO* (June 2003)
SCRYED*
SHAOLIN SISTERS*
SHIRAHIME-SYO* (December 2003)
THE SKULL MAN*
SORCERER HUNTERS
TOKYO MEW MEW*
UNDER THE GLASS MOON (June 2003)
VAMPIRE GAME* (June 2003)
WILD ACT* (July 2003)
WISH*
X-DAY* (August 2003)
ZODIAC P.I.* (July 2003)

CINE-MANGA™

AKIRA*
CARDCAPTORS
JIMMY NEUTRON (COMING SOON)
KIM POSSIBLE
LIZZIE McGUIRE
SPONGEBOB SQUAREPANTS (COMING SOON)
SPY KIDS 2

NOVELS

SAILOR MOON
KARMA CLUB (COMING SOON)

TOKYOPOP KIDS

STRAY SHEEP (September 2003)

ART BOOKS

CARDCAPTOR SAKURA*
MAGIC KNIGHT RAYEARTH*

ANIME GUIDES

GUNDAM TECHNICAL MANUALS
COWBOY BEBOP
SAILOR MOON SCOUT GUIDES

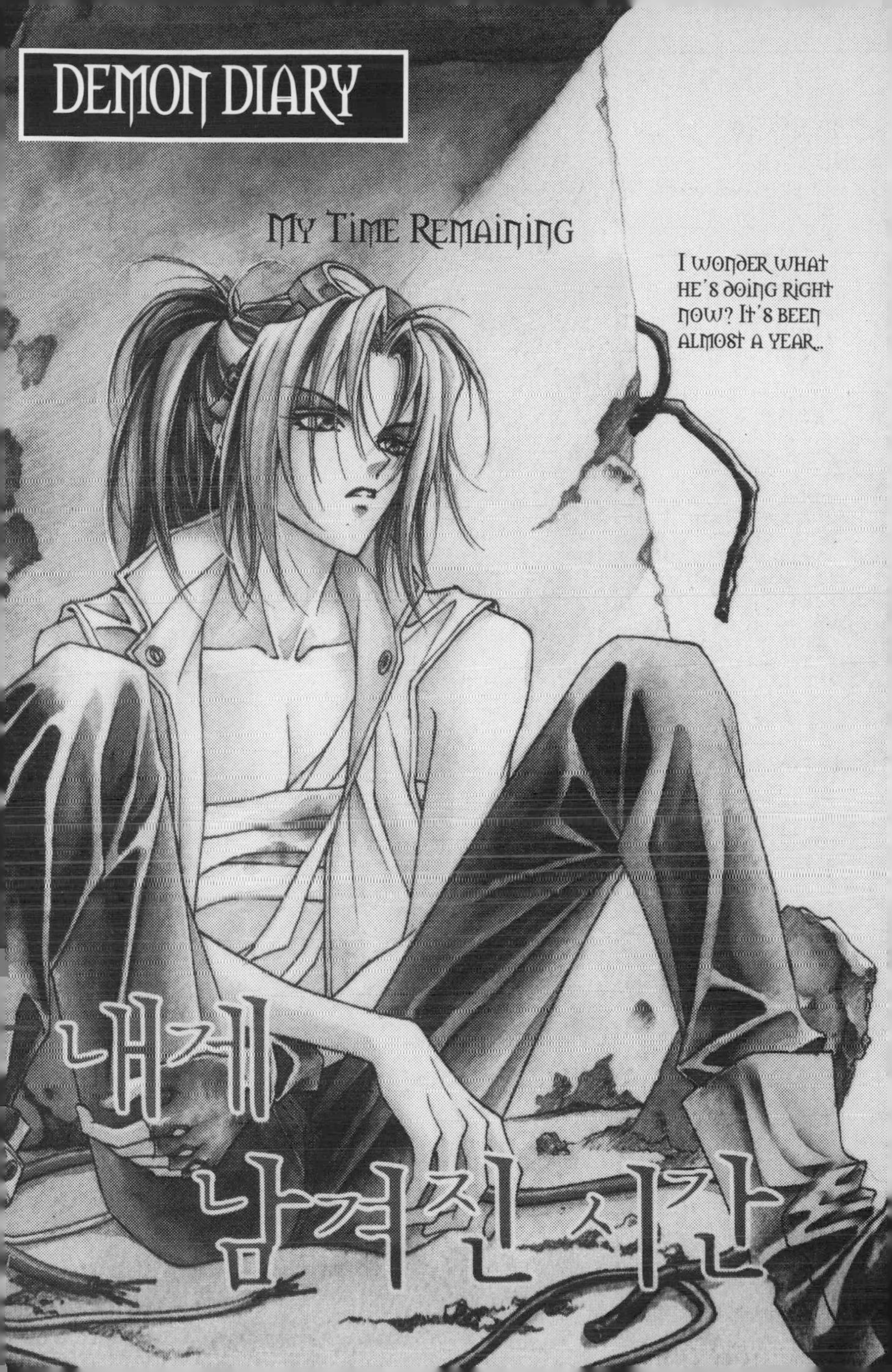
DEMON DIARY
My Time Remaining
I wonder what he's doing right now? It's been almost a year..
내게 남겨진 시간

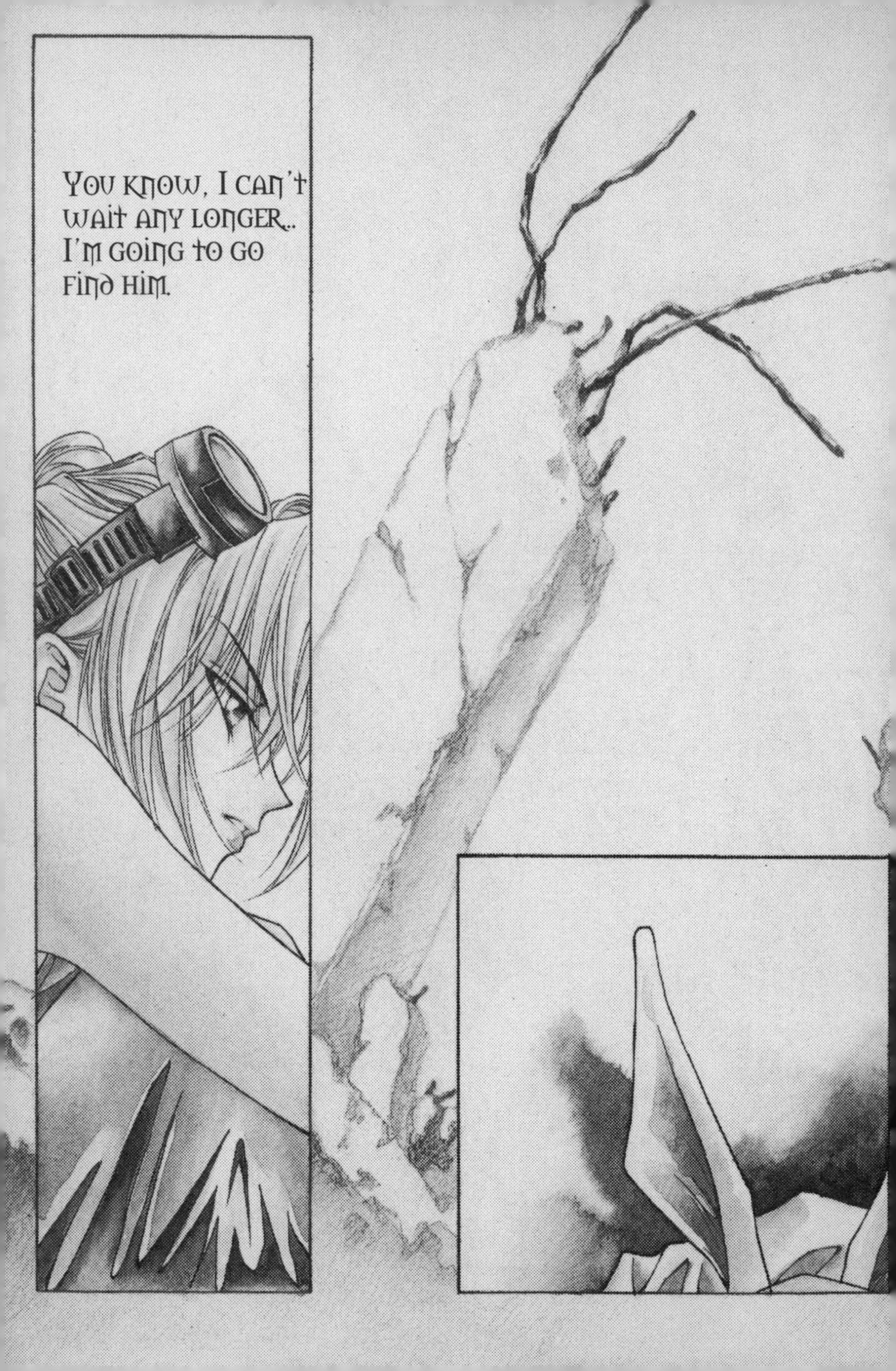
You know, I can't wait any longer.. I'm going to go find him.

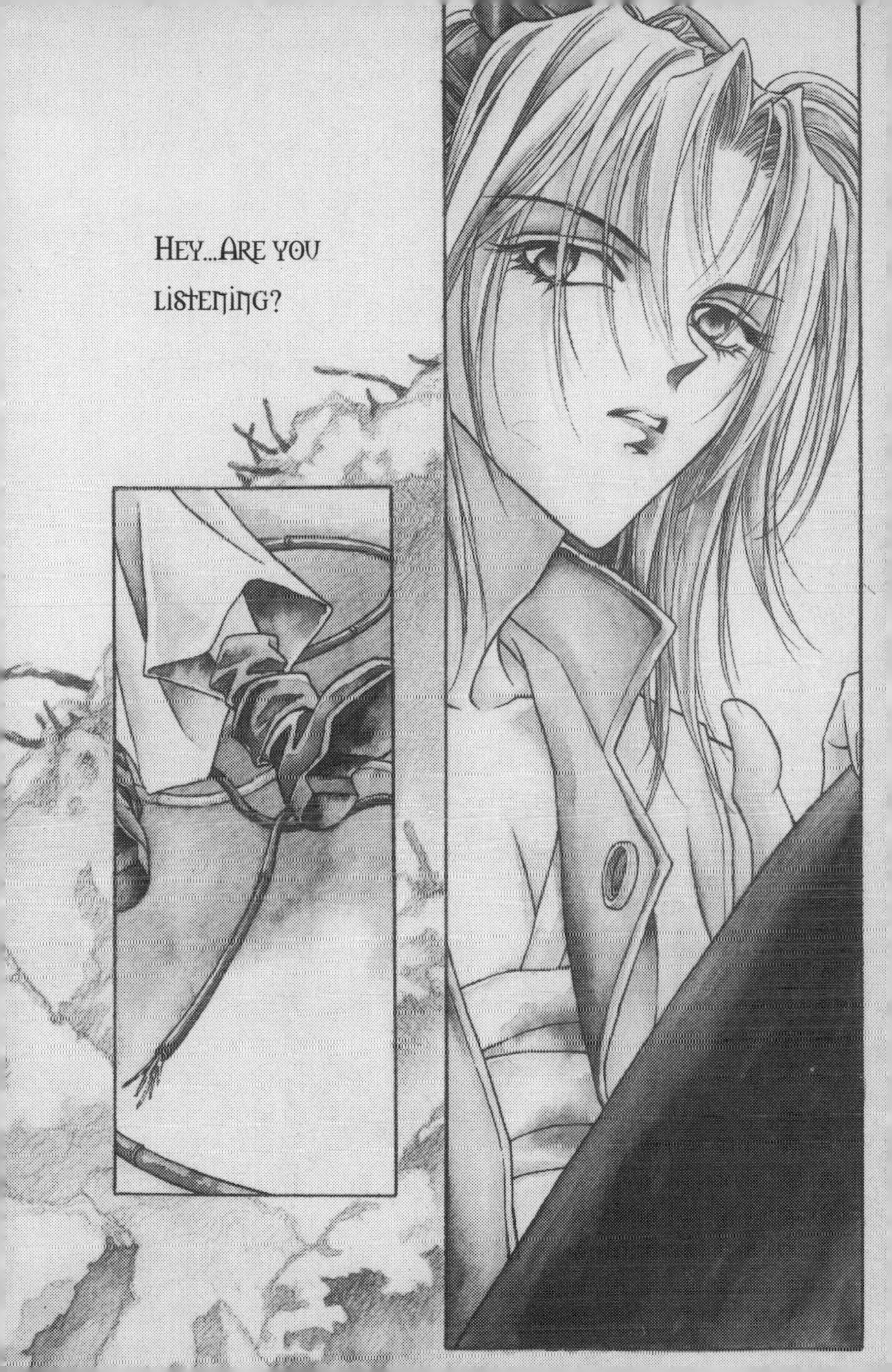
HEY...ARE YOU LISTENING?

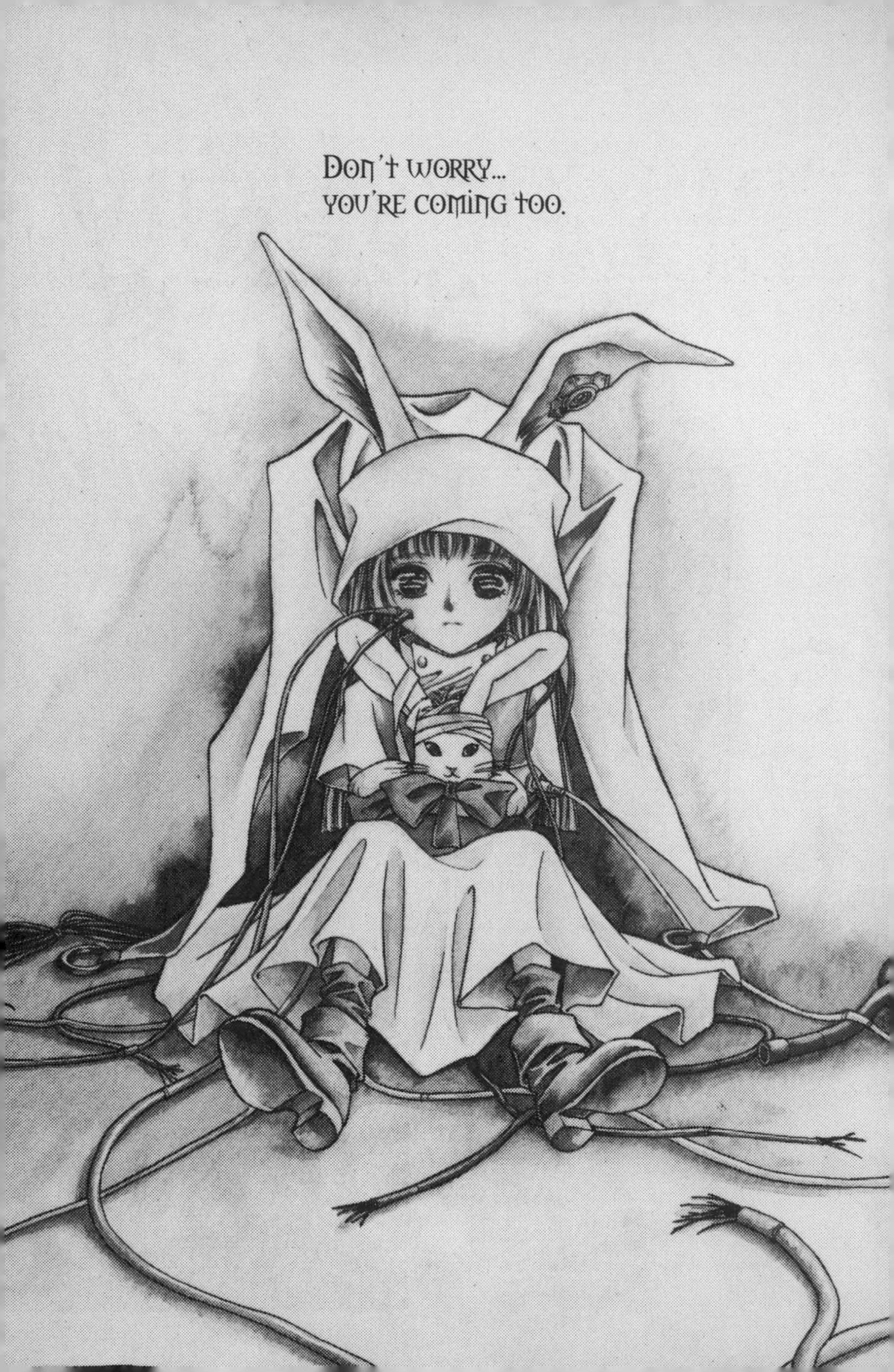
Don't worry...
you're coming too.

DEMON DIARY

Art by Kara
Story by Lee Chi Hyong

Volume 1

Los Angeles • Tokyo

Translator - Lauren Na
English Adaption - Kelly Sue DeConnick
Retouch and Lettering - Monalisa de Asis
Cover Layout - Aaron Suhr

Editors - Jake Forbes and Elizabeth Hurchalla
Managing Editor - Jill Freshney
Production Coordinator - Antonio DePietro
Production Manager - Jennifer Miller
Art Director - Matthew Alford
Editorial Director - Jeremy Ross
VP of Production & Manufacturing - Ron Klamert
President & C.O.O. - John Parker
Publisher & C.E.O. - Stuart Levy

Email: editor@TOKYOPOP.com
Come visit us online at www.TOKYOPOP.com

A **TOKYOPOP**® Manga

TOKYOPOP® is an imprint of Mixx Entertainment, Inc.
5900 Wilshire Blvd., Suite 2000, Los Angeles, CA 90036

ISBN: 1-59182-154-1

First TOKYOPOP® printing: May 2003

10 9 8 7 6 5 4 3 2
Printed in Canada

TABLE OF CONTENTS

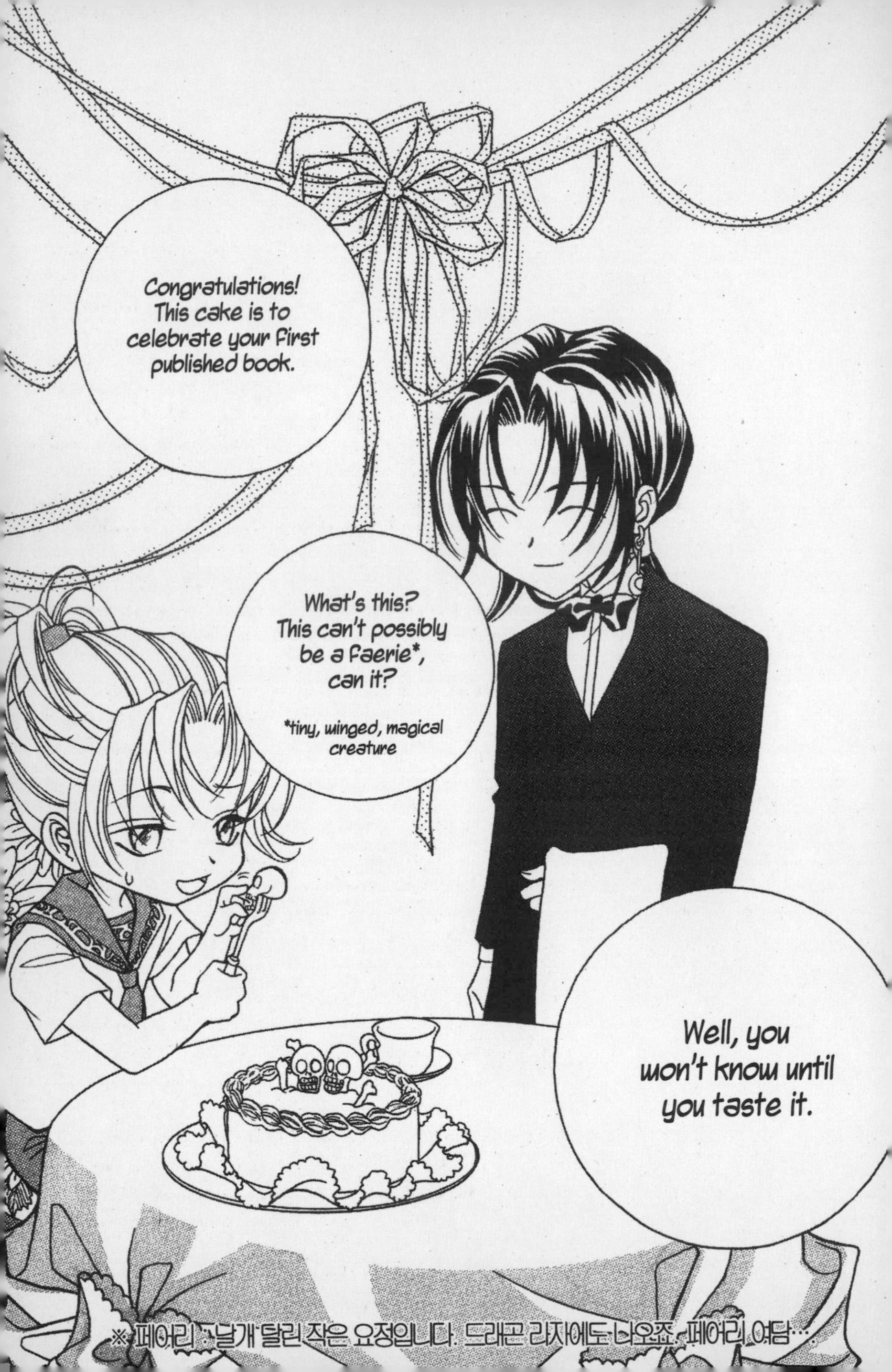
Congratulations! This cake is to celebrate your first published book.
What's this? This can't possibly be a faerie*, can it?
*tiny, winged, magical creature
Well, you won't know until you taste it.
※ 페어리 : 날개 달린 작은 요정입니다. 드래곤 라자에도 나오죠. 페어리 여담…

Wow, I'm so excited my first book is finally out.
It's is the only thing I've been able to think about for a while now.
(I sure hope it sells. Ha ha ha...!)

Let's see, who should I thank? I want to thank God for giving me
the strength to finish, my parents for watching over me
(and for always waiting up for me!) and Cake Publishing for
accepting my work. And I can't forget to thank the readers and
fans for encouraging me and reading my work—thank you!!

And...um...uh...[huddled in a corner, thinking...]

Oof, I didn't have any idea how hard it would be to write an
"Artist's Note." I'm just as nervous and excited writing this as I
was the first time I saw my art in a magazine!

Okay, back to business: what shall I write...?
(Hey—I'm halfway done already!
Just a little more...)

Questions!
Someone asked me, "Do manga-kas take vacations?"
Well, before we became manga kas, we thought that we could take
it easy while everybody else had to work. Now that we've made it,
we're always working while everyone else
gets to play! (Or is that just me...??)

Some people have asked, "Is 'Kara' a man's name or a woman's?"
Of course it's a man's—NOT! Ohohohohoho!
[annoying laughter] I think it's funny that anyone
would think "Kara" was a man's name.

I've used the name Kara from the very beginning, ever since I
was an amateur manga-ka (before the movie of the same name).
It's taken from the Hebrew Bible—Jeremiah 35:17—
and it means "to invite."

So, everyone, I invite you all into Kara's world!

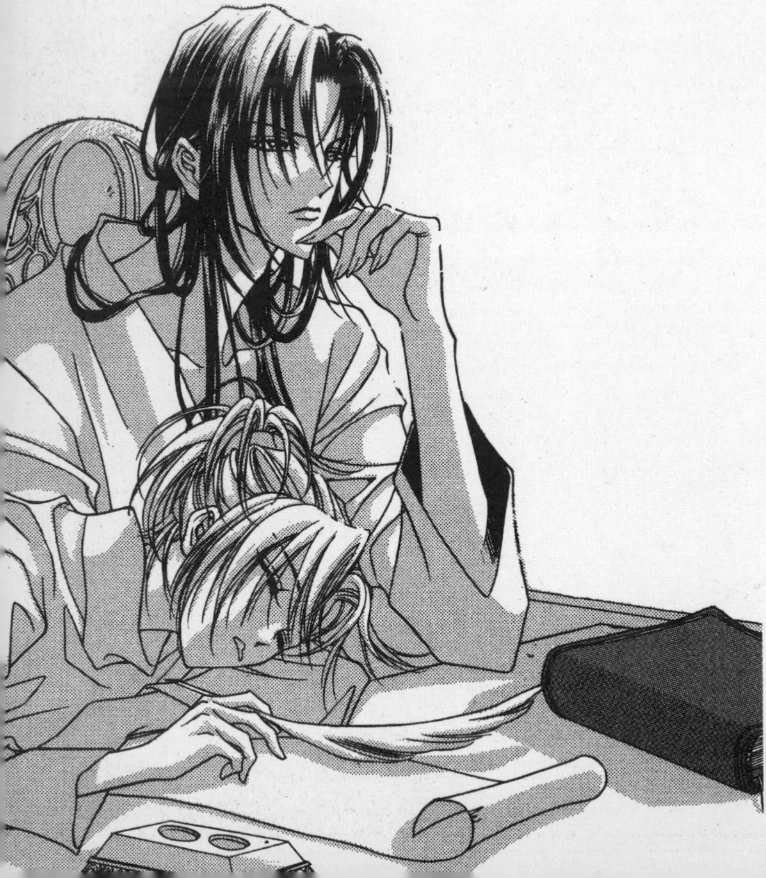

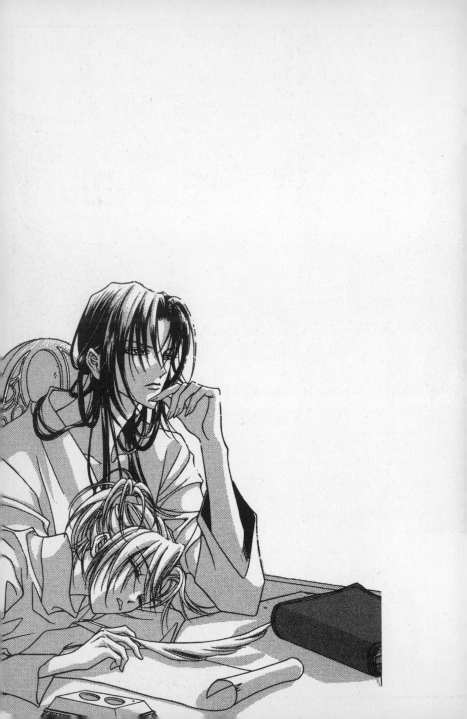

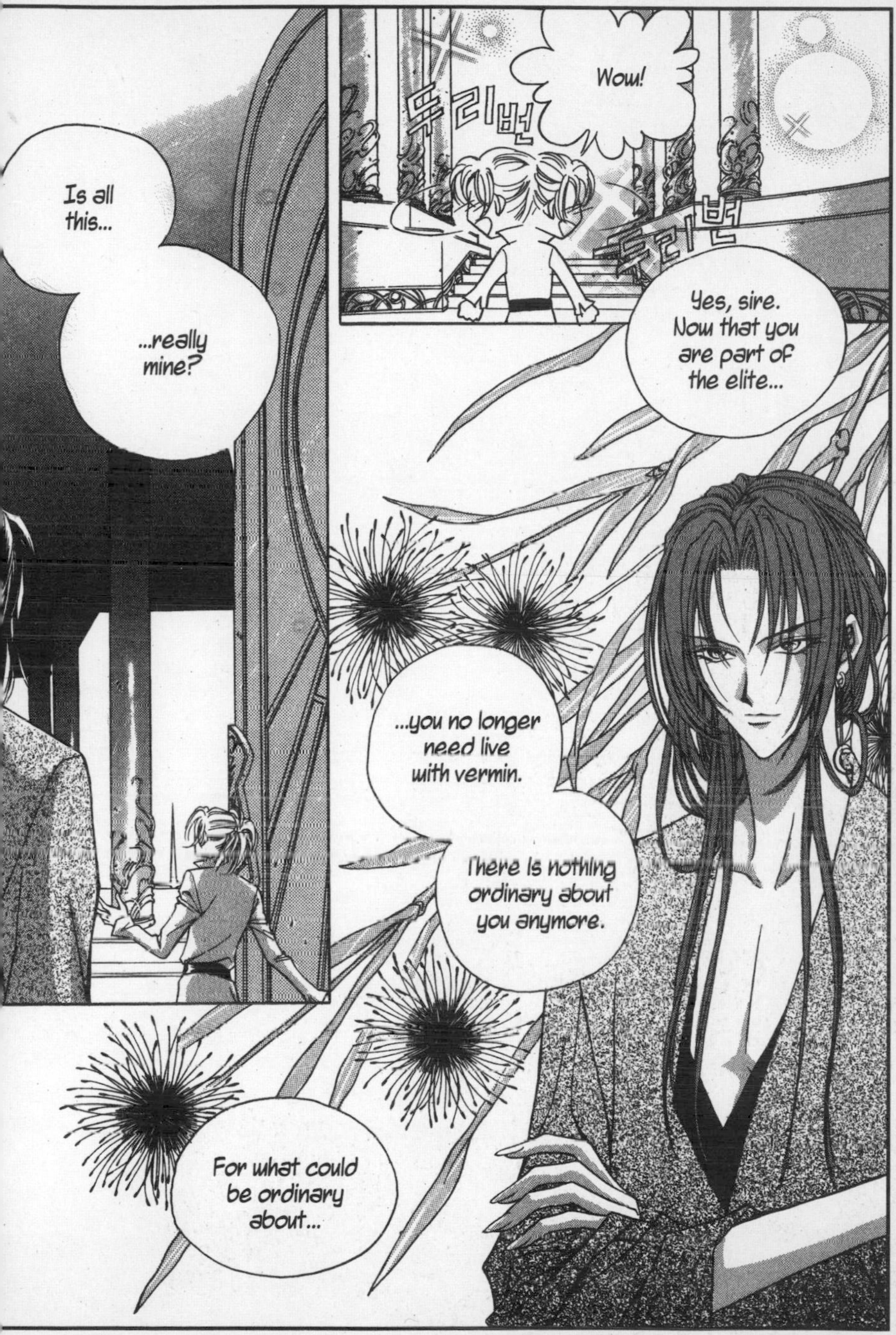
Is all this...
...really mine?
Wow!
두리번
두리번
Yes, sire. Now that you are part of the elite...
...you no longer need live with vermin.
There is nothing ordinary about you anymore.
For what could be ordinary about...

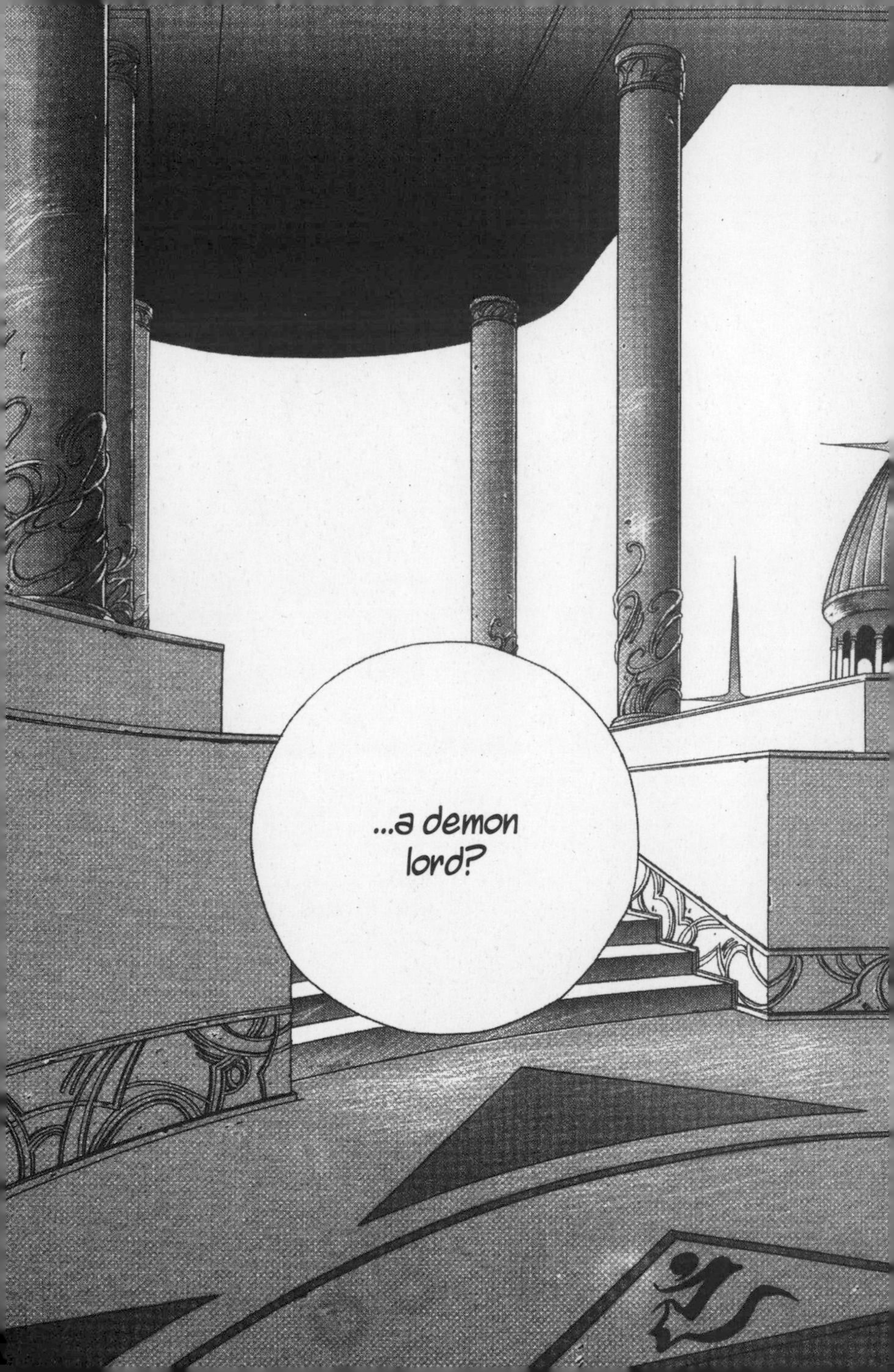
...a demon lord?

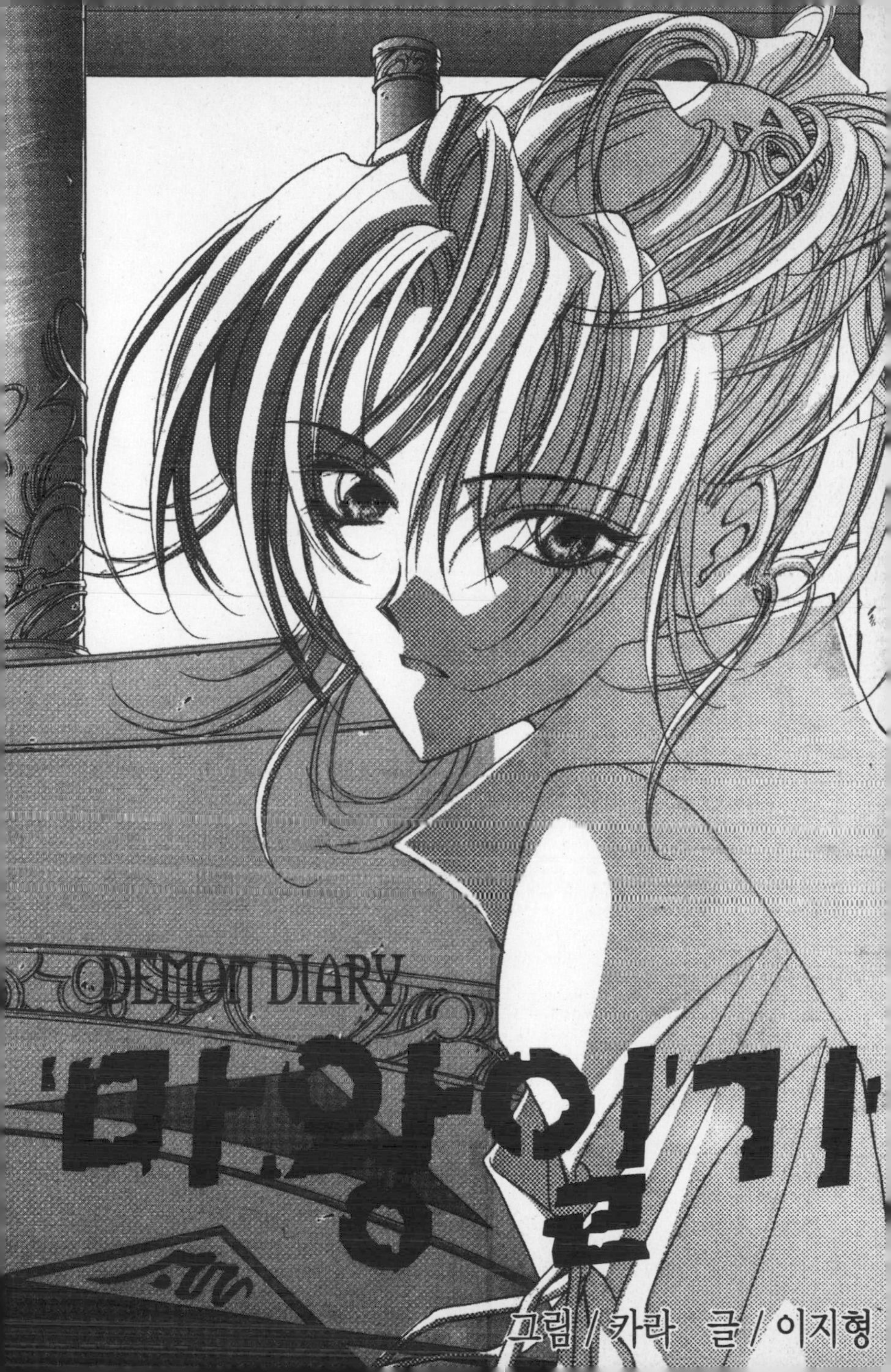

DEMON DIARY
'마왕일기'
그림/카라 글/이지형

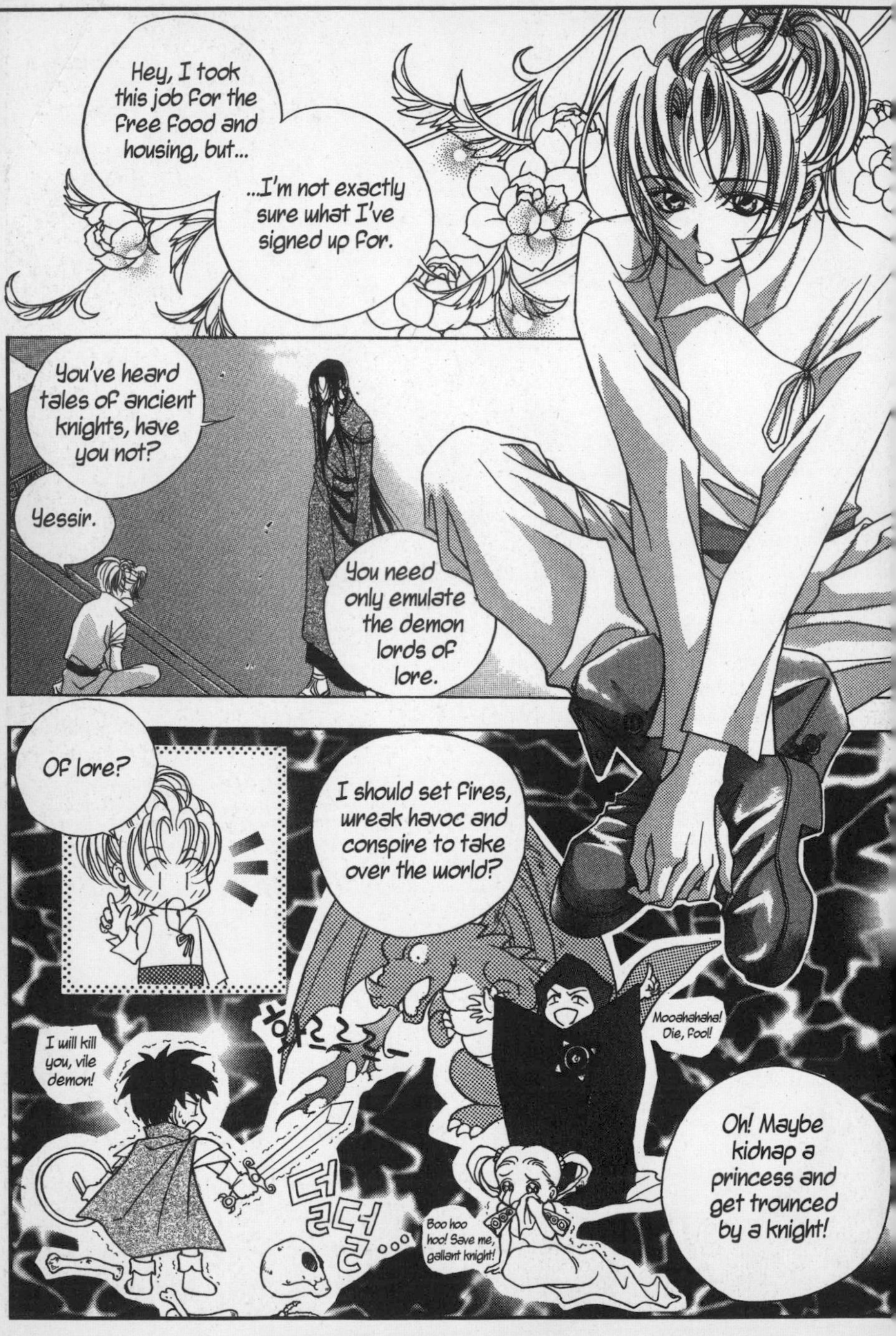
Hey, I took this job for the free food and housing, but...
...I'm not exactly sure what I've signed up for.
You've heard tales of ancient knights, have you not?
Yessir.
You need only emulate the demon lords of lore.
Of lore?
I should set fires, wreak havoc and conspire to take over the world?
I will kill you, vile demon!
Mooahahaha! Die, fool!
Boo hoo hoo! Save me, gallant knight!
Oh! Maybe kidnap a princess and get trounced by a knight!

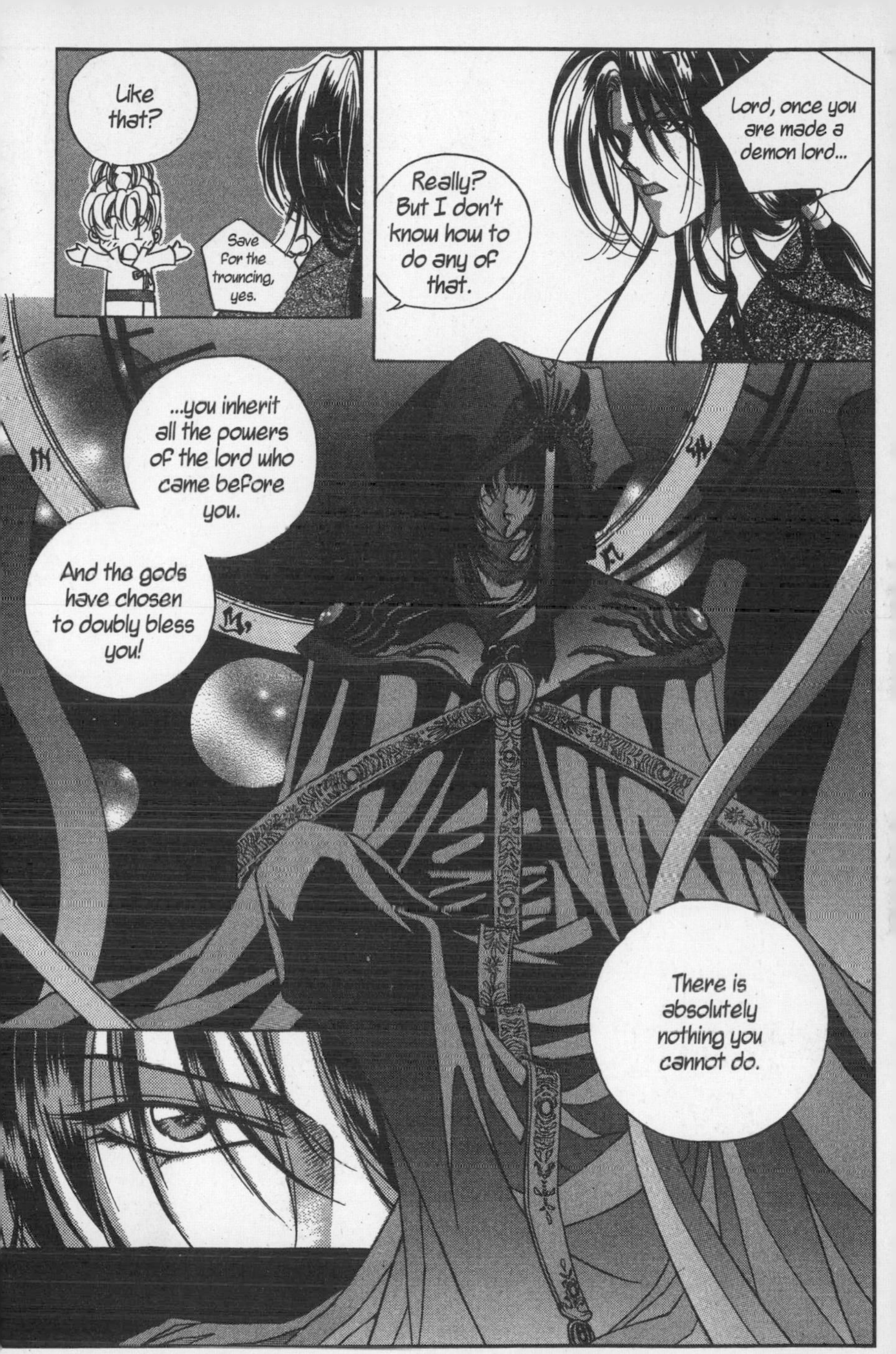
Like that?
Save for the trouncing, yes.
Really? But I don't know how to do any of that.
Lord, once you are made a demon lord...
...you inherit all the powers of the lord who came before you.
And the gods have chosen to doubly bless you!
There is absolutely nothing you cannot do.

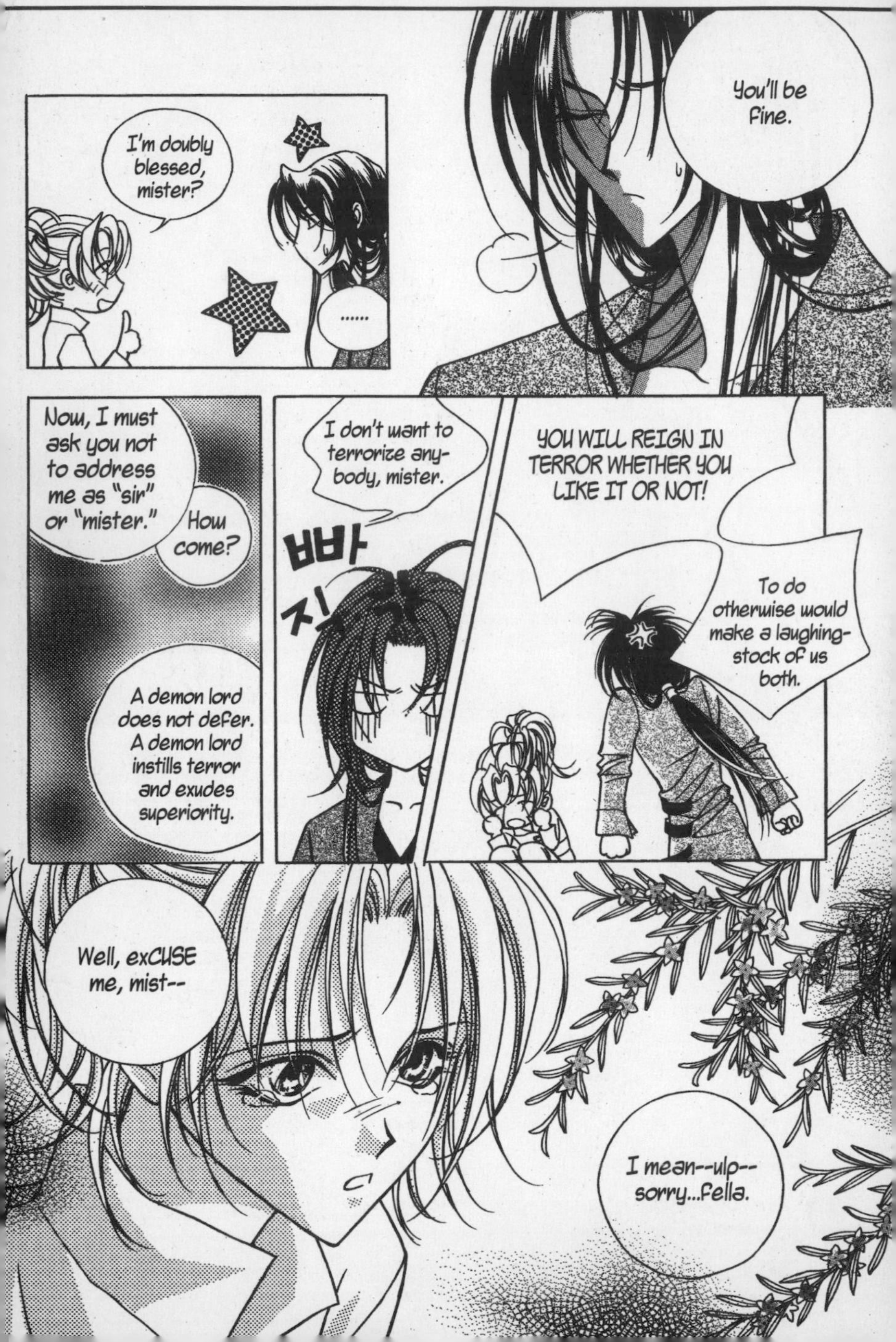
I'm doubly blessed, mister?
......
You'll be fine.
Now, I must ask you not to address me as "sir" or "mister."
How come?
A demon lord does not defer. A demon lord instills terror and exudes superiority.
I don't want to terrorize any-body, mister.
빠직
YOU WILL REIGN IN TERROR WHETHER YOU LIKE IT OR NOT!
To do otherwise would make a laughing-stock of us both.
Well, exCUSE me, mist--
I mean--ulp--sorry...fella.

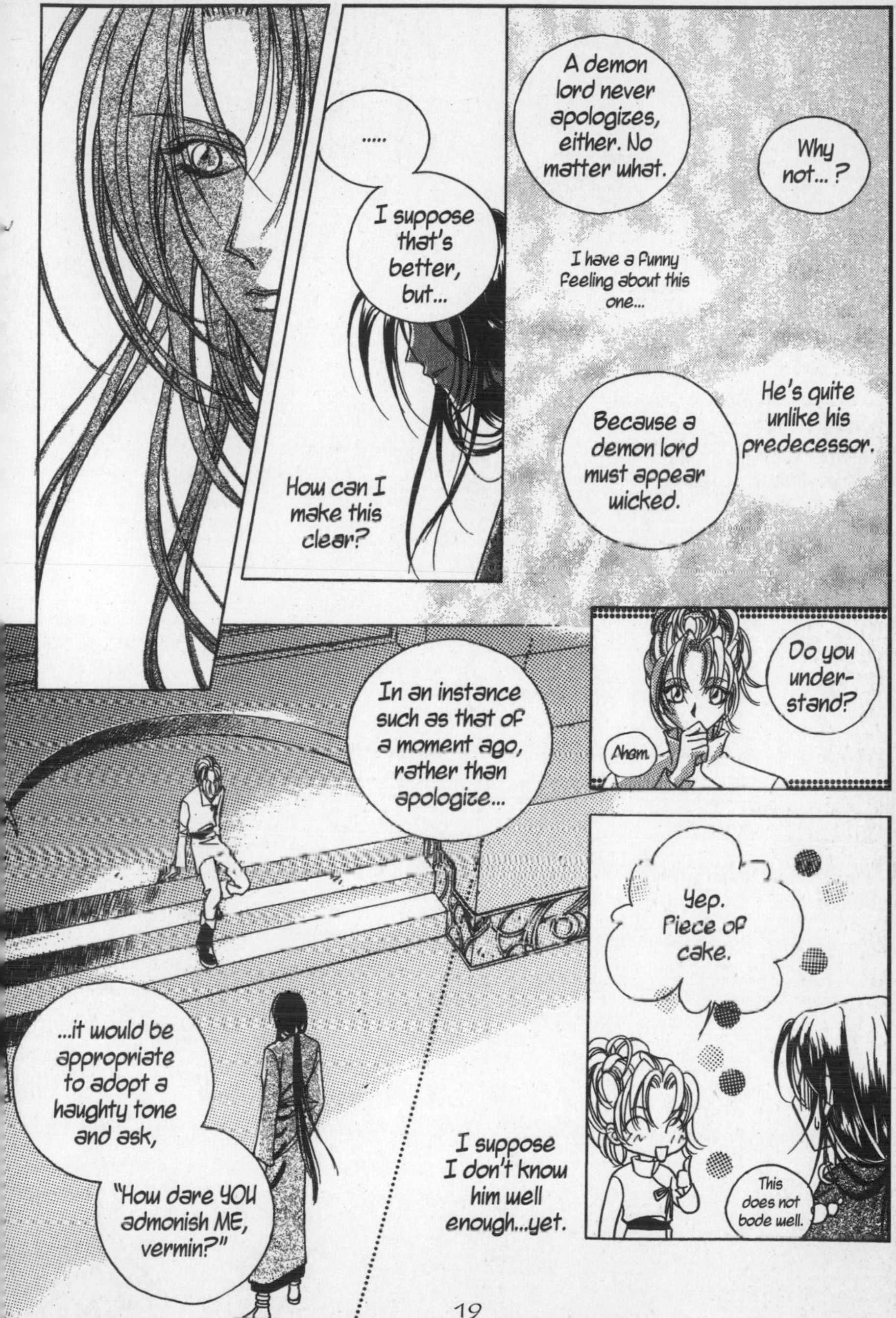
.....
I suppose that's better, but...
How can I make this clear?
A demon lord never apologizes, either. No matter what.
Why not...?
Because a demon lord must appear wicked.
I have a funny feeling about this one...
He's quite unlike his predecessor.
In an instance such as that of a moment ago, rather than apologize...
...it would be appropriate to adopt a haughty tone and ask,
"How dare YOU admonish ME, vermin?"
Ahem.
Do you understand?
Yep. Piece of cake.
I suppose I don't know him well enough...yet.
This does not bode well.

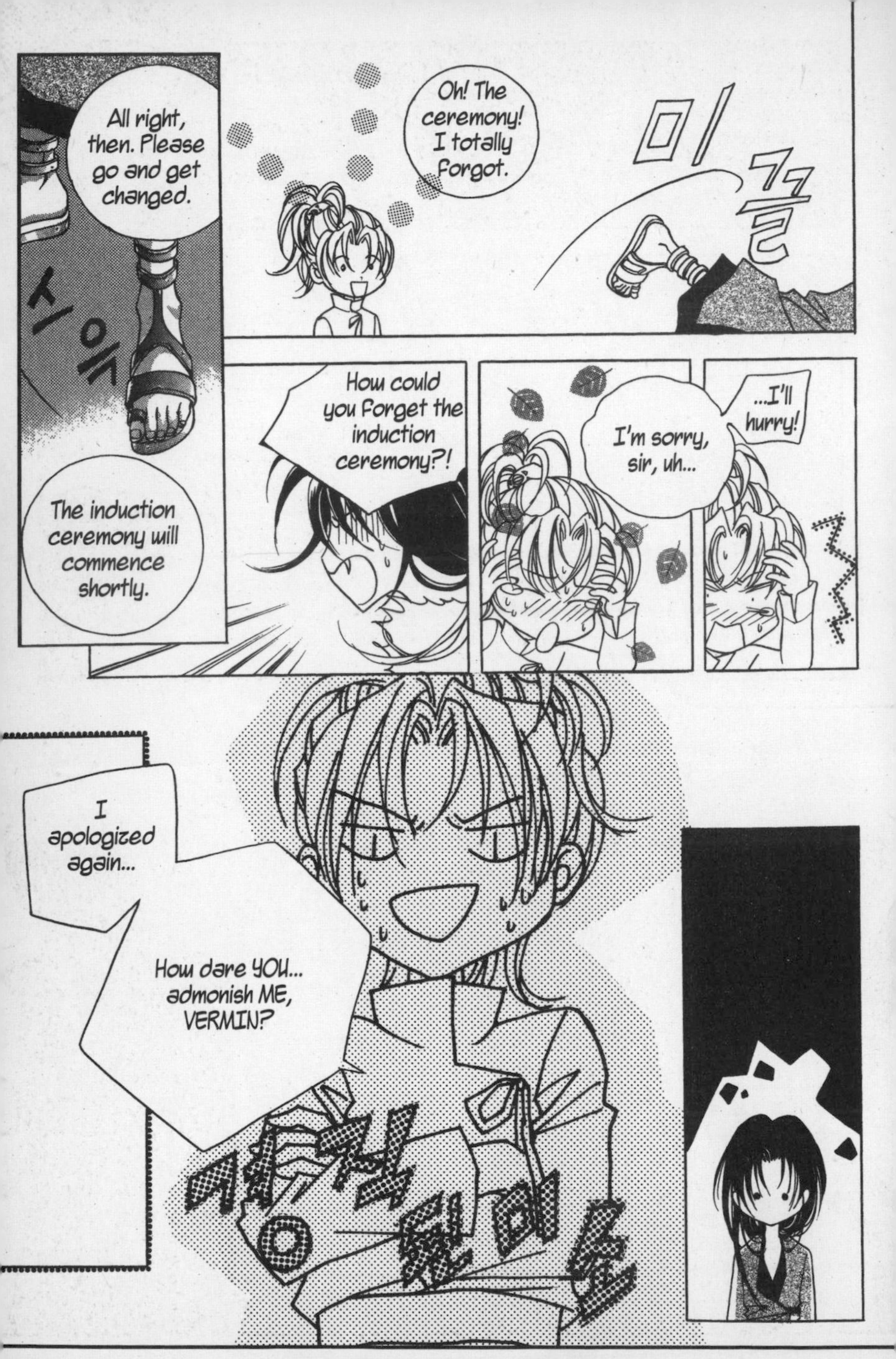
All right, then. Please go and get changed.
Oh! The ceremony! I totally forgot.
The induction ceremony will commence shortly.
How could you forget the induction ceremony?!
I'm sorry, sir, uh...
...I'll hurry!
I apologized again...
How dare YOU... admonish ME, VERMIN?

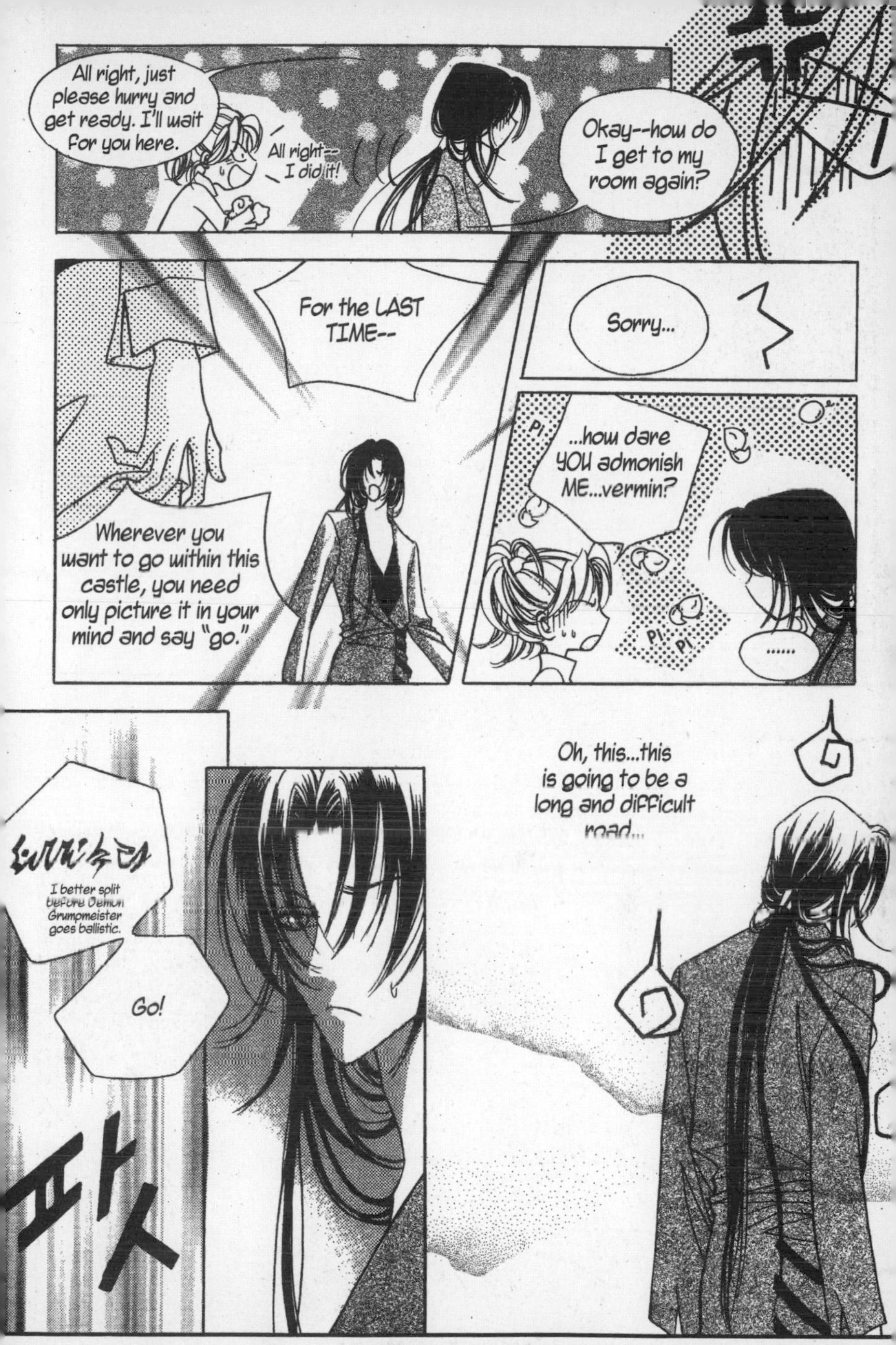
All right, just please hurry and get ready. I'll wait for you here.
All right-- I did it!
Okay--how do I get to my room again?
For the LAST TIME--
Wherever you want to go within this castle, you need only picture it in your mind and say "go."
Sorry...
...how dare YOU admonish ME...vermin?
PI
PI
PI
......
I better split before Demon Grumpmeister goes ballistic.
Go!
Oh, this...this is going to be a long and difficult road...

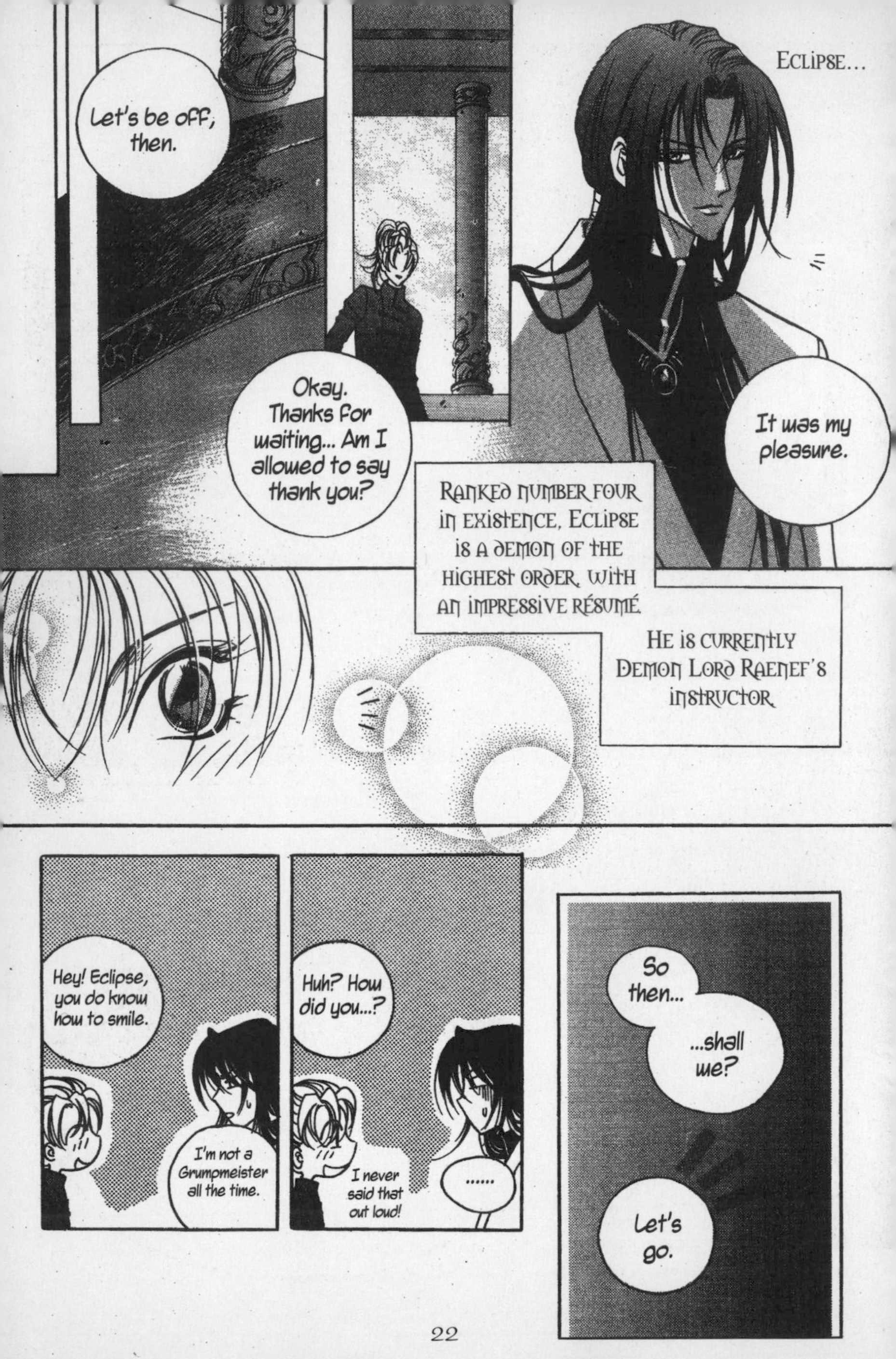
Let's be off, then.
Okay. Thanks for waiting... Am I allowed to say thank you?
Eclipse...
It was my pleasure.
Ranked number four in existence, Eclipse is a demon of the highest order, with an impressive résumé.
He is currently Demon Lord Raenef's instructor.
Hey! Eclipse, you do know how to smile.
I'm not a Grumpmeister all the time.
Huh? How did you...?
I never said that out loud!
......
So then...
...shall we?
Let's go.

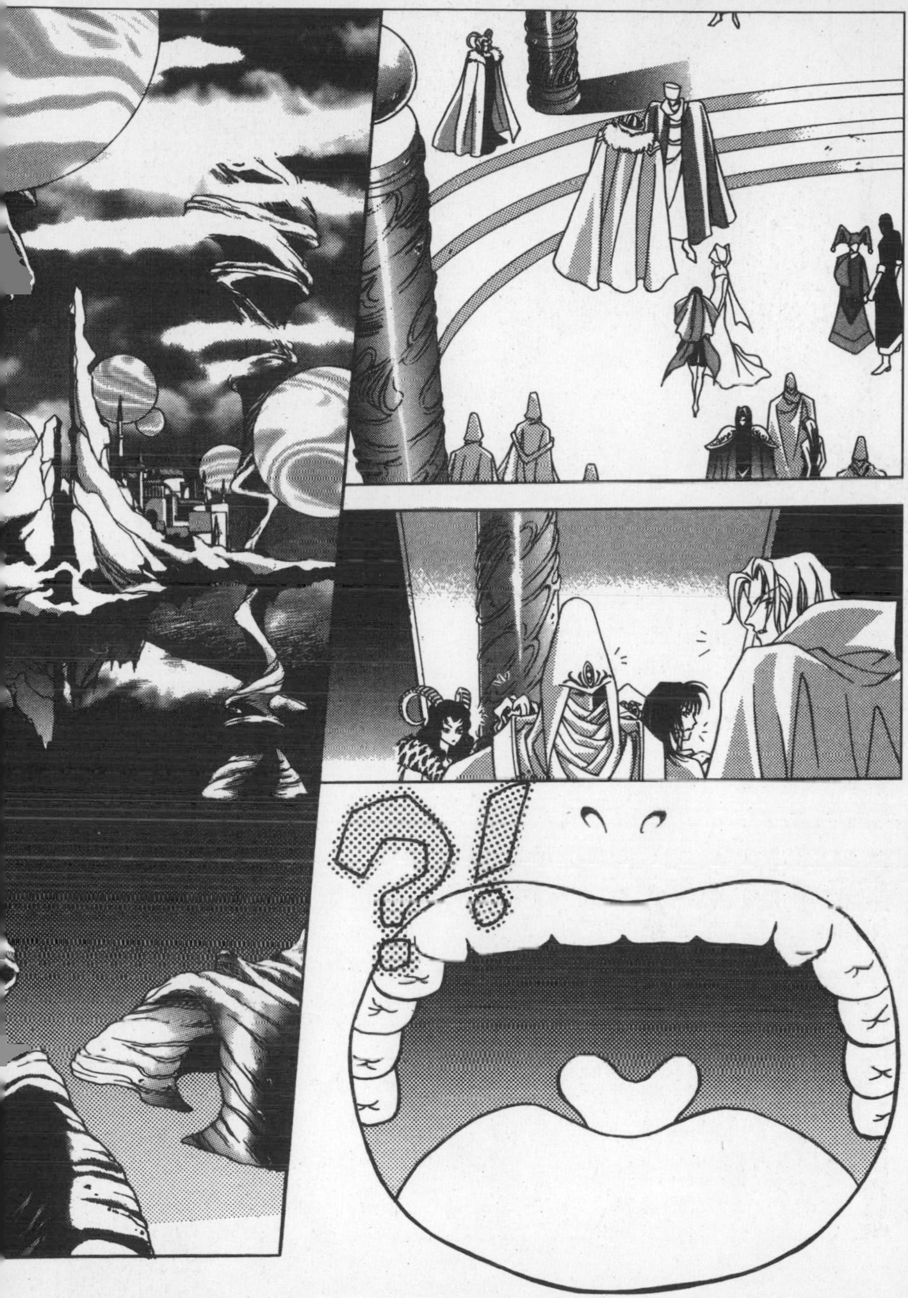
?!

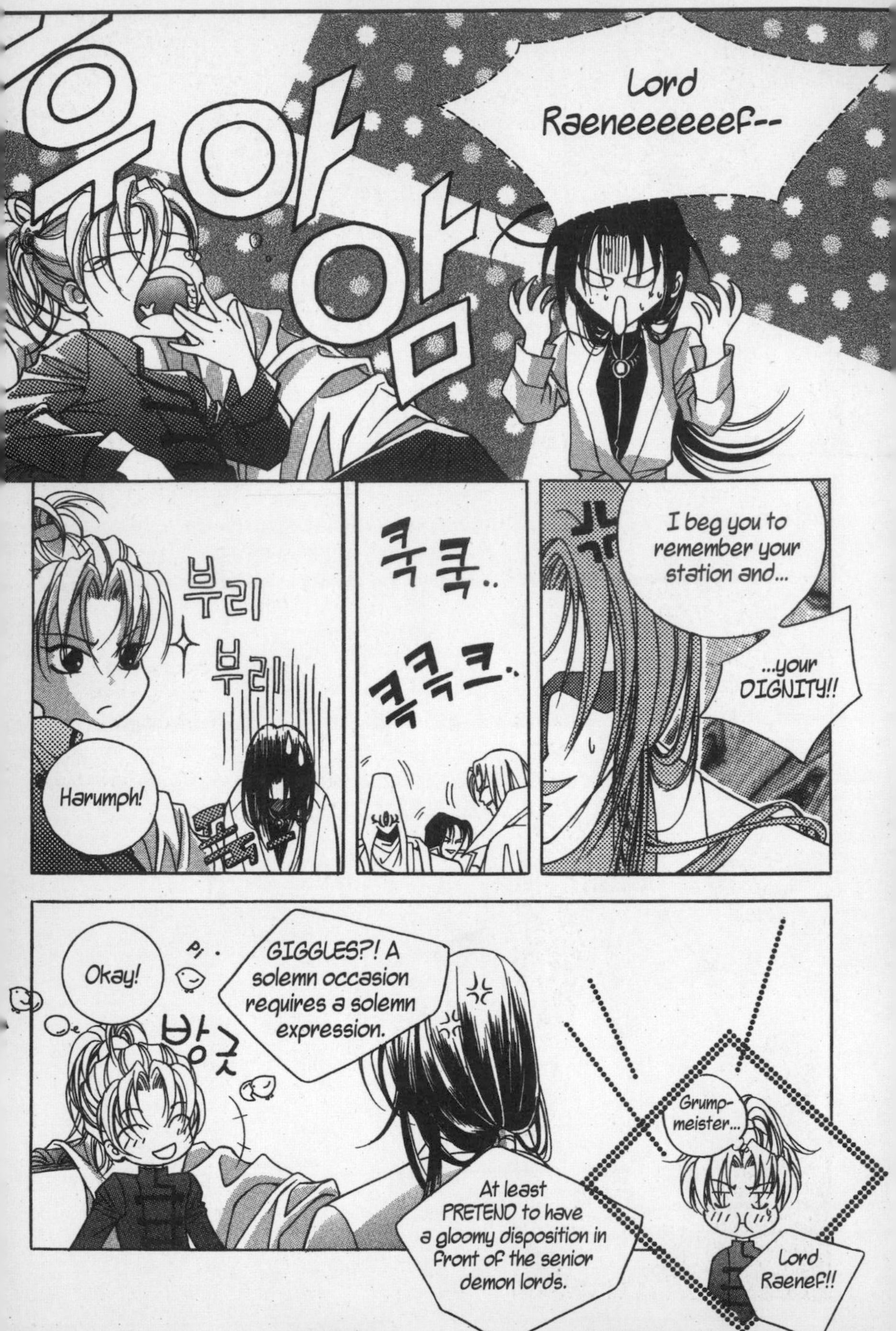
Lord Raeneeeeeeef--
Harumph!
부리 부리
쿡쿡..
I beg you to remember your station and...
...your DIGNITY!!
Okay!
방긋
GIGGLES?! A solemn occasion requires a solemn expression.
At least PRETEND to have a gloomy disposition in front of the senior demon lords.
Grump-meister...
Lord Raenef!!

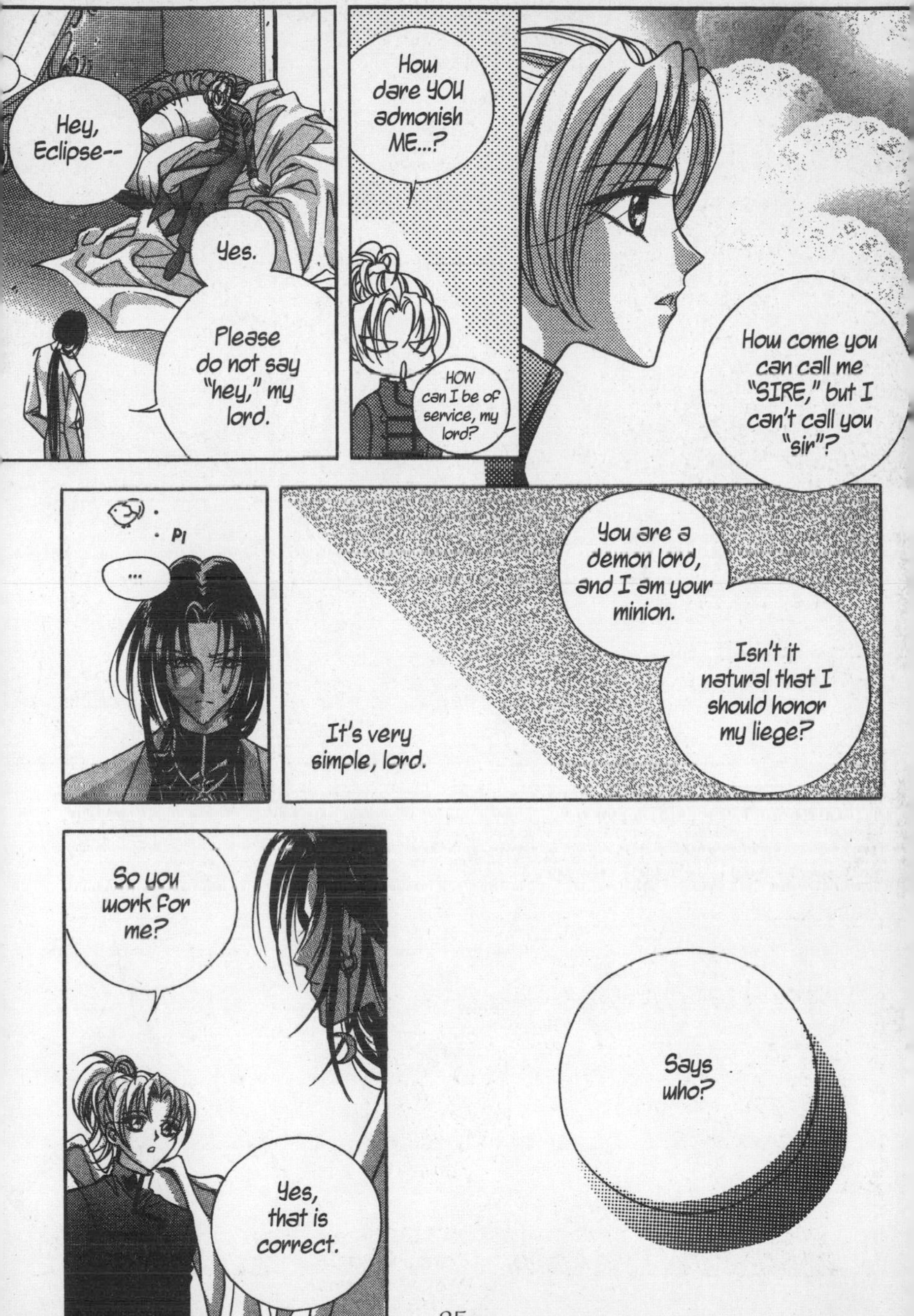

Hey, Eclipse--
Yes.
Please do not say "hey," my lord.
How dare YOU admonish ME...?
HOW can I be of service, my lord?
How come you can call me "SIRE," but I can't call you "sir"?
Pi
...
It's very simple, lord.
You are a demon lord, and I am your minion.
Isn't it natural that I should honor my liege?
So you work for me?
Yes, that is correct.
Says who?

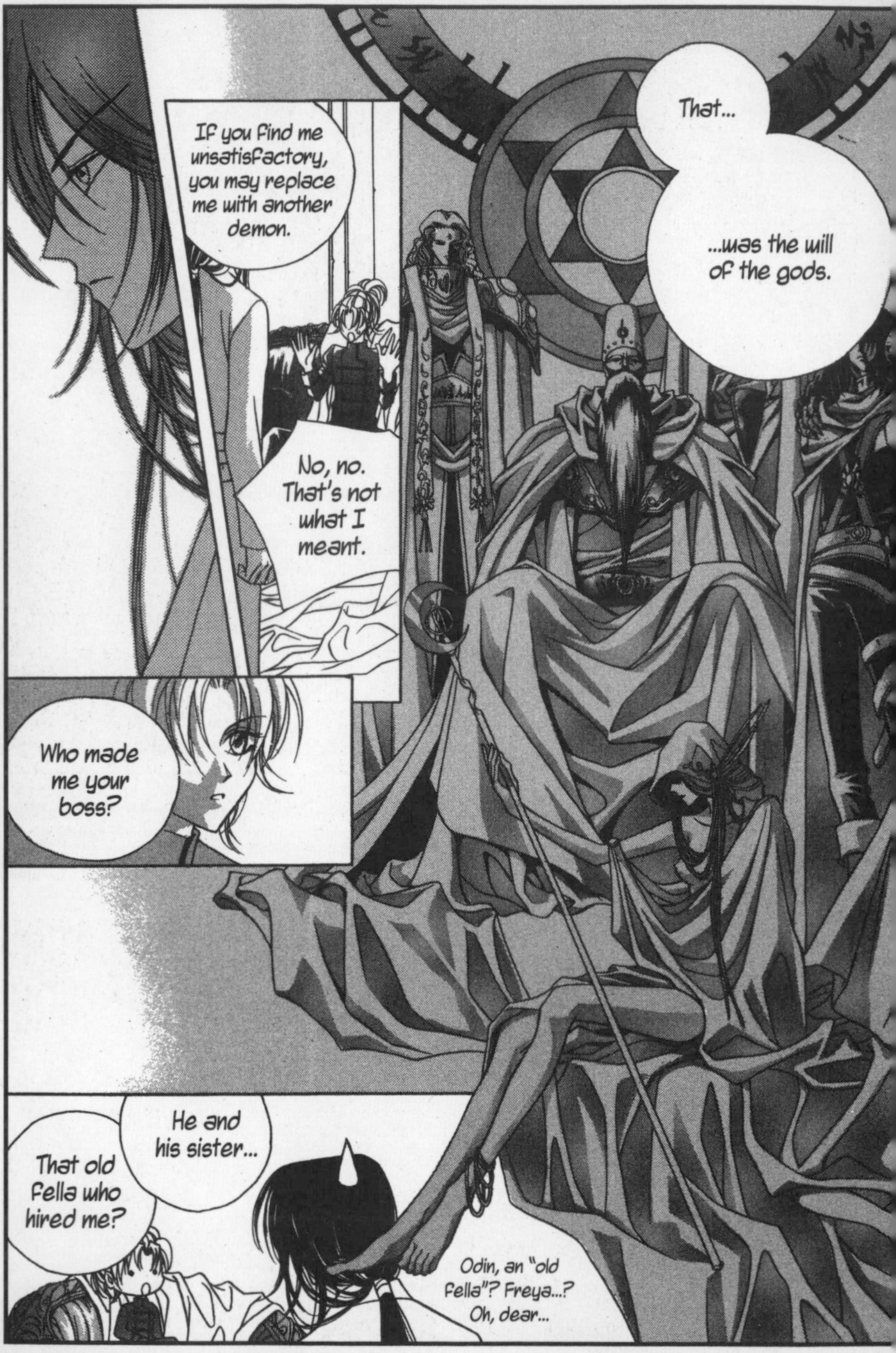
That...
...was the will of the gods.
If you find me unsatisfactory, you may replace me with another demon.
No, no. That's not what I meant.
Who made me your boss?
He and his sister...
That old fella who hired me?
Odin, an "old fella"? Freya...? Oh, dear...

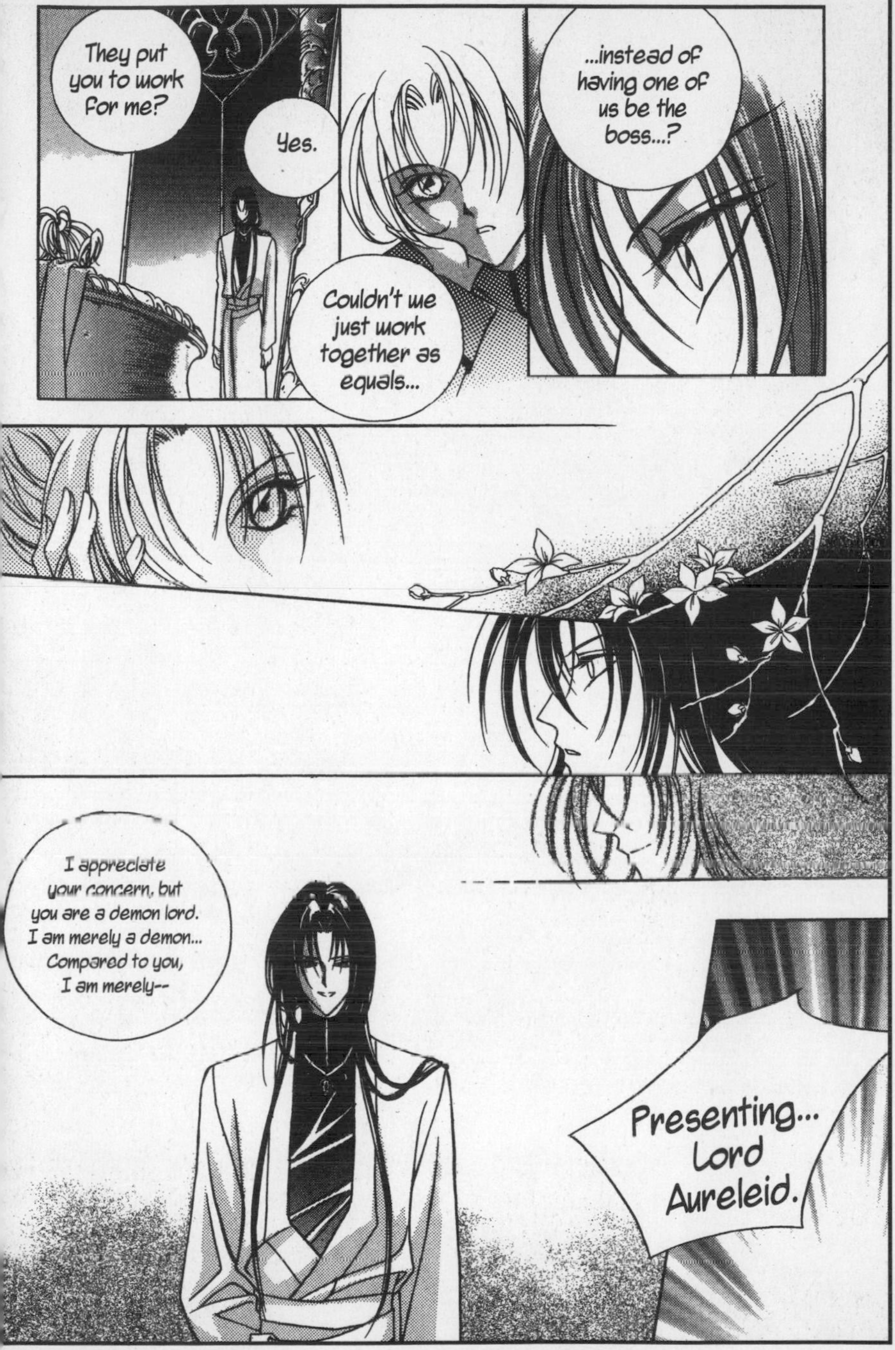
They put you to work for me?
Yes.
Couldn't we just work together as equals...
...instead of having one of us be the boss...?
I appreciate your concern, but you are a demon lord. I am merely a demon... Compared to you, I am merely--
Presenting... Lord Aureleid.

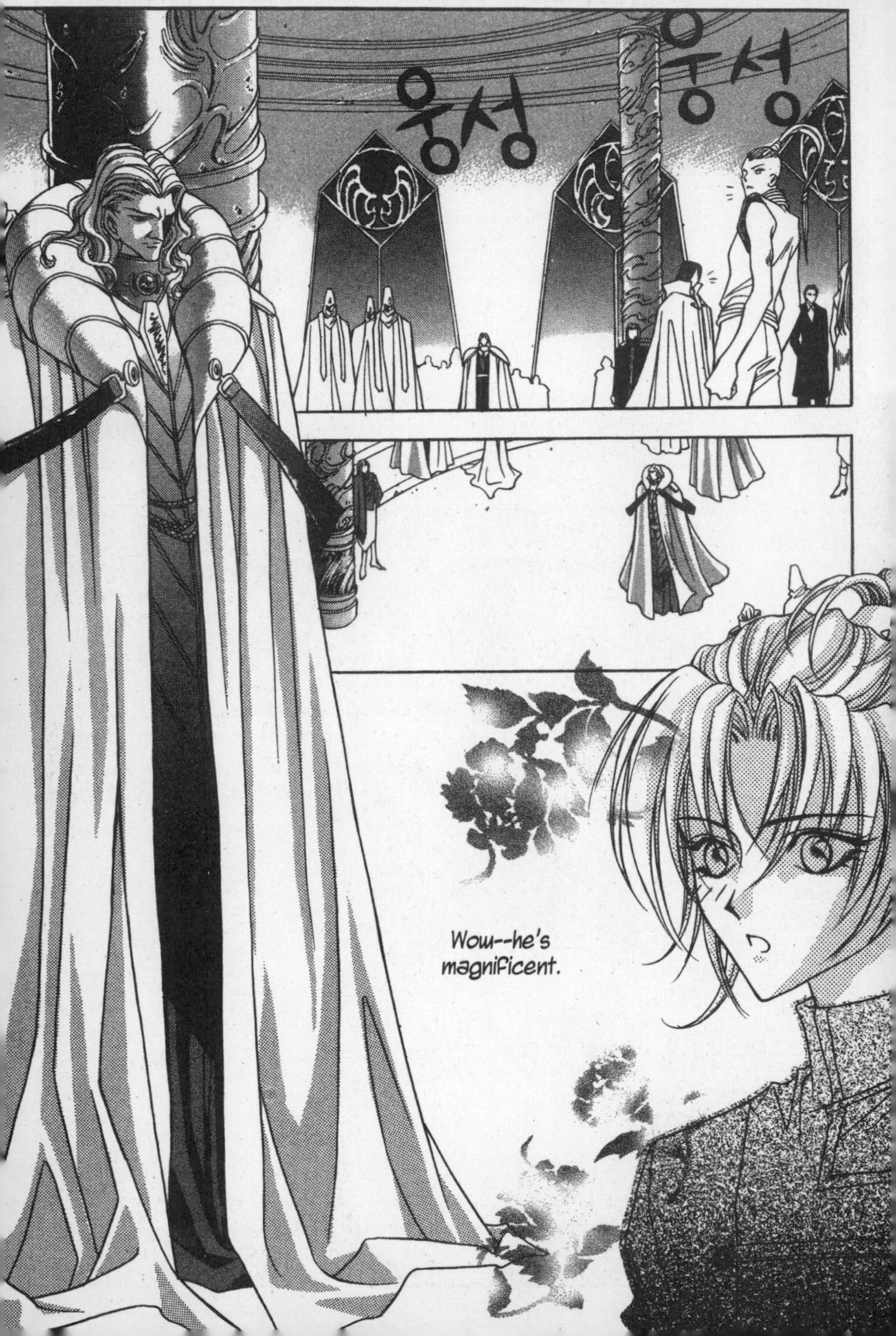
웅성 웅성
Wow--he's magnificent.

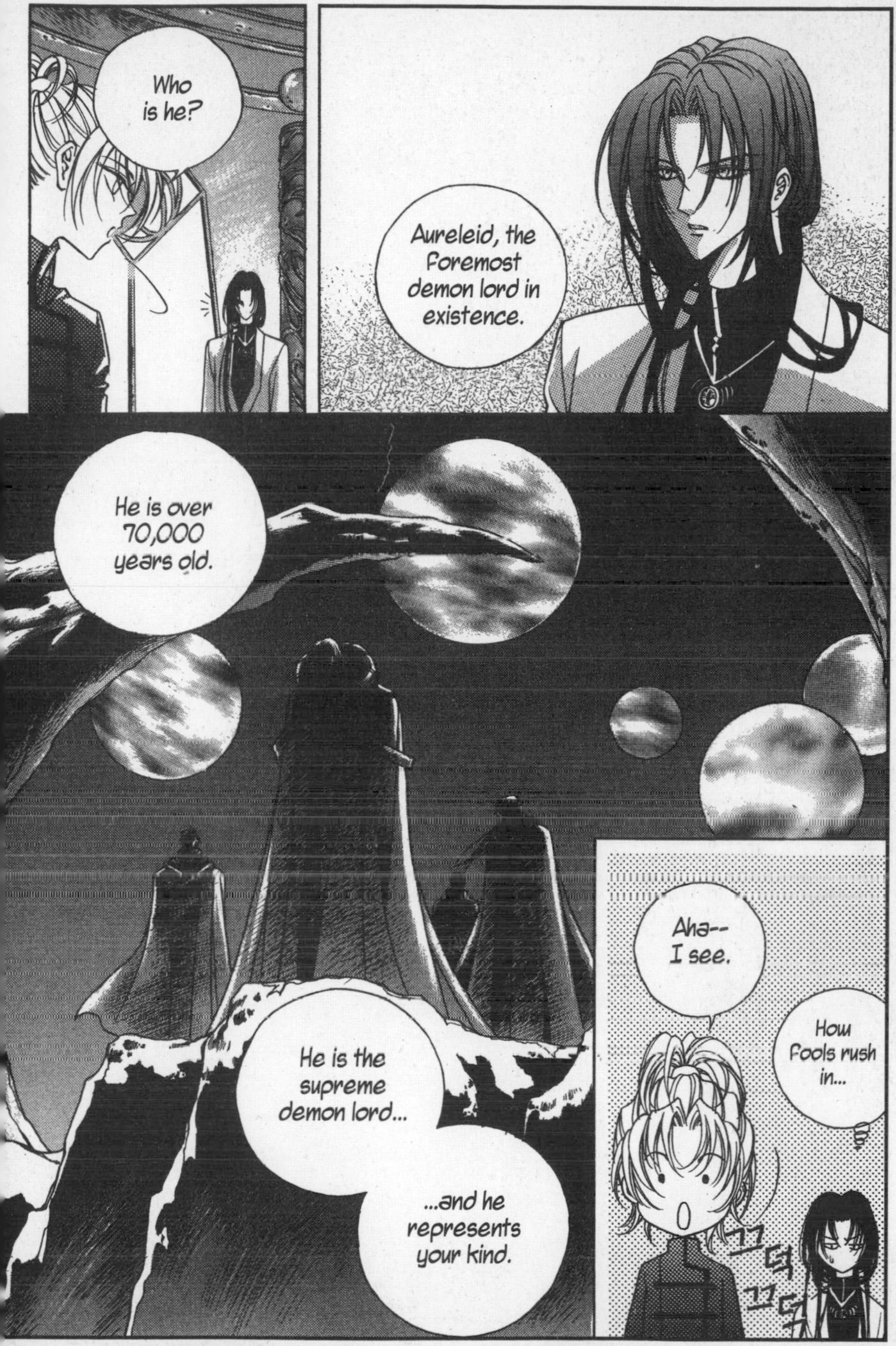
Who is he?
Aureleid, the foremost demon lord in existence.
He is over 70,000 years old.
He is the supreme demon lord...
...and he represents your kind.
Aha-- I see.
How fools rush in...

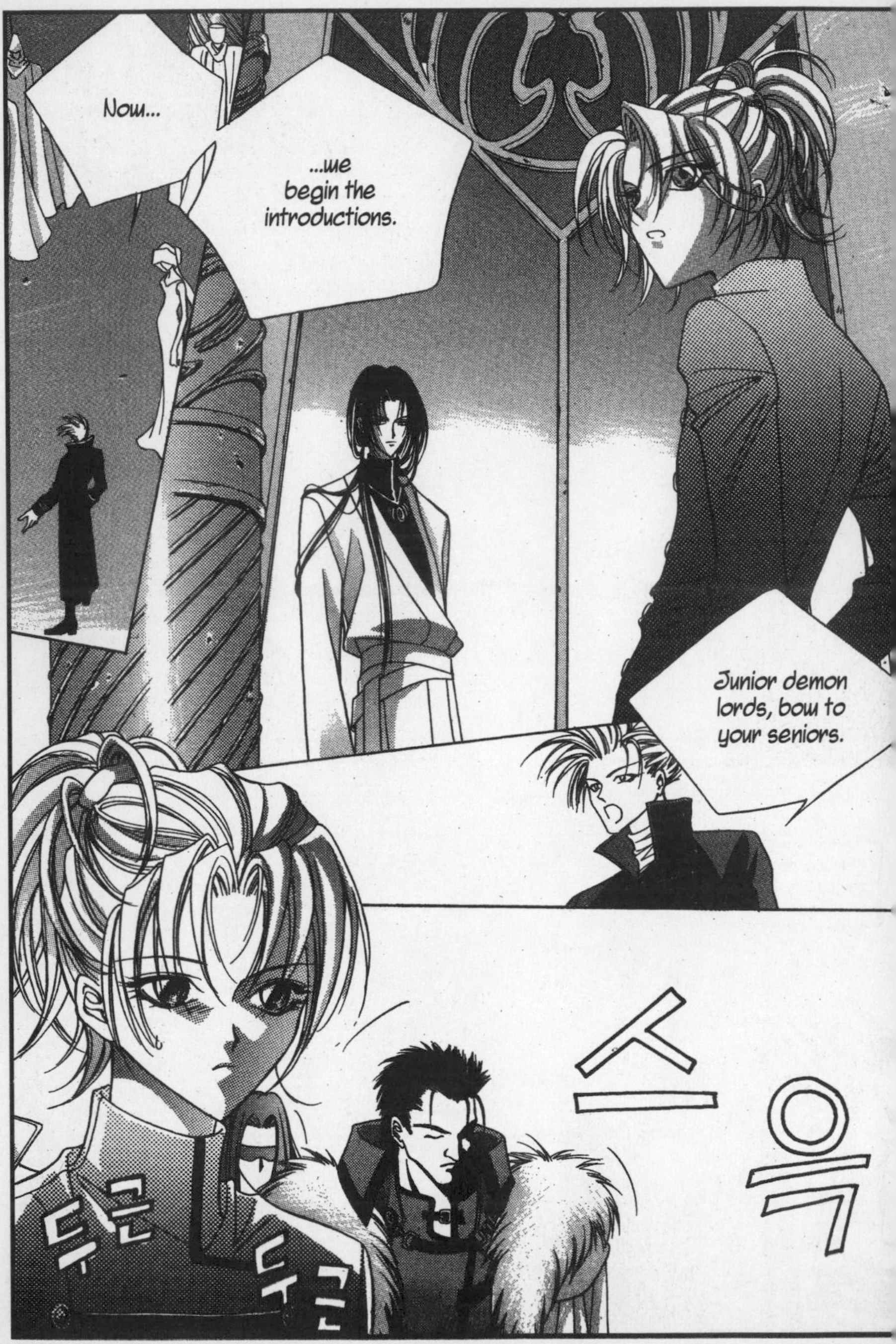
Now...
...we begin the introductions.
Junior demon lords, bow to your seniors.
스윽

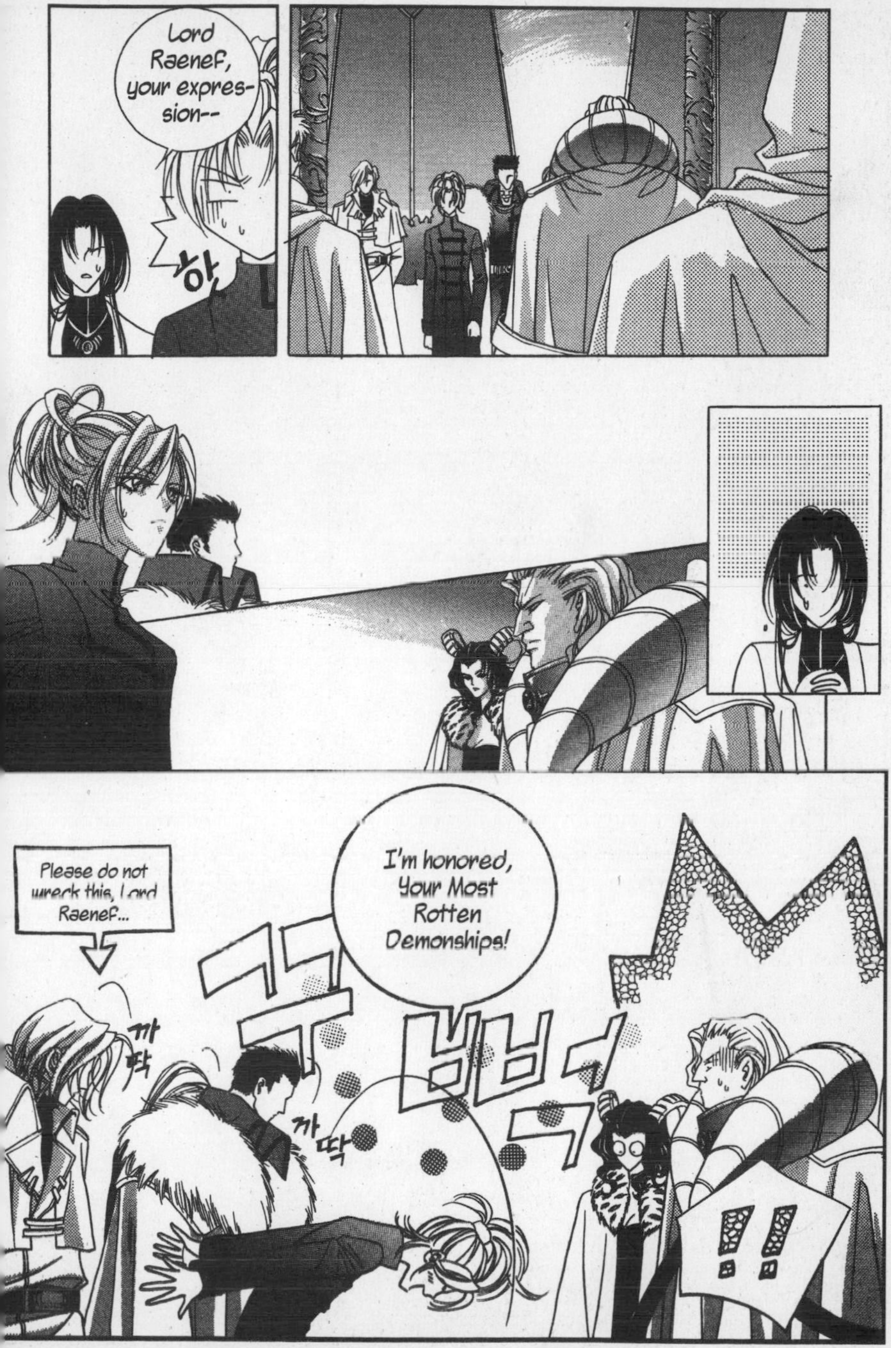
Lord Raenef, your expres-sion--
하
Please do not wreck this, Lord Raenef...
I'm honored, Your Most Rotten Demonships!
까딱
까딱
!!

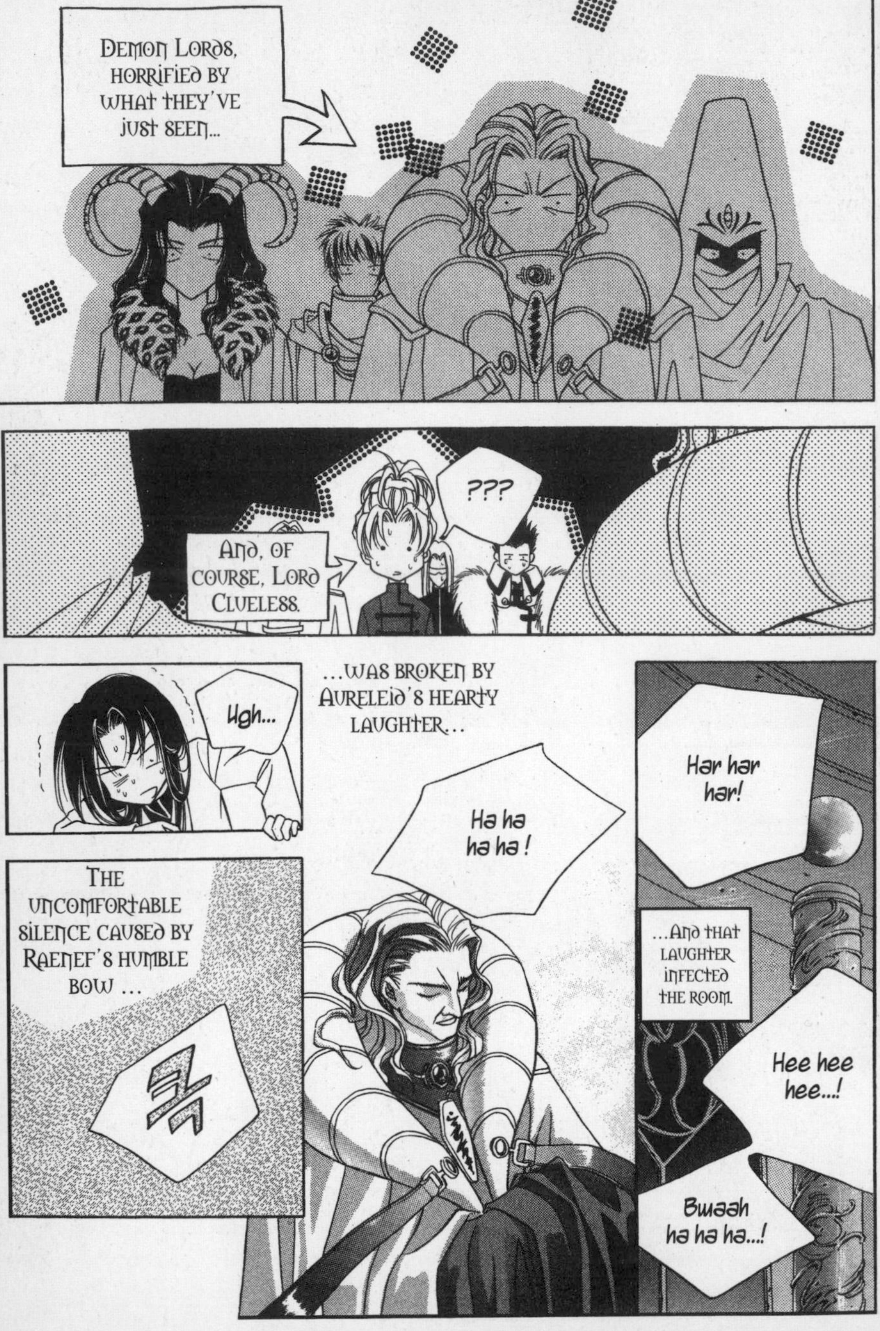

Demon Lords, horrified by what they've just seen...
And, of course, Lord Clueless.
???
Ugh...
The uncomfortable silence caused by Raenef's humble bow ...
...was broken by Aureleid's hearty laughter...
Ha ha ha ha !
Har har har!
...And that laughter infected the room.
Hee hee hee...!
Bwaah ha ha ha...!

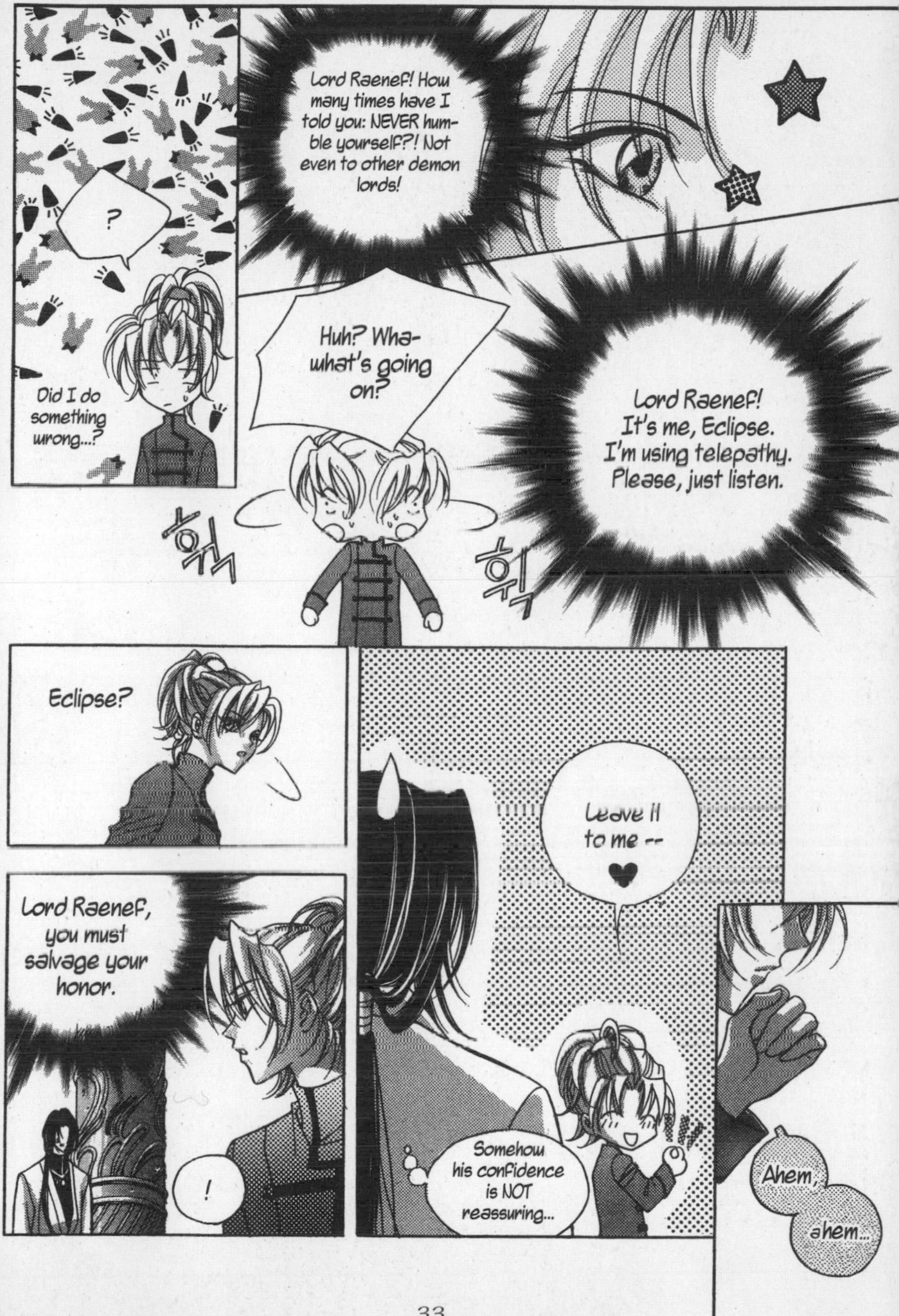
Lord Raenef! How many times have I told you: NEVER humble yourself?! Not even to other demon lords!
?
Did I do something wrong...?
Huh? Wha-what's going on?
Lord Raenef! It's me, Eclipse. I'm using telepathy. Please, just listen.
Eclipse?
Leave it to me --
Lord Raenef, you must salvage your honor.
!
Somehow his confidence is NOT reassuring...
Ahem, ahem...

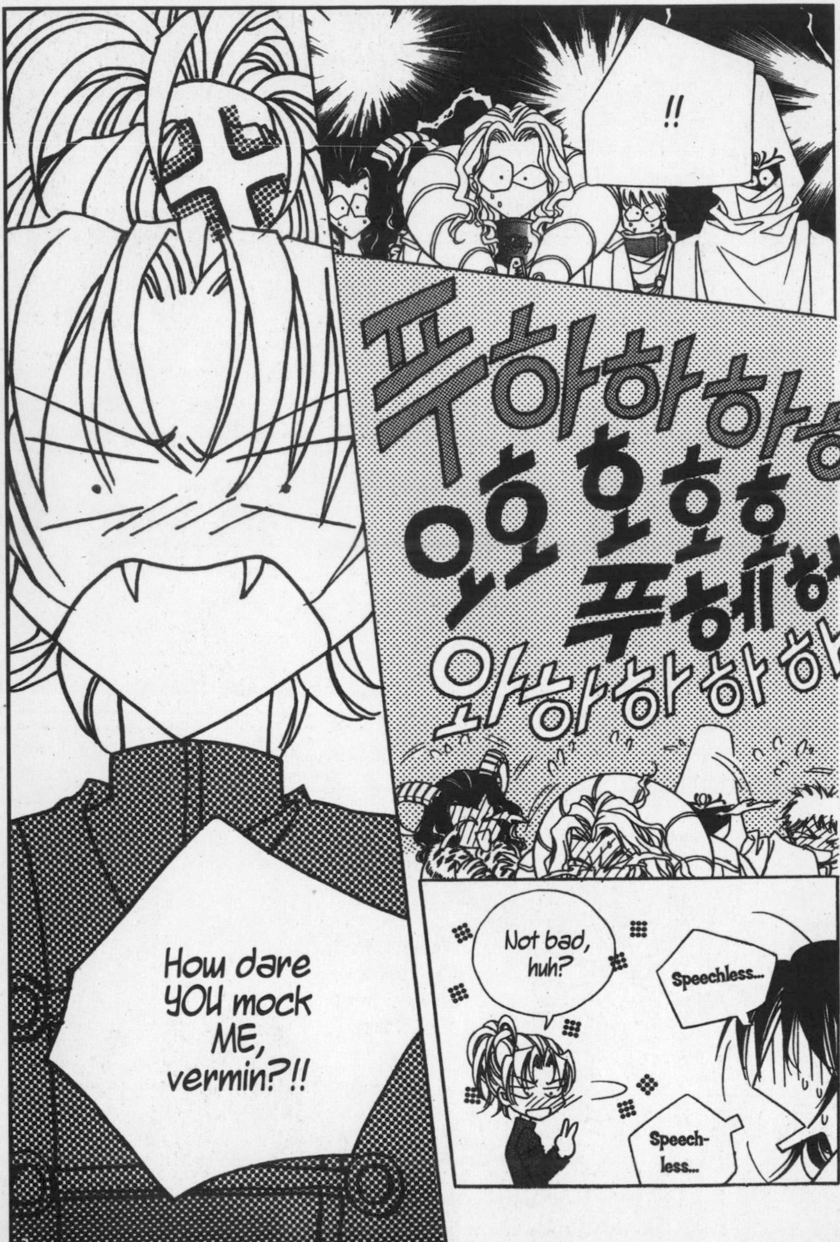
How dare YOU mock ME, vermin?!!
!!
푸하하하하
오호호호
푸헤헤
와하하하하
Not bad, huh?
Speechless...
Speech-less...

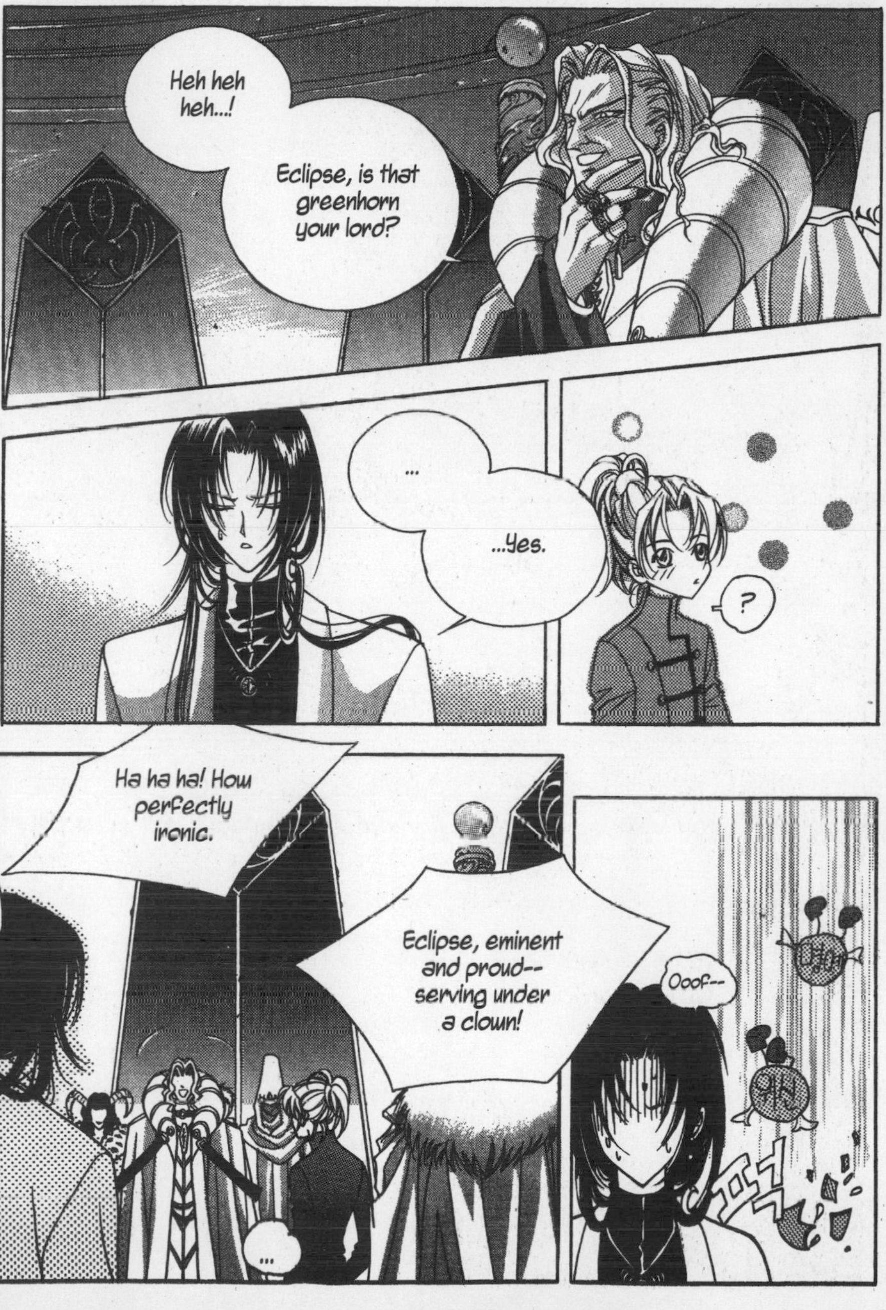
Heh heh heh...!
Eclipse, is that greenhorn your lord?
...
...Yes.
?
Ha ha ha! How perfectly ironic.
Eclipse, eminent and proud-- serving under a clown!
...
Ooof--

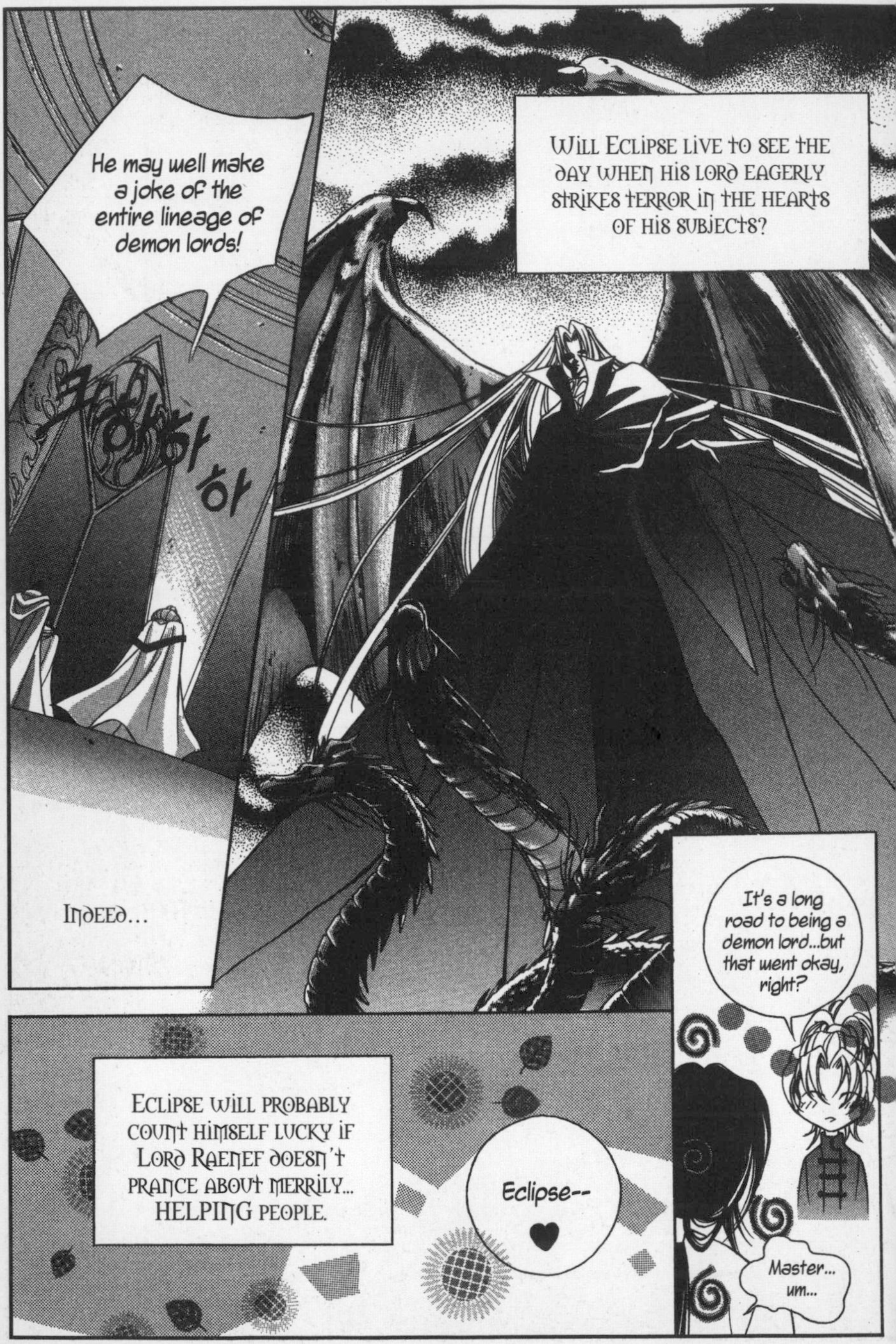
He may well make a joke of the entire lineage of demon lords!
Will Eclipse live to see the day when his lord eagerly strikes terror in the hearts of his subjects?
Indeed...
Eclipse will probably count himself lucky if Lord Raenef doesn't prance about merrily... HELPING people.
Eclipse--
It's a long road to being a demon lord...but that went okay, right?
Master... um...

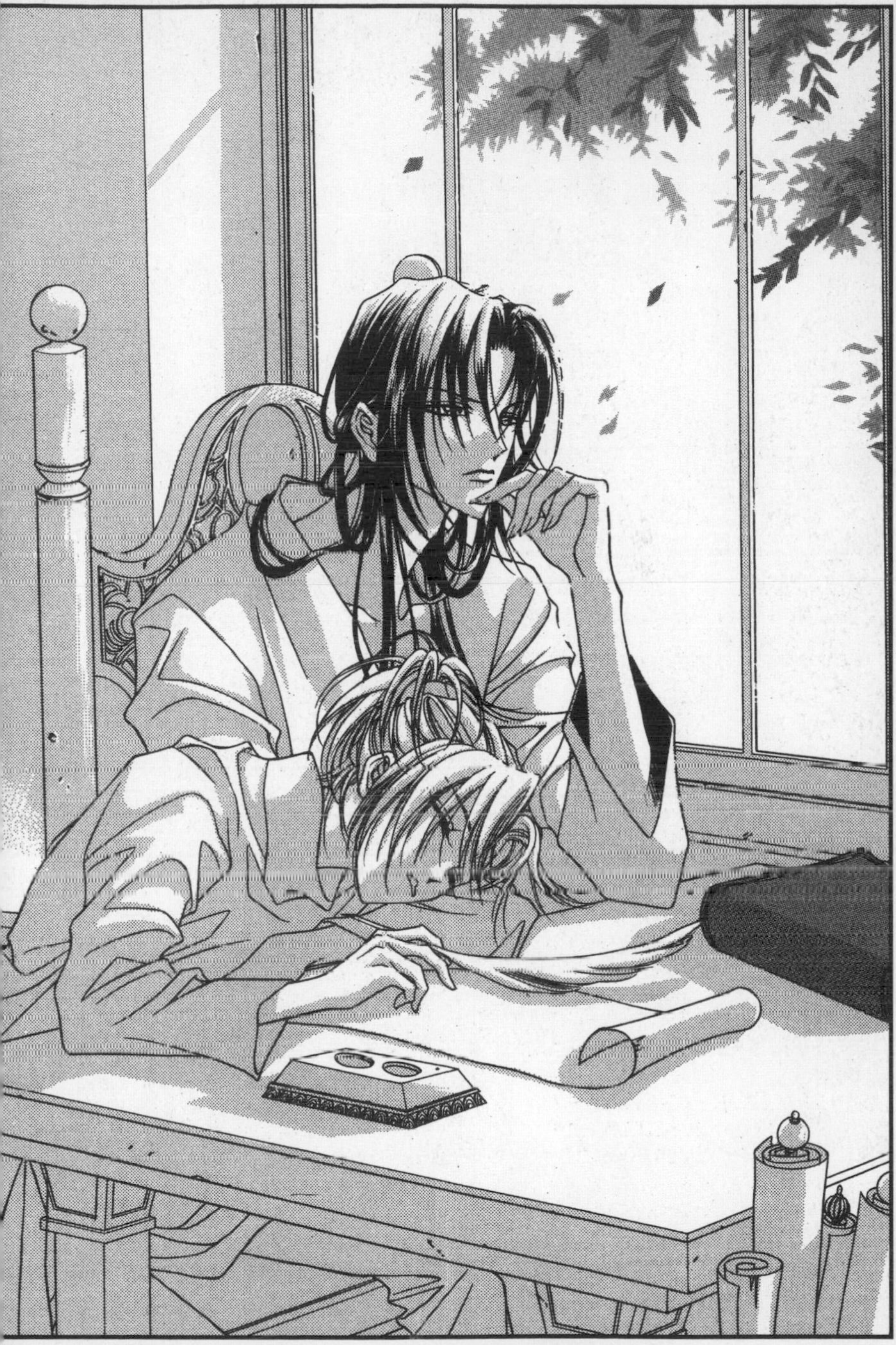

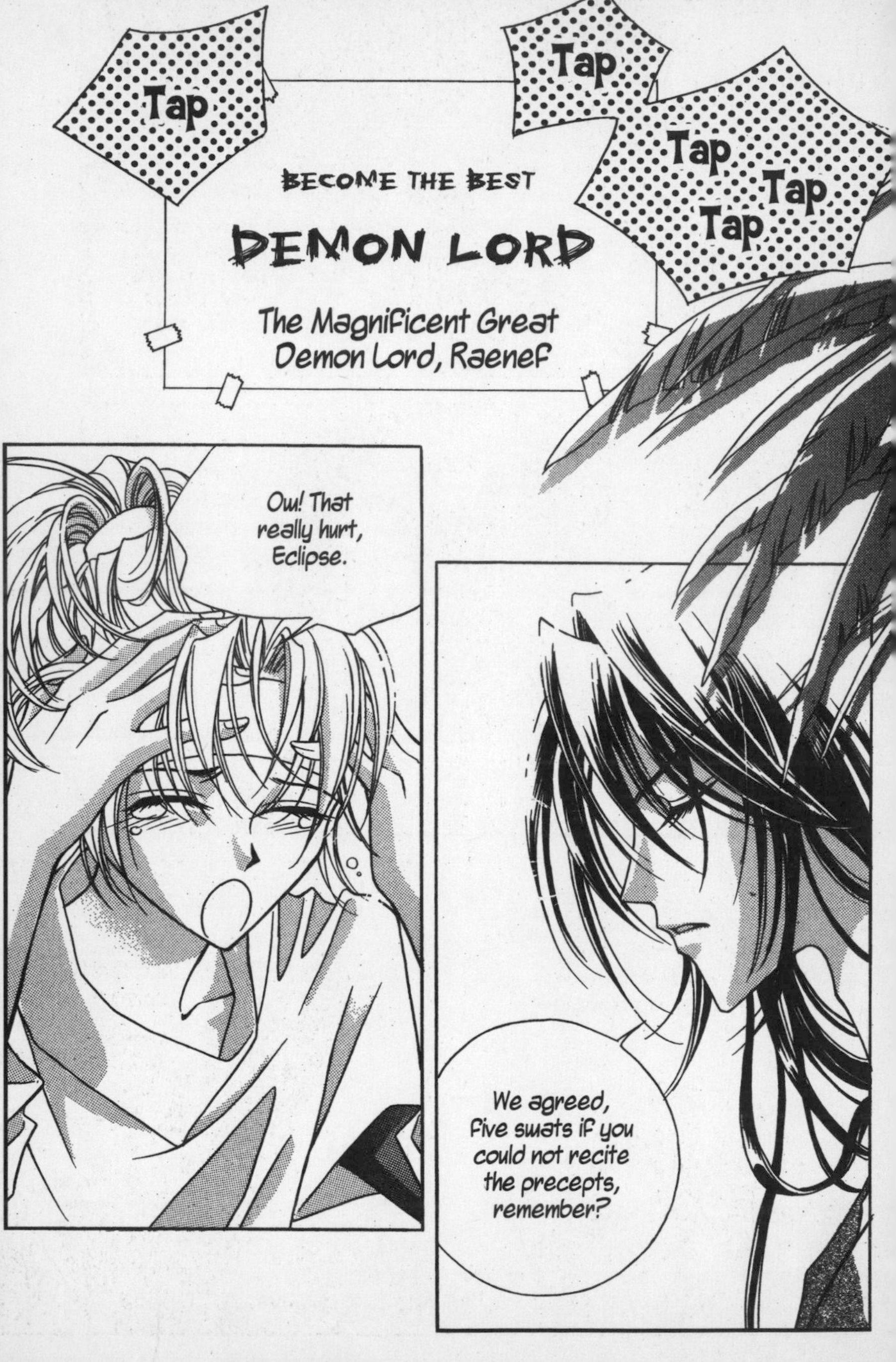
Tap
BECOME THE BEST
DEMON LORD
The Magnificent Great
Demon Lord, Raenef
Tap
Tap
Tap
Tap
Ow! That really hurt, Eclipse.
We agreed, five swats if you could not recite the precepts, remember?

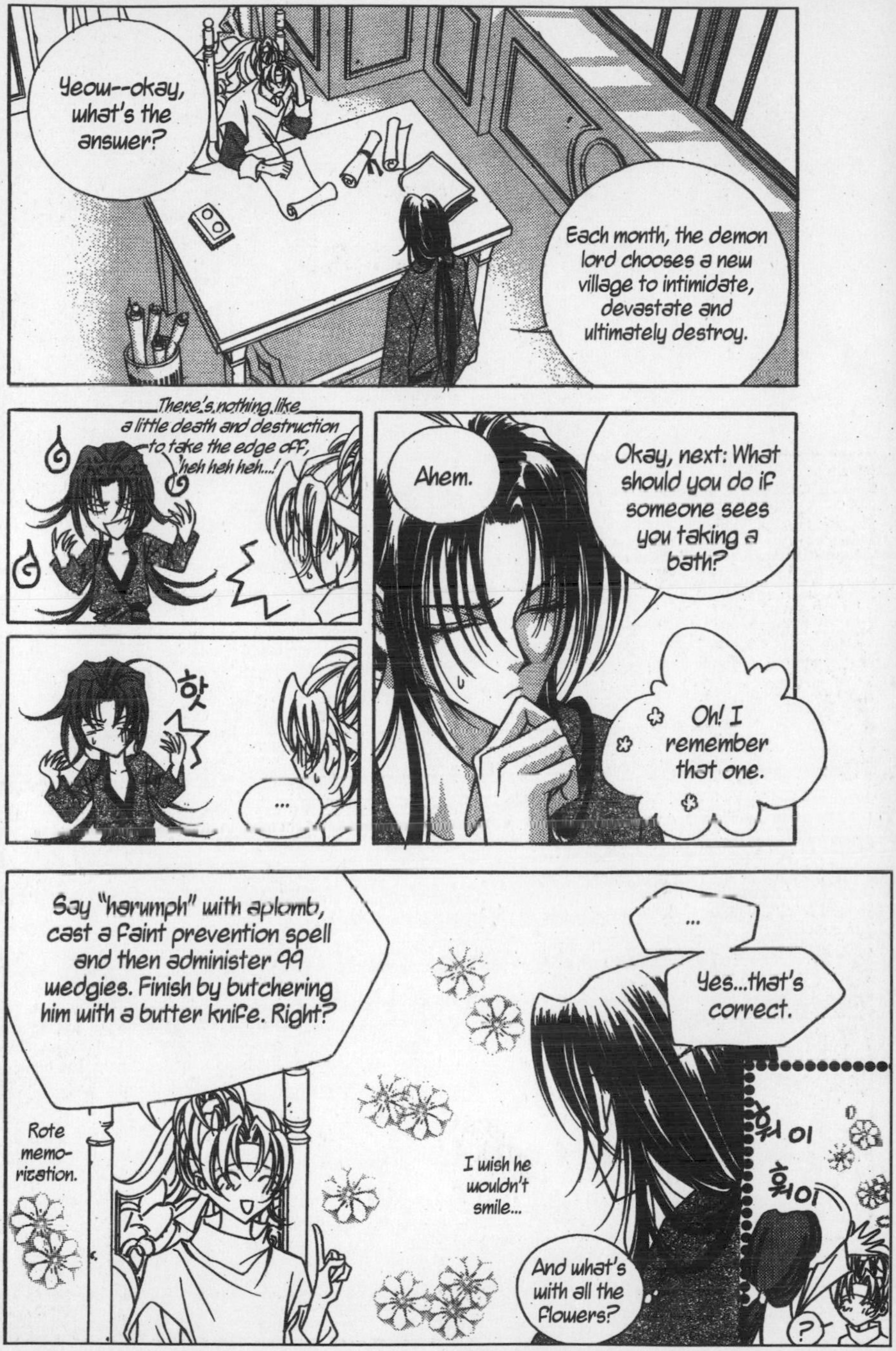
Yeow--okay, what's the answer?
Each month, the demon lord chooses a new village to intimidate, devastate and ultimately destroy.
There's nothing like a little death and destruction to take the edge off, heh heh heh...!
Ahem.
Okay, next: What should you do if someone sees you taking a bath?
핫
...
Oh! I remember that one.
Say "harumph" with aplomb, cast a faint prevention spell and then administer 99 wedgies. Finish by butchering him with a butter knife. Right?
...
Yes...that's correct.
Rote memorization.
I wish he wouldn't smile...
And what's with all the flowers?
훠이
훠이
?

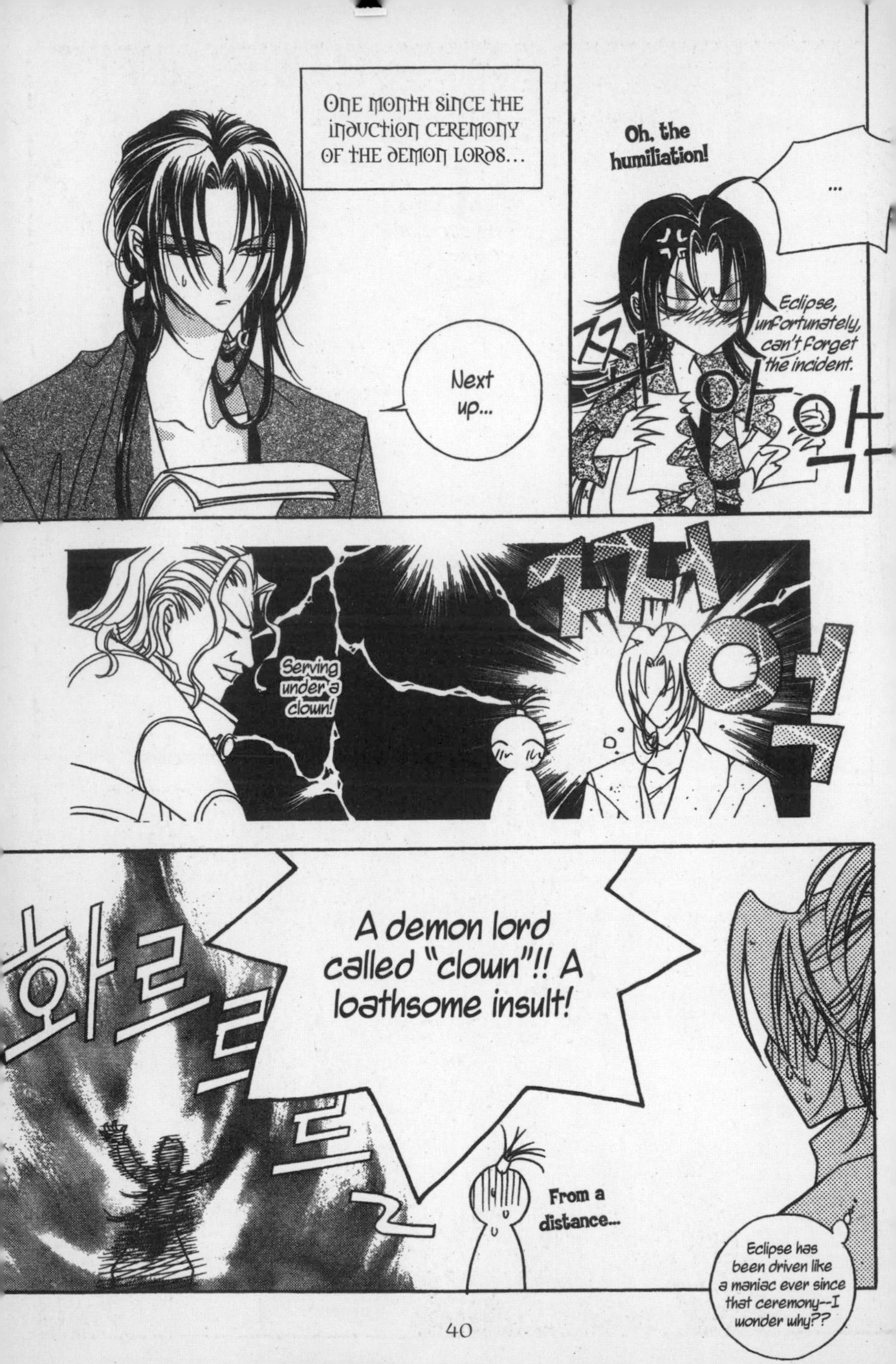
ONE MONTH SINCE THE INDUCTION CEREMONY OF THE DEMON LORDS...
Next up...
Oh, the humiliation!
...
Eclipse, unfortunately, can't forget the incident.
Serving under a clown!
A demon lord called "clown"!! A loathsome insult!
From a distance...
Eclipse has been driven like a maniac ever since that ceremony--I wonder why??

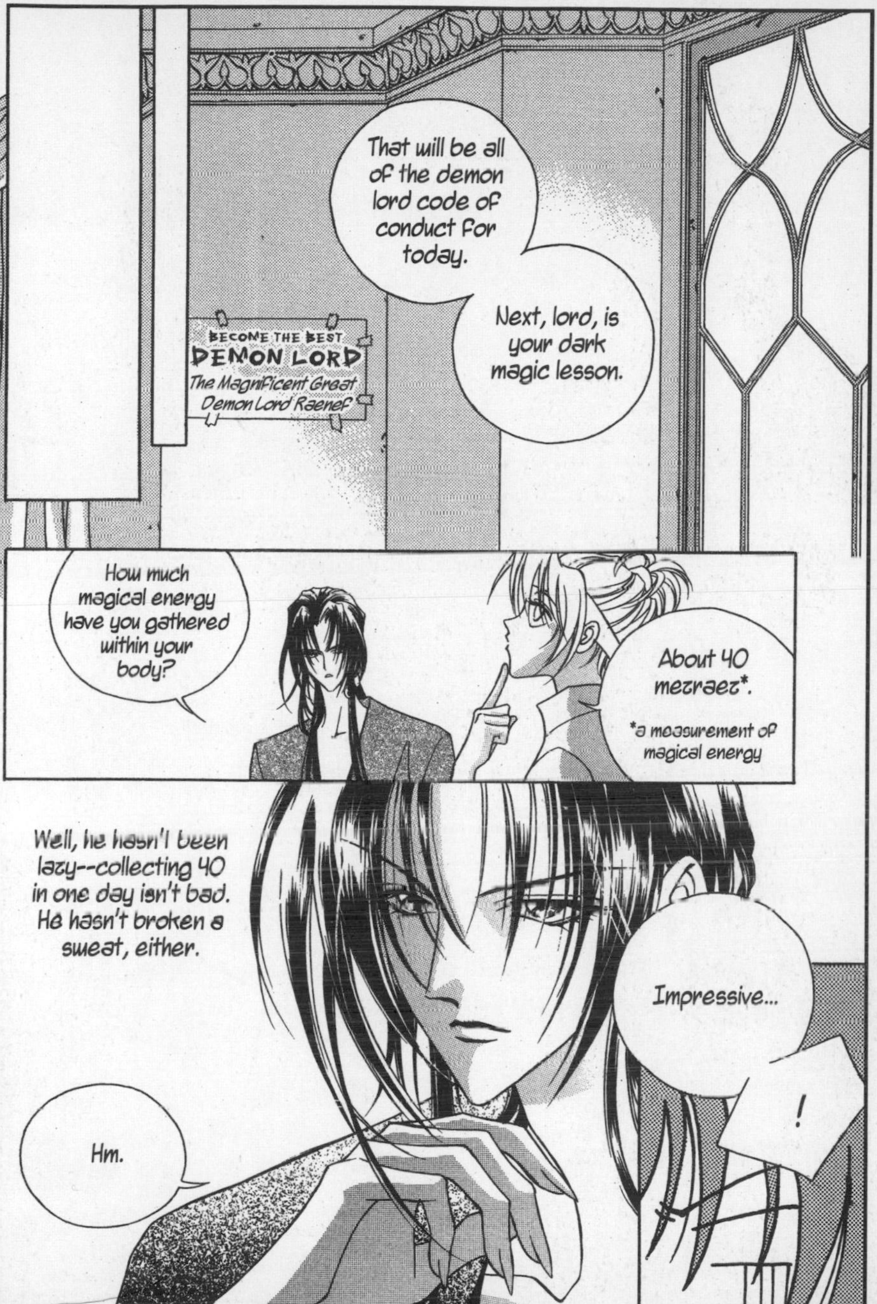
That will be all of the demon lord code of conduct for today.
Next, lord, is your dark magic lesson.
BECOME THE BEST DEMON LORD The Magnificent Great Demon Lord Raenef
How much magical energy have you gathered within your body?
About 40 merraer*.
*a measurement of magical energy
Well, he hasn't been lazy--collecting 40 in one day isn't bad. He hasn't broken a sweat, either.
Impressive...
!
Hm.

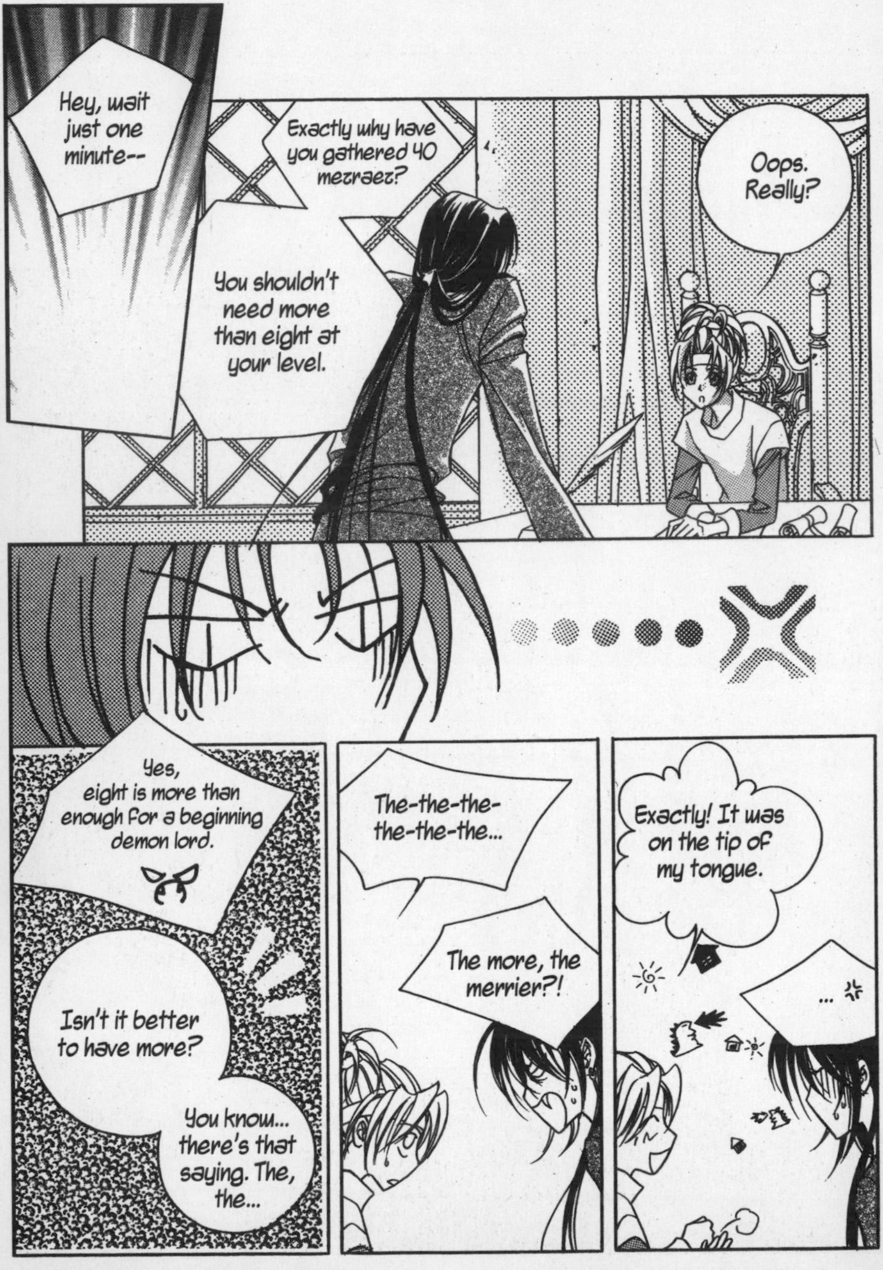
Hey, wait just one minute--
Exactly why have you gathered 40 mezraez?
You shouldn't need more than eight at your level.
Oops. Really?
Yes, eight is more than enough for a beginning demon lord.
Isn't it better to have more?
You know... there's that saying. The, the...
The-the-the-the-the-the...
The more, the merrier?!
Exactly! It was on the tip of my tongue.
...

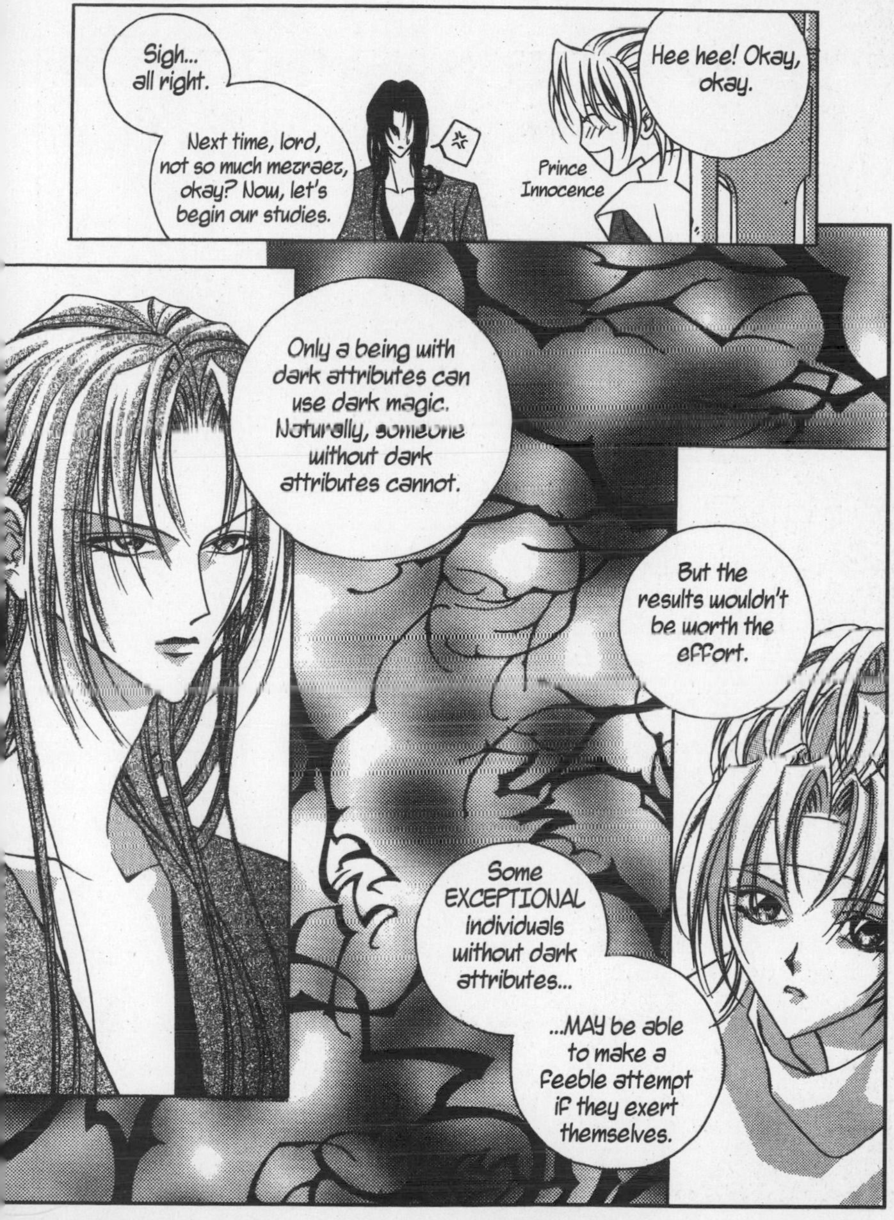
Hee hee! Okay, okay.
Prince Innocence
Sigh... all right.
Next time, lord, not so much mezraez, okay? Now, let's begin our studies.
Only a being with dark attributes can use dark magic. Naturally, someone without dark attributes cannot.
But the results wouldn't be worth the effort.
Some EXCEPTIONAL individuals without dark attributes...
...MAY be able to make a feeble attempt if they exert themselves.

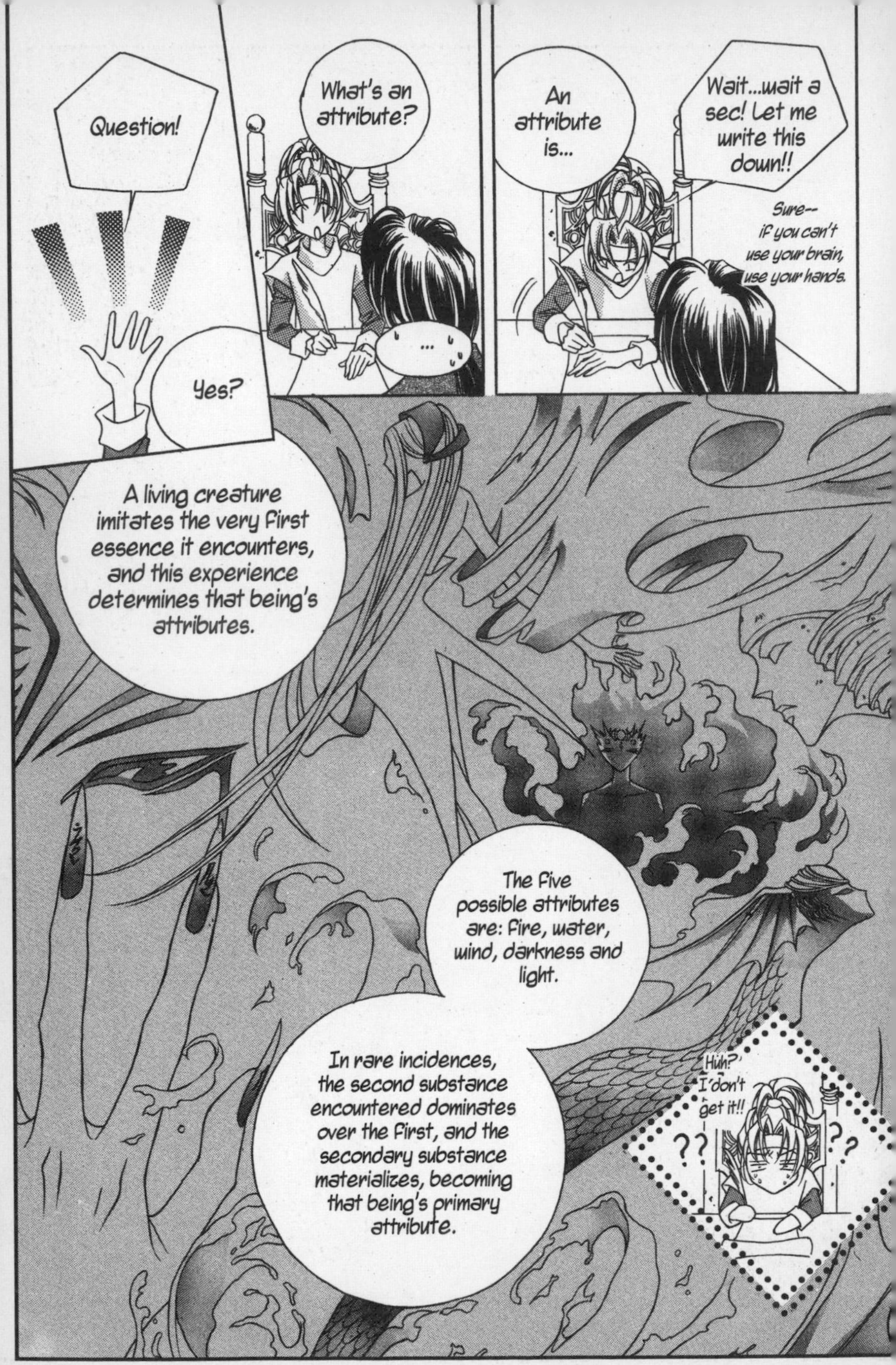
Question!
Yes?
What's an attribute?
...
An attribute is...
Wait...wait a sec! Let me write this down!!
Sure-- if you can't use your brain, use your hands.
A living creature imitates the very first essence it encounters, and this experience determines that being's attributes.
The five possible attributes are: fire, water, wind, darkness and light.
In rare incidences, the second substance encountered dominates over the first, and the secondary substance materializes, becoming that being's primary attribute.
Huh? I don't get it!!
??
??

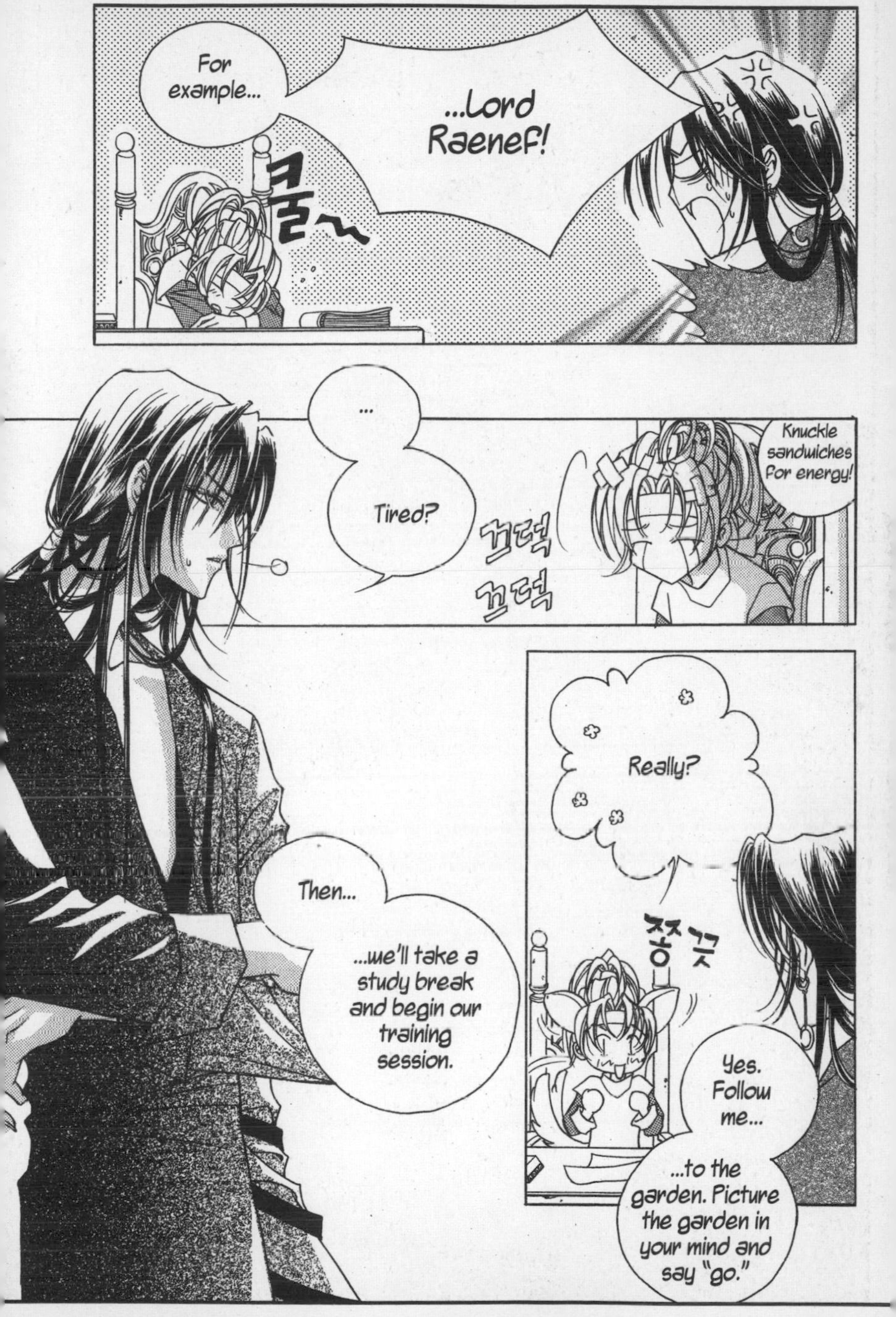
For example...
...Lord Raenef!
쿨~
...
Tired?
끄덕
끄덕
Knuckle sandwiches for energy!
Really?
Then...
...we'll take a study break and begin our training session.
쫑긋
Yes. Follow me...
...to the garden. Picture the garden in your mind and say "go."

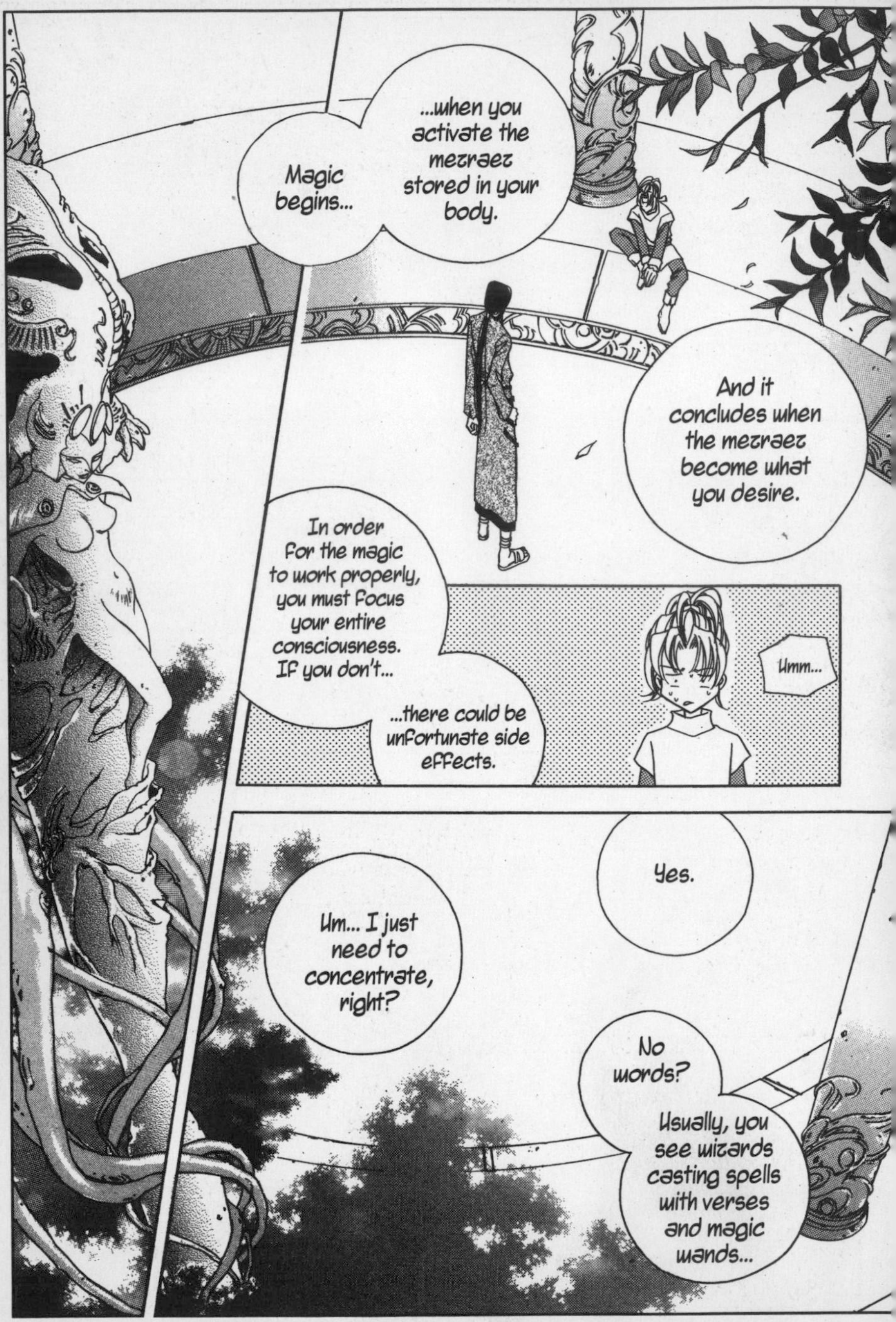

Magic begins...
...when you activate the metraet stored in your body.
And it concludes when the metraet become what you desire.
In order for the magic to work properly, you must focus your entire consciousness. If you don't...
...there could be unfortunate side effects.
Umm...
Yes.
Um... I just need to concentrate, right?
No words?
Usually, you see wizards casting spells with verses and magic wands...

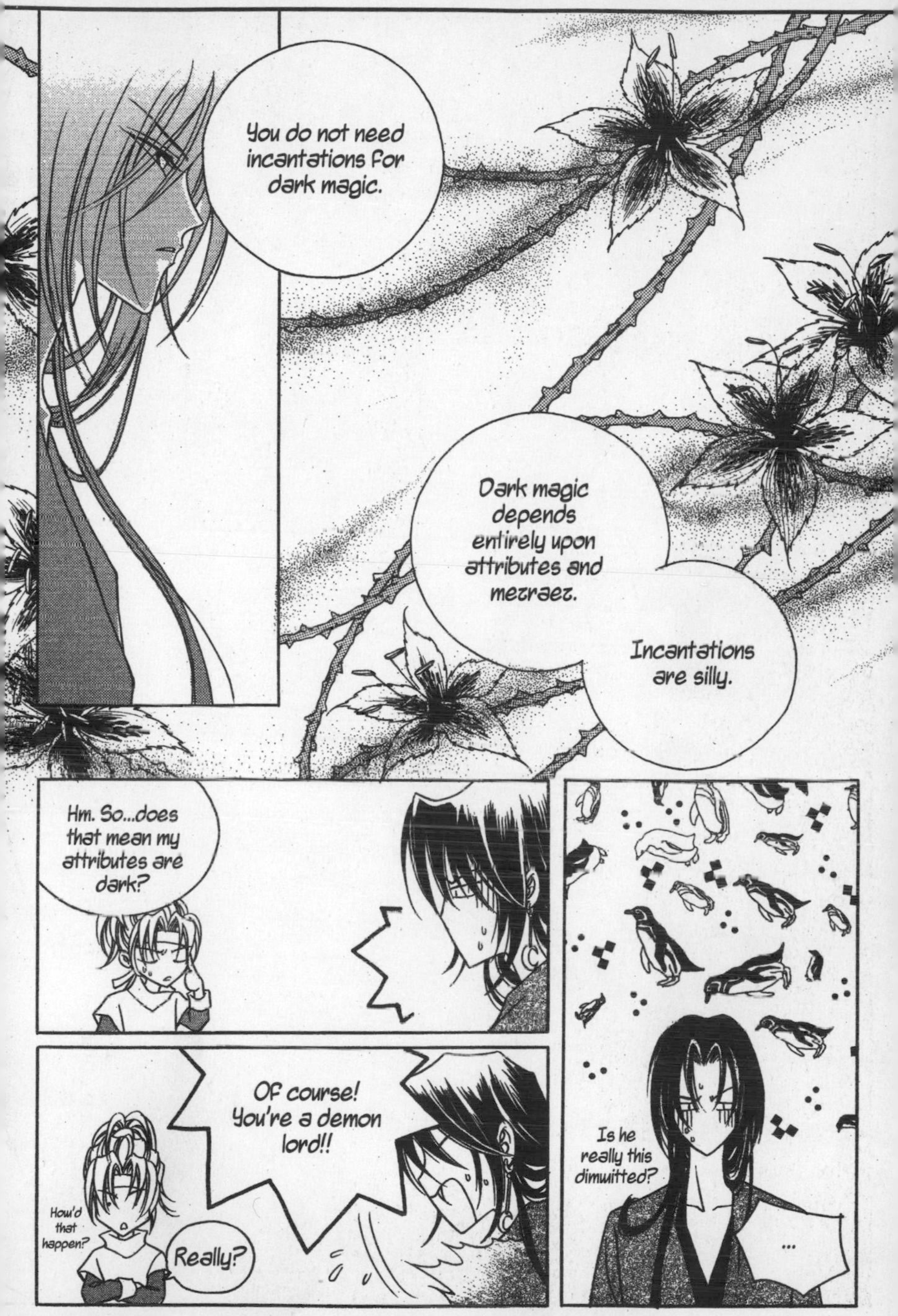
You do not need incantations for dark magic.
Dark magic depends entirely upon attributes and mezraez.
Incantations are silly.
Hm. So...does that mean my attributes are dark?
Of course! You're a demon lord!!
How'd that happen?
Really?
Is he really this dimwitted?
...

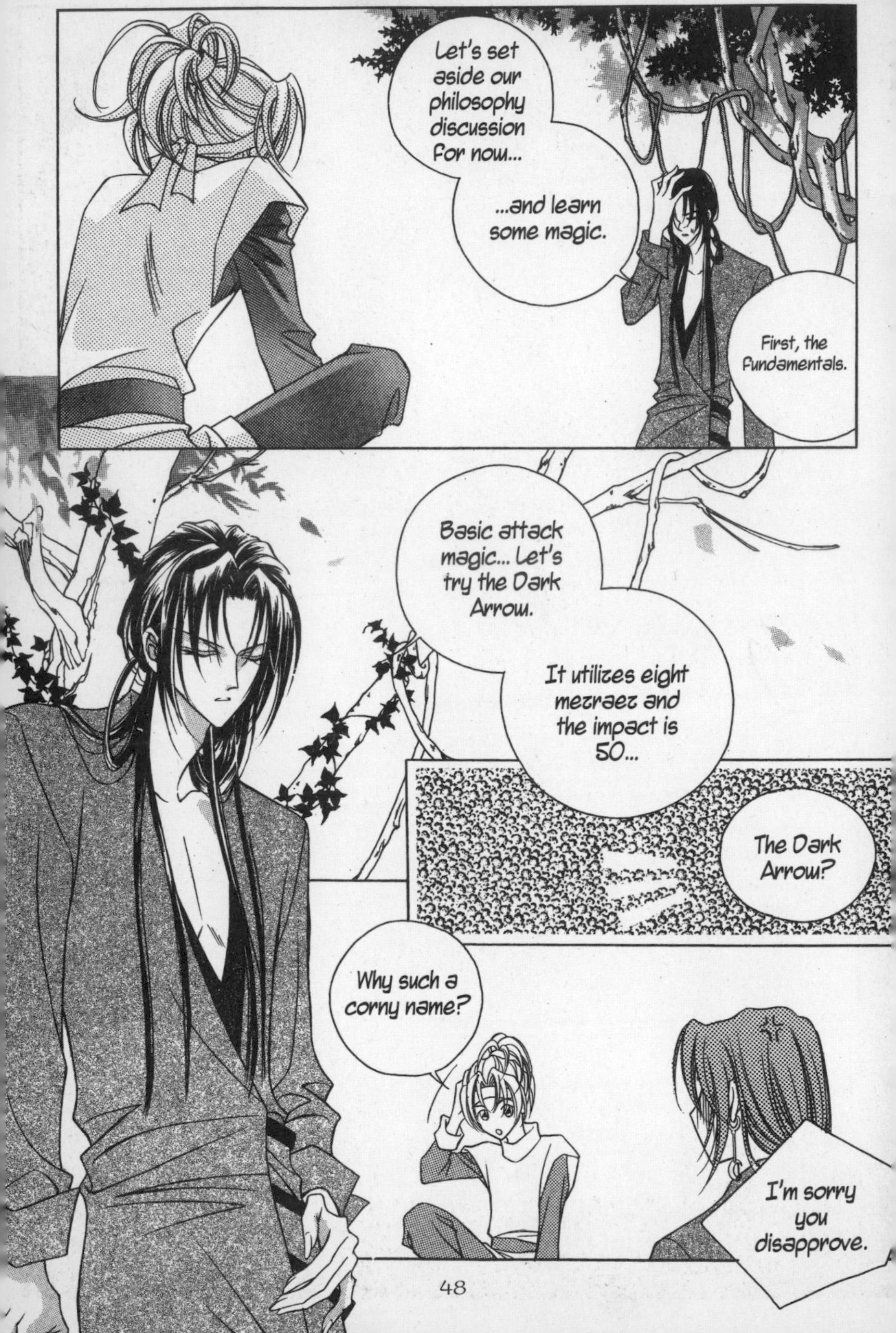
Let's set aside our philosophy discussion for now...
...and learn some magic.
First, the fundamentals.
Basic attack magic... Let's try the Dark Arrow.
It utilizes eight mezraez and the impact is 50...
The Dark Arrow?
Why such a corny name?
I'm sorry you disapprove.

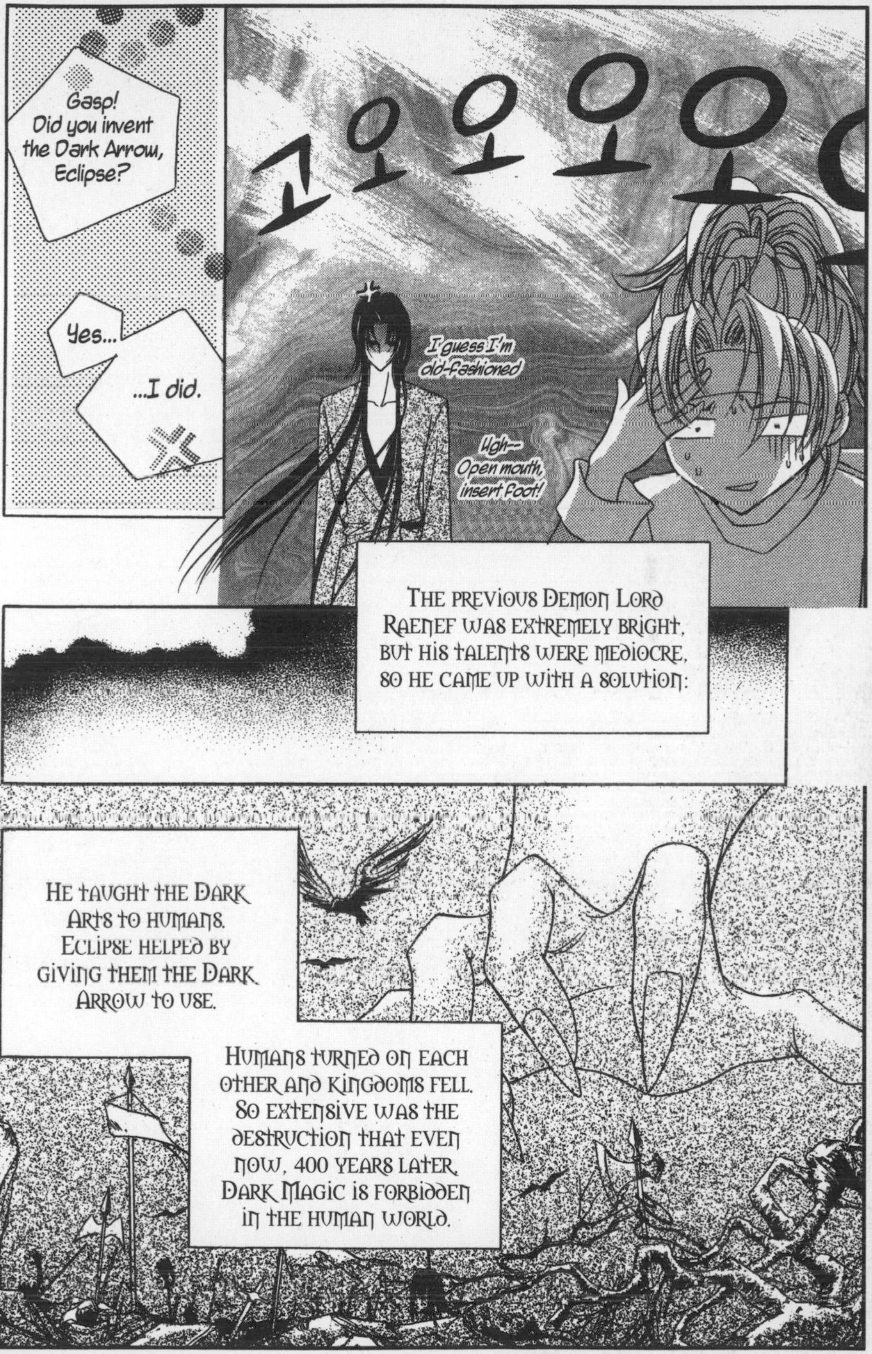

Gasp! Did you invent the Dark Arrow, Eclipse?
고오오오오
Yes...
...I did.
I guess I'm old-fashioned
Ugh-- Open mouth, insert foot!
The previous Demon Lord Raenef was extremely bright, but his talents were mediocre, so he came up with a solution:
He taught the Dark Arts to humans. Eclipse helped by giving them the Dark Arrow to use.
Humans turned on each other and kingdoms fell. So extensive was the destruction that even now, 400 years later, Dark Magic is forbidden in the human world.

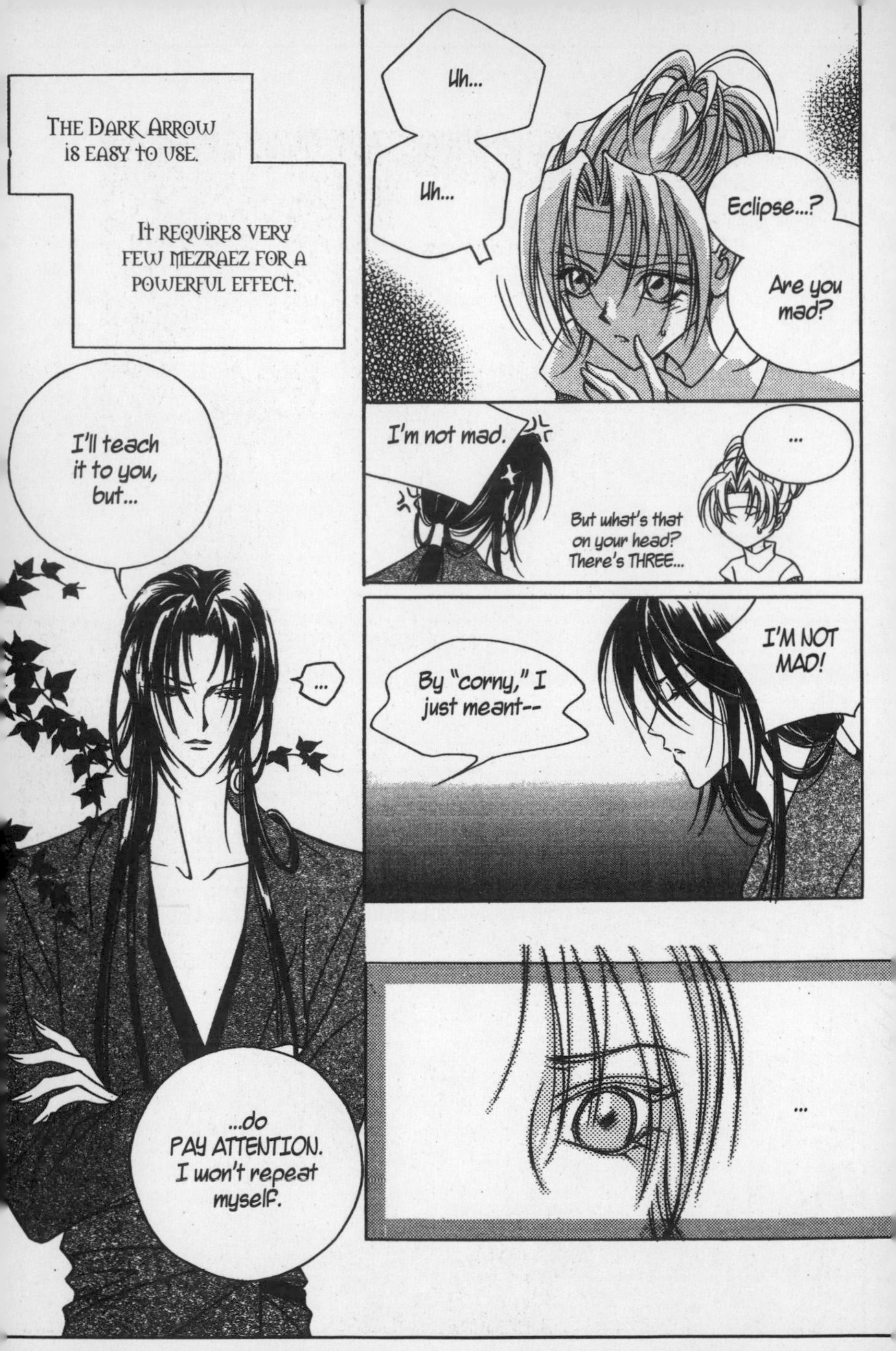
The Dark Arrow is easy to use.
It requires very few mezraez for a powerful effect.
I'll teach it to you, but...
...
...do PAY ATTENTION. I won't repeat myself.
Uh...
Uh...
Eclipse...?
Are you mad?
I'm not mad.
...
But what's that on your head? There's THREE...
By "corny," I just meant--
I'M NOT MAD!
...

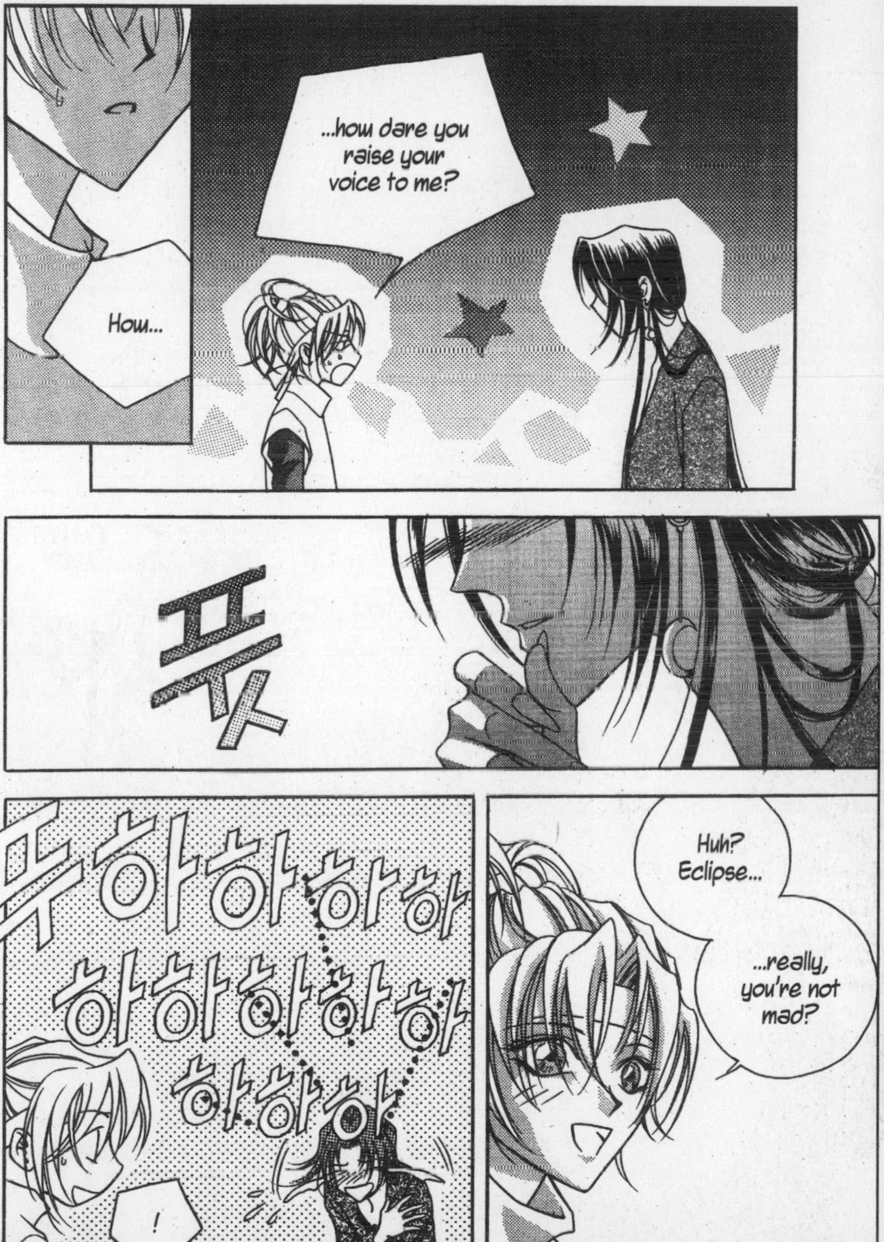
How...
...how dare you raise your voice to me?
!
Huh? Eclipse...
...really, you're not mad?

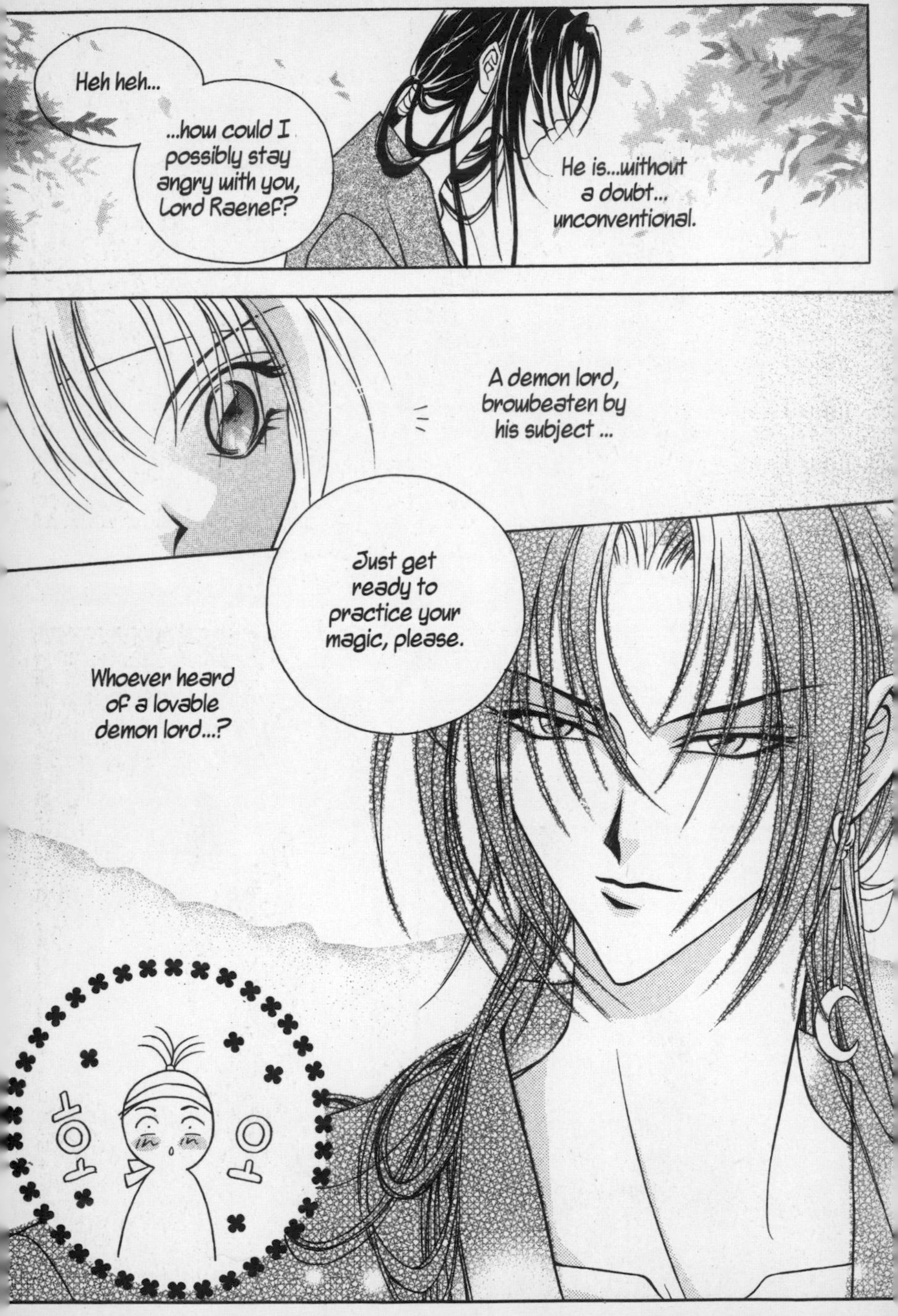

Heh heh...
...how could I possibly stay angry with you, Lord Raenef?
He is...without a doubt... unconventional.
A demon lord, browbeaten by his subject ...
Just get ready to practice your magic, please.
Whoever heard of a lovable demon lord...?

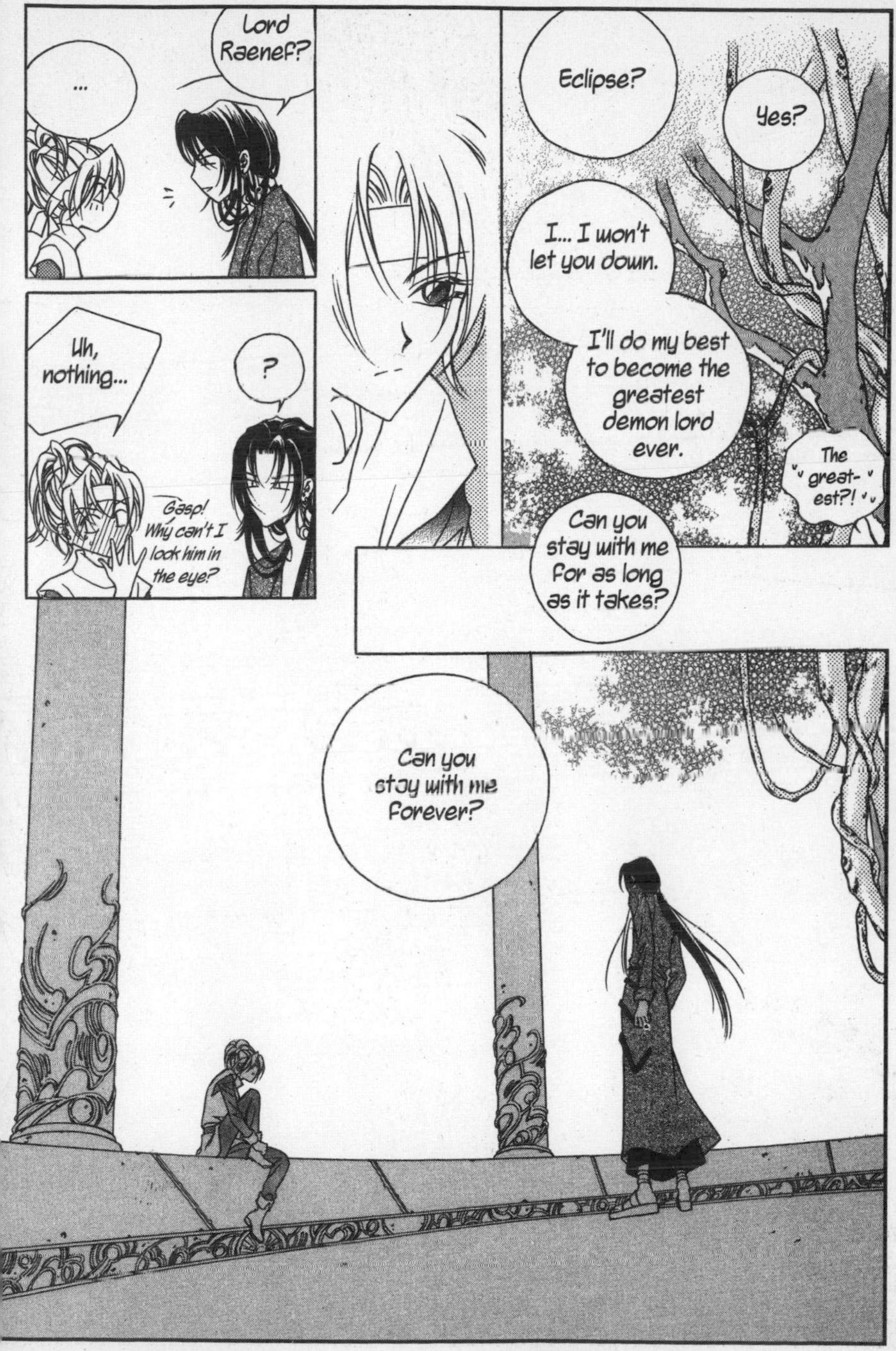
Eclipse?
Yes?
I... I won't let you down.
I'll do my best to become the greatest demon lord ever.
The greatest?!
Lord Raenef?
...
?
Uh, nothing...
Gasp! Why can't I look him in the eye?
Can you stay with me for as long as it takes?
Can you stay with me forever?

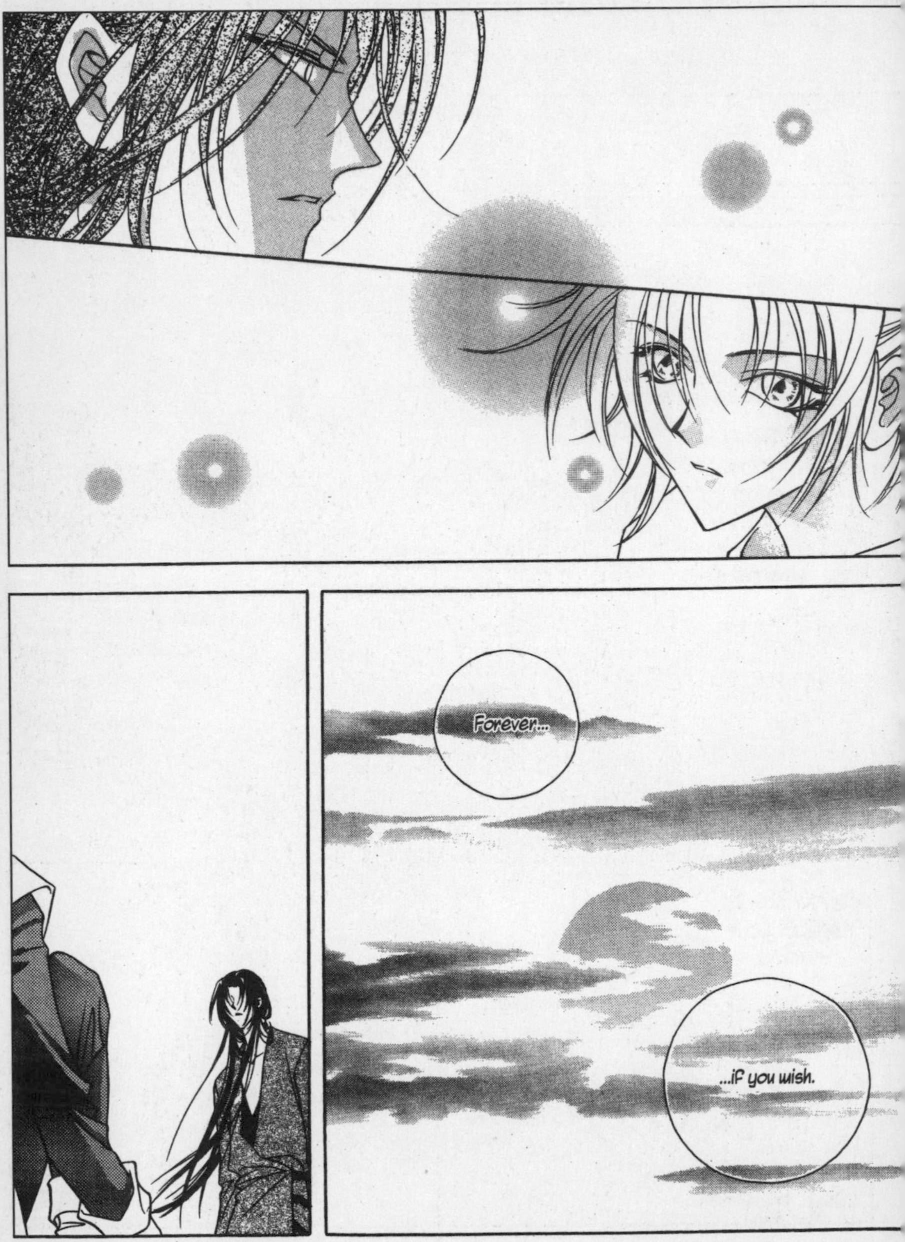
Forever...
...if you wish.

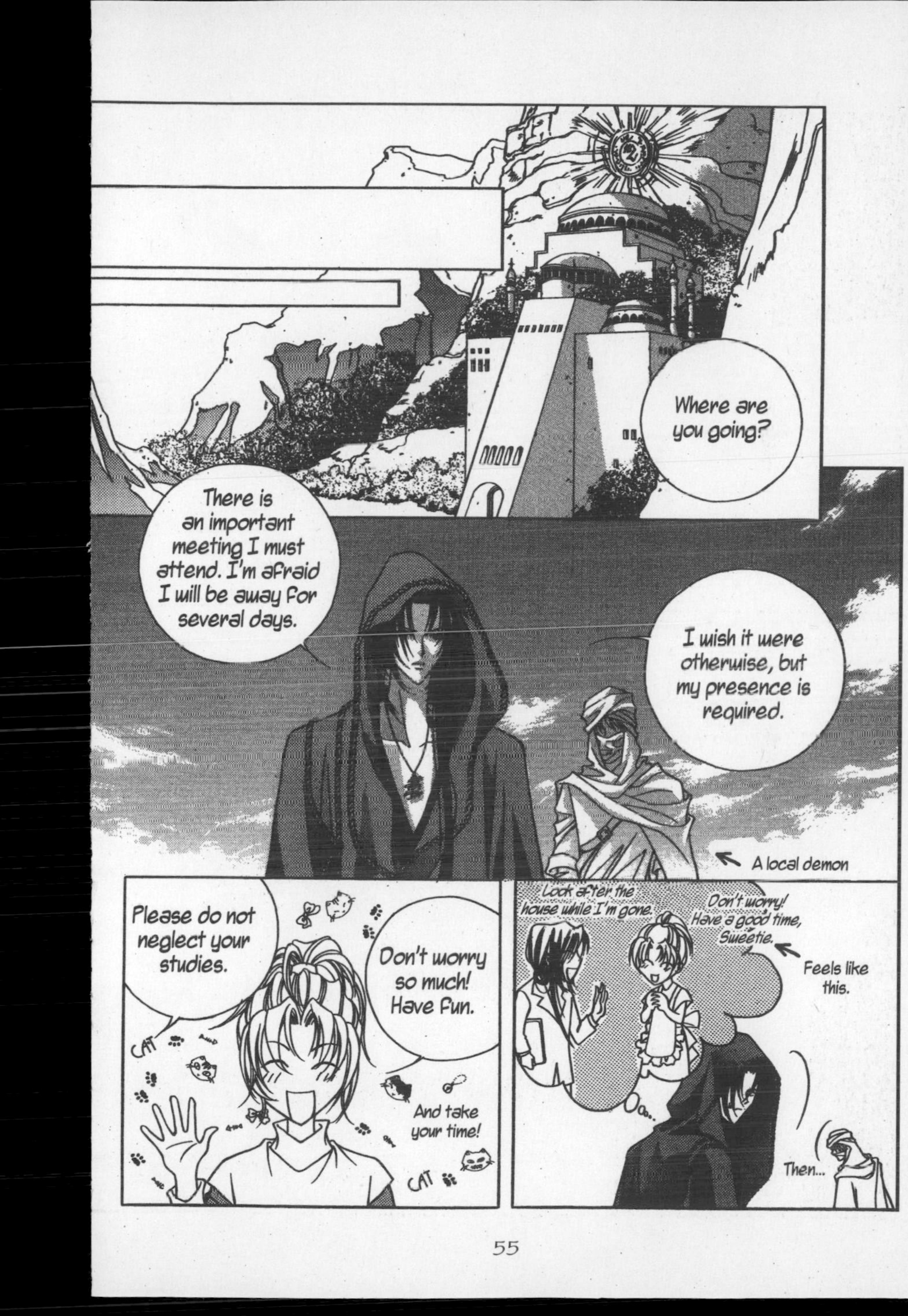
Where are you going?
There is an important meeting I must attend. I'm afraid I will be away for several days.
I wish it were otherwise, but my presence is required.
A local demon
Please do not neglect your studies.
Don't worry so much! Have fun.
And take your time!
CAT
CAT
Look after the house while I'm gone.
Don't worry! Have a good time, Sweetie.
Feels like this.
Then...

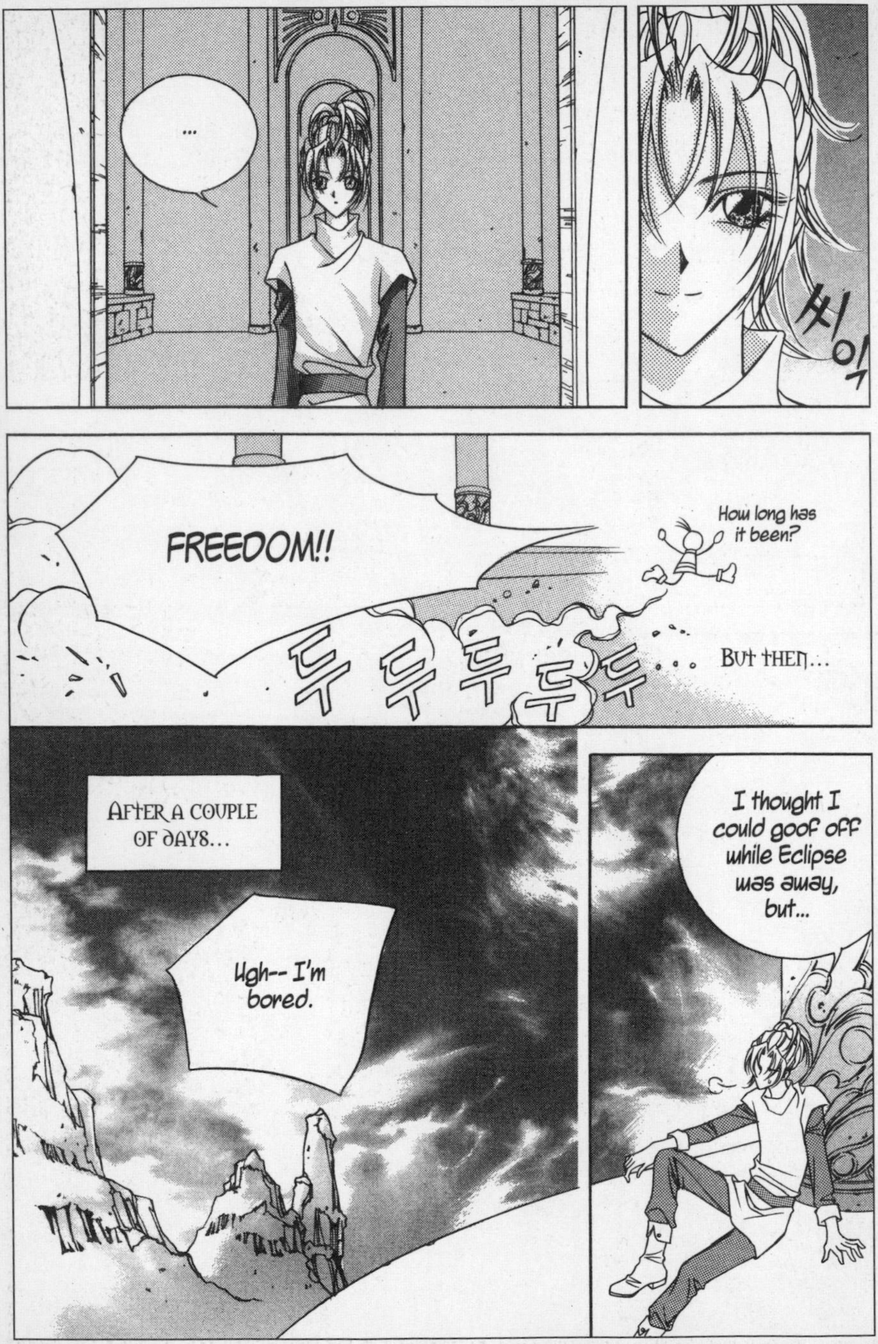
...
씨익
FREEDOM!!
How long has it been?
두두두두두...
But then...
After a couple of days...
Ugh-- I'm bored.
I thought I could goof off while Eclipse was away, but...

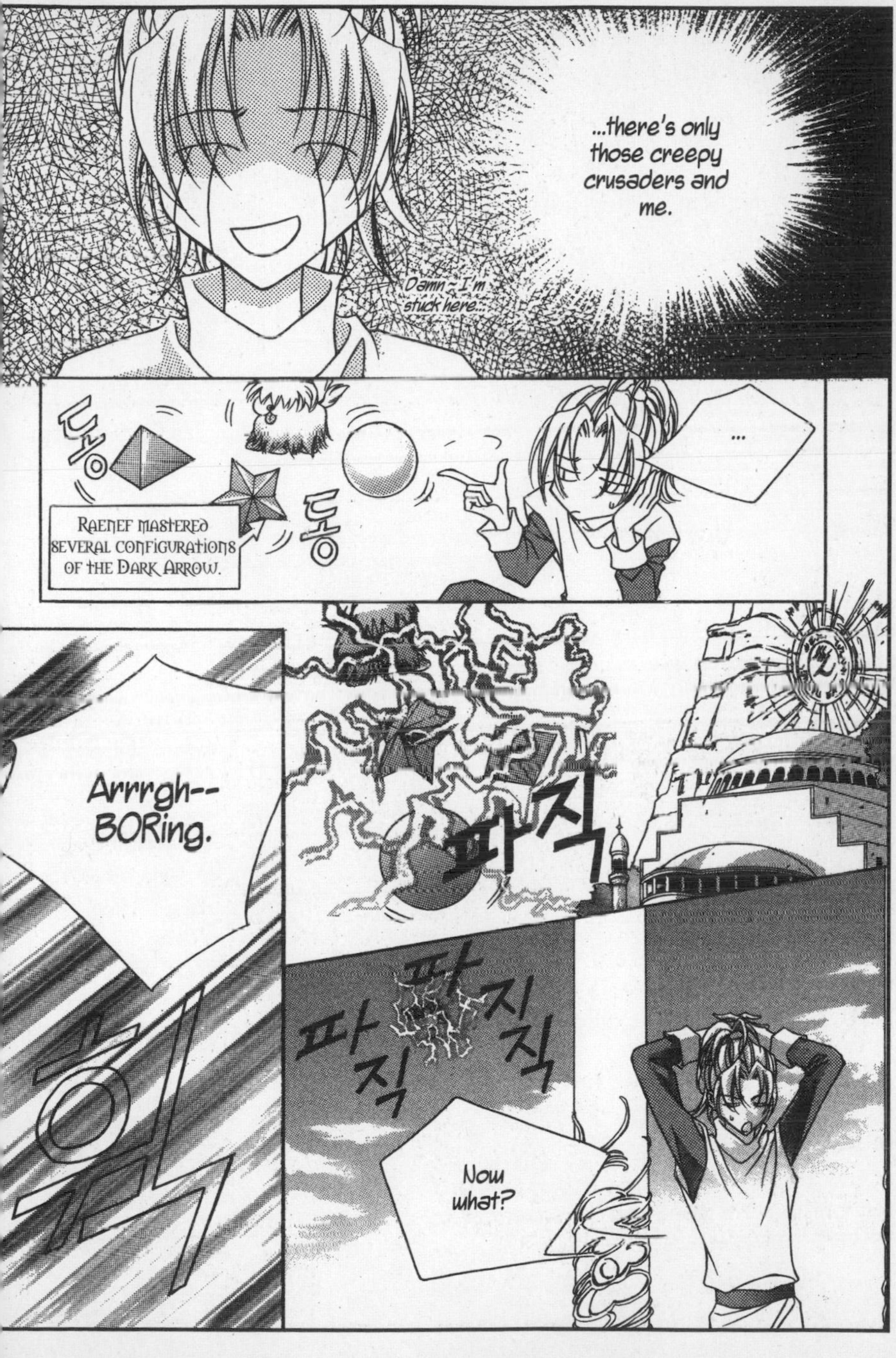
...there's only those creepy crusaders and me.
Damn~ I'm stuck here...
...
동
동
Raenef mastered several configurations of the Dark Arrow.
Arrrgh-- BORing.
파직
파직
파지직
Now what?

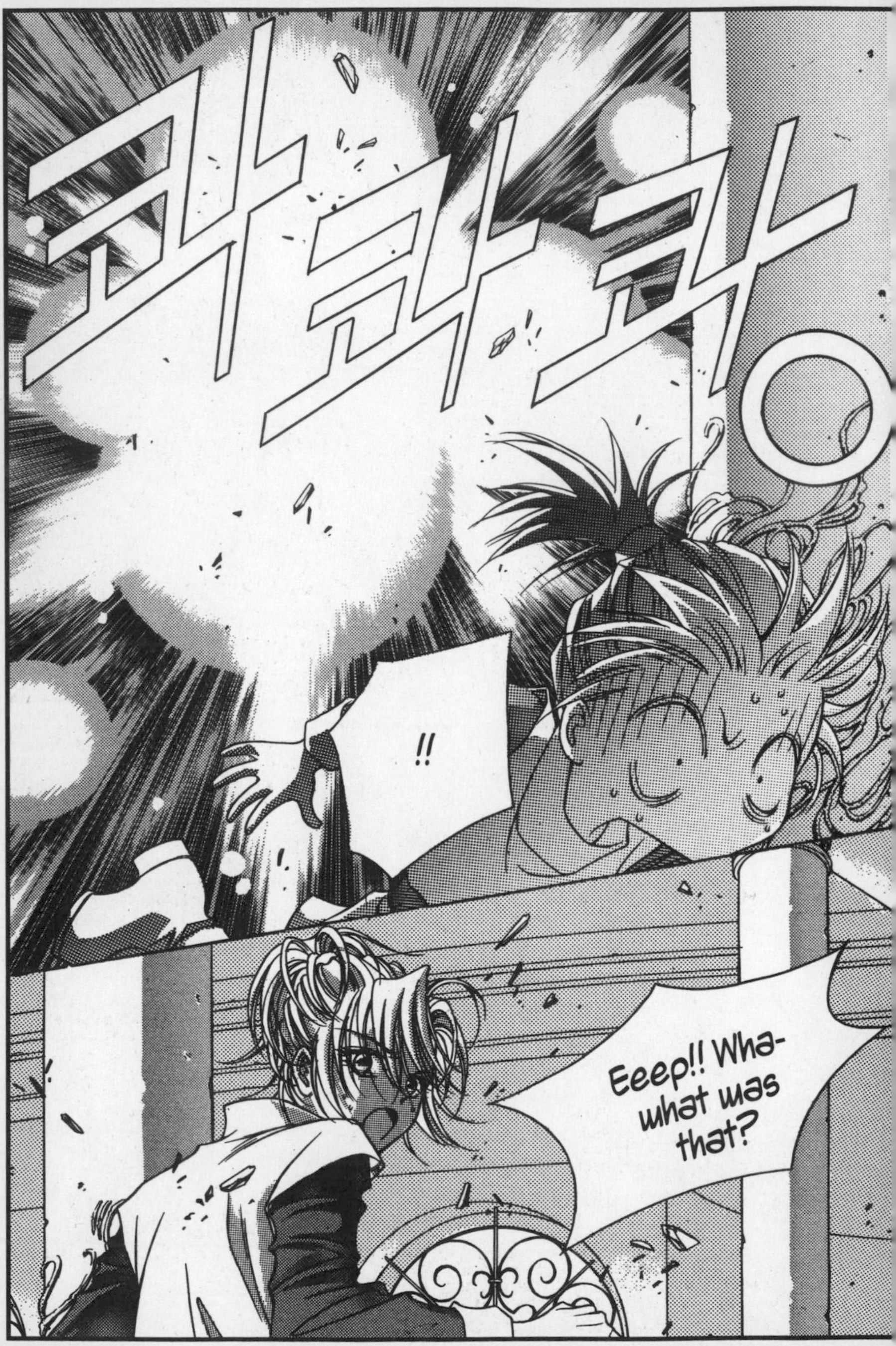
!!
Eeep!! Wha-what was that?

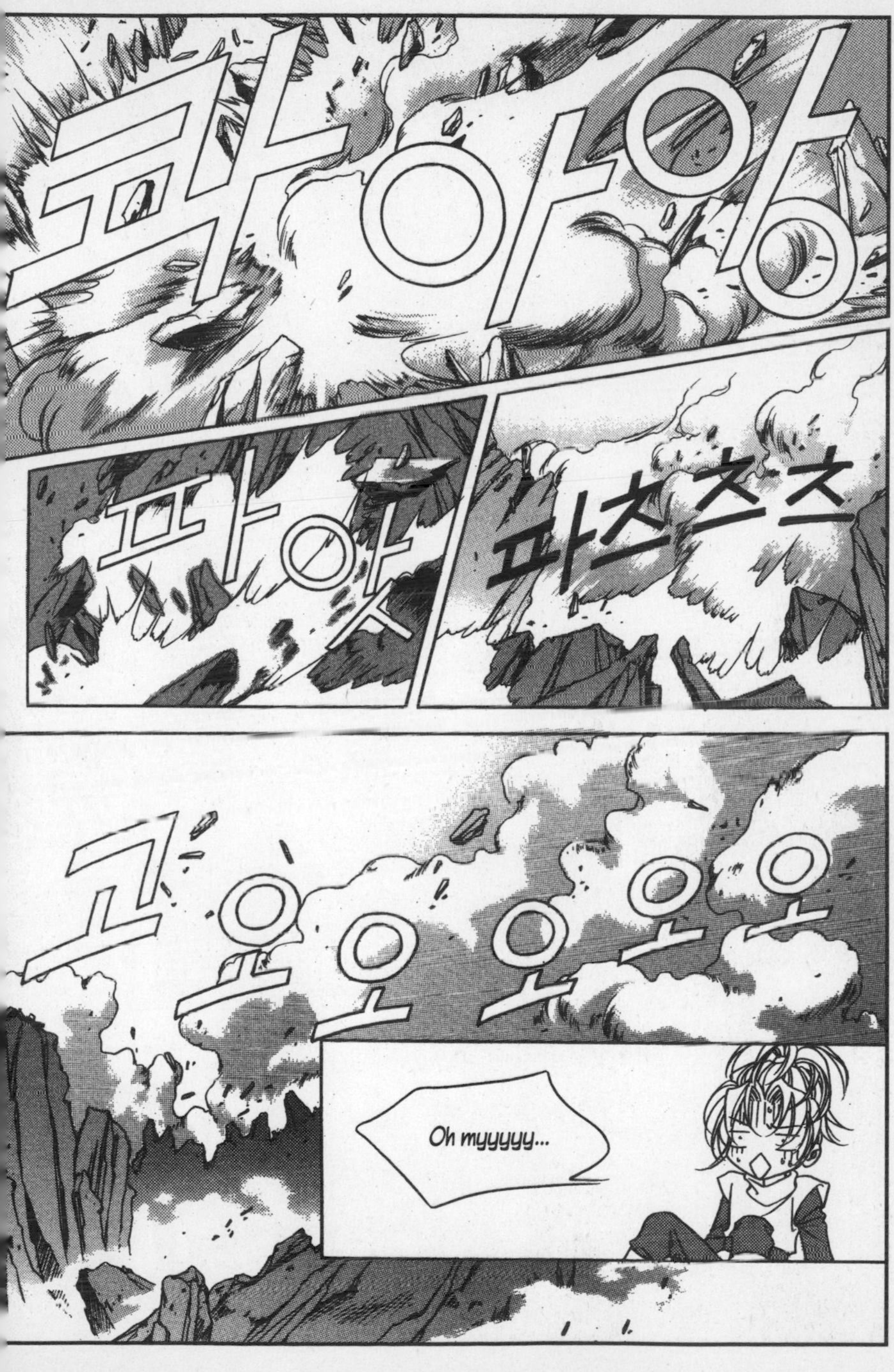
콰아앙
파앗
파츠츠
고오오오오오
Oh myyyyy...

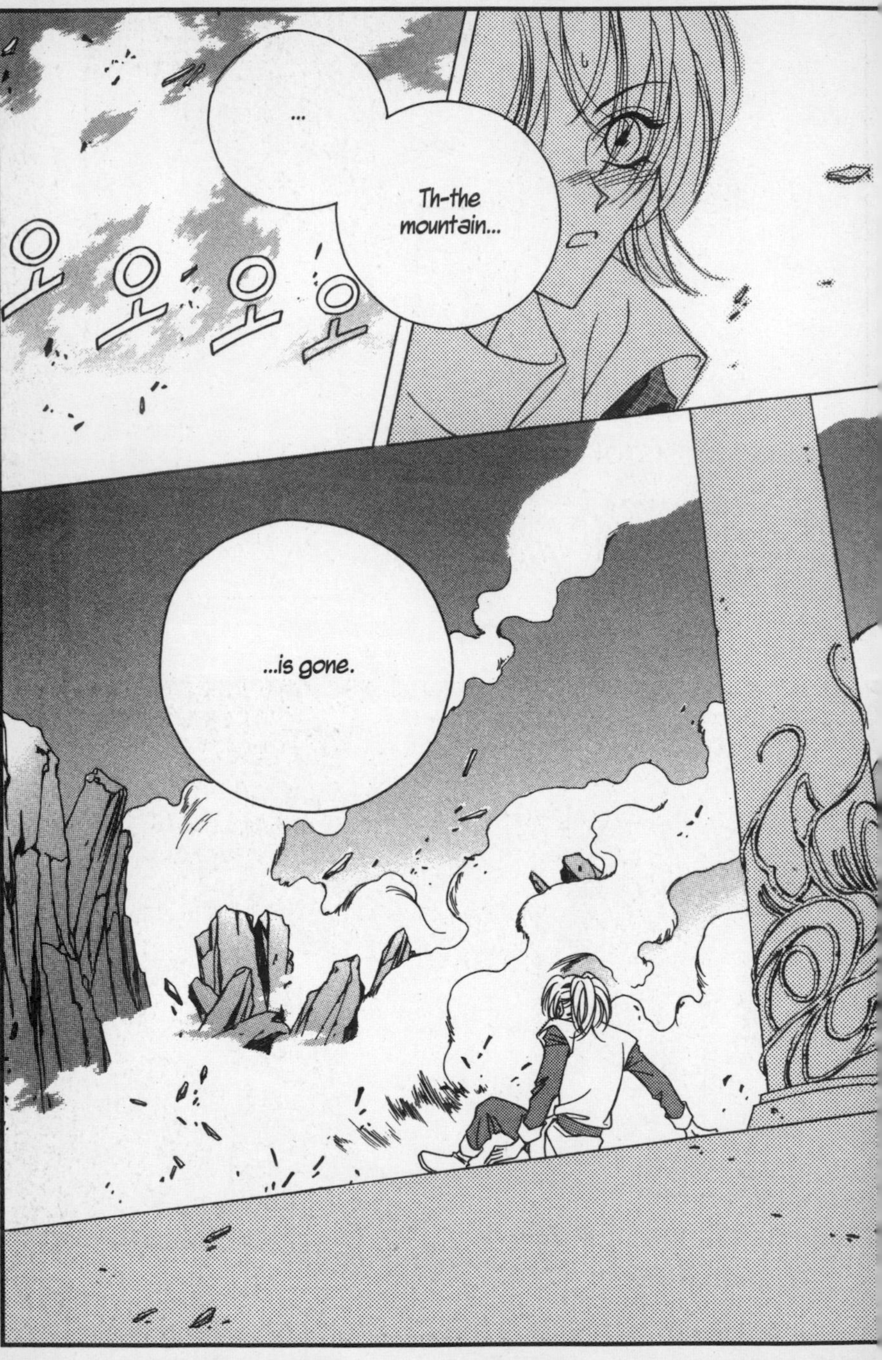
...
Th-the mountain...
오오오오
...is gone.

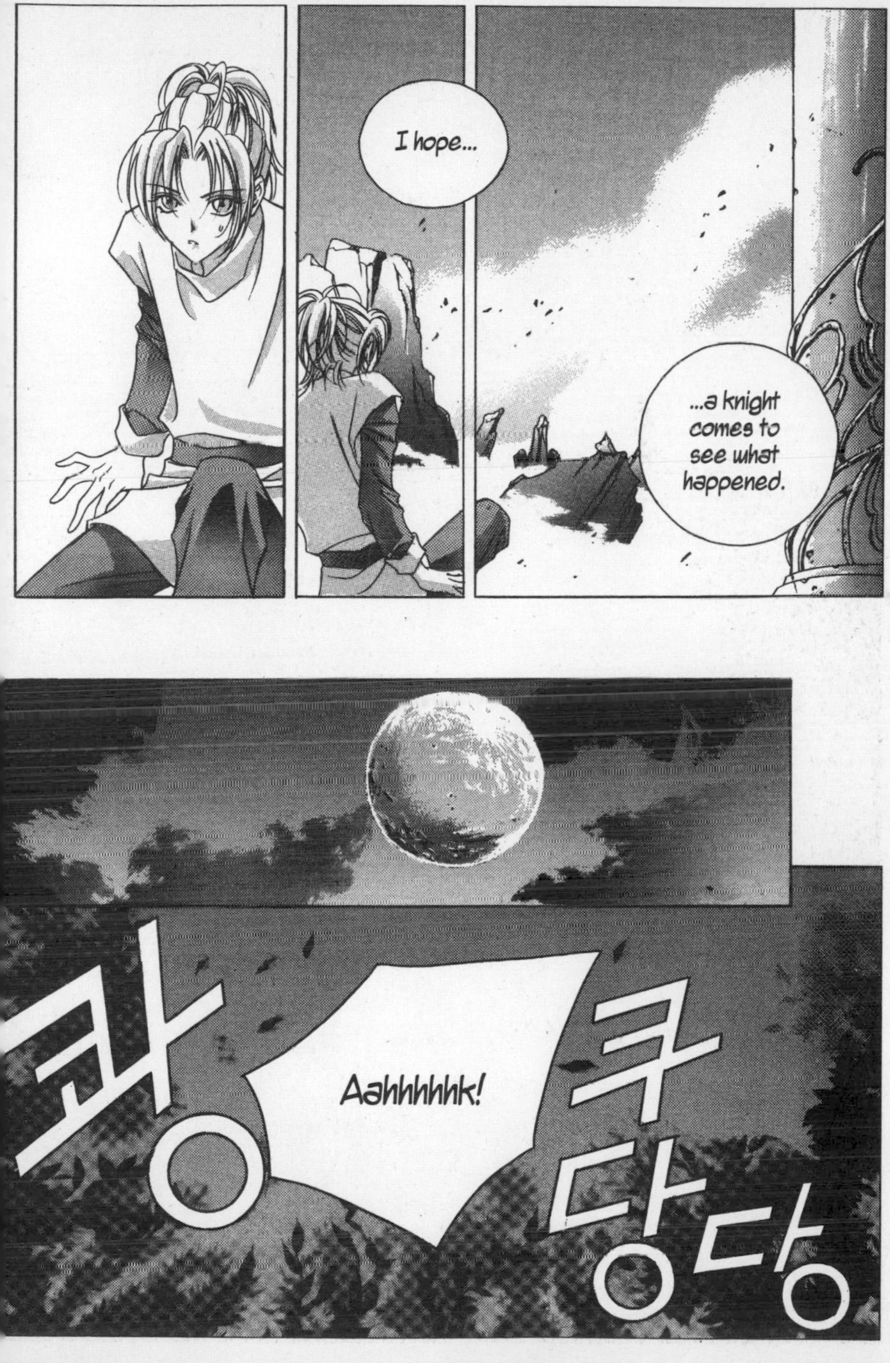
I hope...
...a knight comes to see what happened.
콰앙
Aahhhhhk!
쿠다당

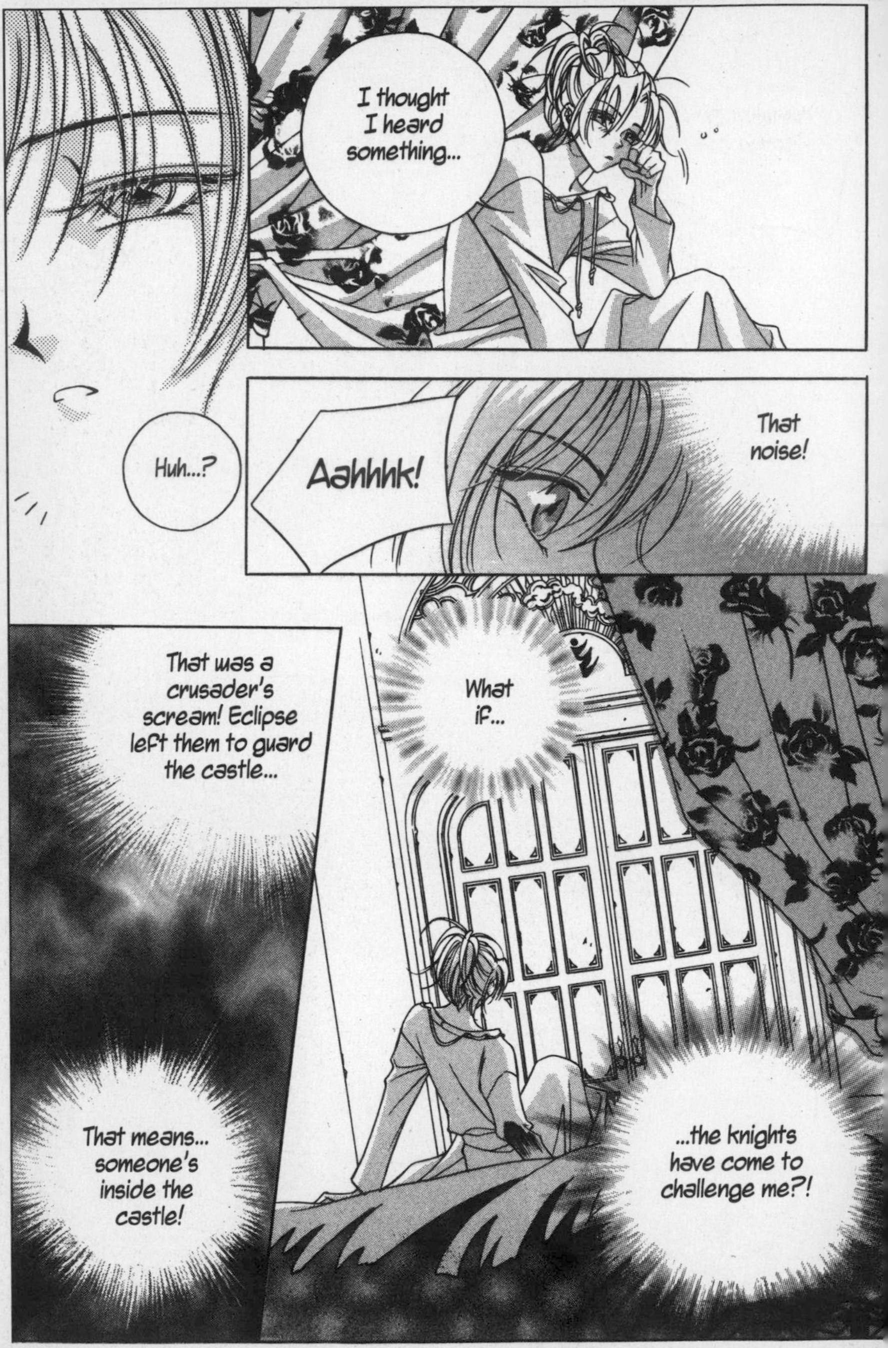
Huh...?
I thought I heard something...
Aahhhk!
That noise!
That was a crusader's scream! Eclipse left them to guard the castle...
That means... someone's inside the castle!
What if...
...the knights have come to challenge me?!

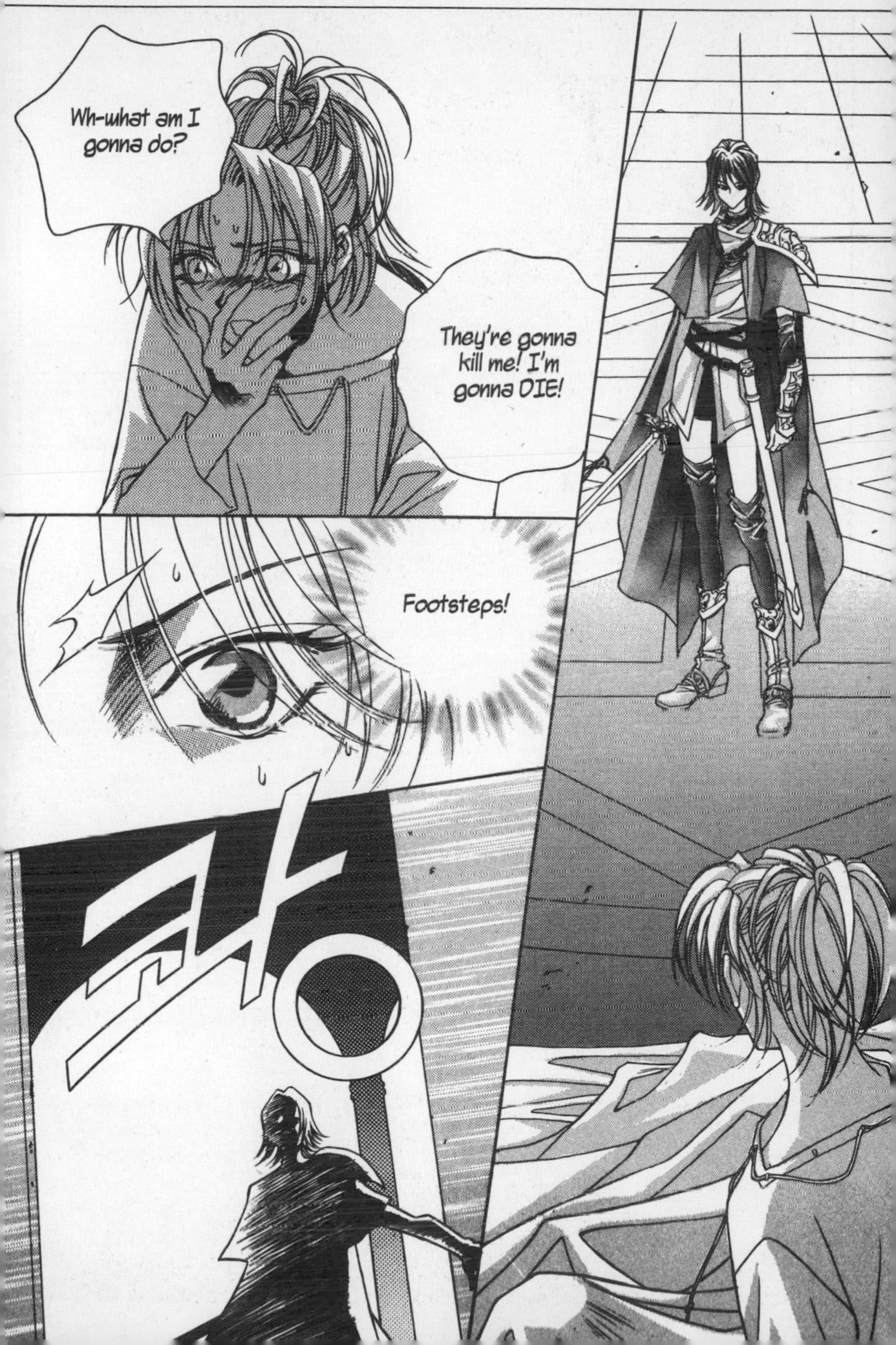
Wh-what am I gonna do?
They're gonna kill me! I'm gonna DIE!
Footsteps!

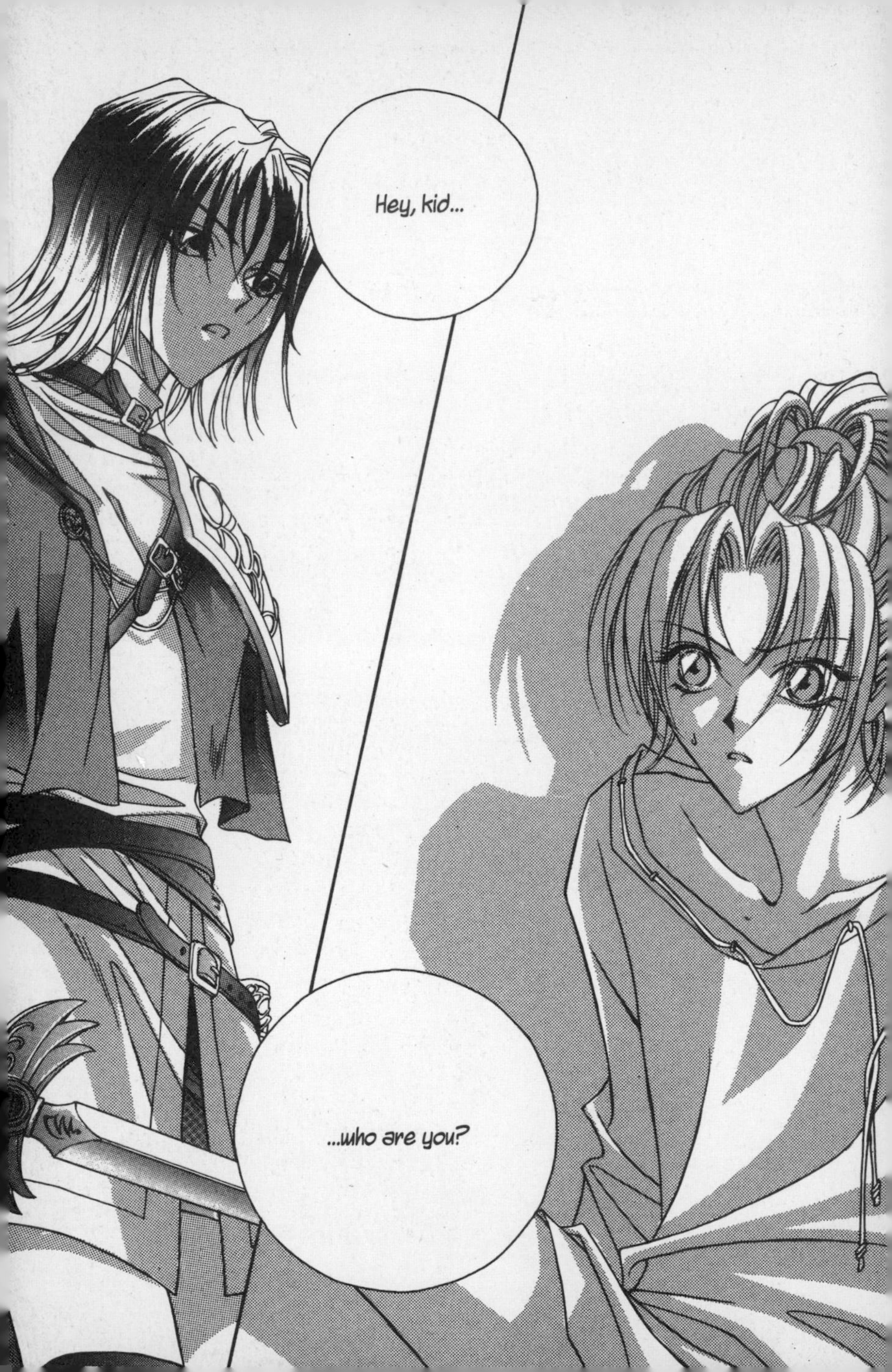
Hey, kid...
...who are you?

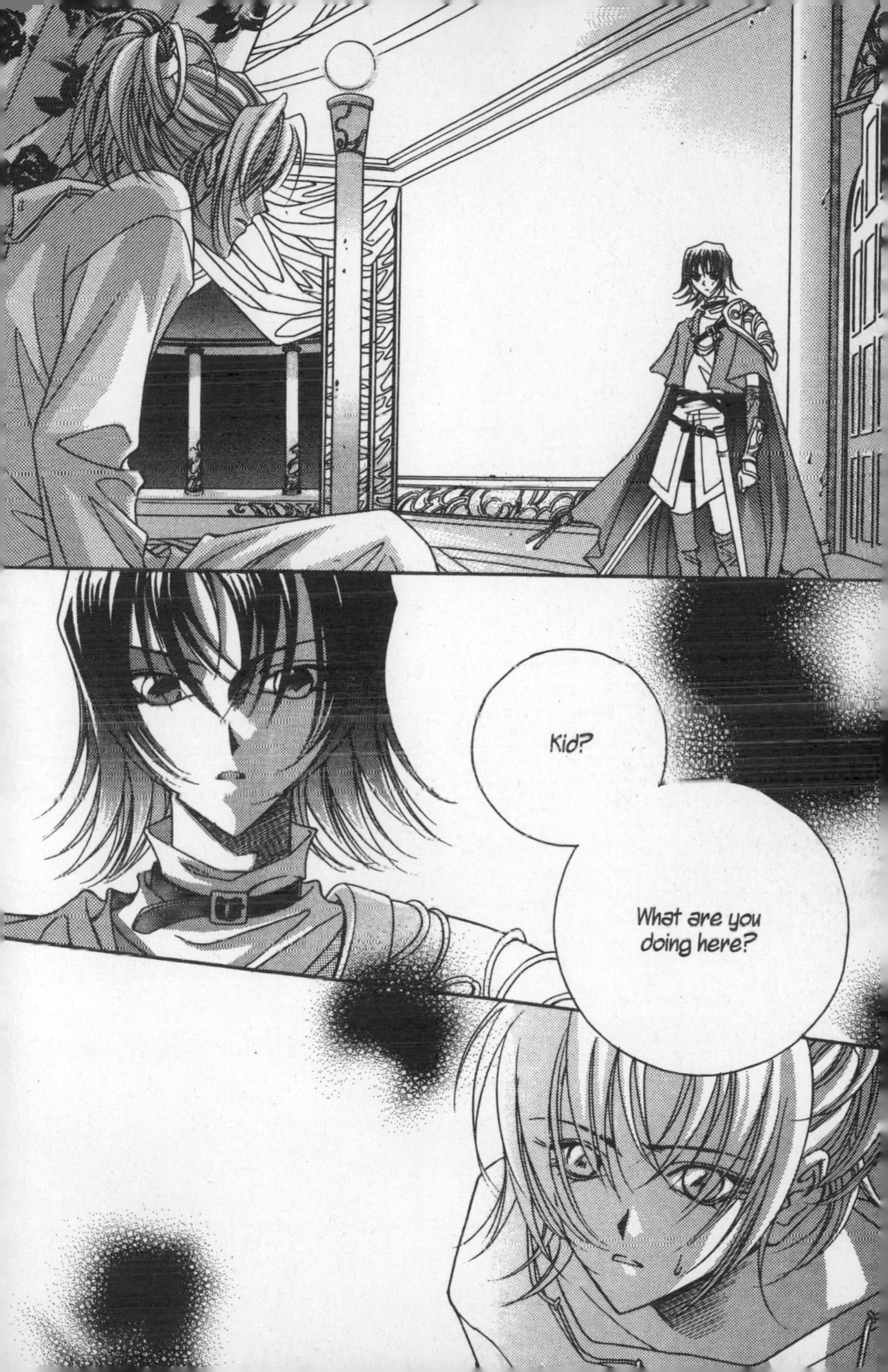
Kid?
What are you doing here?

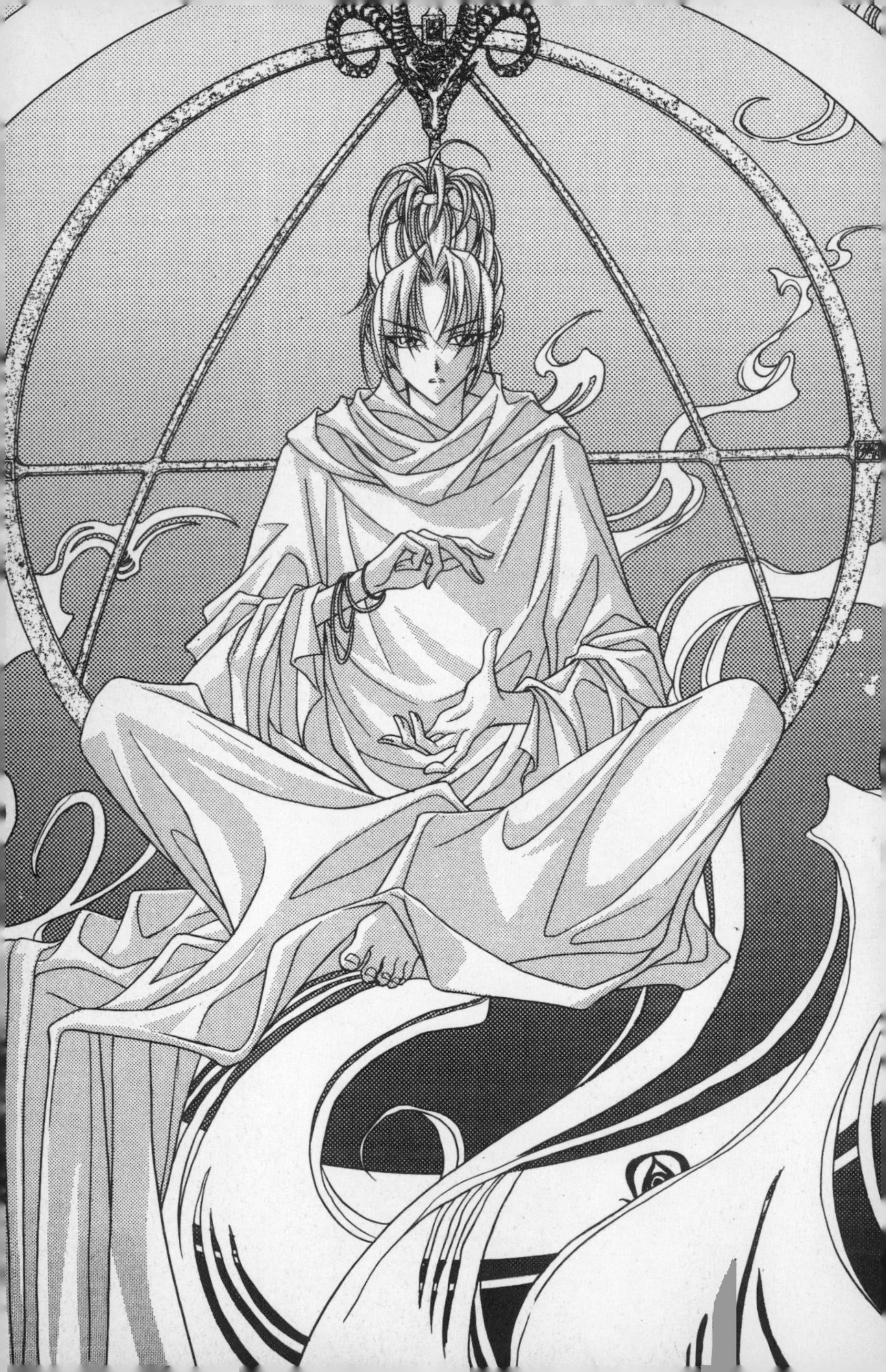

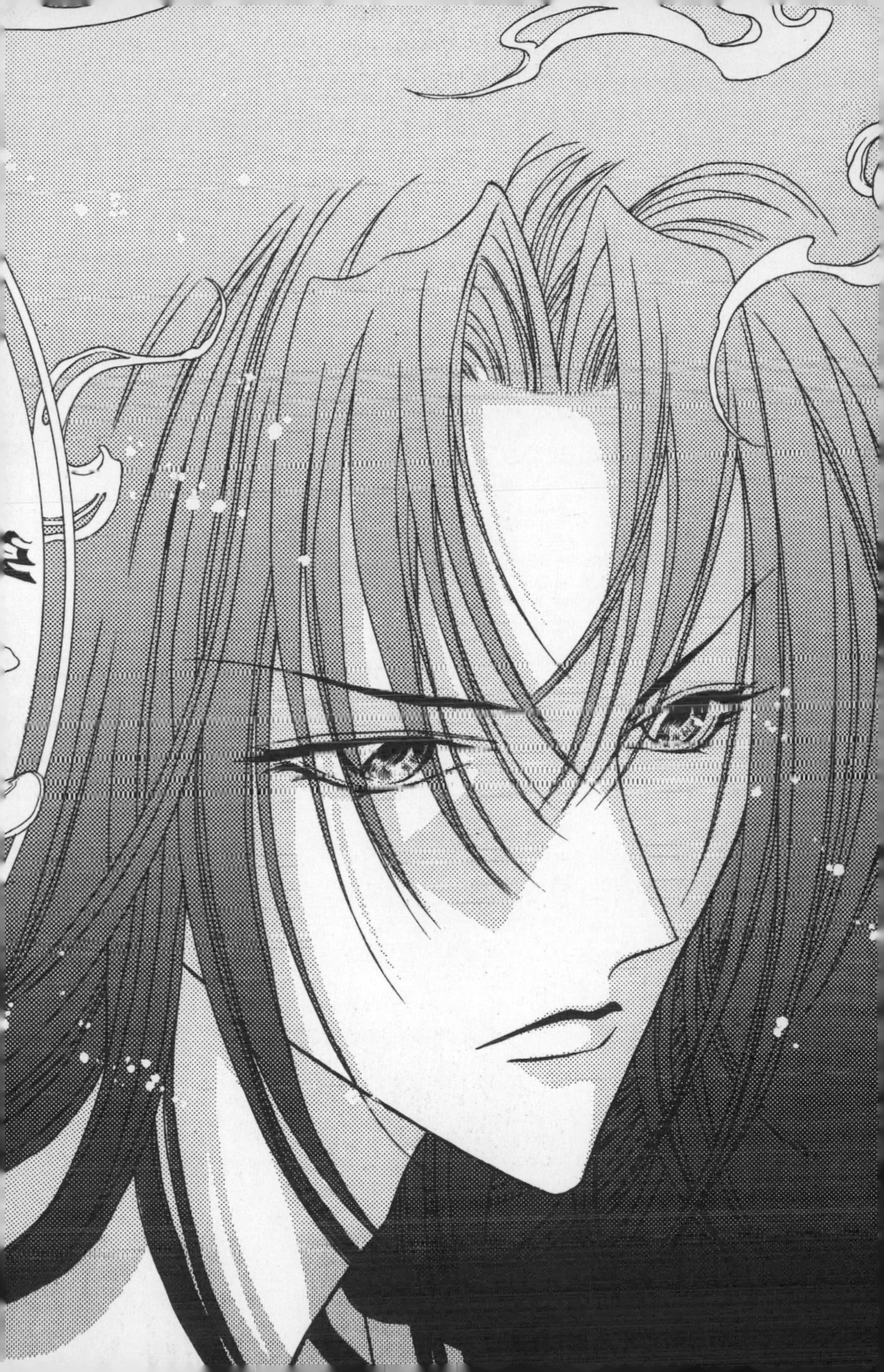

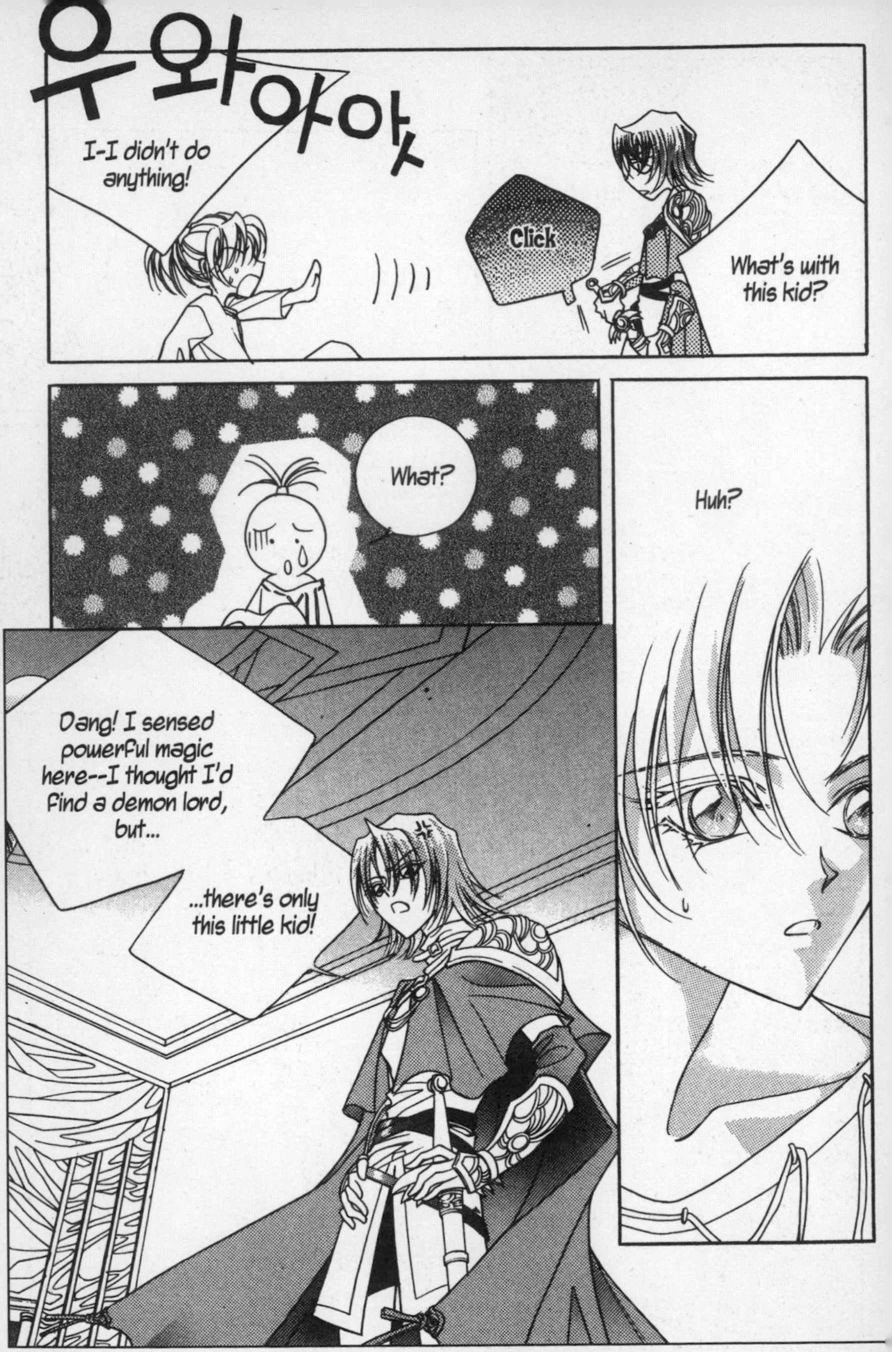
우와야야
I-I didn't do anything!
Click
What's with this kid?
What?
Huh?
Dang! I sensed powerful magic here--I thought I'd find a demon lord, but...
...there's only this little kid!

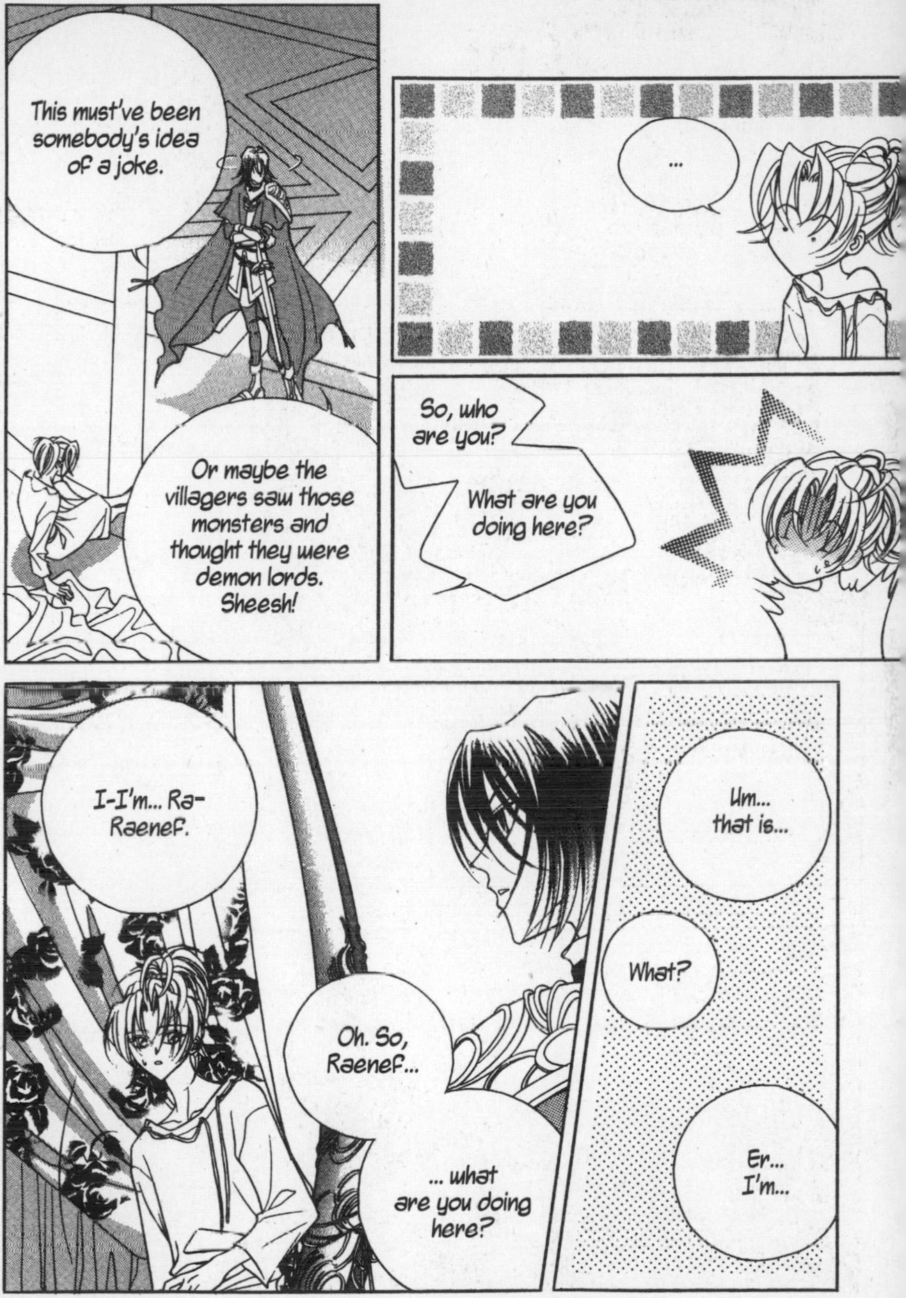
This must've been somebody's idea of a joke.
Or maybe the villagers saw those monsters and thought they were demon lords. Sheesh!
...
So, who are you?
What are you doing here?
I-I'm... Ra-Raenef.
Oh. So, Raenef...
... what are you doing here?
Um... that is...
What?
Er... I'm...

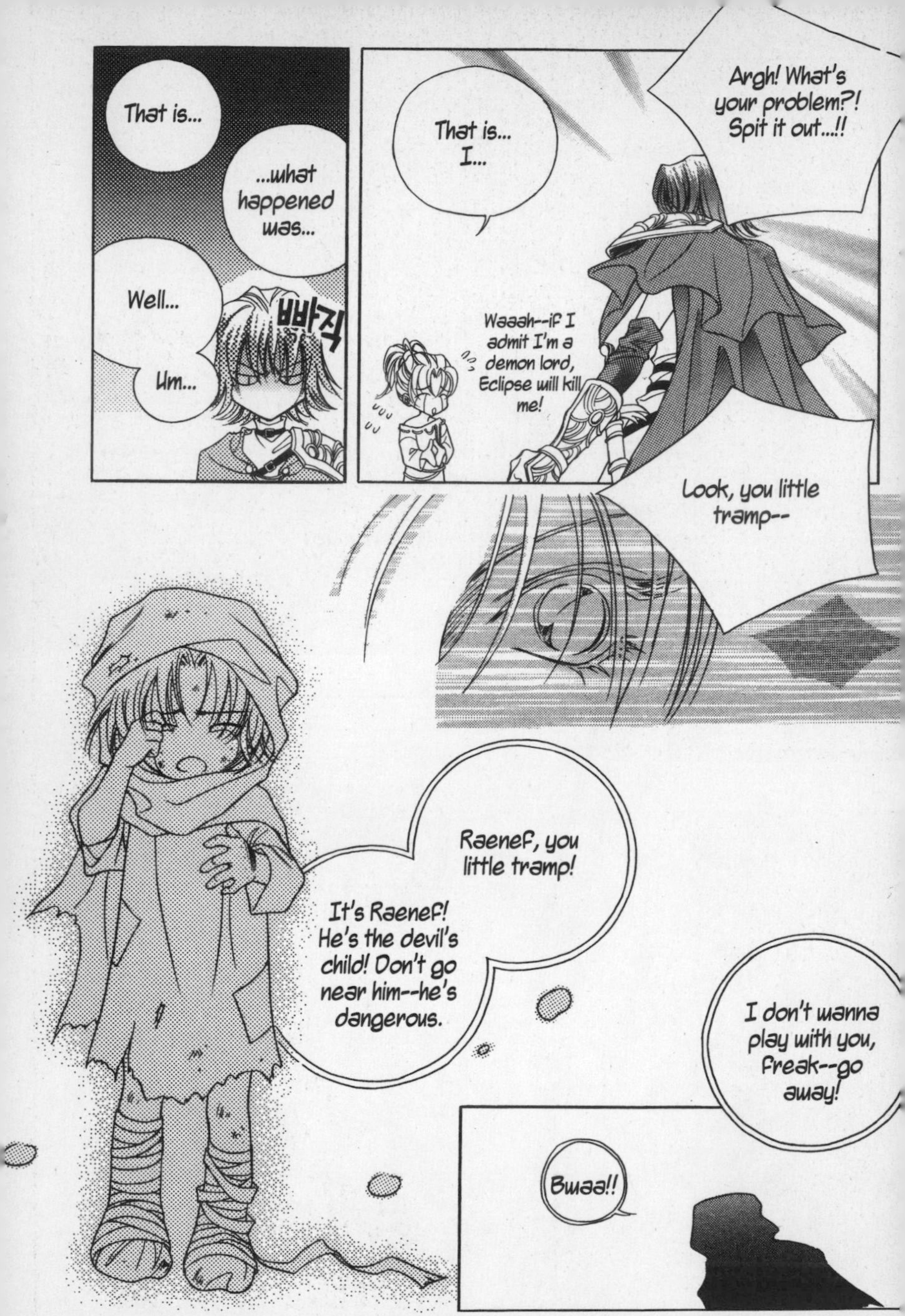
That is...
...what happened was...
Well...
Um...
빠직
That is... I...
Argh! What's your problem?! Spit it out...!!
Waaah--if I admit I'm a demon lord, Eclipse will kill me!
Look, you little tramp--
Raenef, you little tramp!
It's Raenef! He's the devil's child! Don't go near him--he's dangerous.
I don't wanna play with you, freak--go away!
Bwaa!!

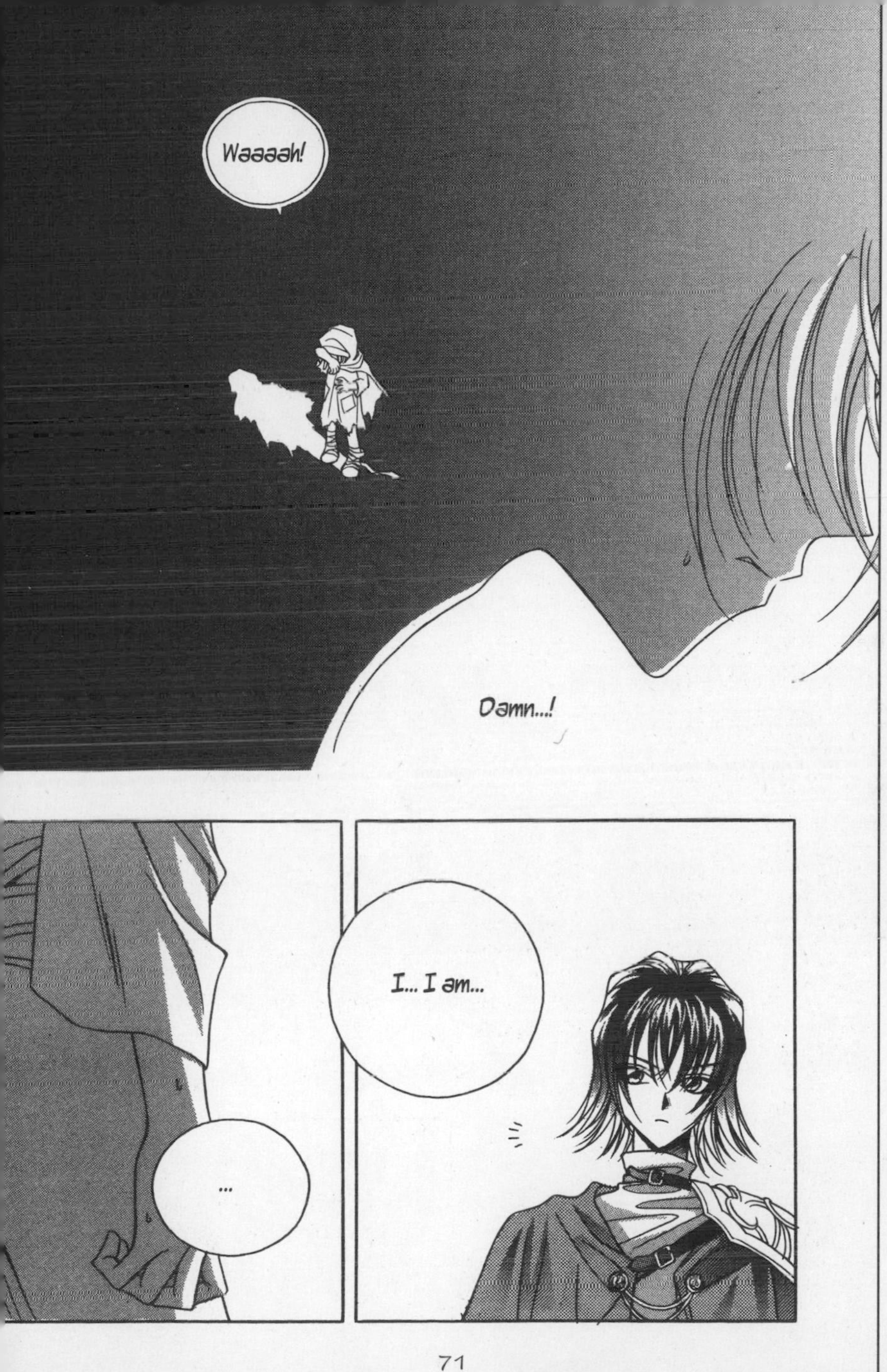
Waaaah!
Damn...!
I... I am...
...

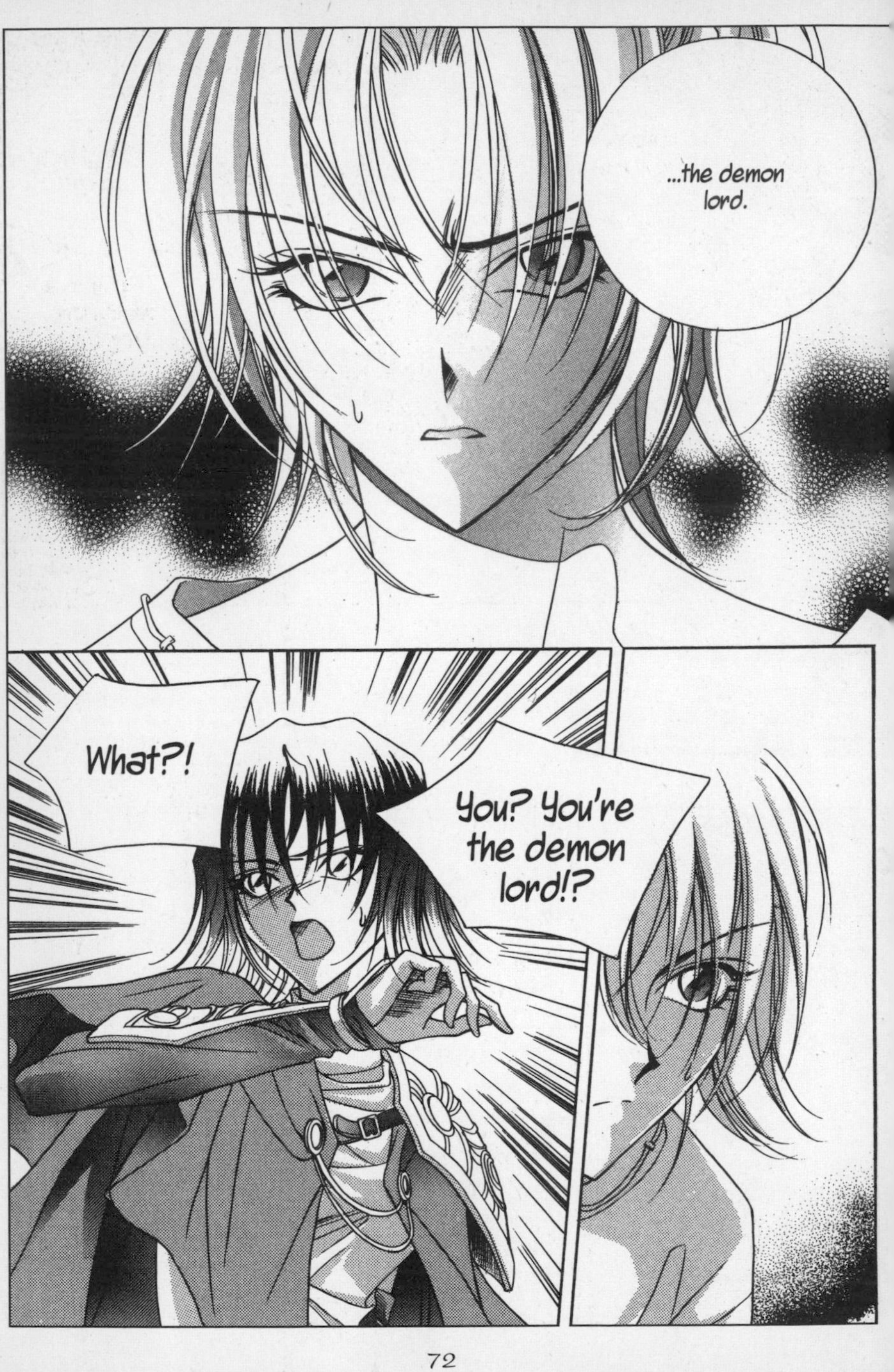
...the demon lord.
What?!
You? You're the demon lord!?

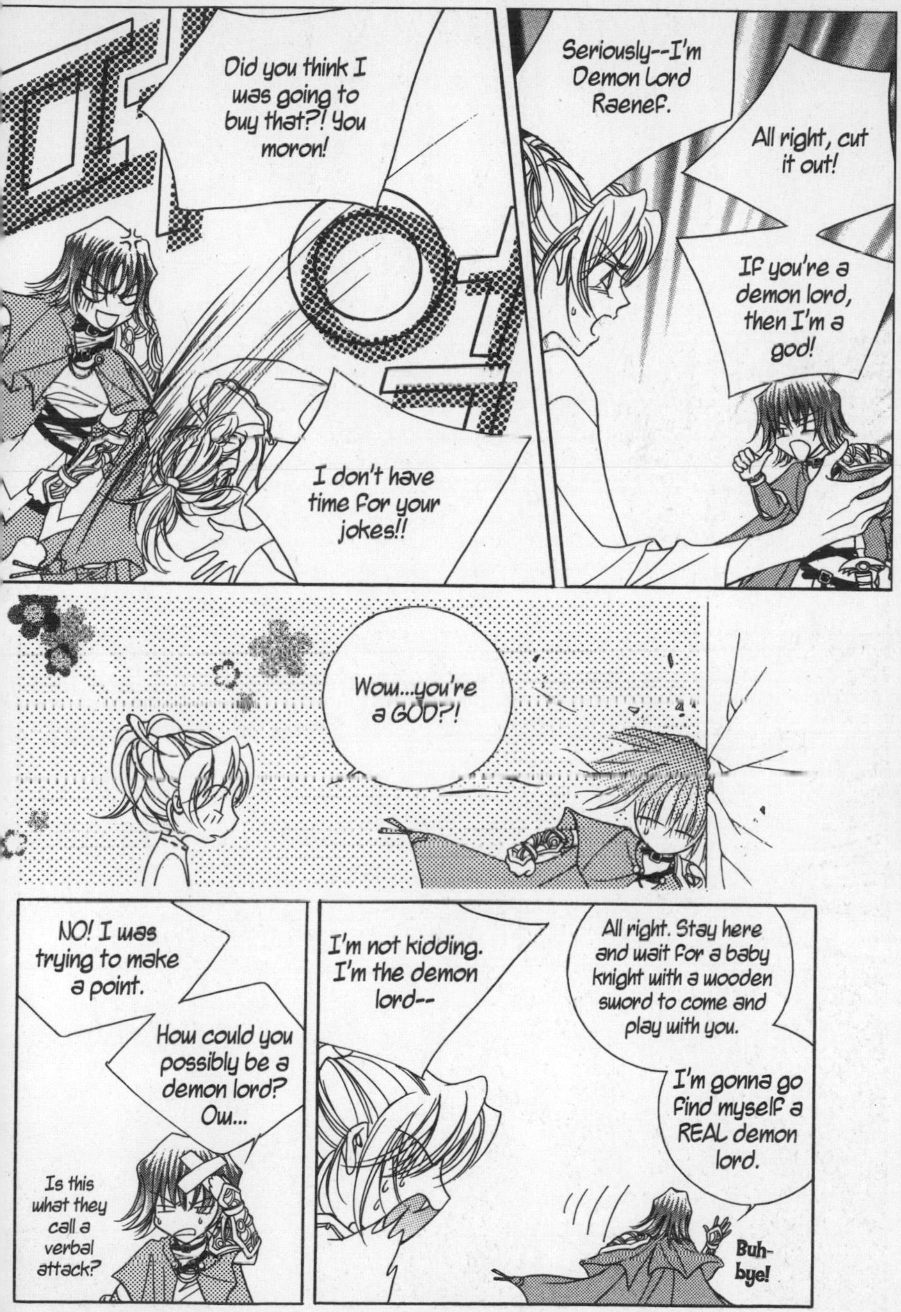
Did you think I was going to buy that?! You moron!
I don't have time for your jokes!!
Seriously--I'm Demon Lord Raenef.
All right, cut it out!
If you're a demon lord, then I'm a god!
Wow...you're a GOD?!
NO! I was trying to make a point.
How could you possibly be a demon lord? Ow...
Is this what they call a verbal attack?
I'm not kidding. I'm the demon lord--
All right. Stay here and wait for a baby knight with a wooden sword to come and play with you.
I'm gonna go find myself a REAL demon lord.
Buh-bye!

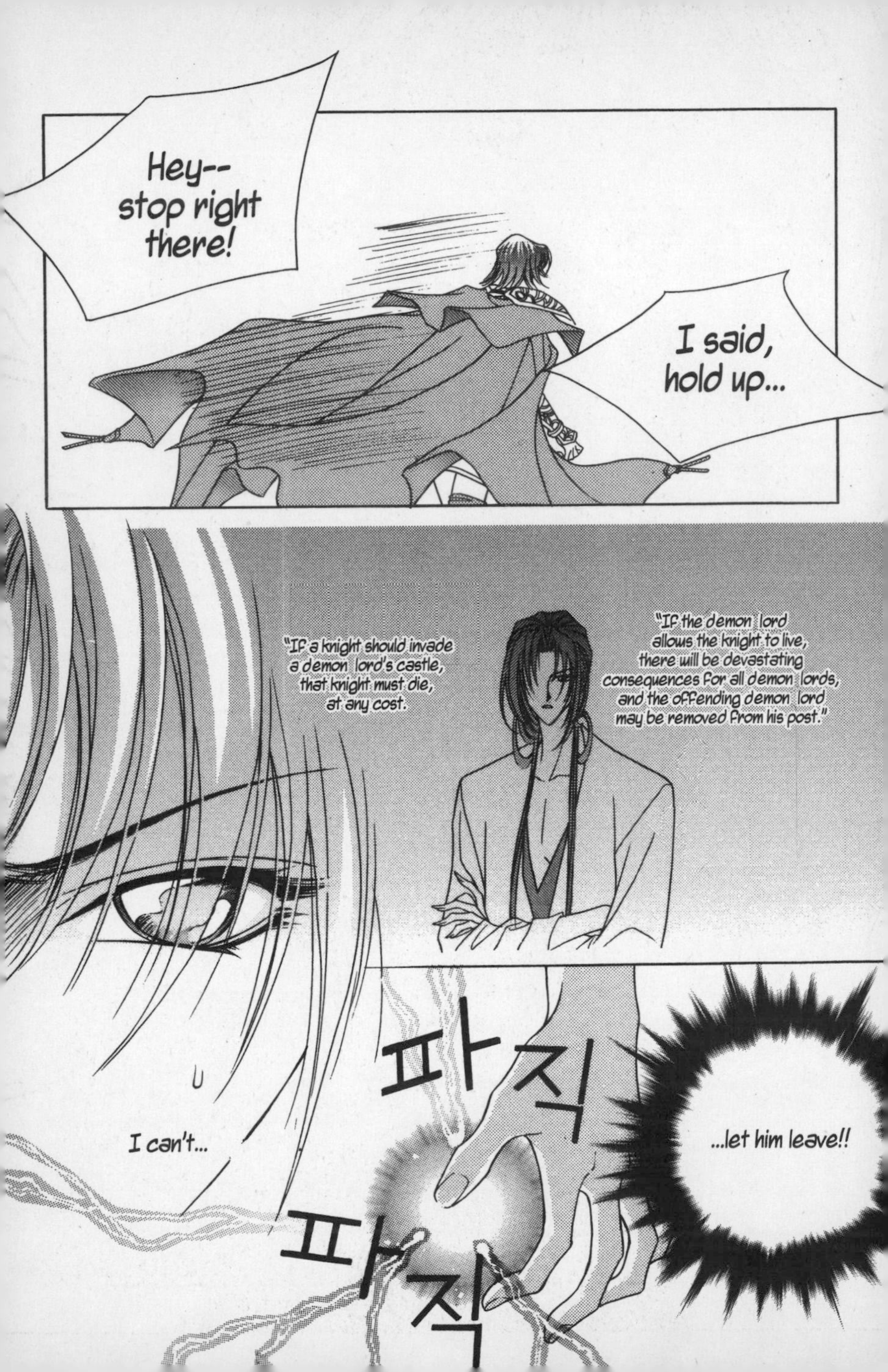
Hey--
stop right
there!
I said,
hold up...
"If a knight should invade a demon lord's castle, that knight must die, at any cost.
"If the demon lord allows the knight to live, there will be devastating consequences for all demon lords, and the offending demon lord may be removed from his post."
I can't...
파직
파직
...let him leave!!

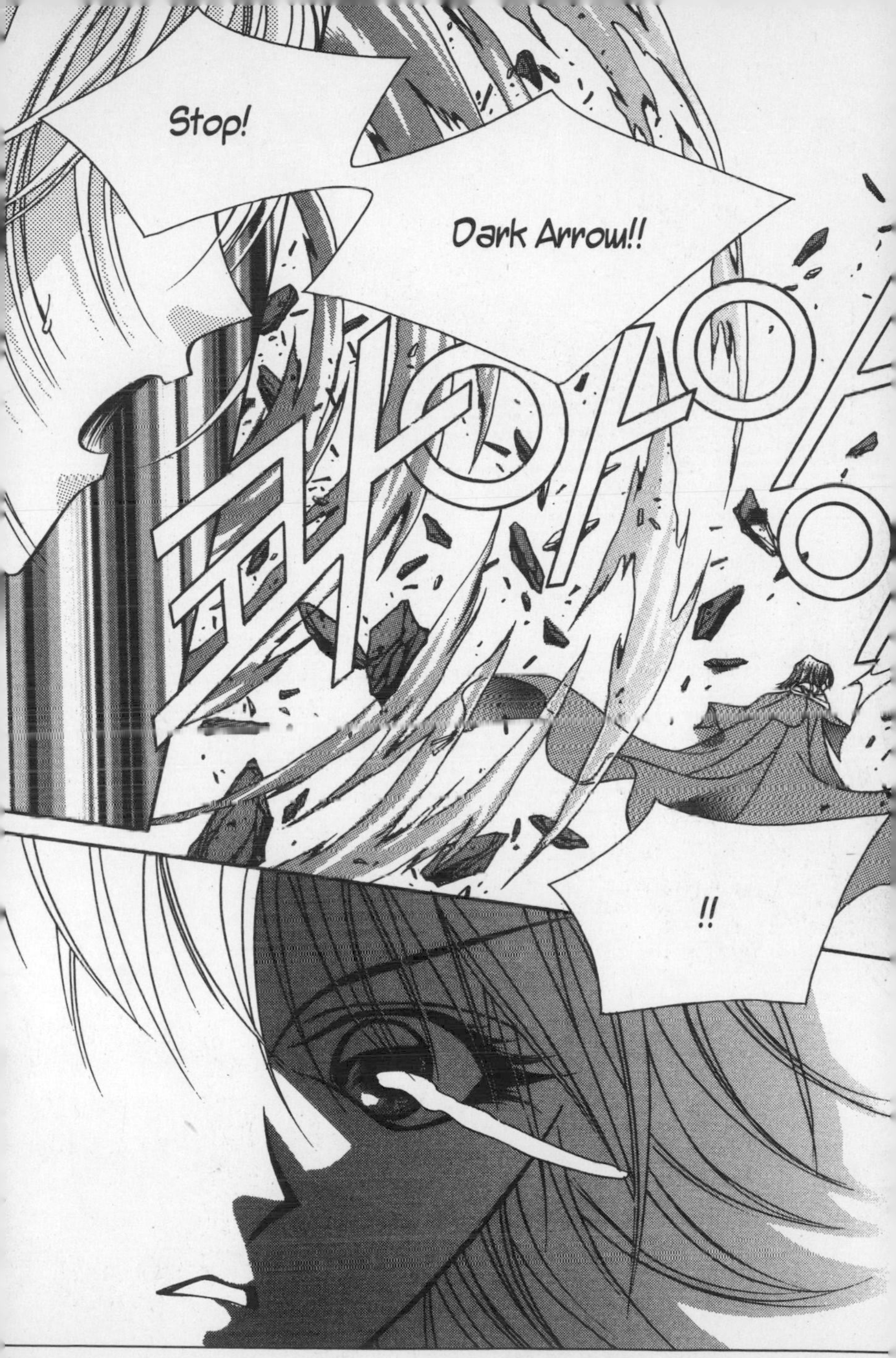
Stop!
Dark Arrow!!
!!

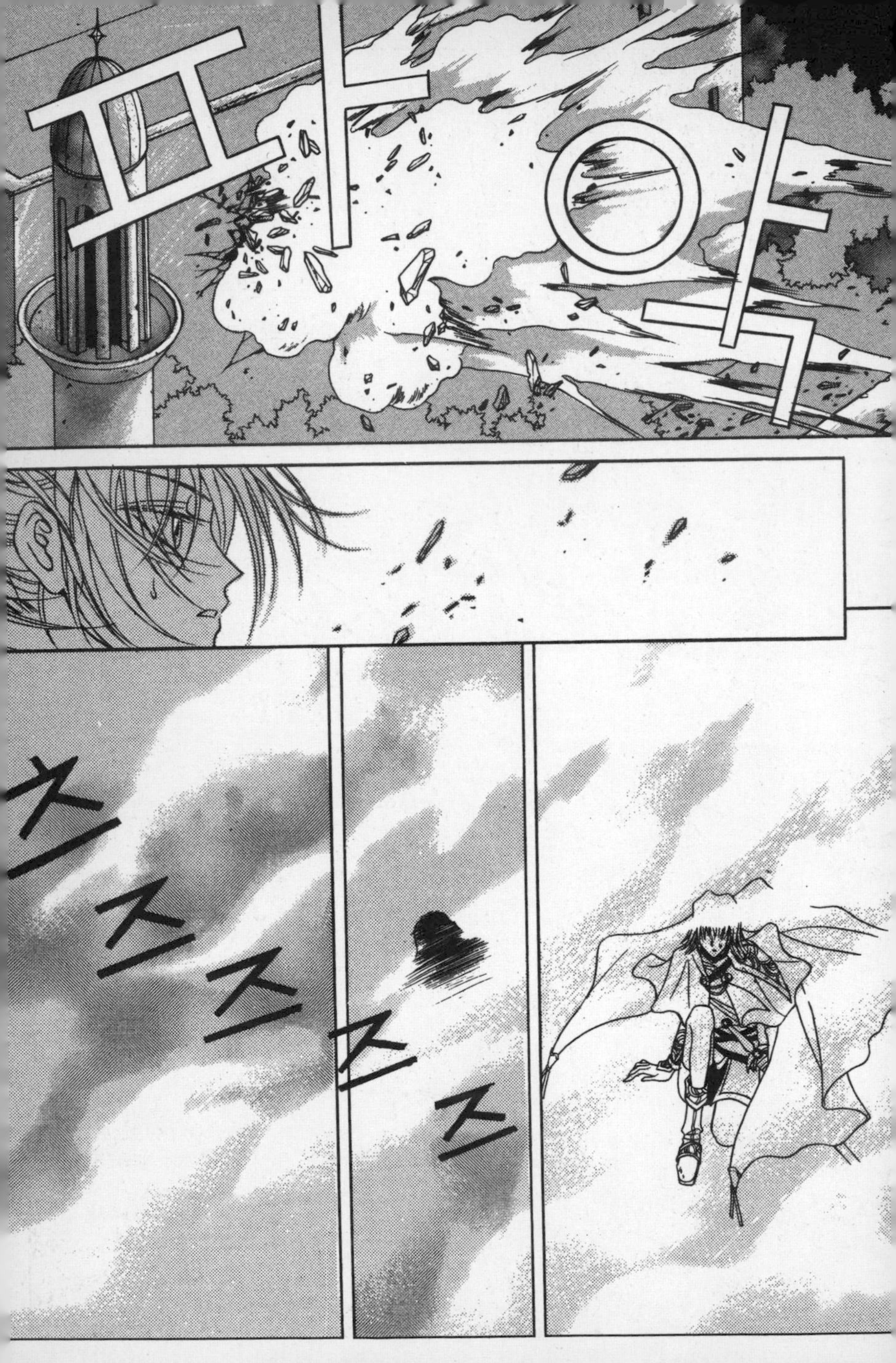

파약

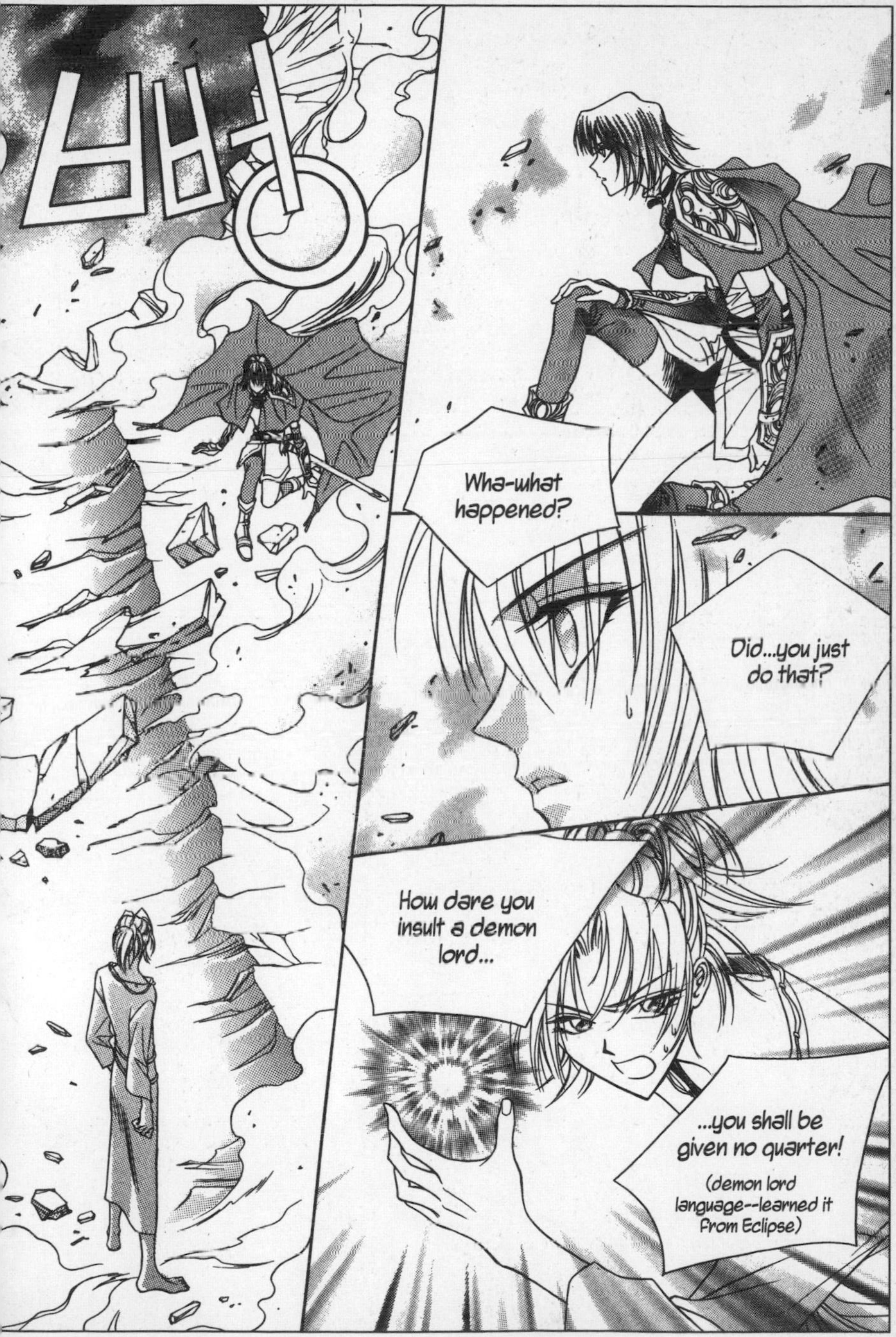
Wha-what happened?
Did...you just do that?
How dare you insult a demon lord...
...you shall be given no quarter!
(demon lord language--learned it from Eclipse)

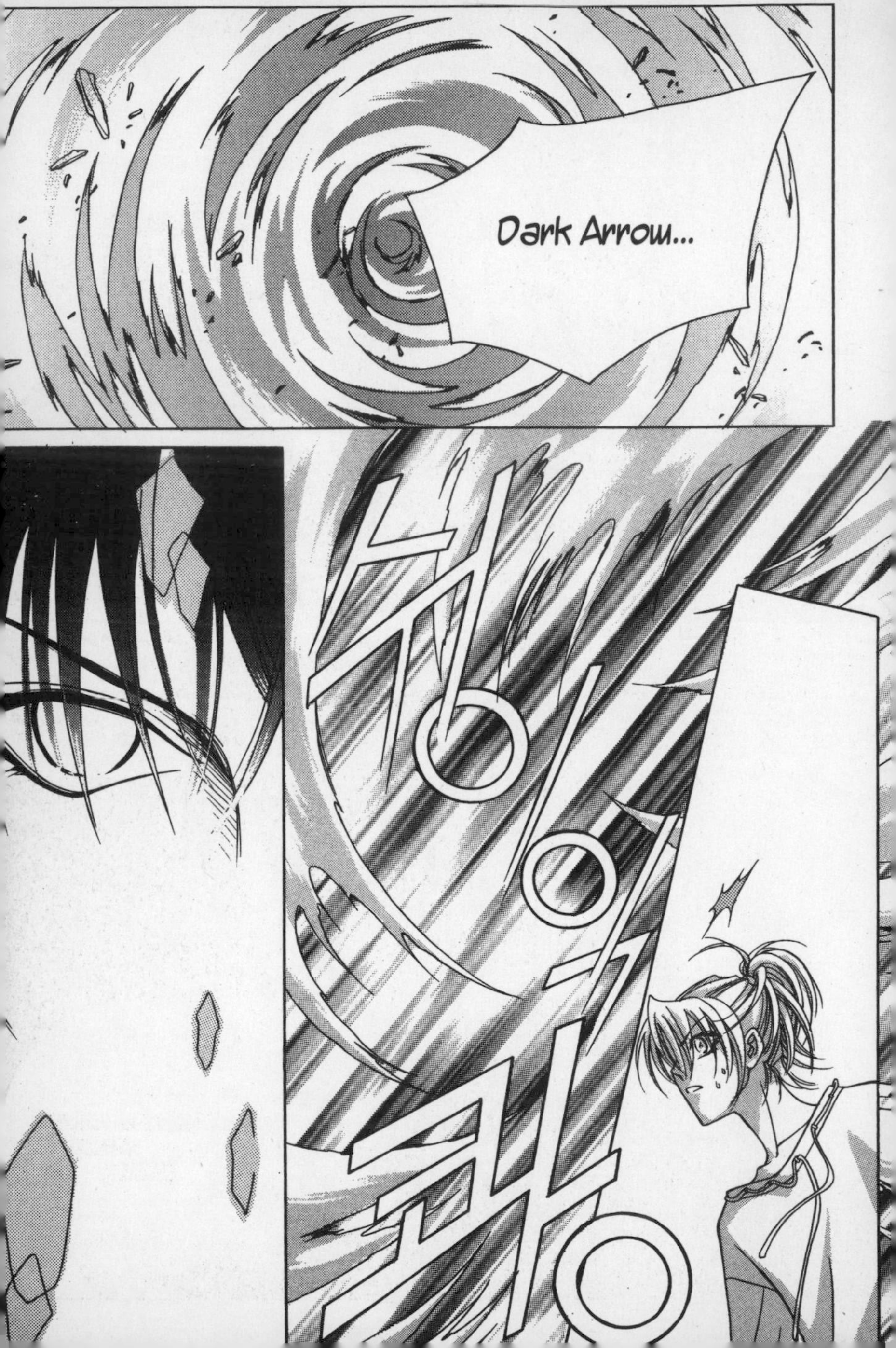
Dark Arrow...

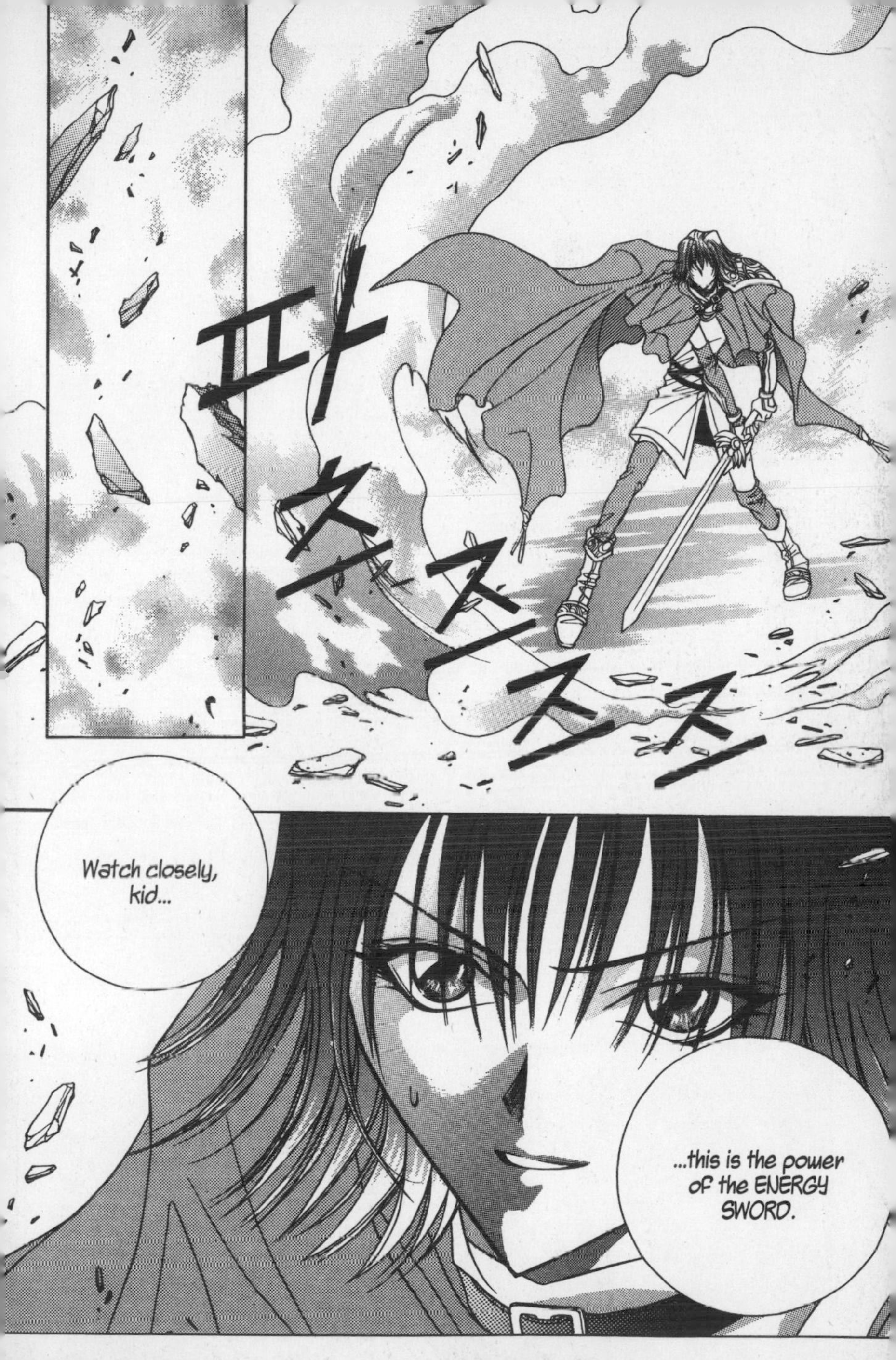
Watch closely, kid...
...this is the power of the ENERGY SWORD.

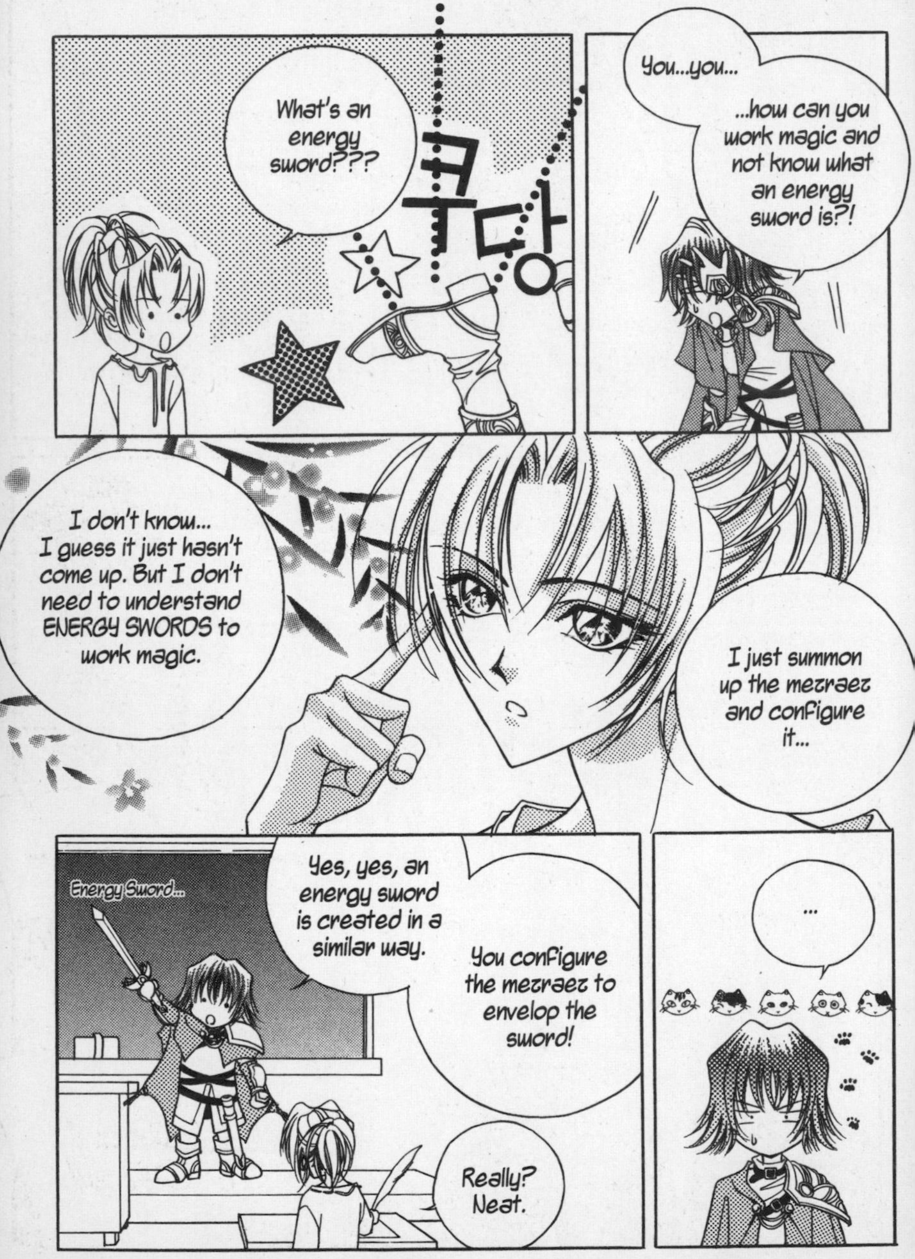
What's an energy sword???
카다앙
You...you...
...how can you work magic and not know what an energy sword is?!
I don't know... I guess it just hasn't come up. But I don't need to understand ENERGY SWORDS to work magic.
I just summon up the metraet and configure it...
Energy Sword...
Yes, yes, an energy sword is created in a similar way.
You configure the metraet to envelop the sword!
Really? Neat.
...

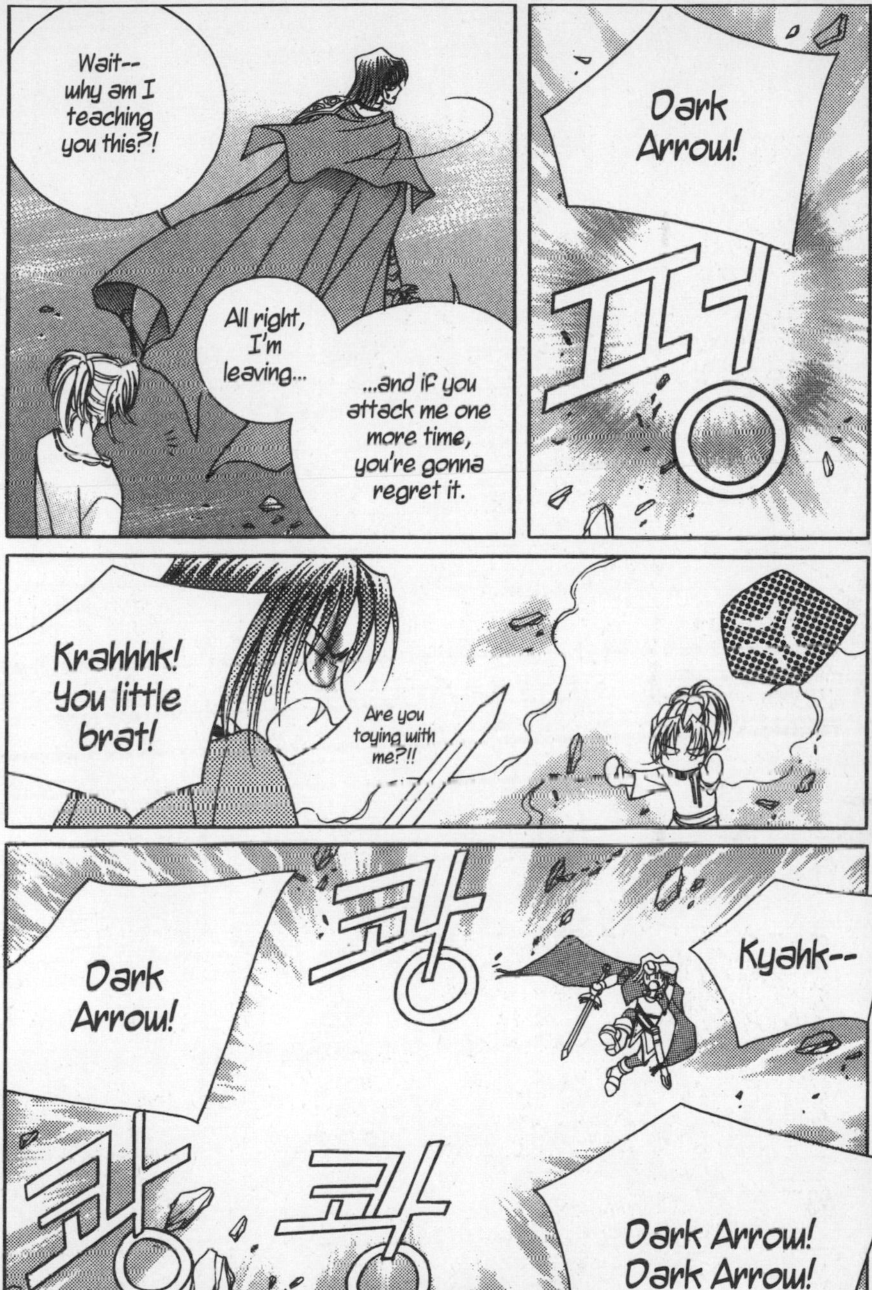

Wait-- why am I teaching you this?!
All right, I'm leaving...
...and if you attack me one more time, you're gonna regret it.
Dark Arrow!
펑
Krahhhk! You little brat!
Are you toying with me?!!
Dark Arrow!
쾅
Kyahk--
쾅
쾅
Dark Arrow! Dark Arrow!

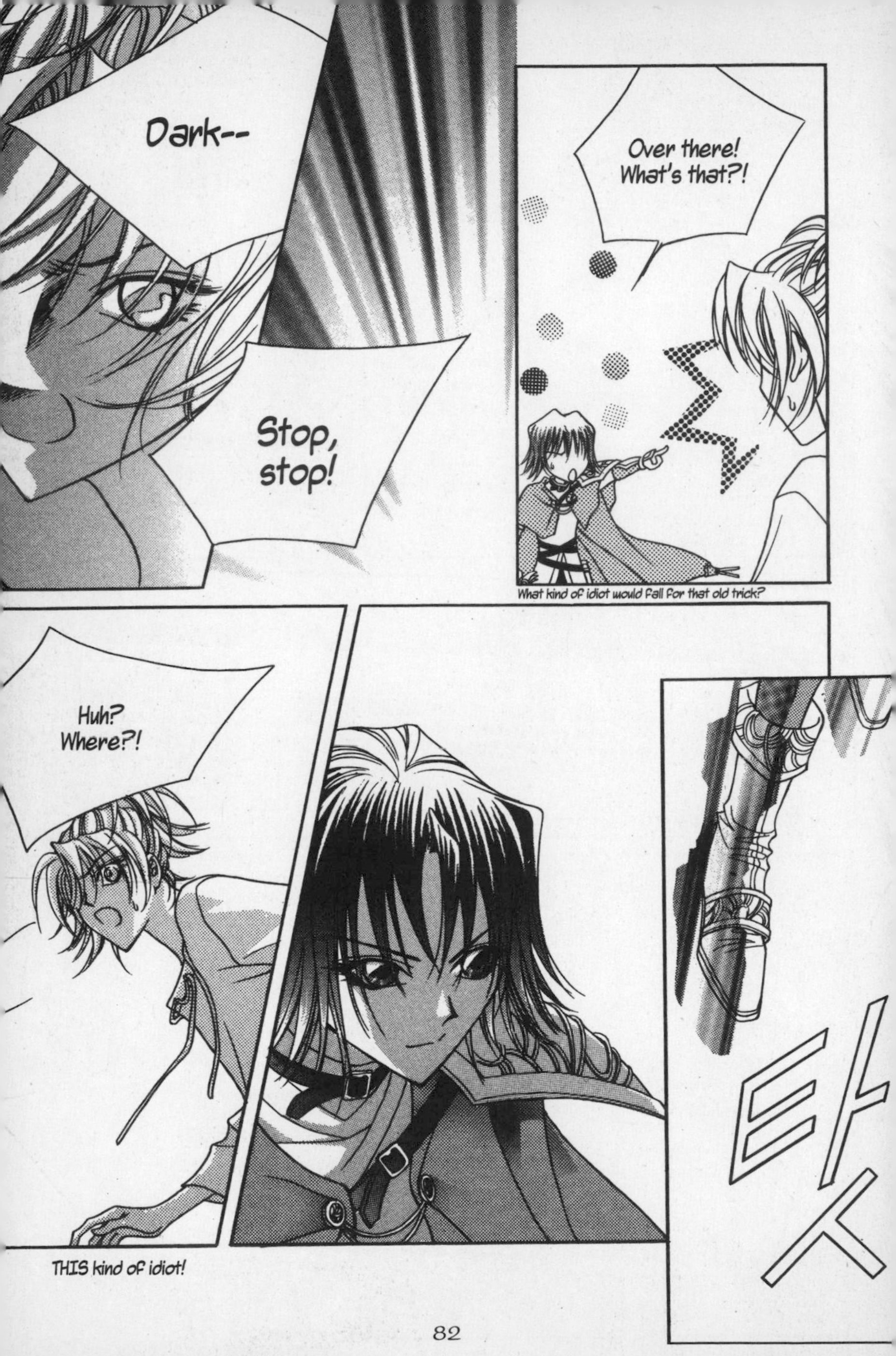
Dark--
Stop, stop!
Over there! What's that?!
What kind of idiot would fall for that old trick?
Huh? Where?!
THIS kind of idiot!

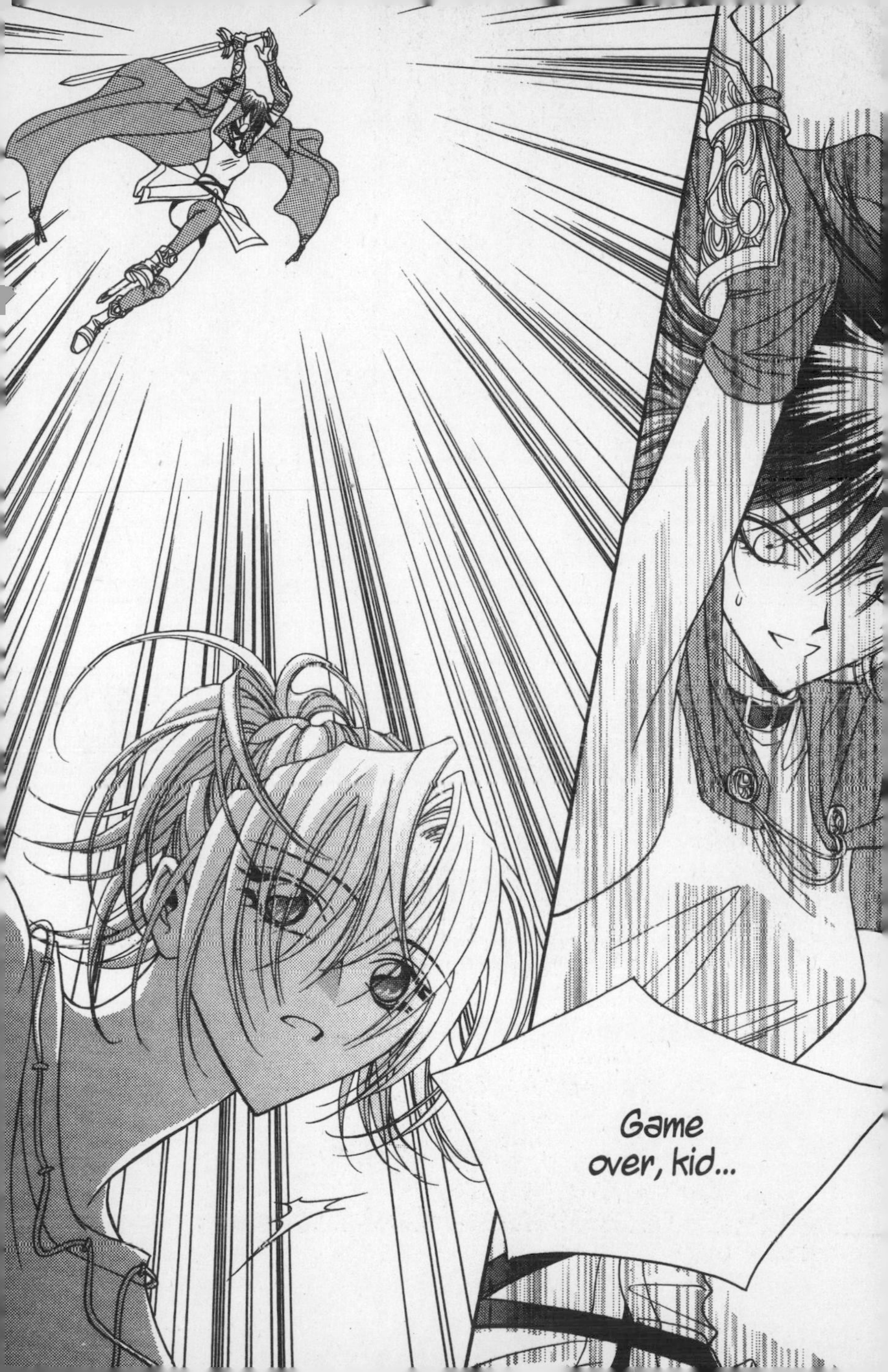
Game over, kid...

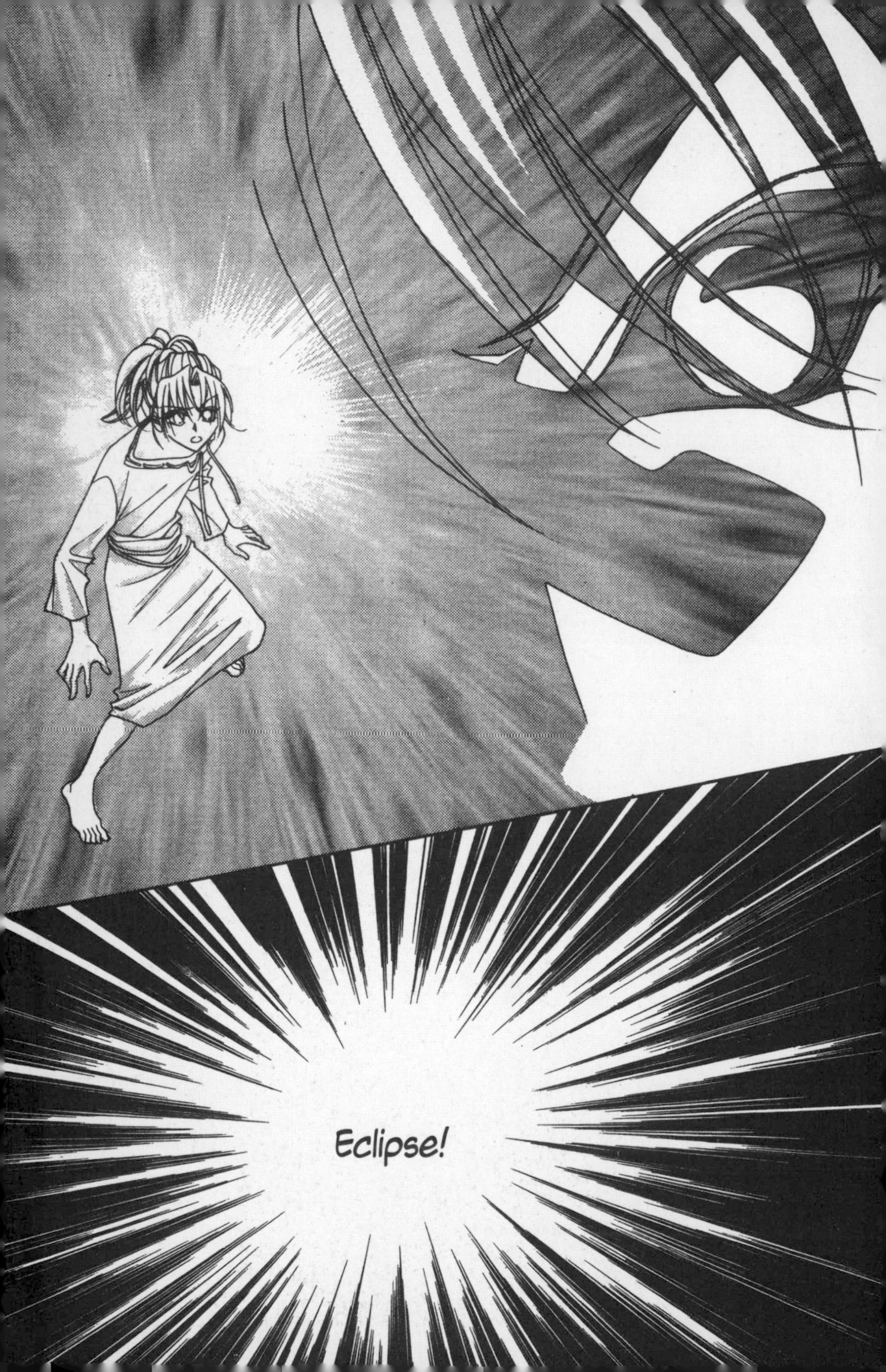
Eclipse!

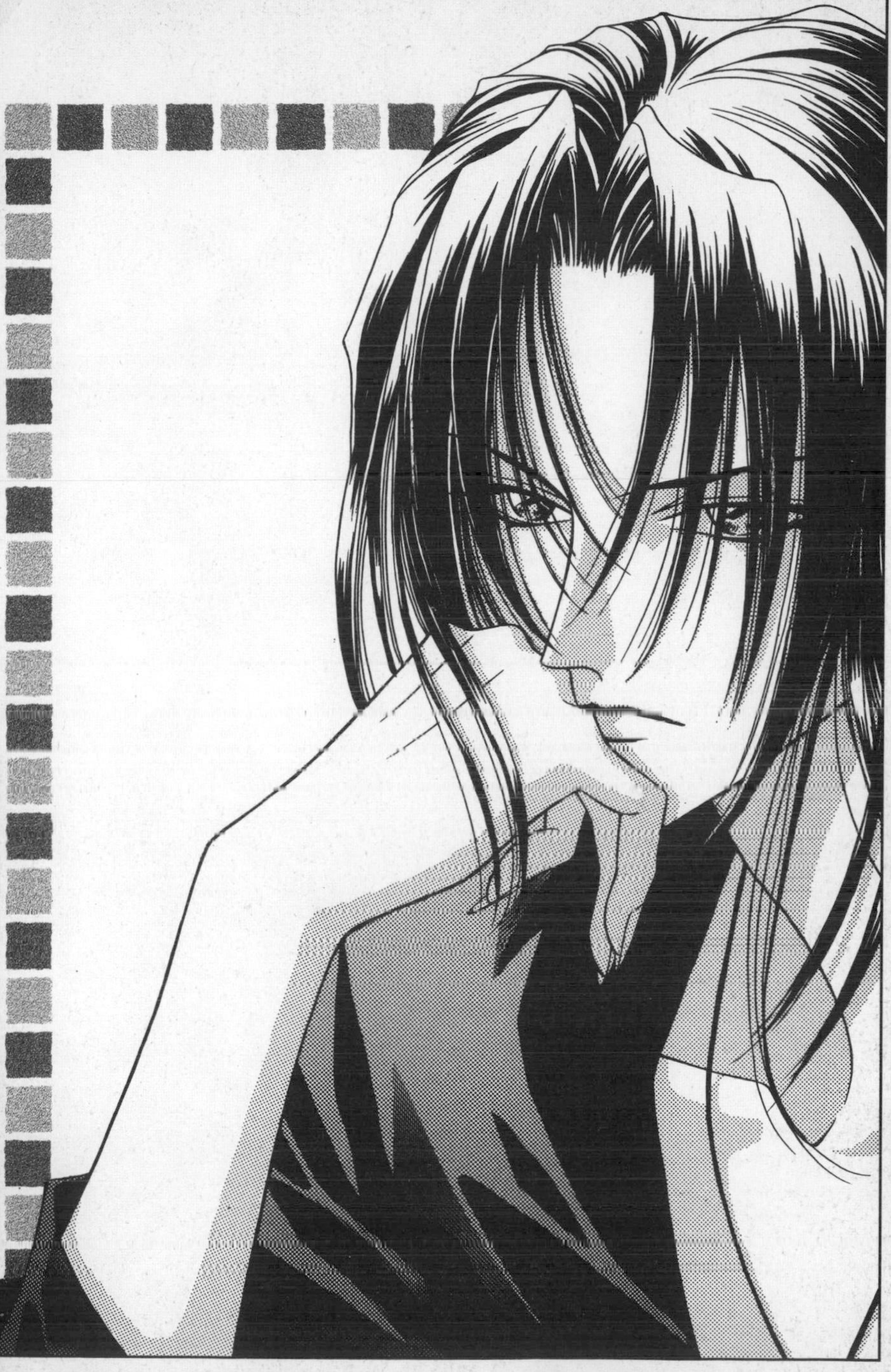

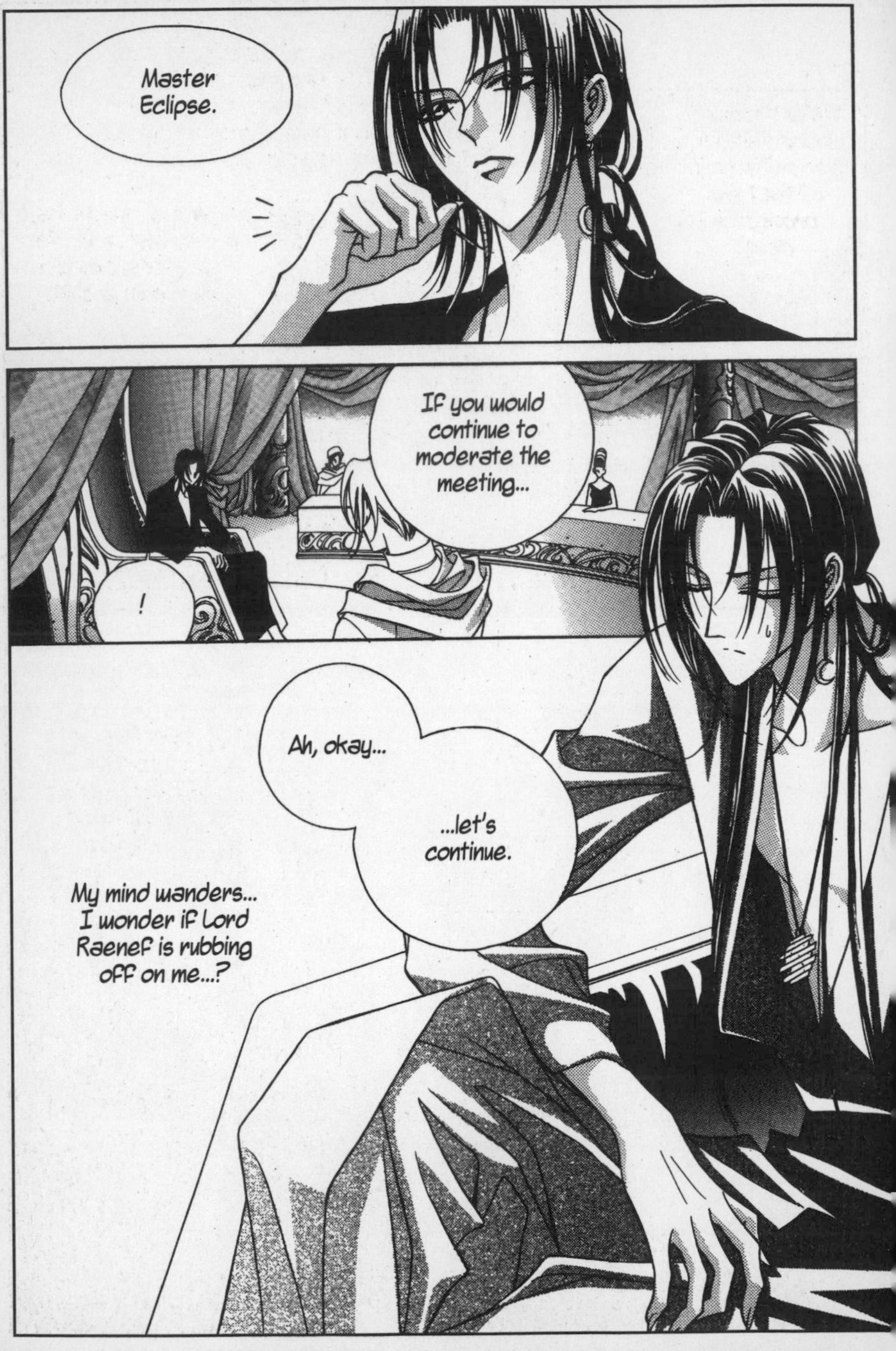
Master Eclipse.
If you would continue to moderate the meeting...
!
Ah, okay...
...let's continue.
My mind wanders... I wonder if Lord Raenef is rubbing off on me...?

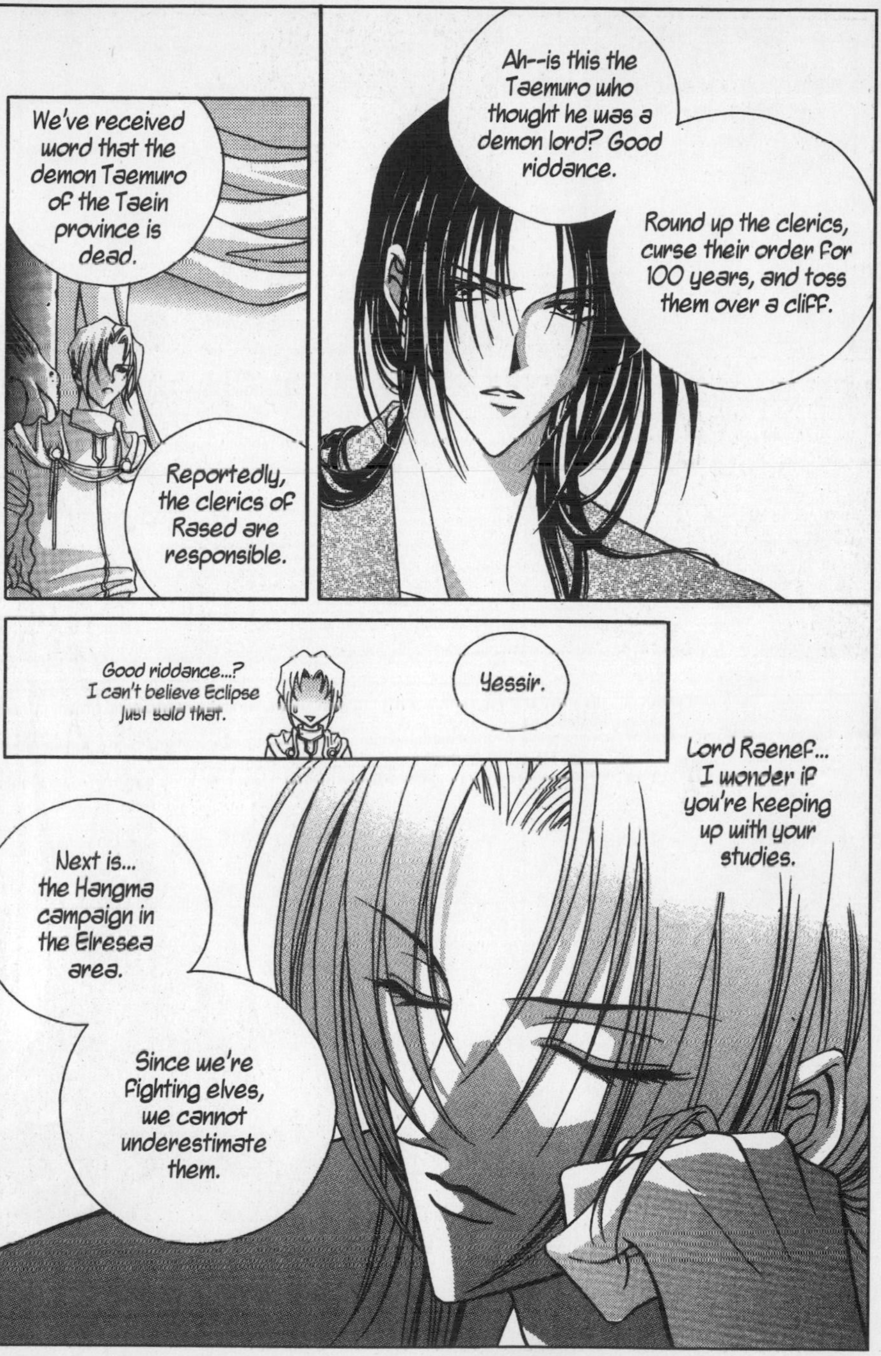
We've received word that the demon Taemuro of the Taein province is dead.
Reportedly, the clerics of Rased are responsible.
Ah--is this the Taemuro who thought he was a demon lord? Good riddance.
Round up the clerics, curse their order for 100 years, and toss them over a cliff.
Yessir.
Good riddance...? I can't believe Eclipse just said that.
Lord Raenef... I wonder if you're keeping up with your studies.
Next is... the Hangma campaign in the Elresea area.
Since we're fighting elves, we cannot underestimate them.

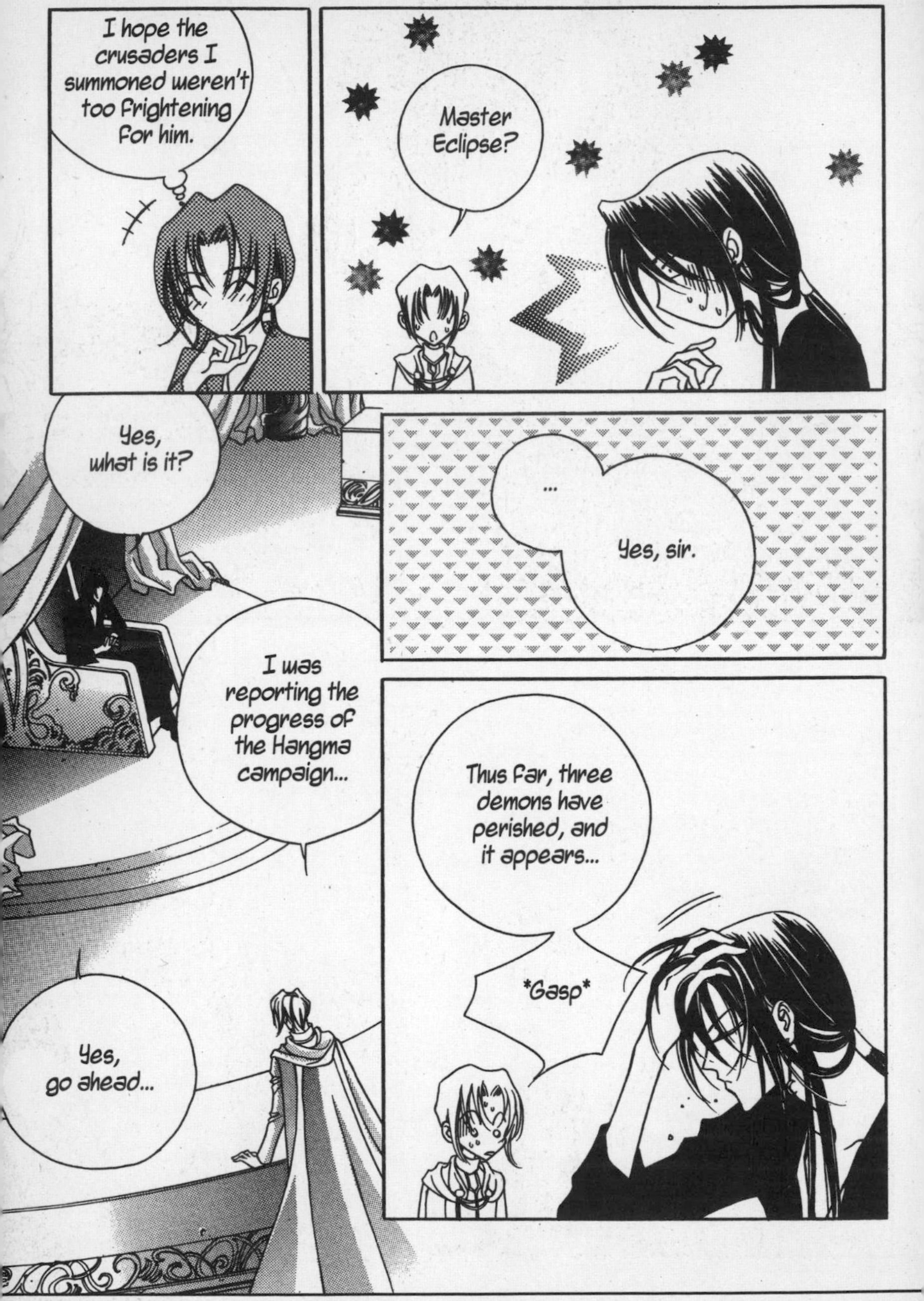
I hope the crusaders I summoned weren't too frightening for him.
Master Eclipse?
Yes, what is it?
...
Yes, sir.
I was reporting the progress of the Hangma campaign...
Yes, go ahead...
Thus far, three demons have perished, and it appears...
Gasp

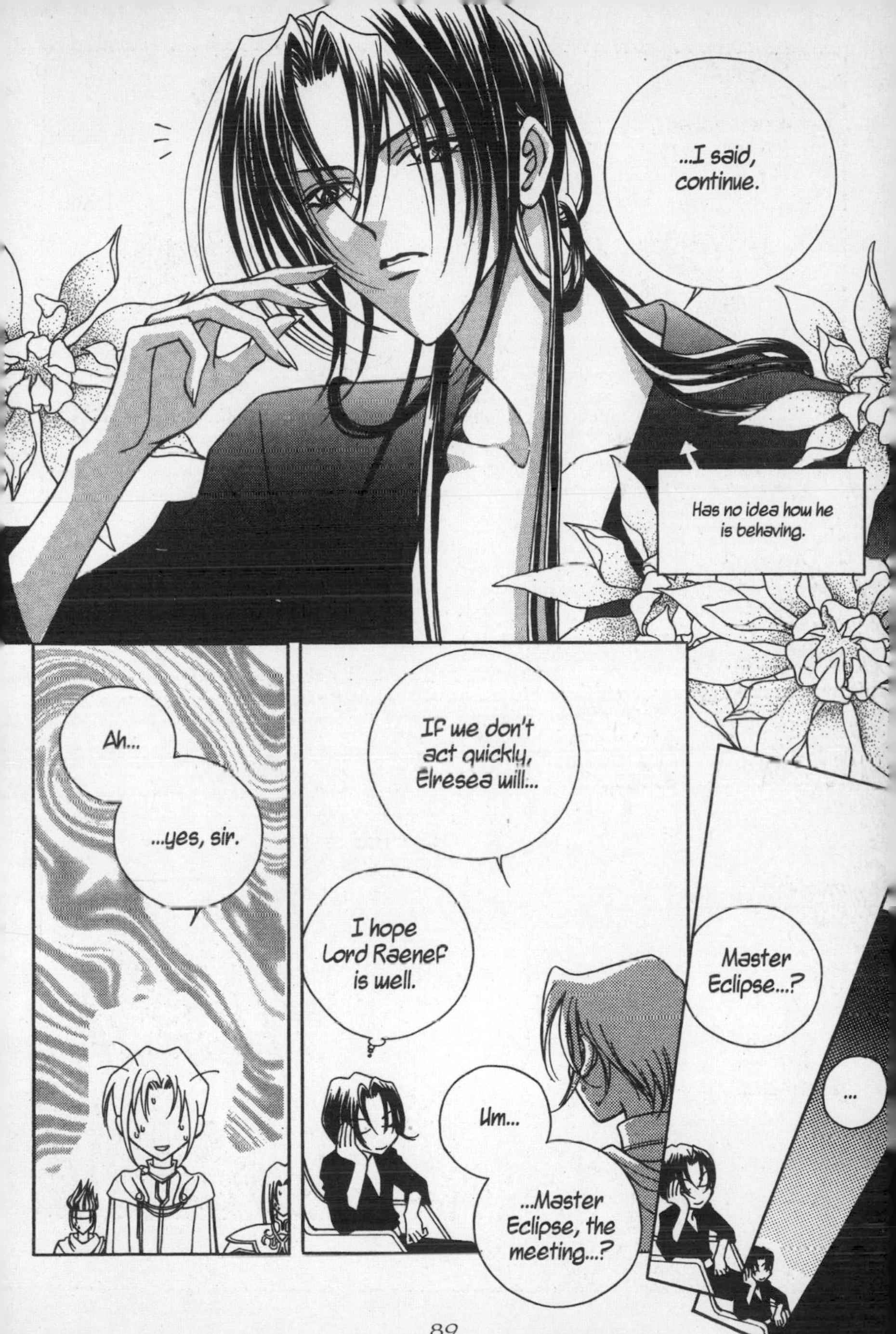
...I said, continue.
Has no idea how he is behaving.
Ah...
...yes, sir.
If we don't act quickly, Elresea will...
I hope Lord Raenef is well.
Um...
...Master Eclipse, the meeting...?
Master Eclipse...?
...

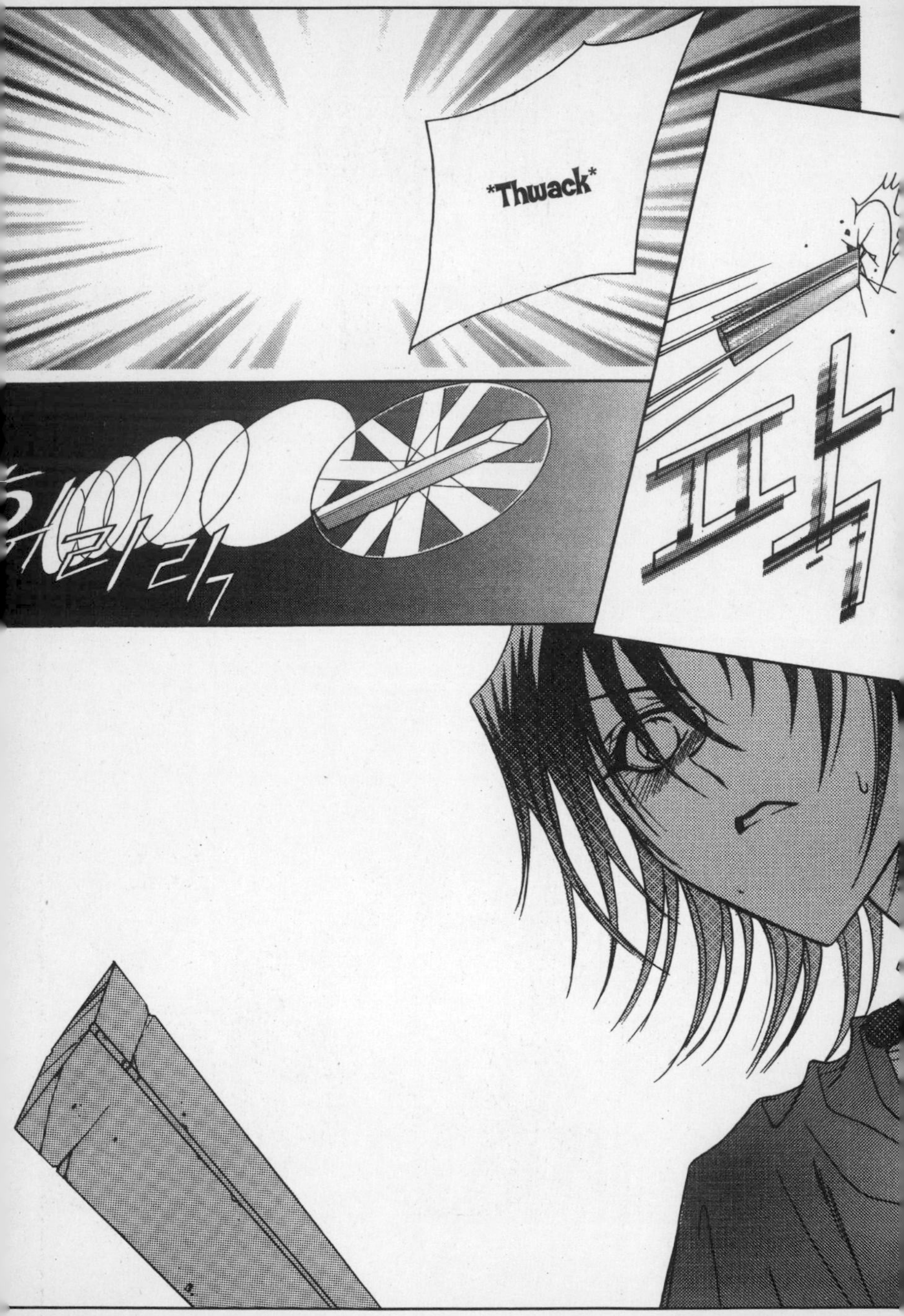
Thwack

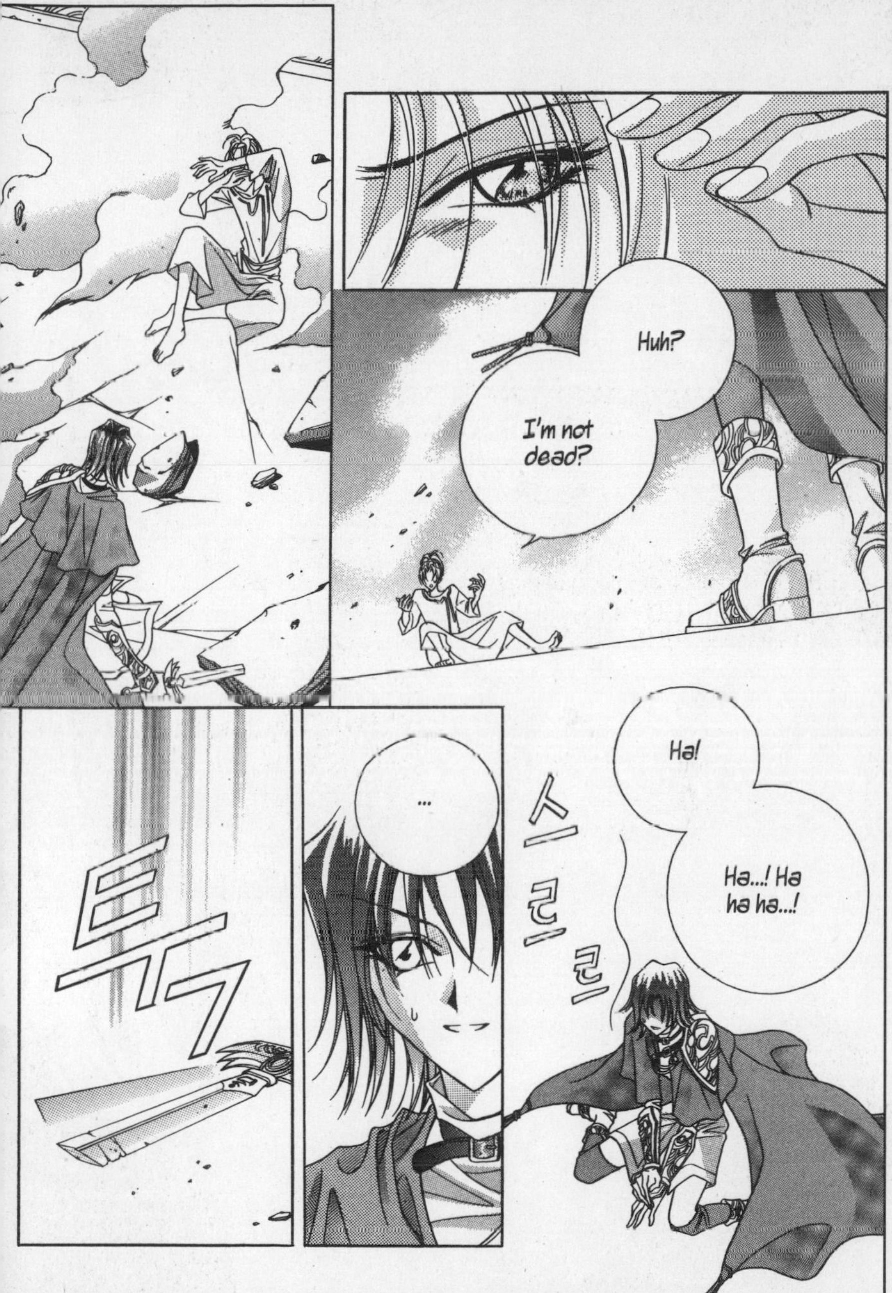

Huh?
I'm not dead?
...
Ha!
Ha...! Ha ha ha...!

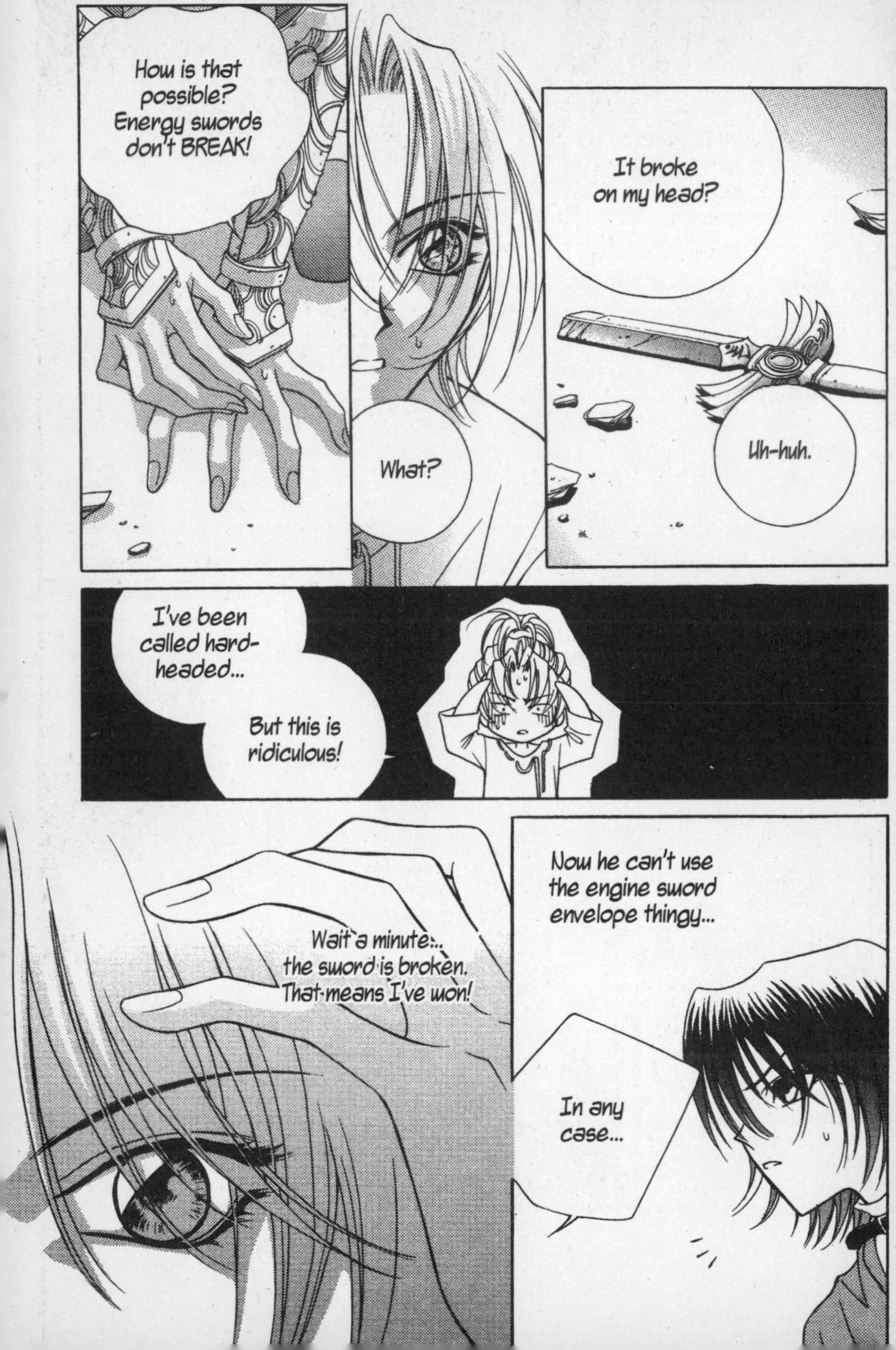

It broke on my head?
Uh-huh.
How is that possible? Energy swords don't BREAK!
What?
I've been called hard-headed...
But this is ridiculous!
Now he can't use the engine sword envelope thingy...
In any case...
Wait a minute... the sword is broken. That means I've won!

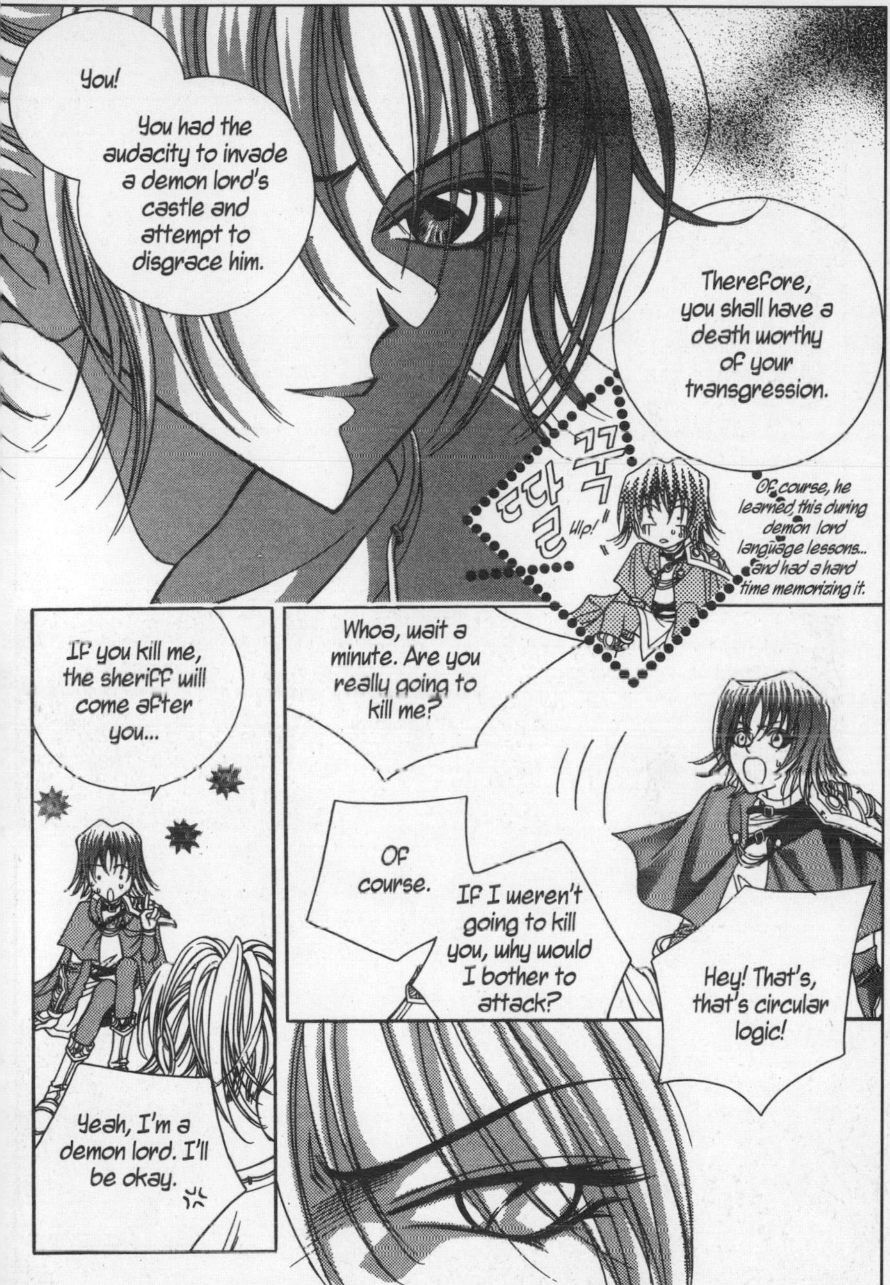
You!
You had the audacity to invade a demon lord's castle and attempt to disgrace him.
Therefore, you shall have a death worthy of your transgression.
Ulp!
Of course, he learned this during demon lord language lessons... and had a hard time memorizing it.
If you kill me, the sheriff will come after you...
Yeah, I'm a demon lord. I'll be okay.
Whoa, wait a minute. Are you really going to kill me?
Of course.
If I weren't going to kill you, why would I bother to attack?
Hey! That's, that's circular logic!

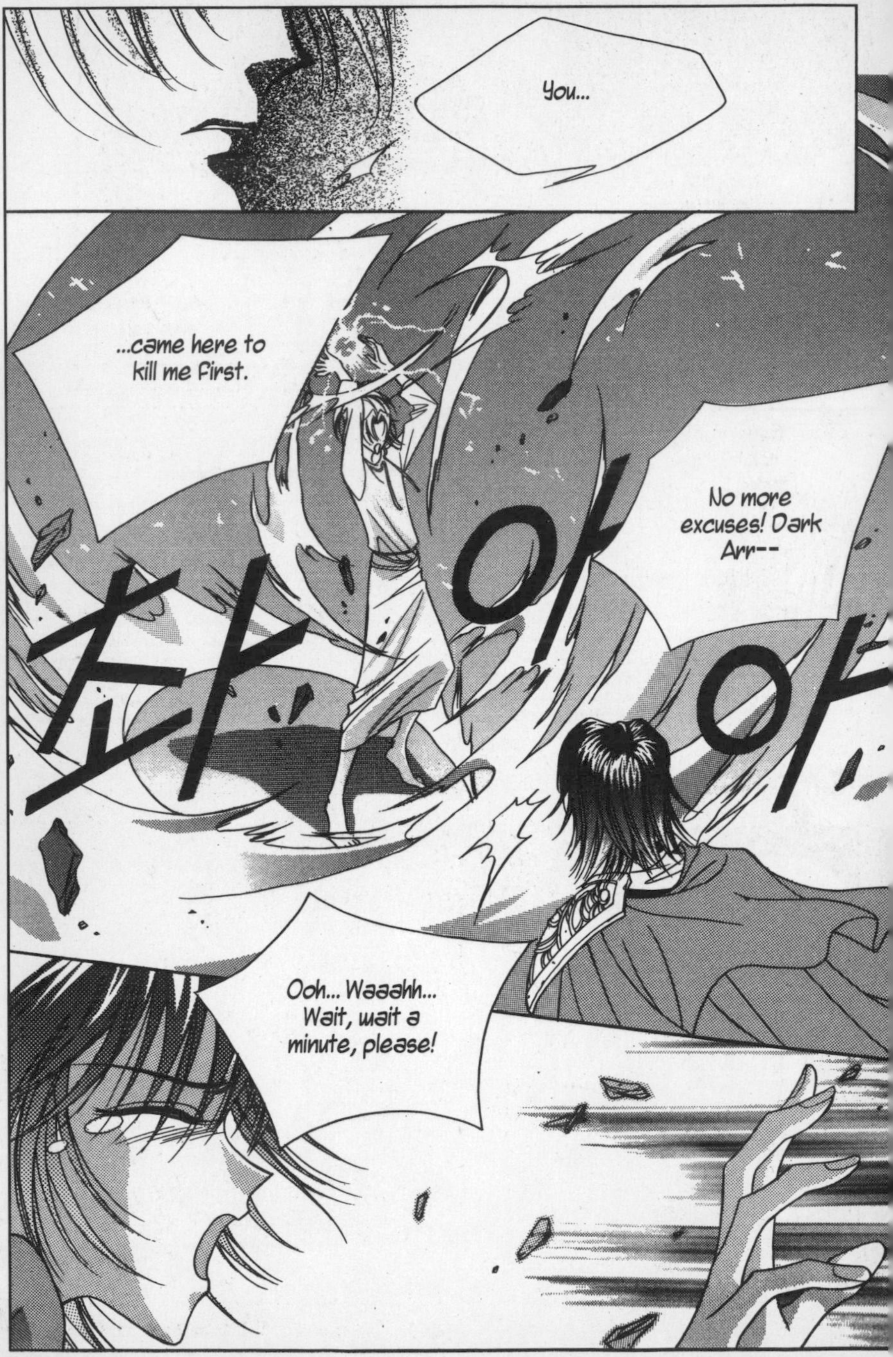
You...
No more excuses! Dark Arr--
...came here to kill me first.
Ooh... Waaahh... Wait, wait a minute, please!

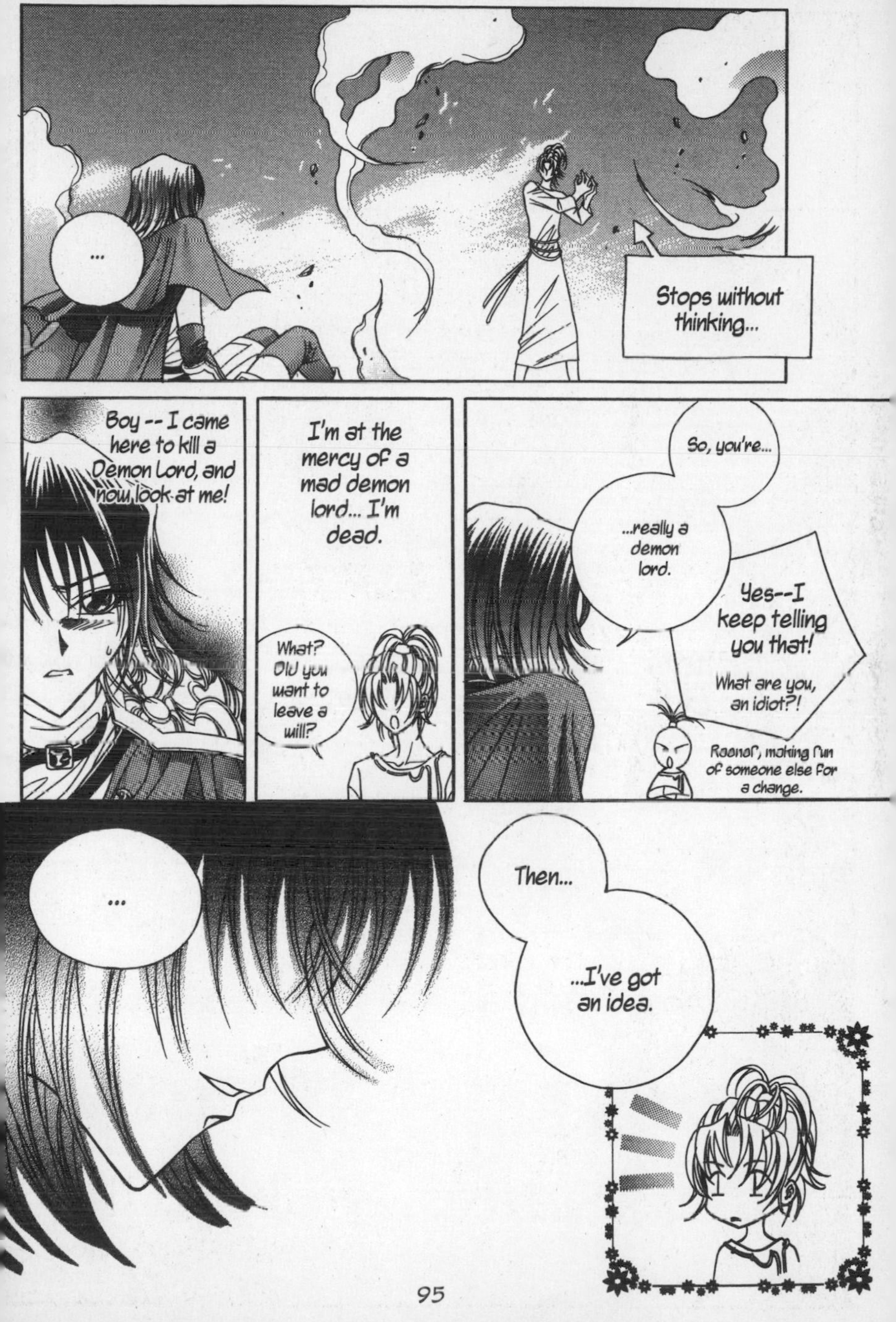
Stops without thinking...
...
So, you're...
...really a demon lord.
Yes--I keep telling you that!
What are you, an idiot?!
Raenef, making fun of someone else for a change.
I'm at the mercy of a mad demon lord... I'm dead.
What? Did you want to leave a will?
Boy -- I came here to kill a Demon Lord, and now look at me!
Then...
...I've got an idea.
...

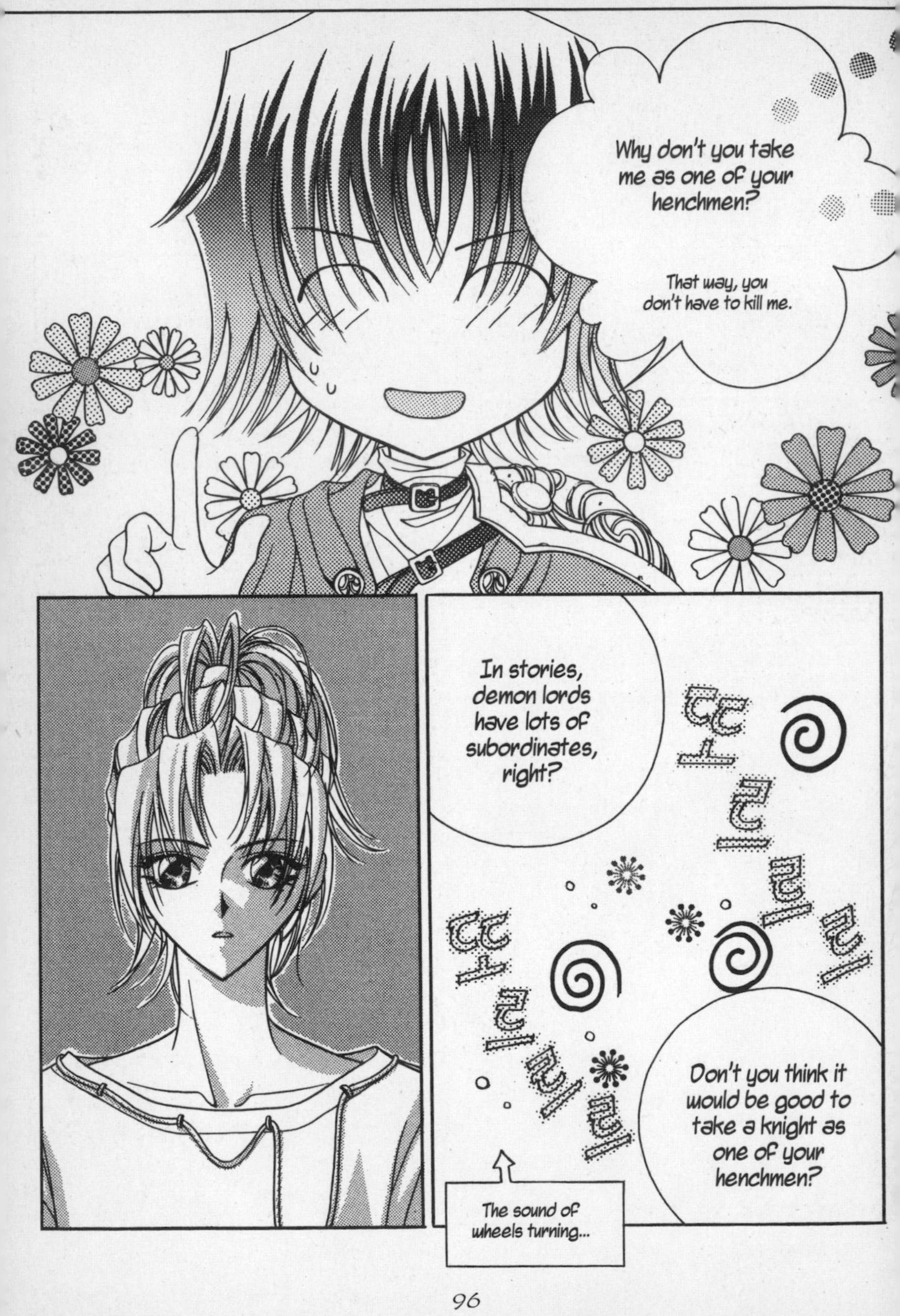
Why don't you take me as one of your henchmen?
That way, you don't have to kill me.
In stories, demon lords have lots of subordinates, right?
Don't you think it would be good to take a knight as one of your henchmen?
The sound of wheels turning...

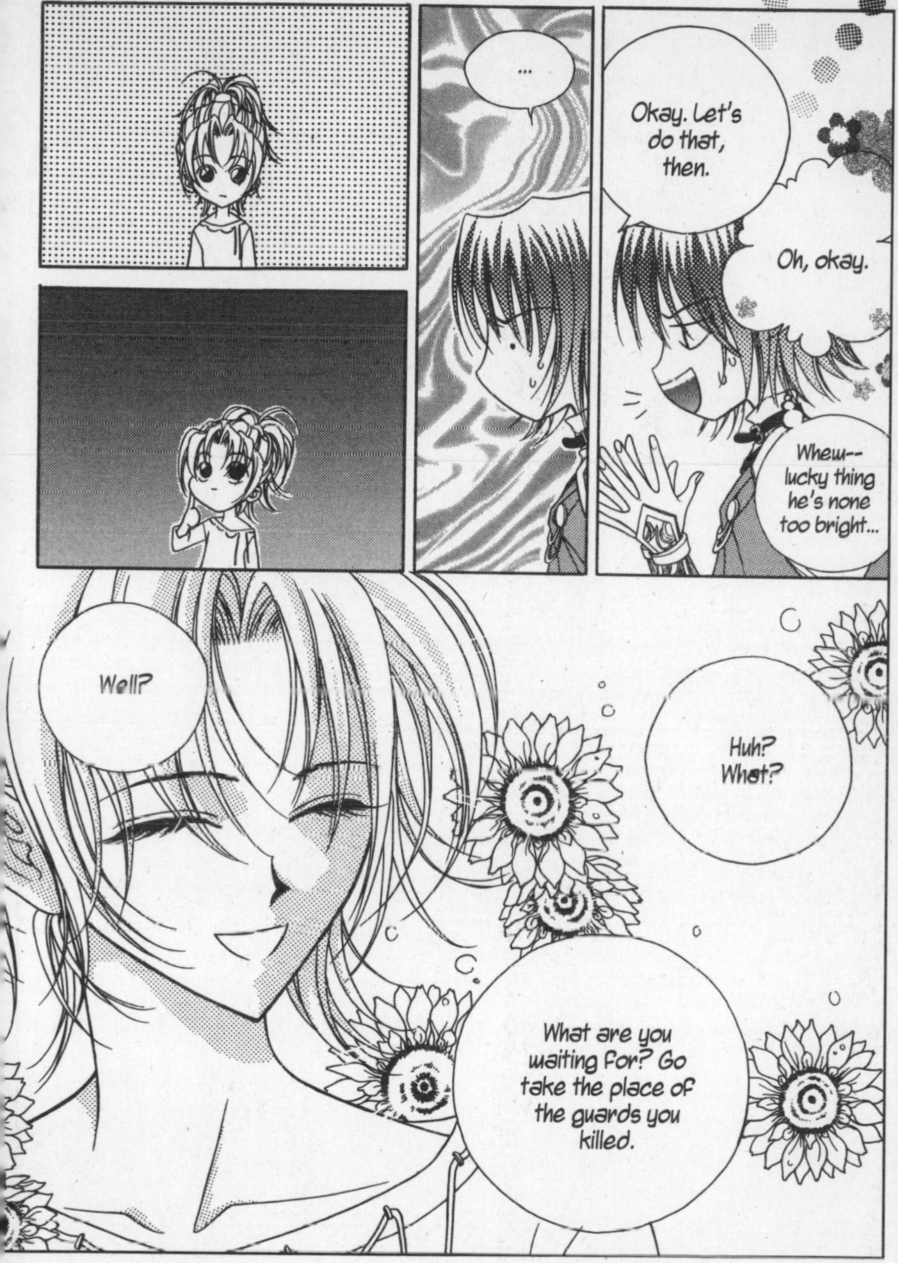
Okay. Let's do that, then.
Oh, okay.
Whew-- lucky thing he's none too bright...
...
Well?
Huh? What?
What are you waiting for? Go take the place of the guards you killed.

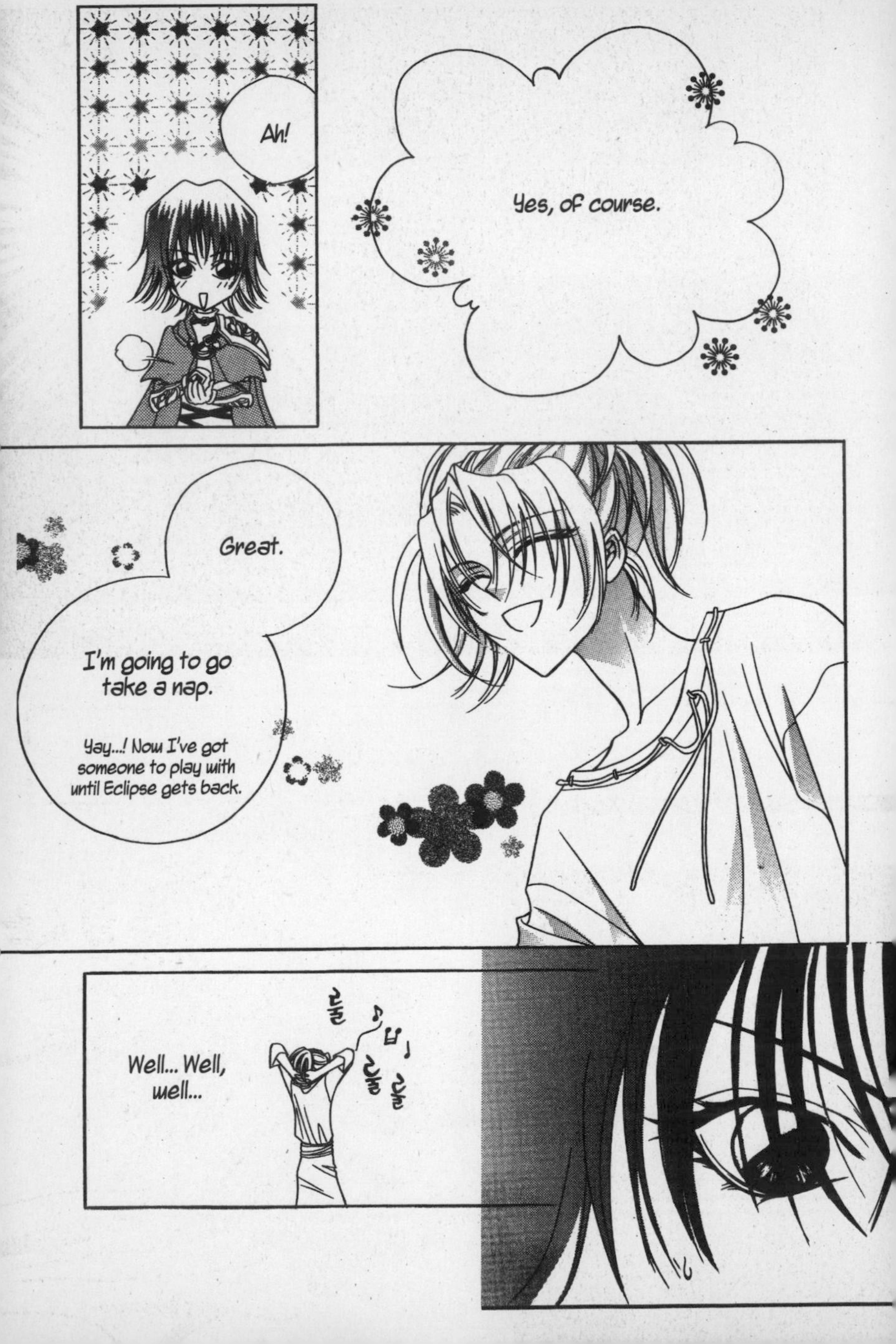
Ah!
Yes, of course.
Great.
I'm going to go take a nap.
Yay...! Now I've got someone to play with until Eclipse gets back.
Well... Well, well...

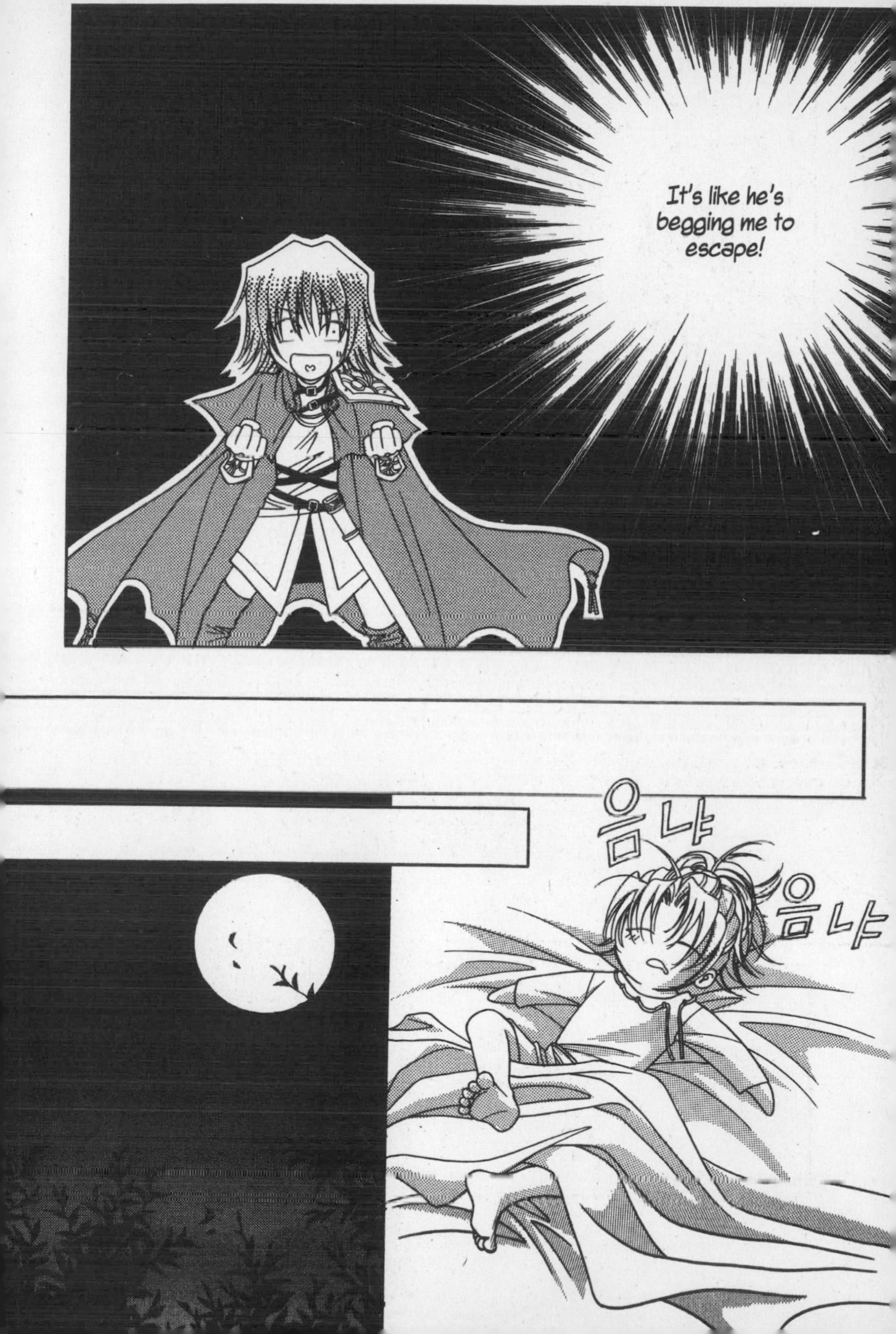
It's like he's begging me to escape!
음냐
음냐

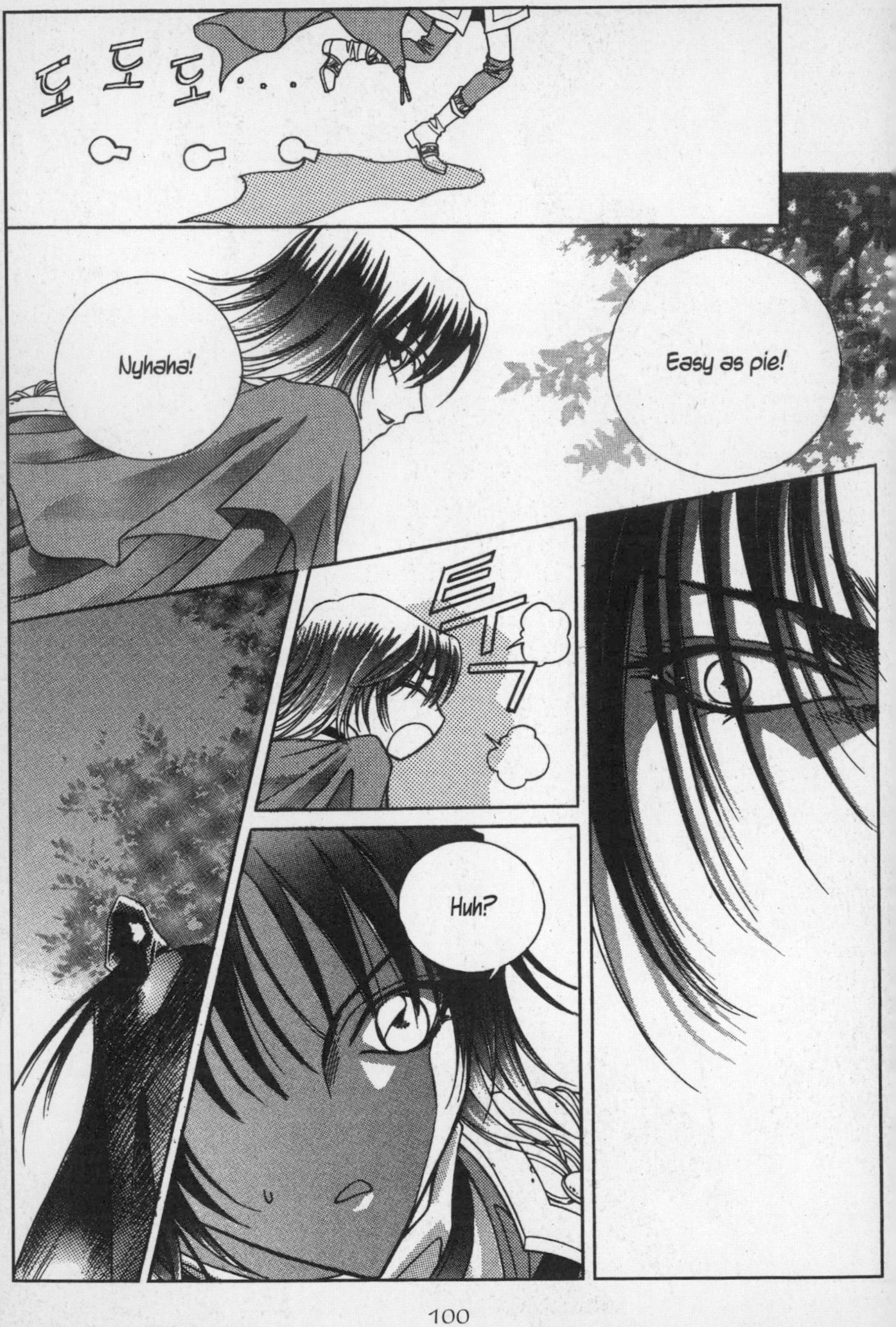

Nyhaha!
Easy as pie!
Huh?

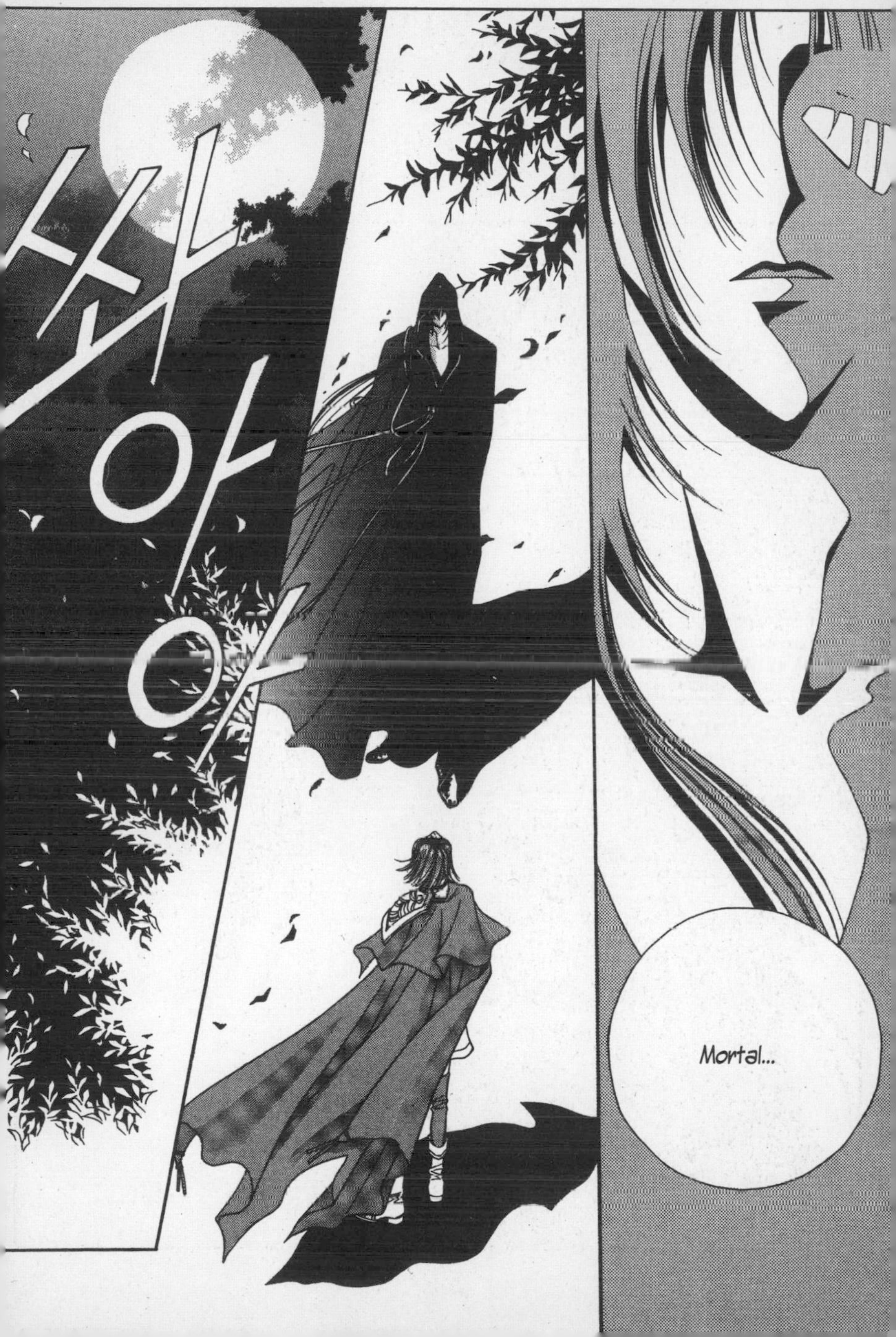
솨아아
Mortal...

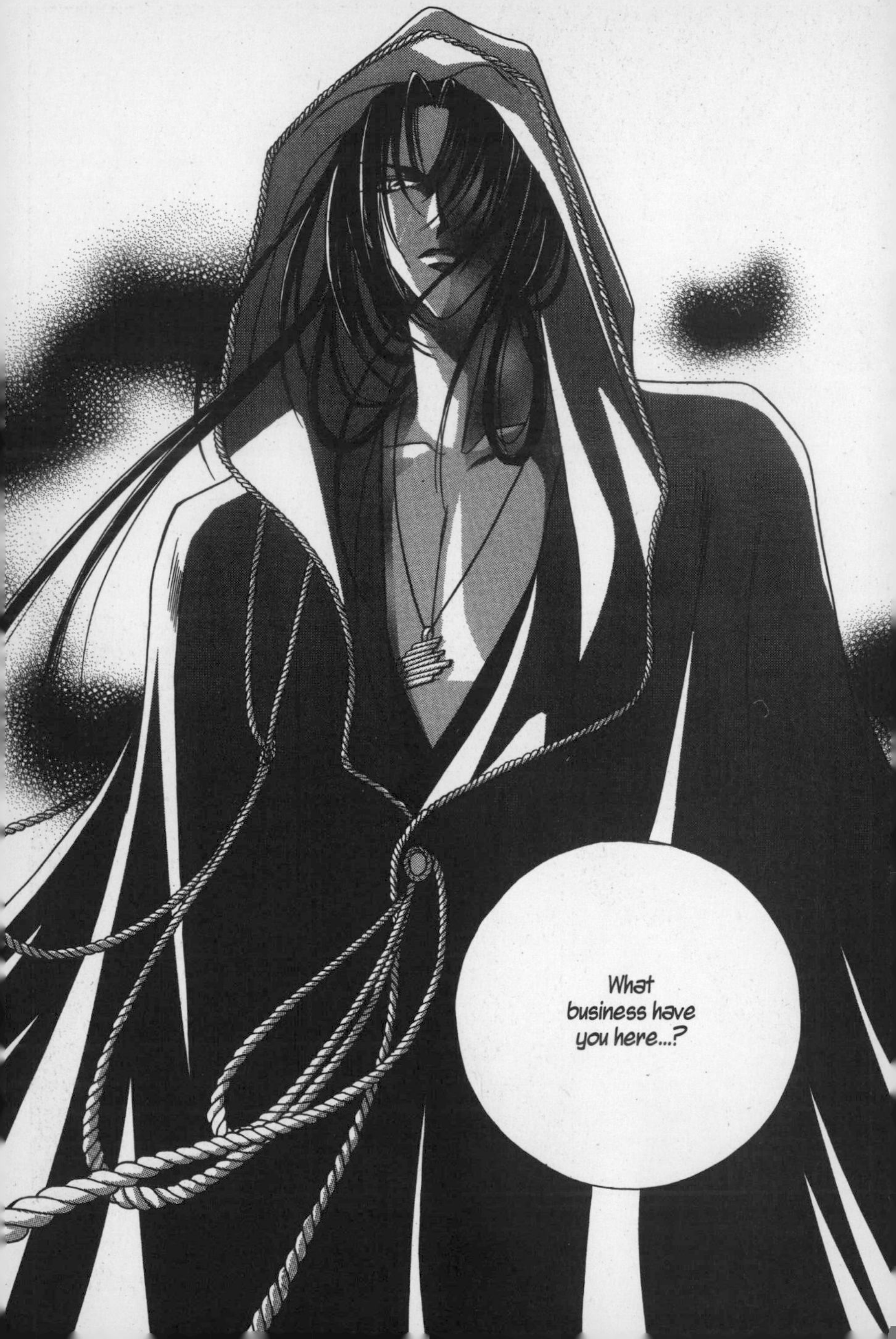
What business have you here...?

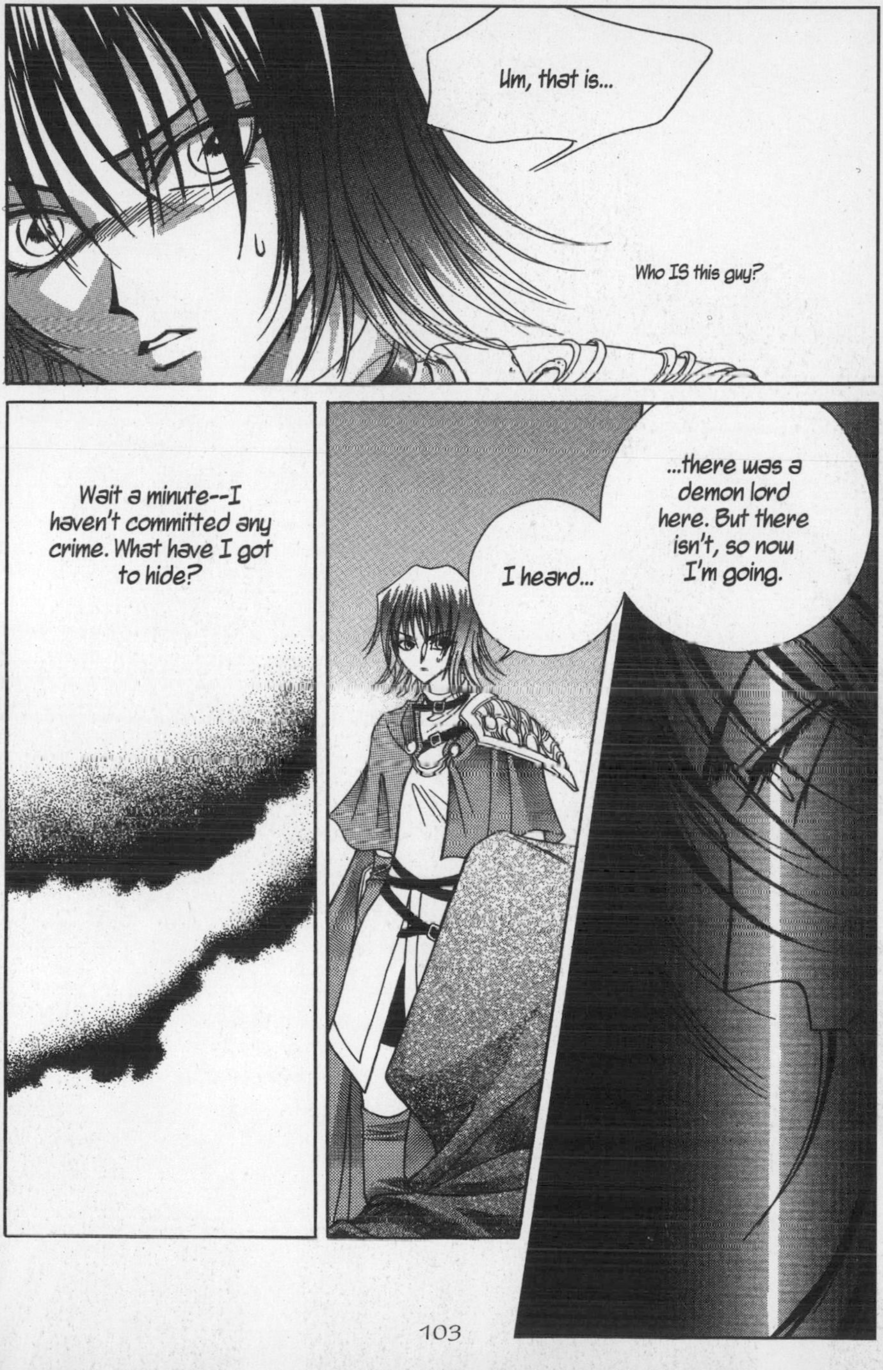
Um, that is...
Who IS this guy?
...there was a demon lord here. But there isn't, so now I'm going.
I heard...
Wait a minute--I haven't committed any crime. What have I got to hide?

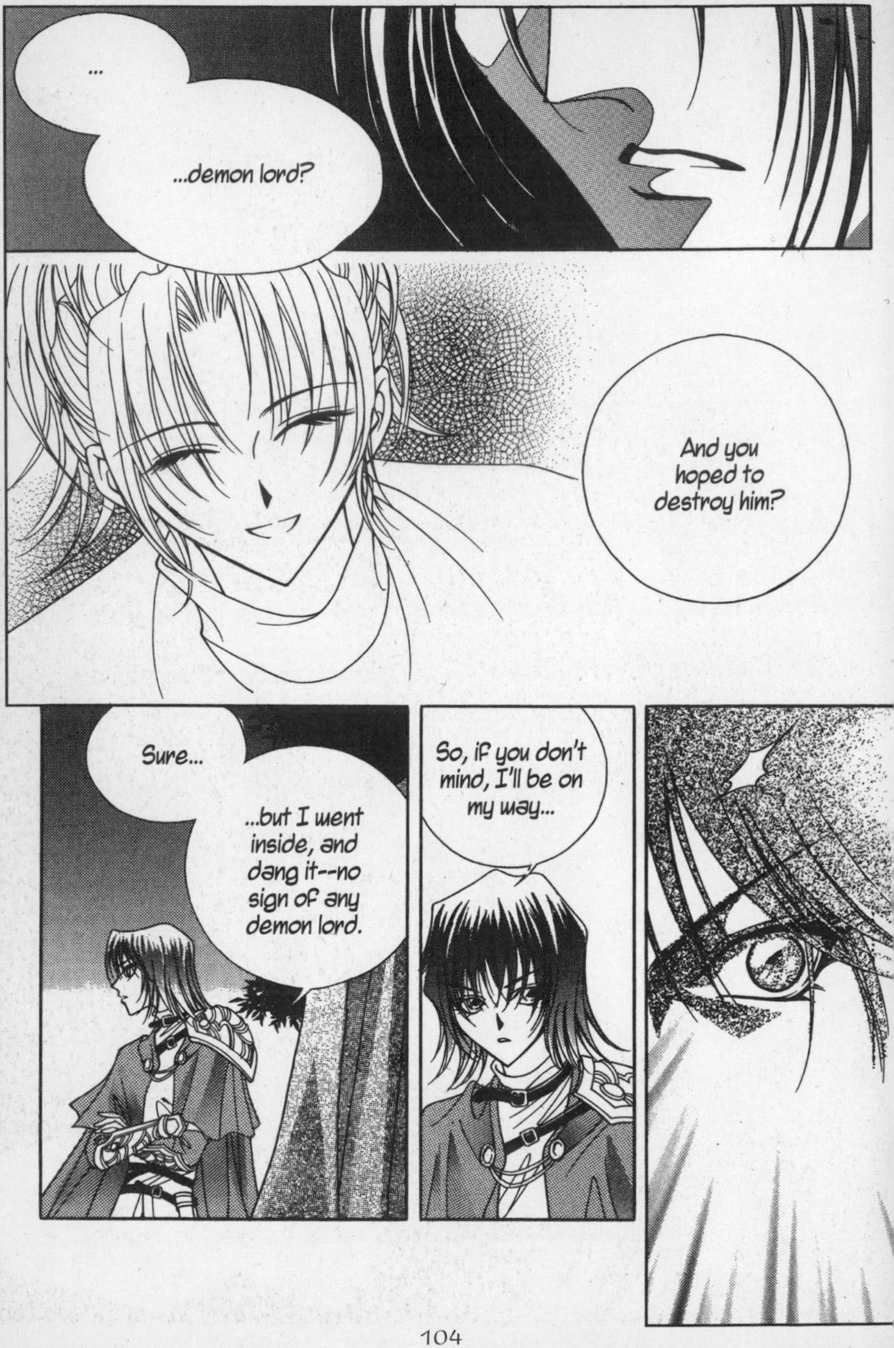
...
...demon lord?
And you hoped to destroy him?
Sure...
...but I went inside, and dang it--no sign of any demon lord.
So, if you don't mind, I'll be on my way...

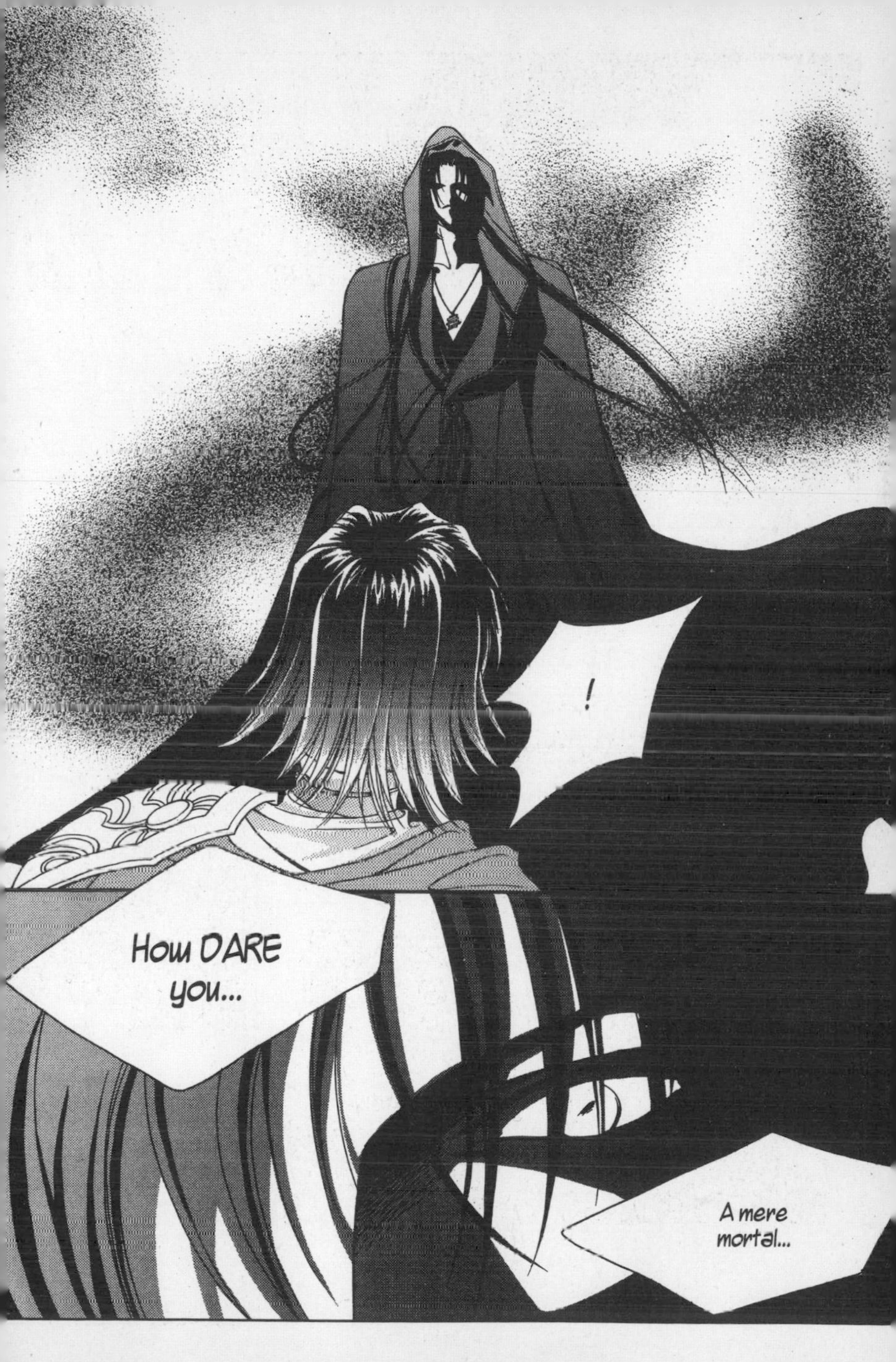
!
How DARE you...
A mere mortal...

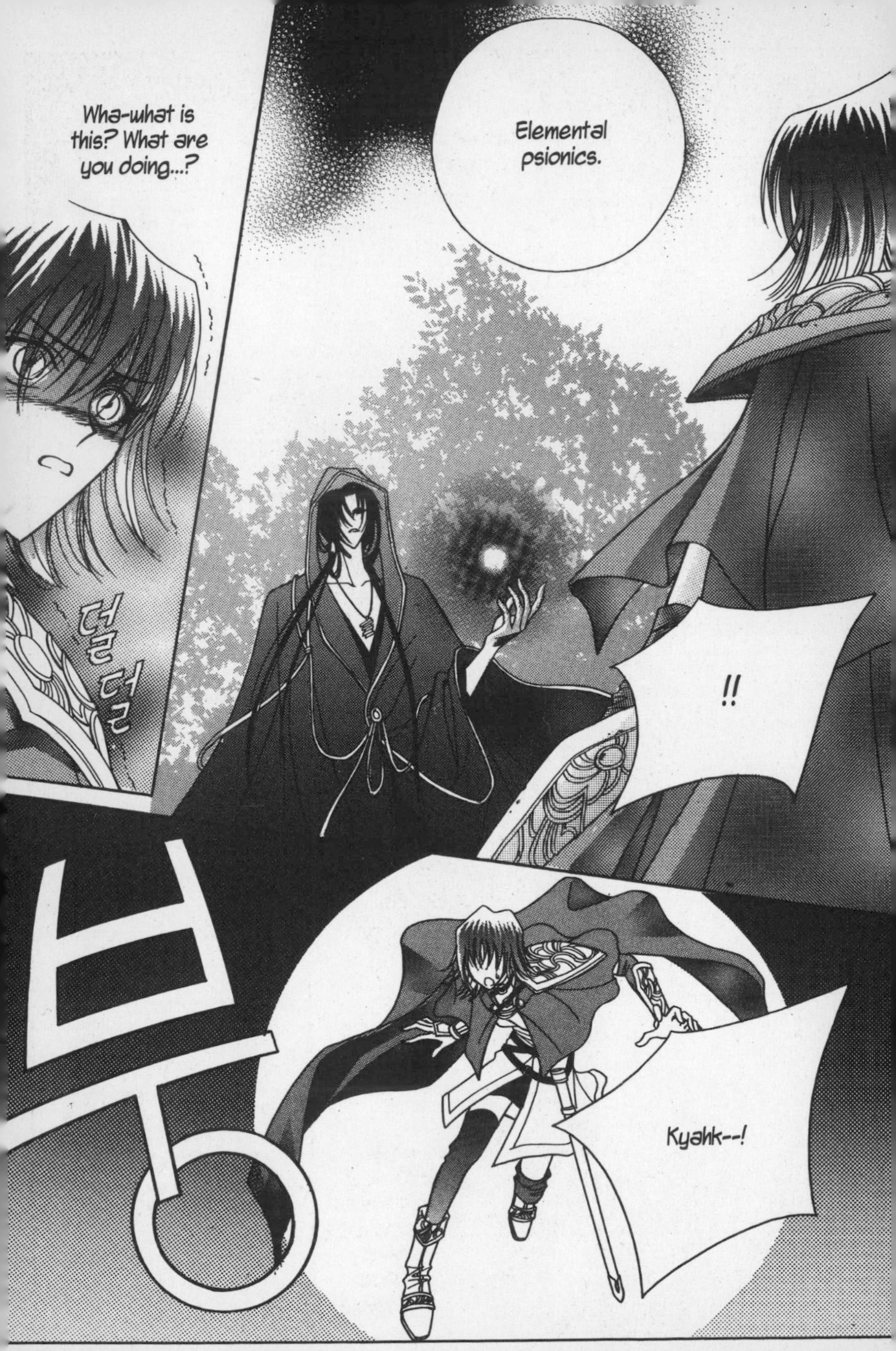
Wha-what is this? What are you doing...?
Elemental psionics.
!!
Kyahk--!

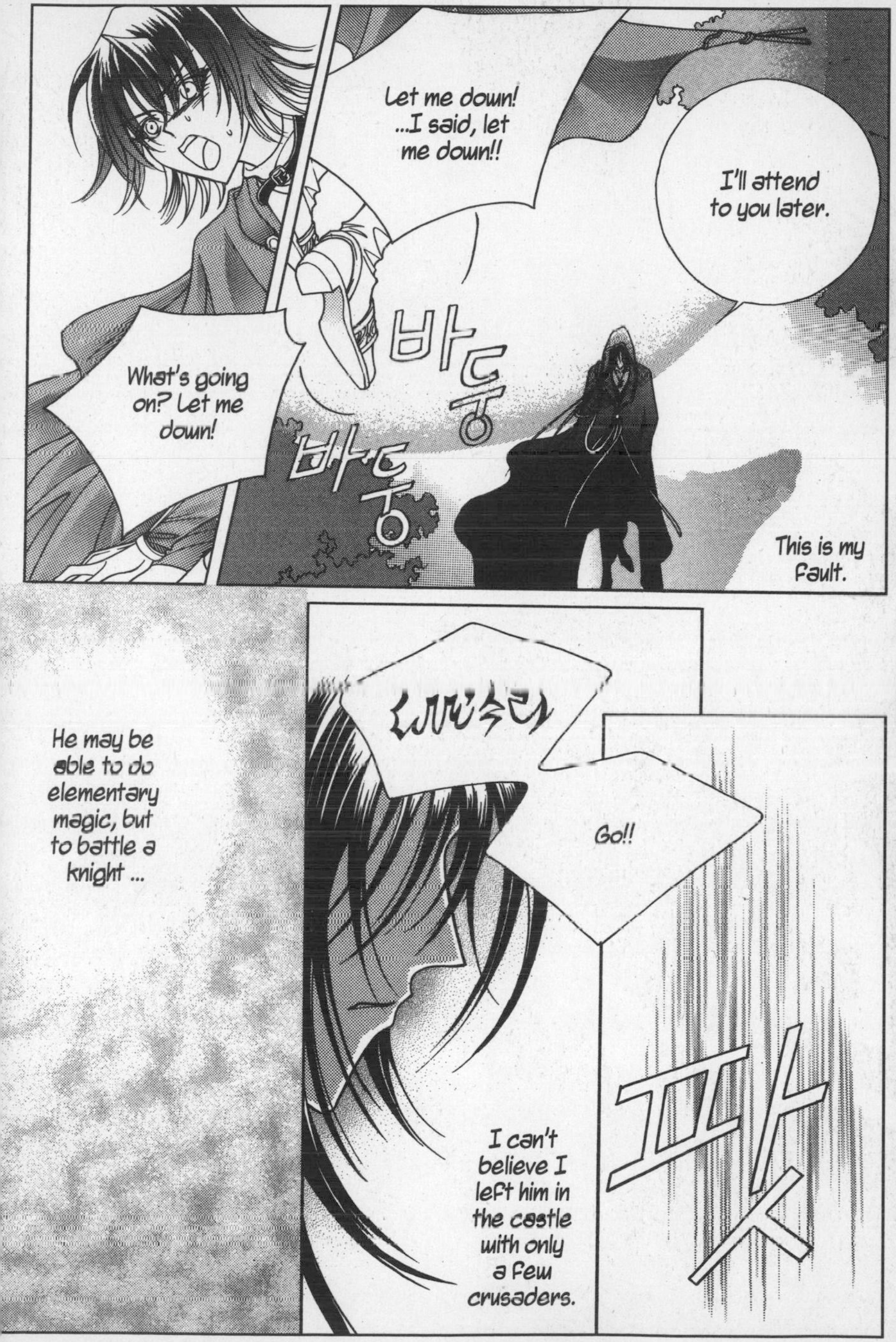
What's going on? Let me down!
Let me down! ...I said, let me down!!
바둥
바둥
I'll attend to you later.
This is my fault.
He may be able to do elementary magic, but to battle a knight ...
Go!!
I can't believe I left him in the castle with only a few crusaders.
팟

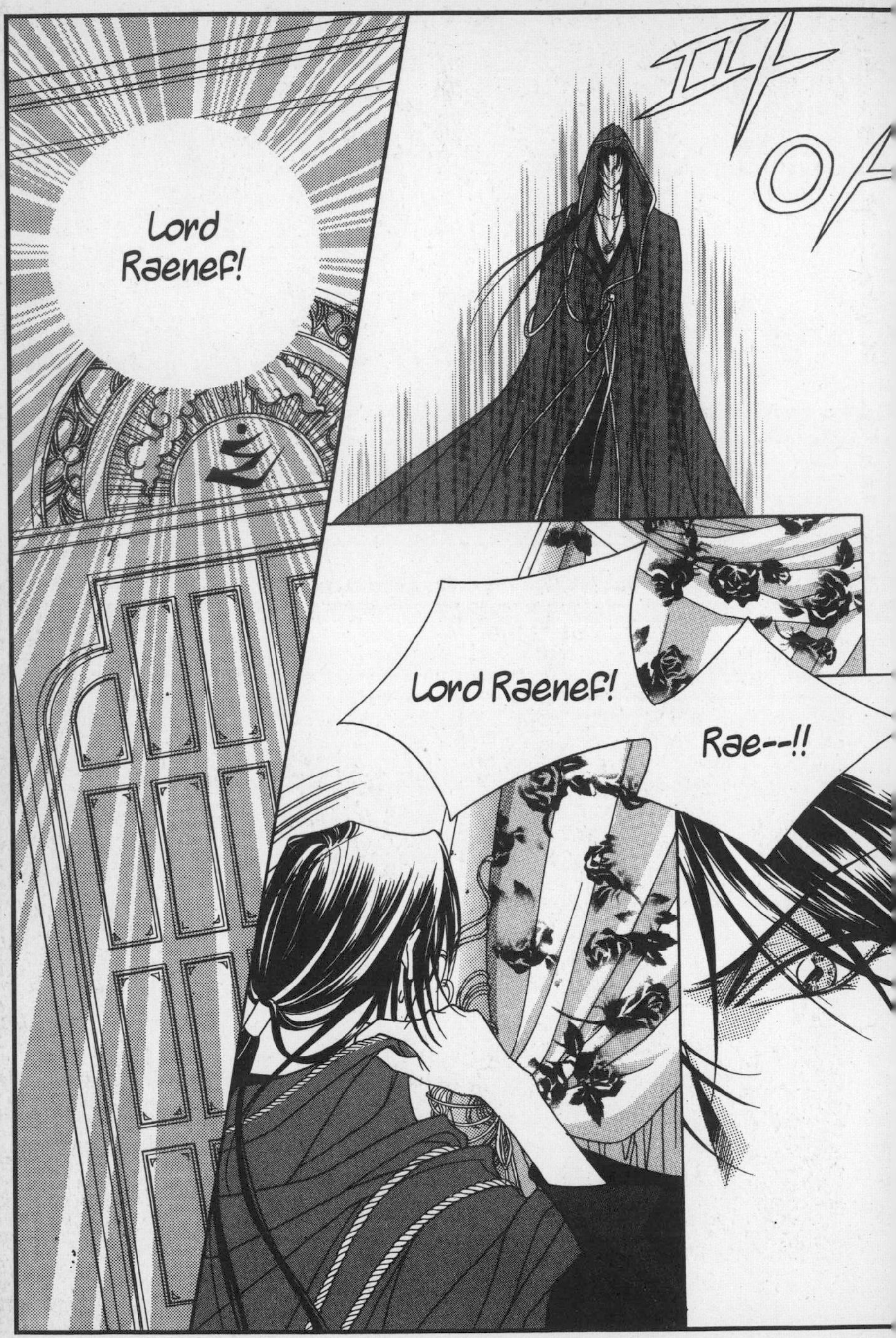
Lord Raenef!
Lord Raenef!
Rae--!!

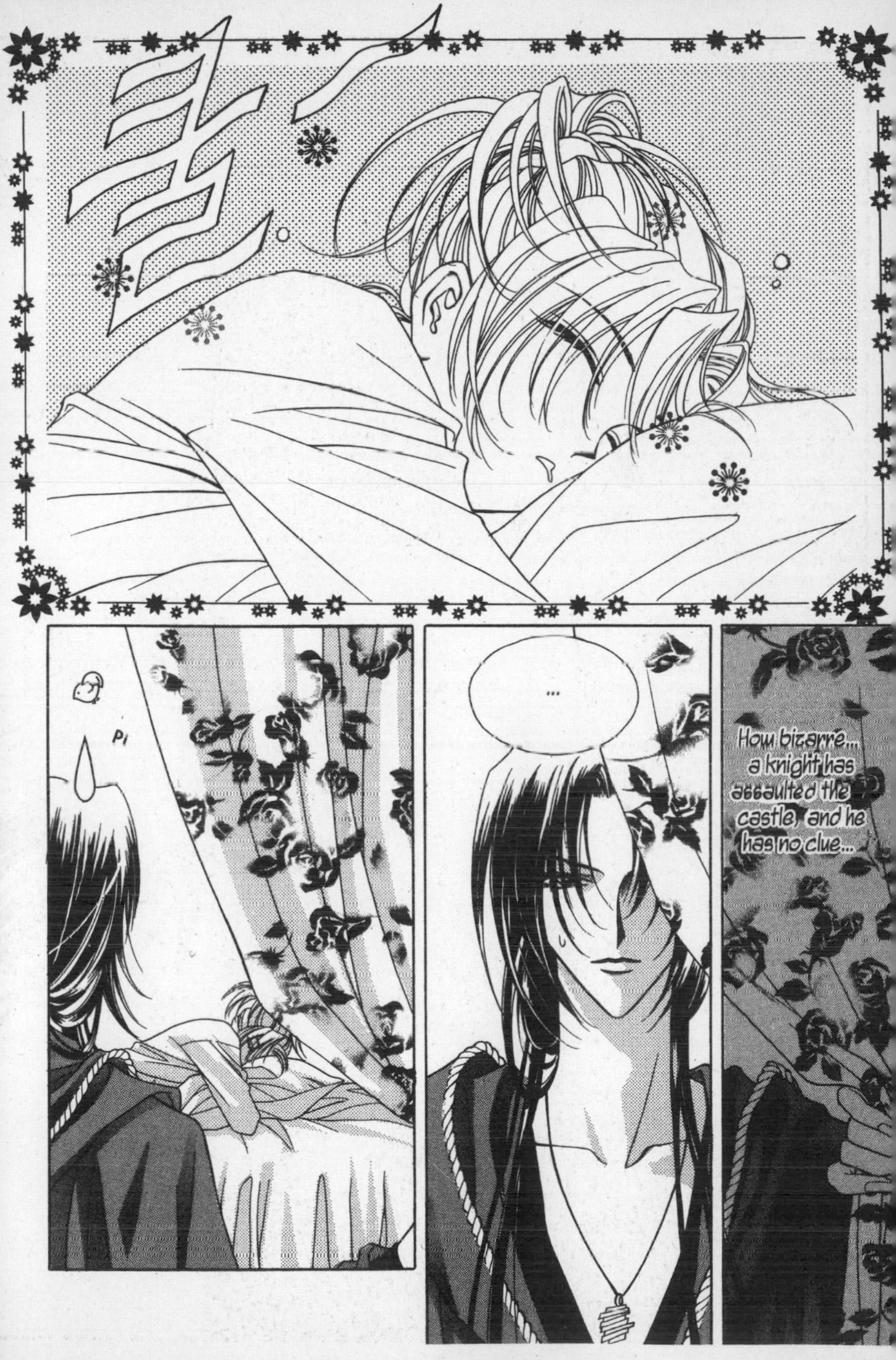
How bizarre... a knight has assaulted the castle, and he has no clue...
...
Pi

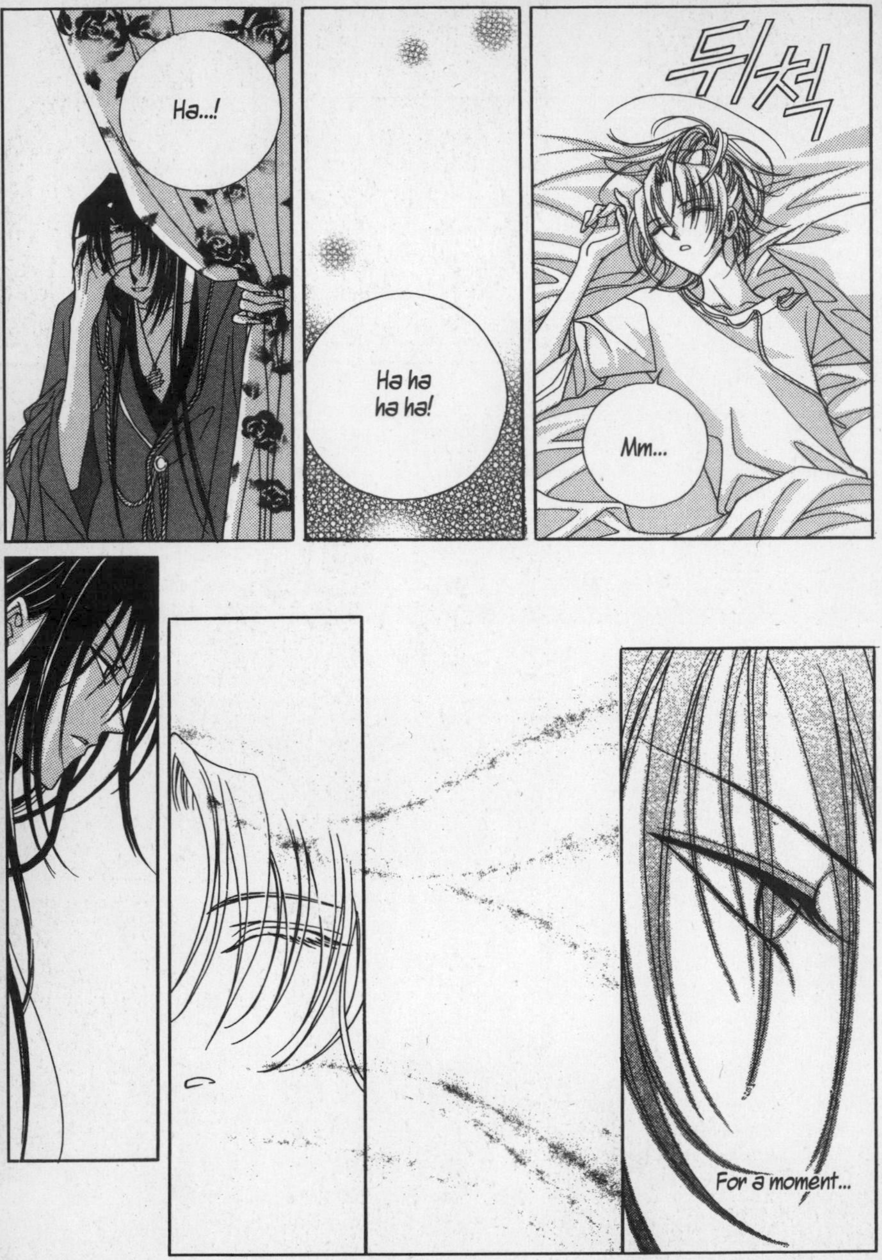
Ha...!
Ha ha ha ha!
뒤척
Mm...
For a moment...

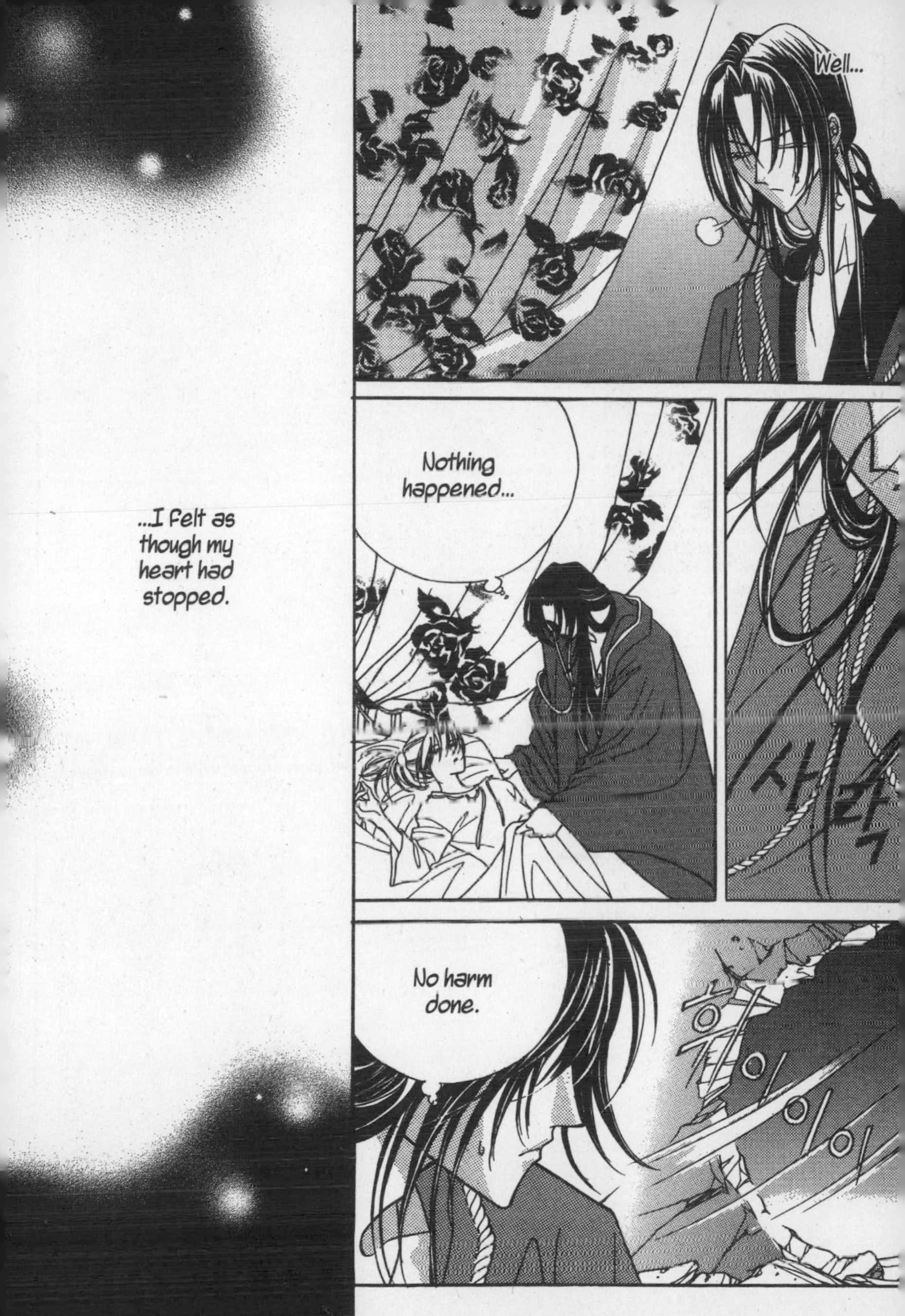

...I felt as though my heart had stopped.
Well...
Nothing happened...
No harm done.

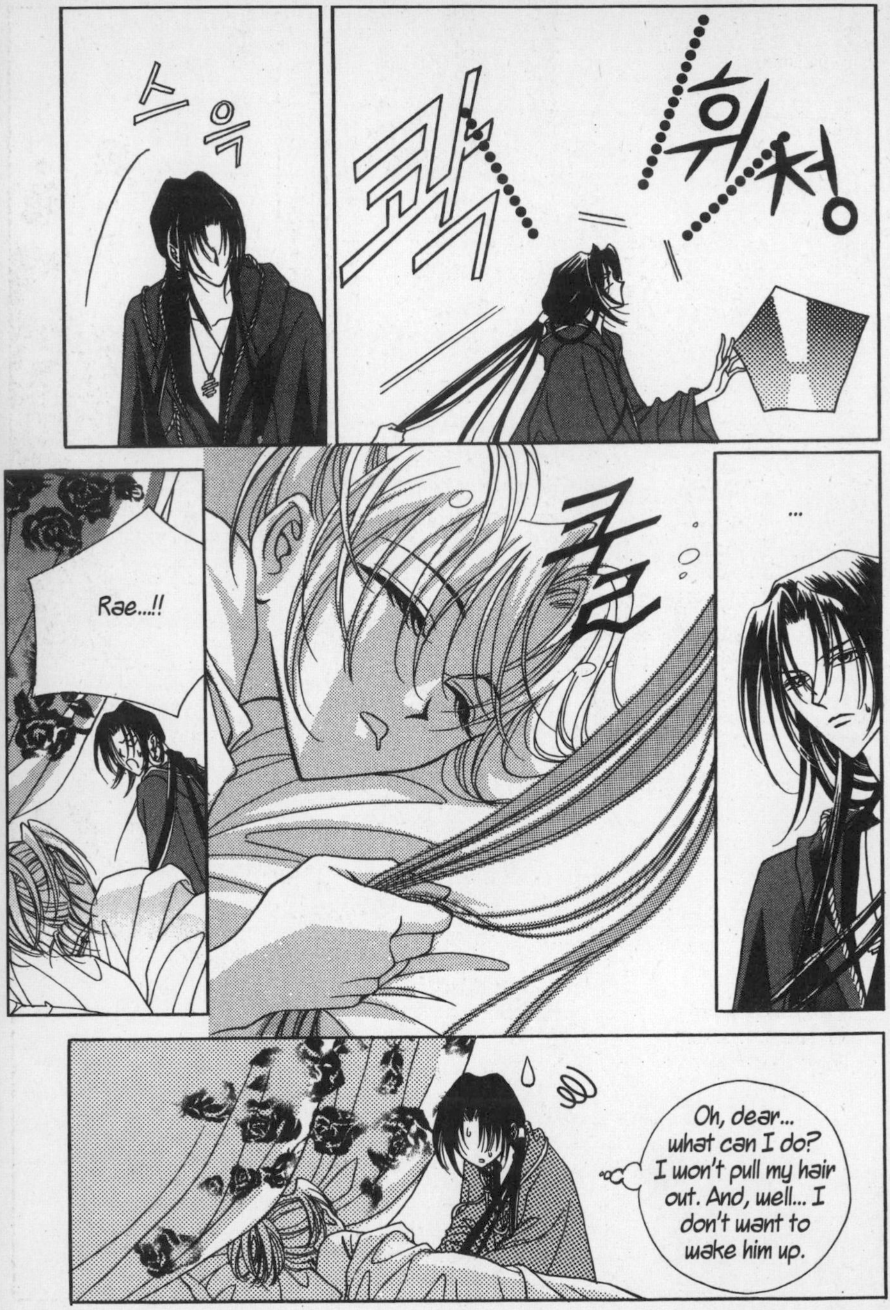
스윽
콰각
휘청
Rae...!!
...
Oh, dear... what can I do? I won't pull my hair out. And, well... I don't want to make him up.

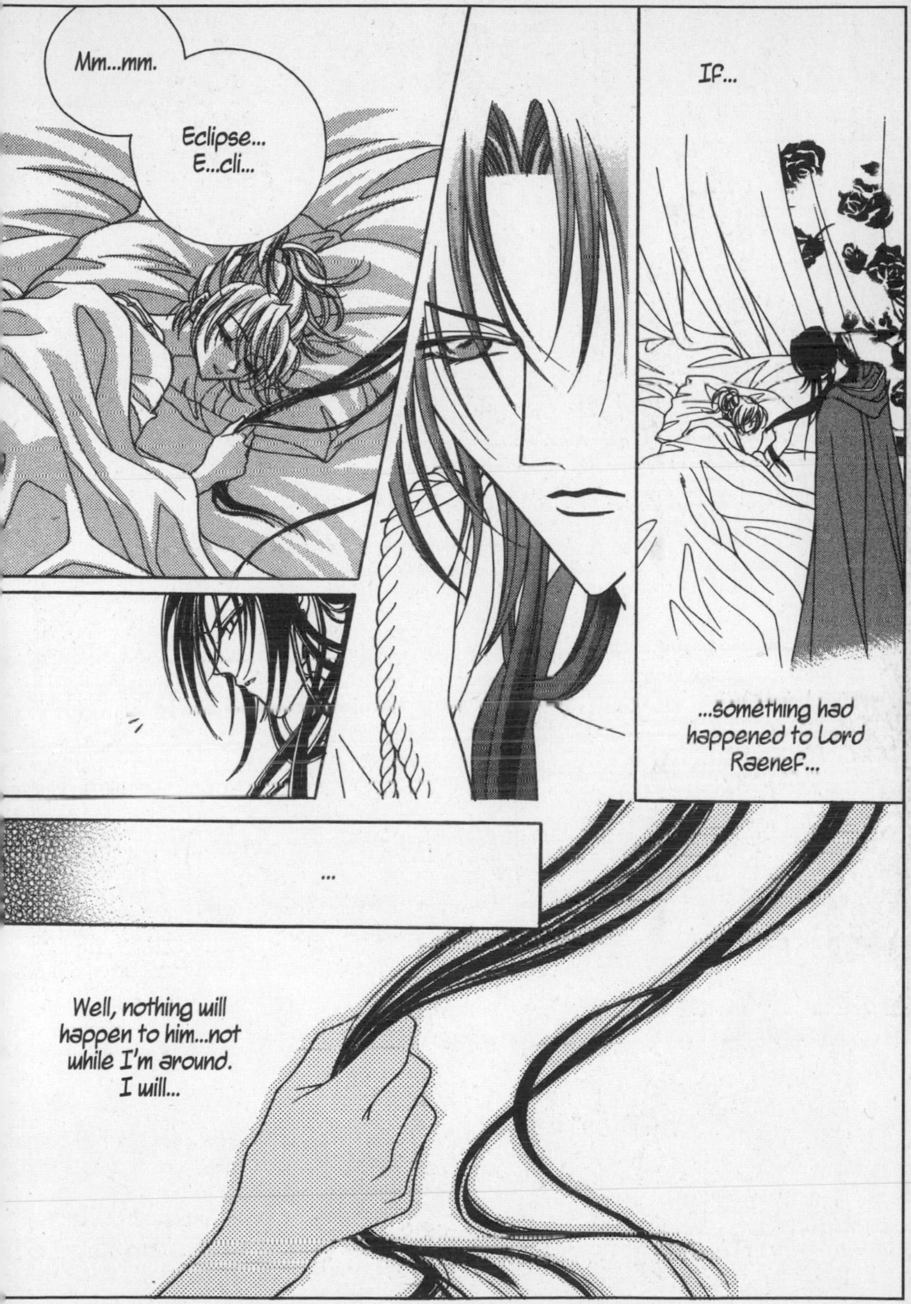
Mm...mm.
Eclipse... E...cli...
If...
...something had happened to Lord Raenef...
...
Well, nothing will happen to him...not while I'm around. I will...

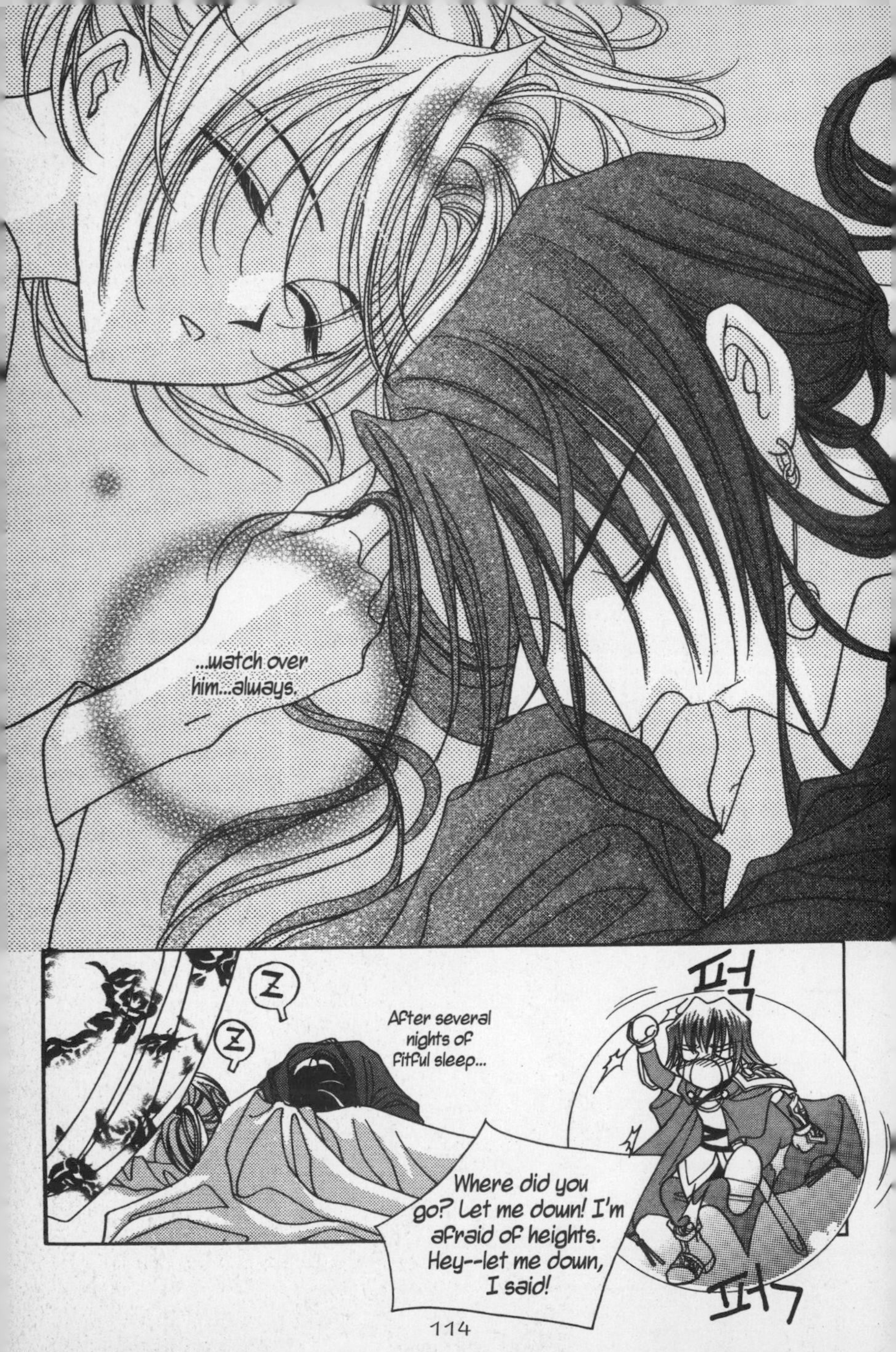
...watch over him...always.
After several nights of fitful sleep...
Where did you go? Let me down! I'm afraid of heights. Hey--let me down, I said!

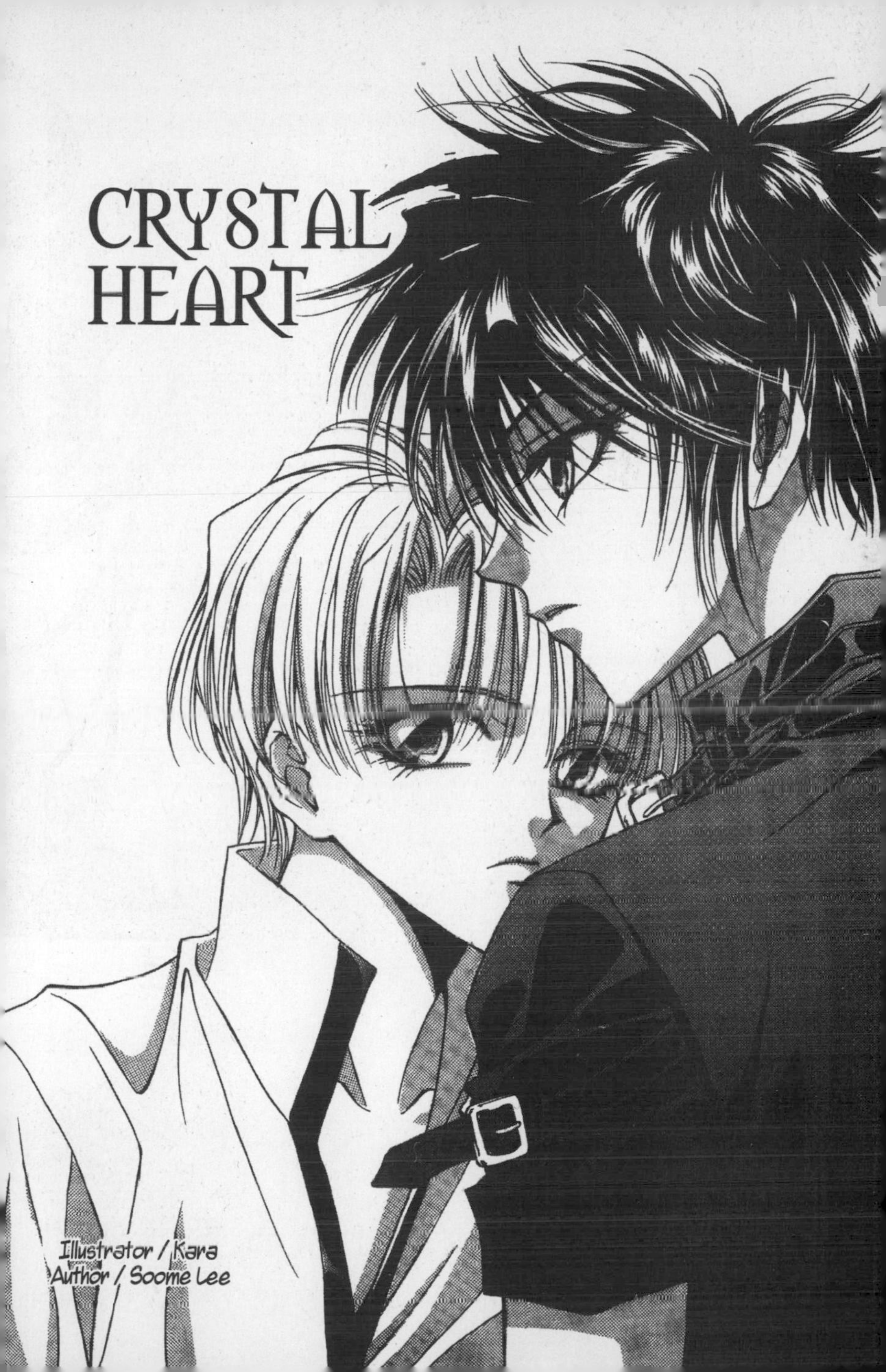
CRYSTAL HEART
Illustrator / Kara
Author / Soome Lee

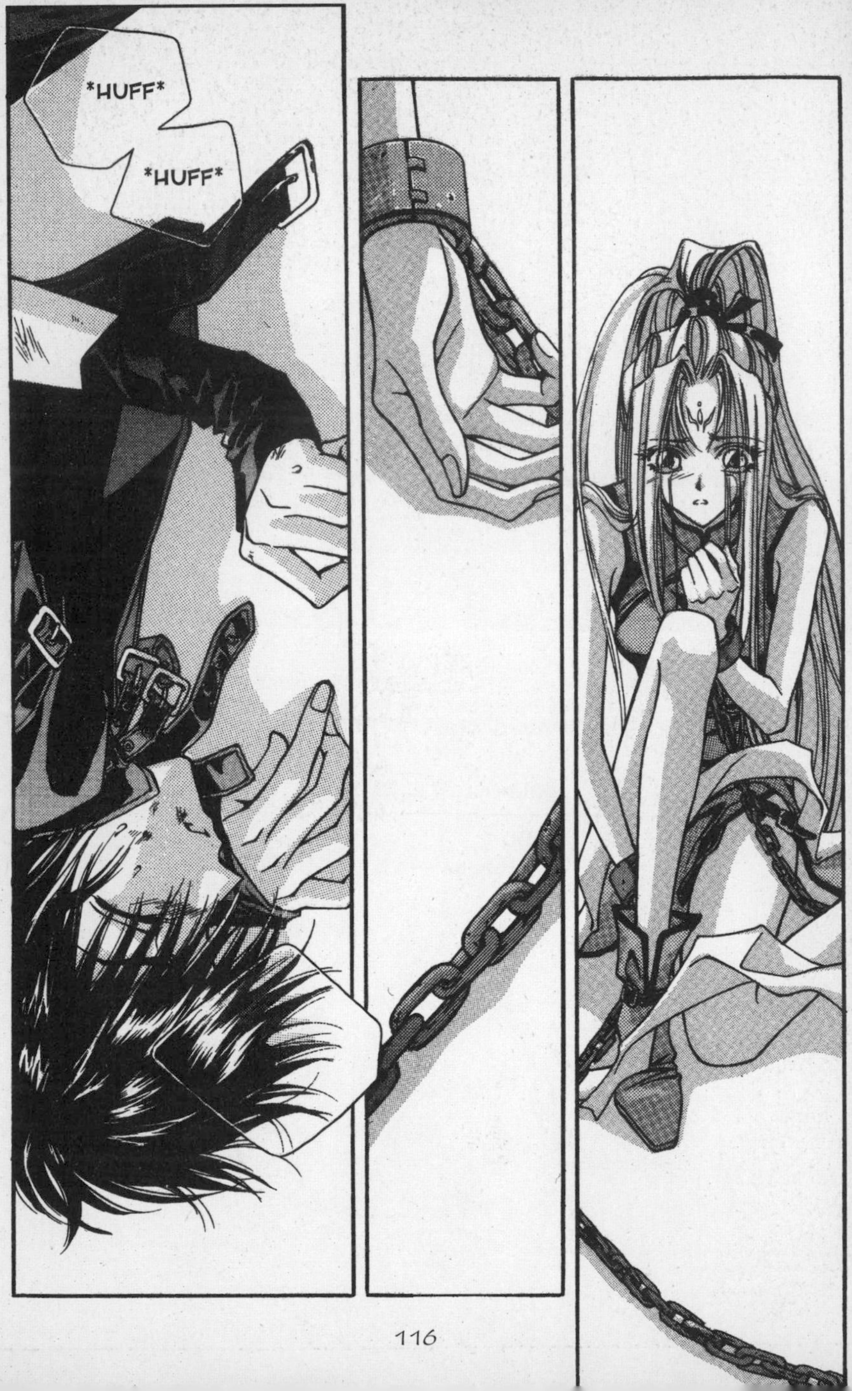
HUFF
HUFF

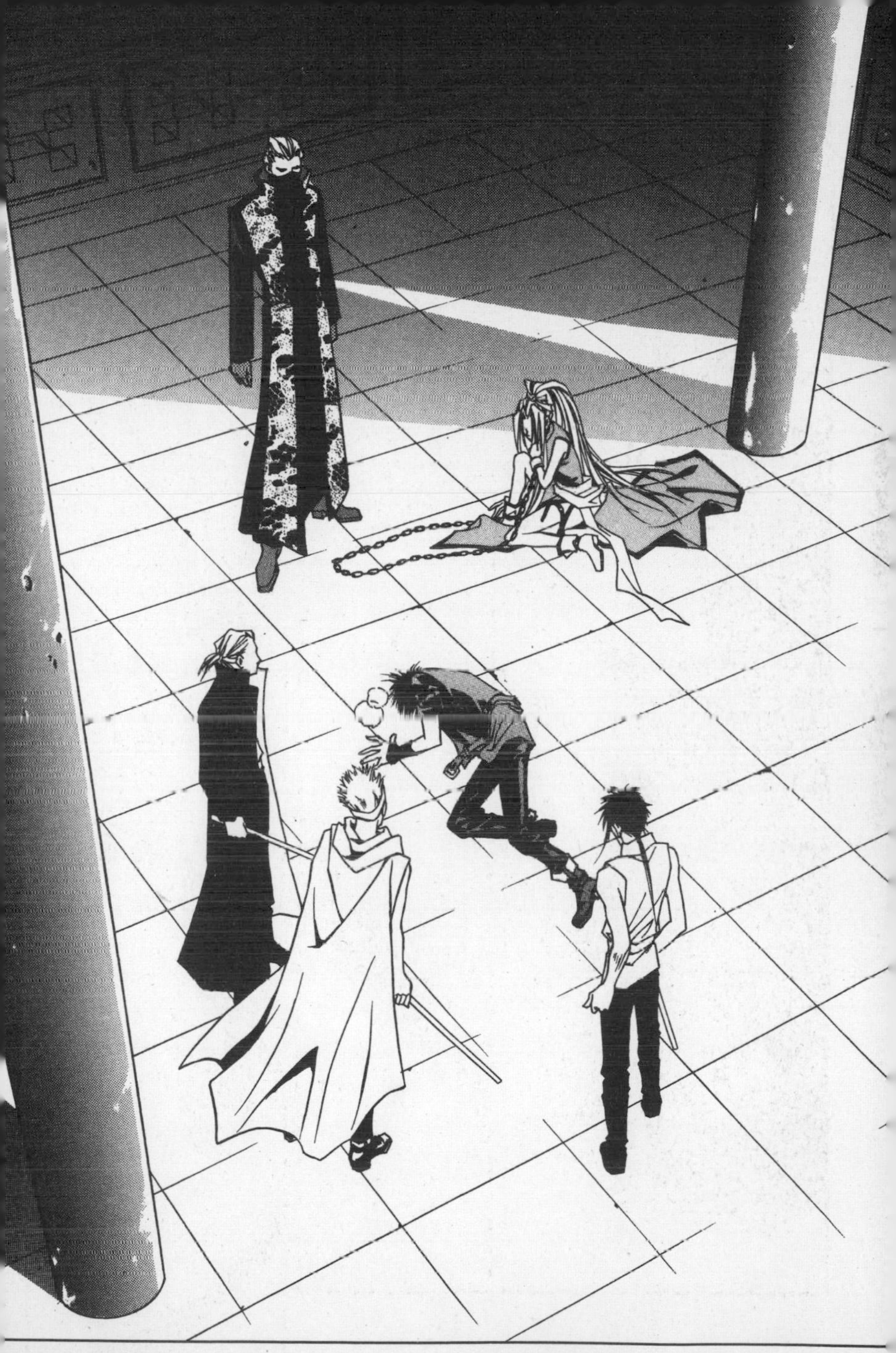

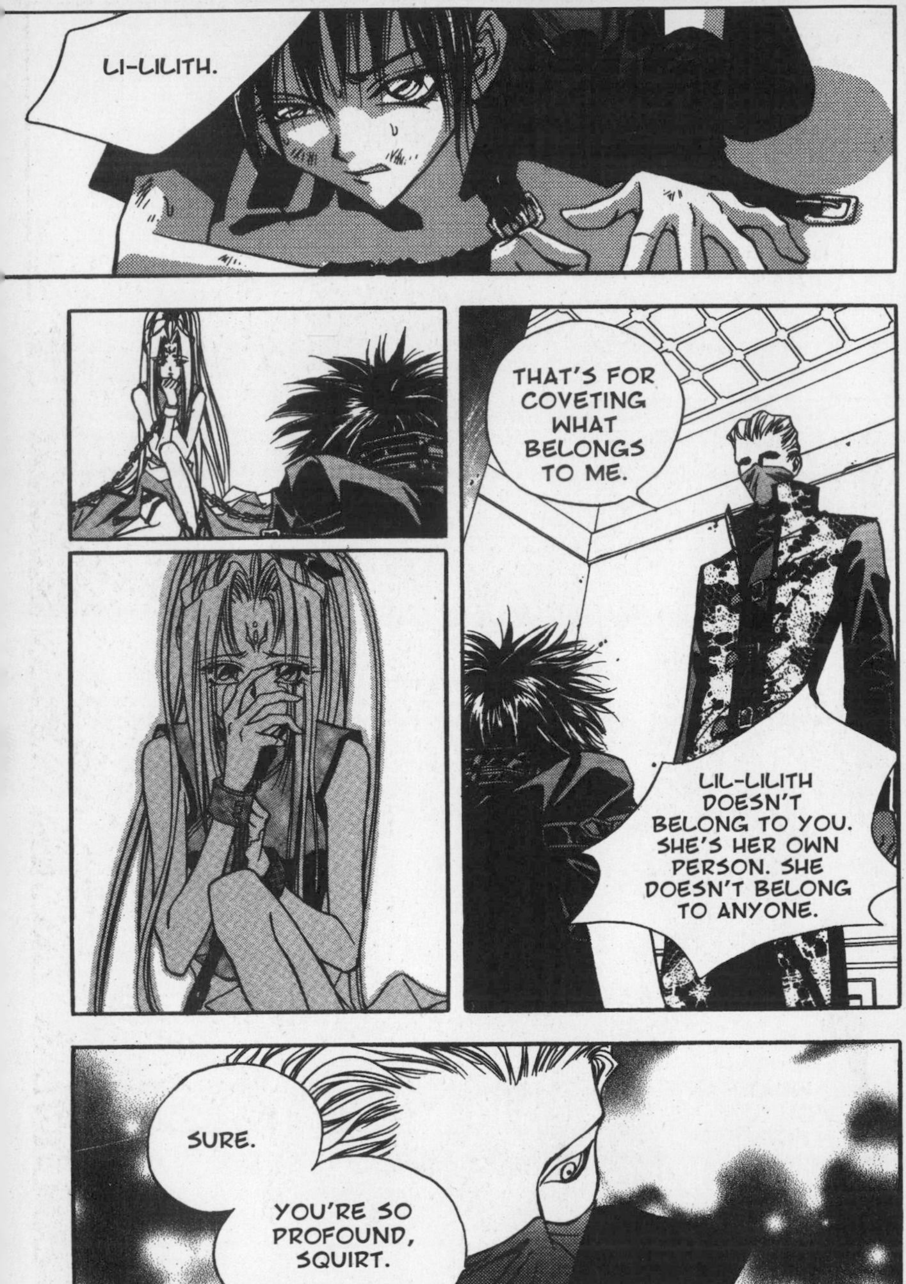
LI-LILITH.
THAT'S FOR COVETING WHAT BELONGS TO ME.
LIL-LILITH DOESN'T BELONG TO YOU. SHE'S HER OWN PERSON. SHE DOESN'T BELONG TO ANYONE.
SURE.
YOU'RE SO PROFOUND, SQUIRT.

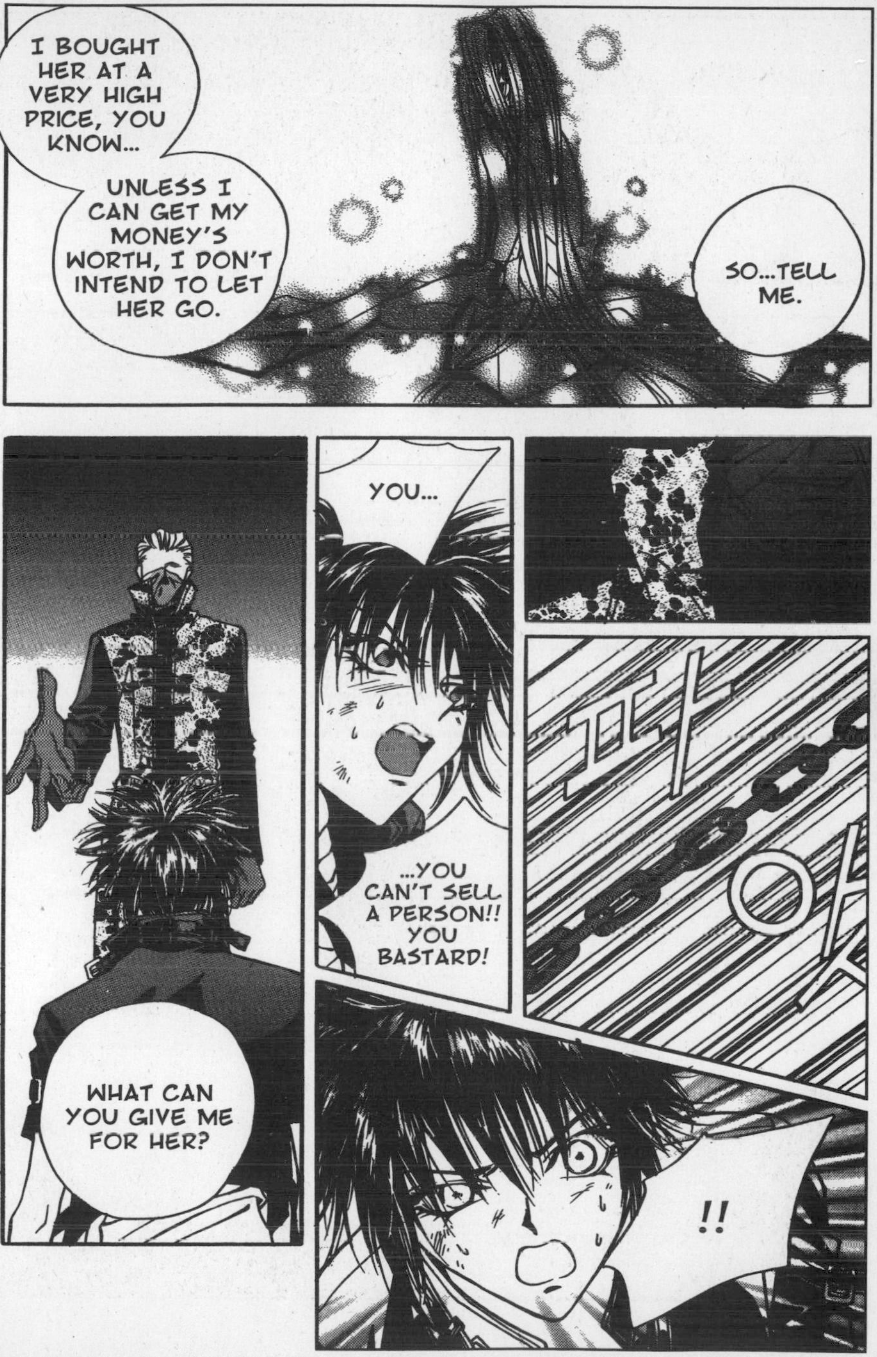
SO...TELL ME.
I BOUGHT HER AT A VERY HIGH PRICE, YOU KNOW...
UNLESS I CAN GET MY MONEY'S WORTH, I DON'T INTEND TO LET HER GO.
YOU...
...YOU CAN'T SELL A PERSON!! YOU BASTARD!
WHAT CAN YOU GIVE ME FOR HER?
!!

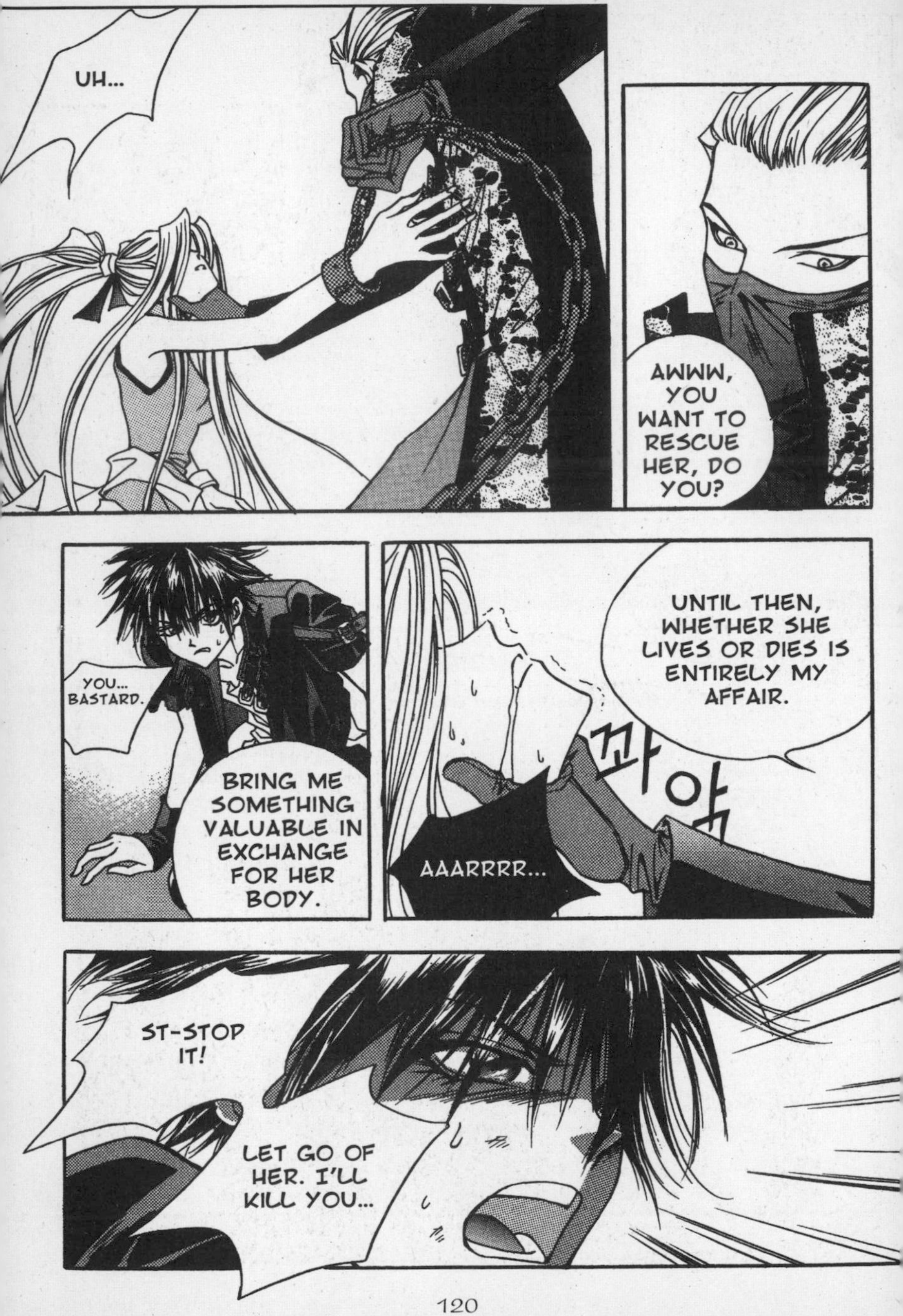
UH...
AWWW, YOU WANT TO RESCUE HER, DO YOU?
YOU... BASTARD.
BRING ME SOMETHING VALUABLE IN EXCHANGE FOR HER BODY.
UNTIL THEN, WHETHER SHE LIVES OR DIES IS ENTIRELY MY AFFAIR.
꽈악
AAARRRR...
ST-STOP IT!
LET GO OF HER. I'LL KILL YOU...

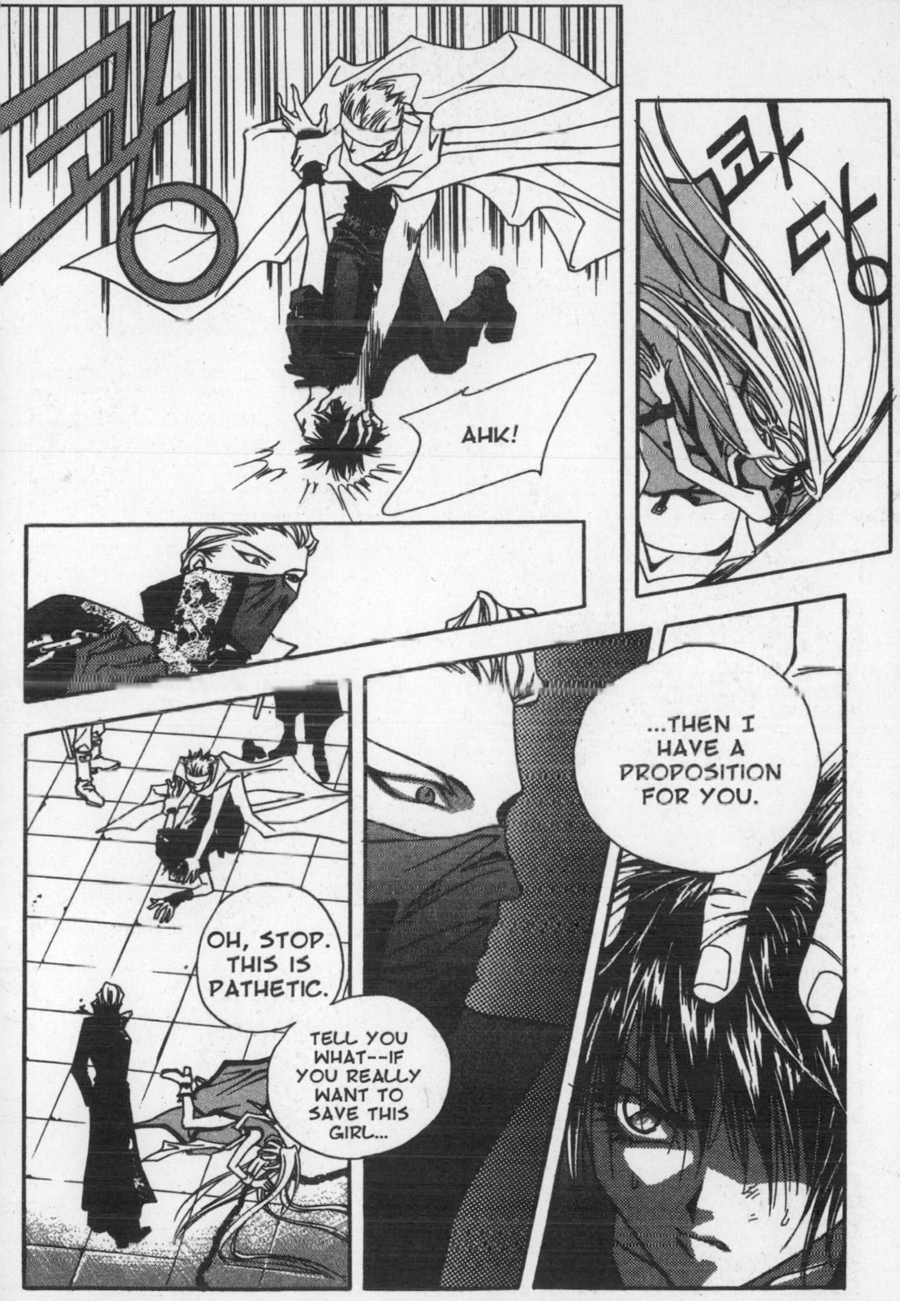

AHK!
OH, STOP. THIS IS PATHETIC.
TELL YOU WHAT--IF YOU REALLY WANT TO SAVE THIS GIRL...
...THEN I HAVE A PROPOSITION FOR YOU.

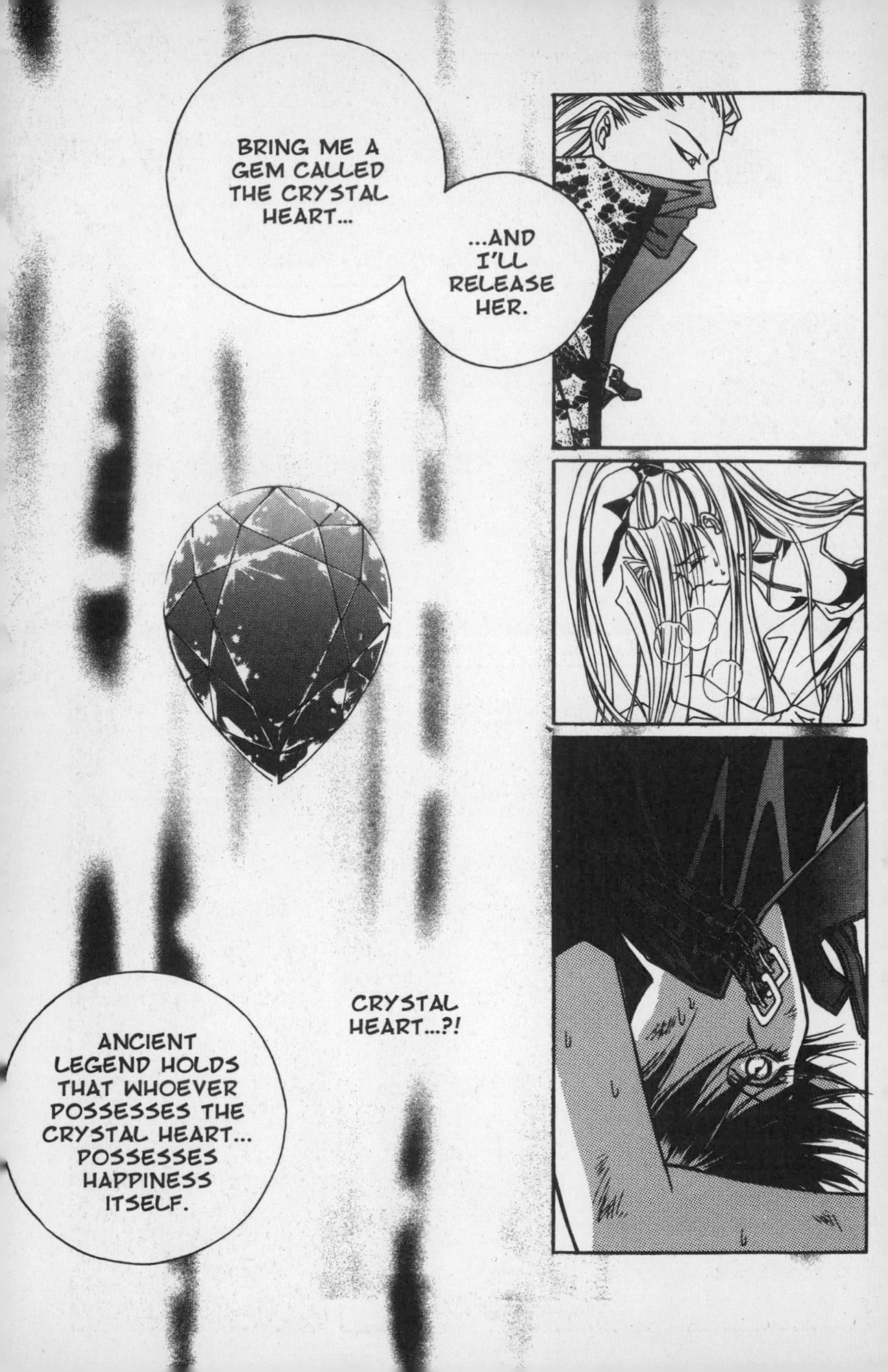
BRING ME A GEM CALLED THE CRYSTAL HEART...
...AND I'LL RELEASE HER.
CRYSTAL HEART...?!
ANCIENT LEGEND HOLDS THAT WHOEVER POSSESSES THE CRYSTAL HEART... POSSESSES HAPPINESS ITSELF.

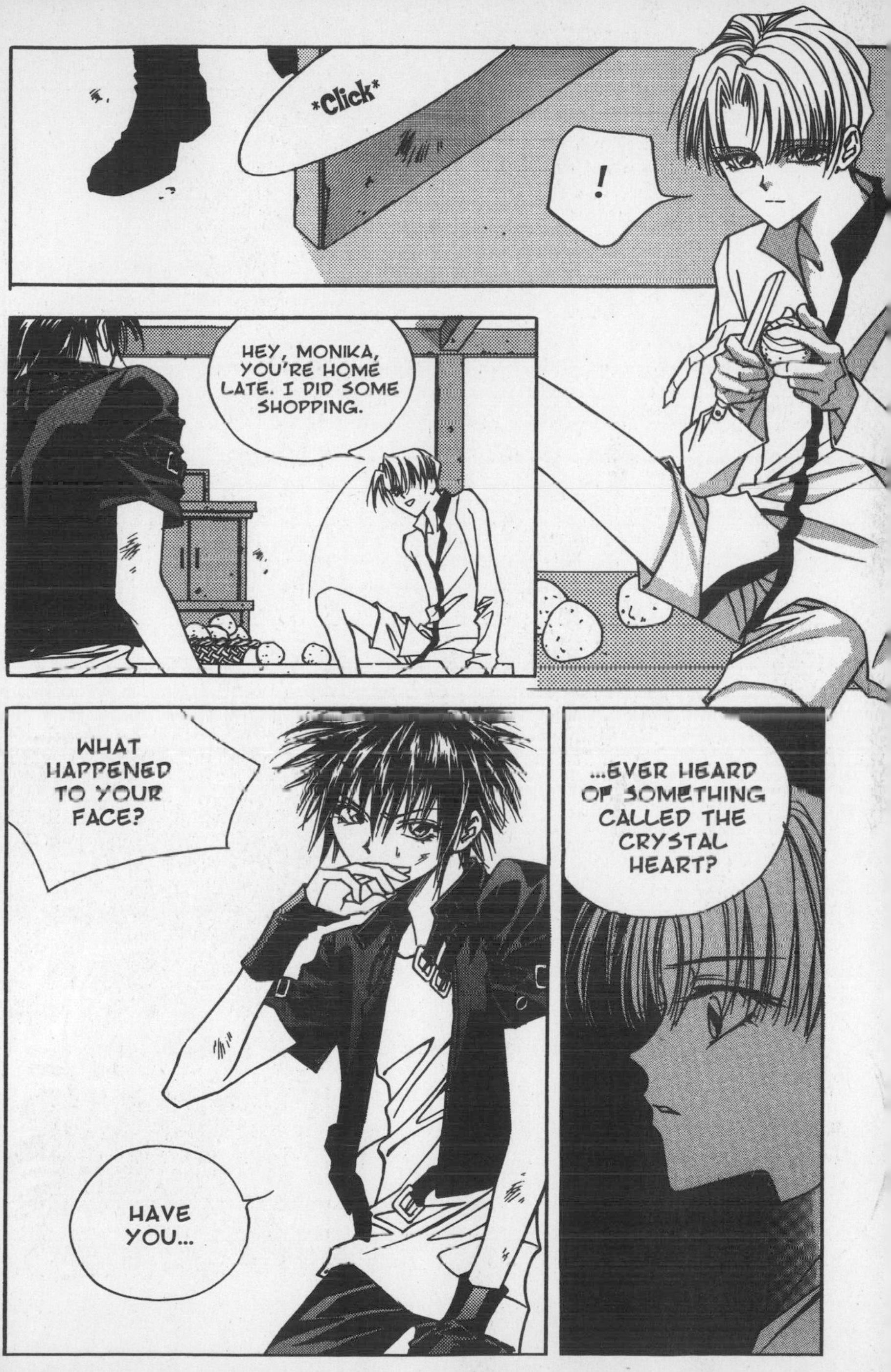
Click
!
HEY, MONIKA, YOU'RE HOME LATE. I DID SOME SHOPPING.
...EVER HEARD OF SOMETHING CALLED THE CRYSTAL HEART?
WHAT HAPPENED TO YOUR FACE?
HAVE YOU...

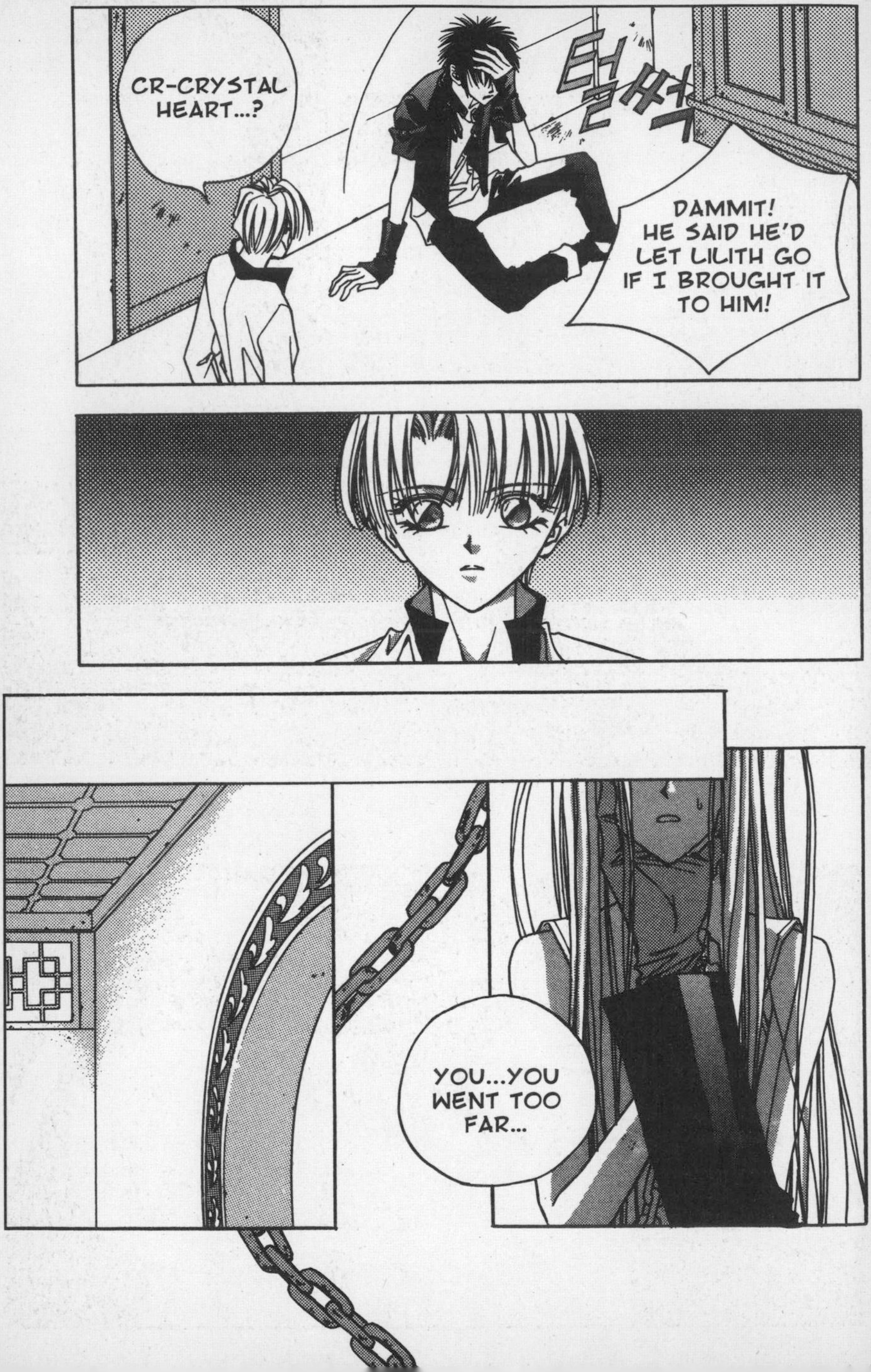
CR-CRYSTAL HEART...?
털썩
DAMMIT! HE SAID HE'D LET LILITH GO IF I BROUGHT IT TO HIM!
YOU...YOU WENT TOO FAR...

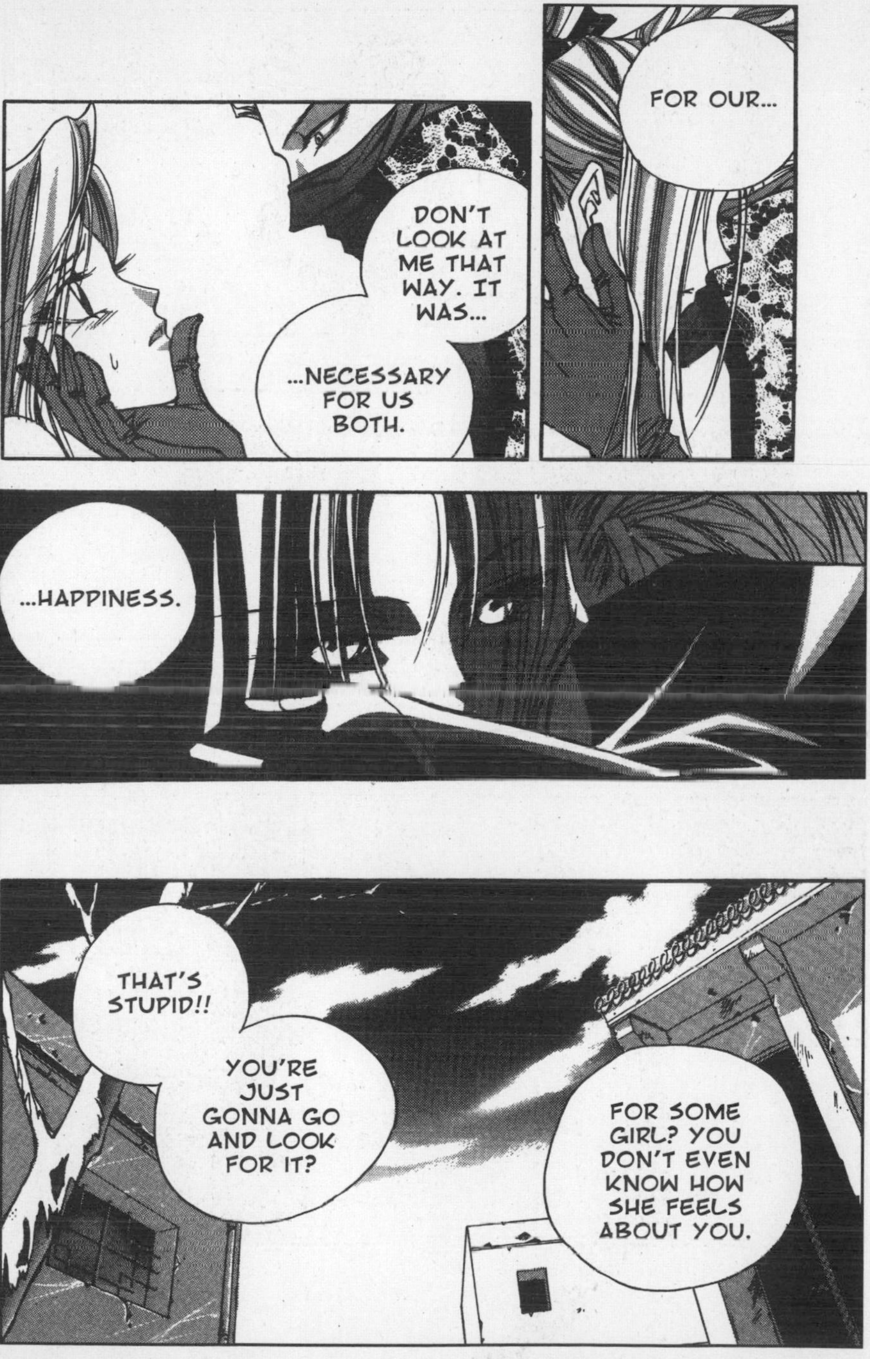
DON'T LOOK AT ME THAT WAY. IT WAS...
...NECESSARY FOR US BOTH.
FOR OUR...
...HAPPINESS.
THAT'S STUPID!!
YOU'RE JUST GONNA GO AND LOOK FOR IT?
FOR SOME GIRL? YOU DON'T EVEN KNOW HOW SHE FEELS ABOUT YOU.

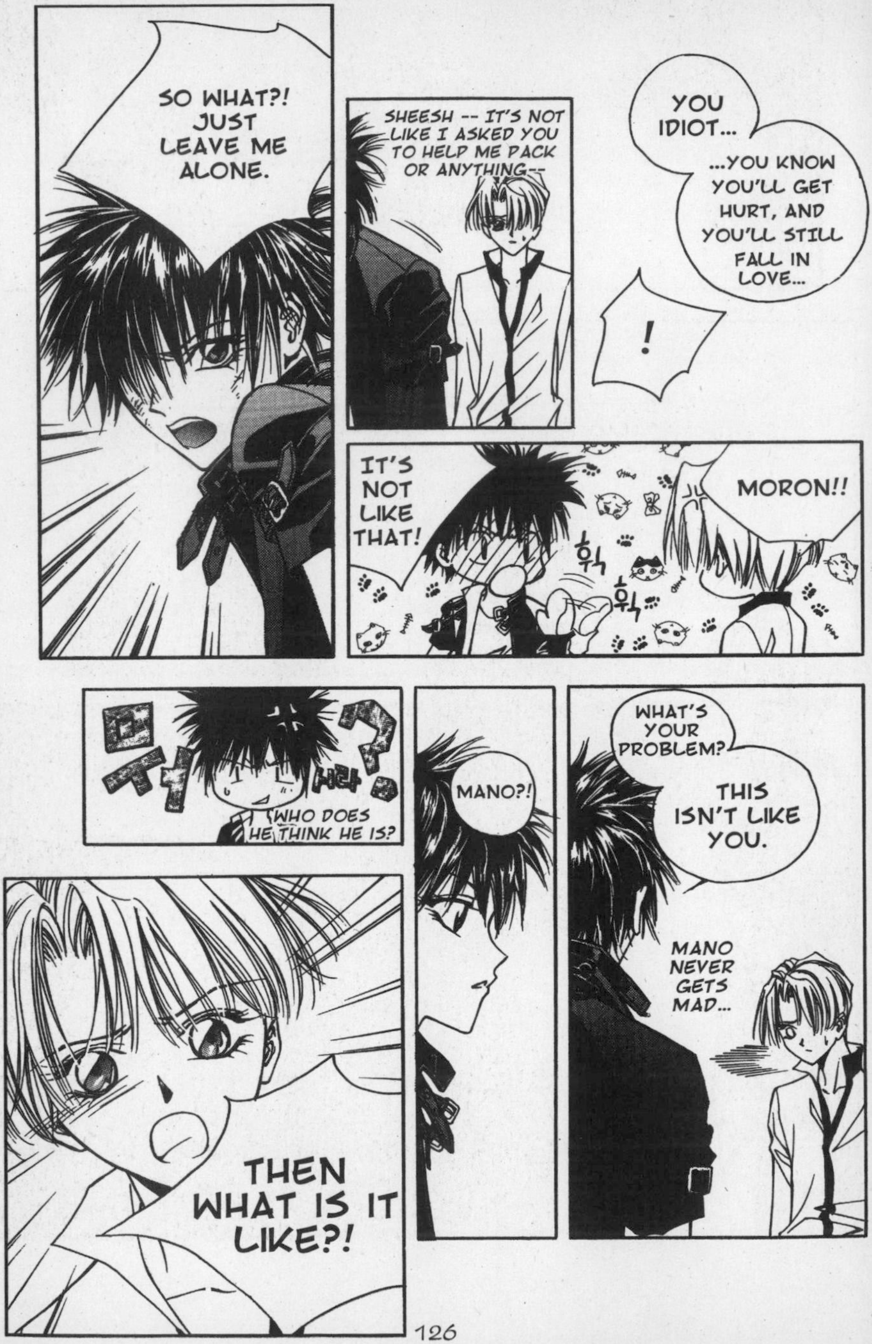
YOU IDIOT...
...YOU KNOW YOU'LL GET HURT, AND YOU'LL STILL FALL IN LOVE...
!
SHEESH -- IT'S NOT LIKE I ASKED YOU TO HELP ME PACK OR ANYTHING--
SO WHAT?! JUST LEAVE ME ALONE.
MORON!!
IT'S NOT LIKE THAT!
WHO DOES HE THINK HE IS?
WHAT'S YOUR PROBLEM?
THIS ISN'T LIKE YOU.
MANO NEVER GETS MAD...
MANO?!
THEN WHAT IS IT LIKE?!

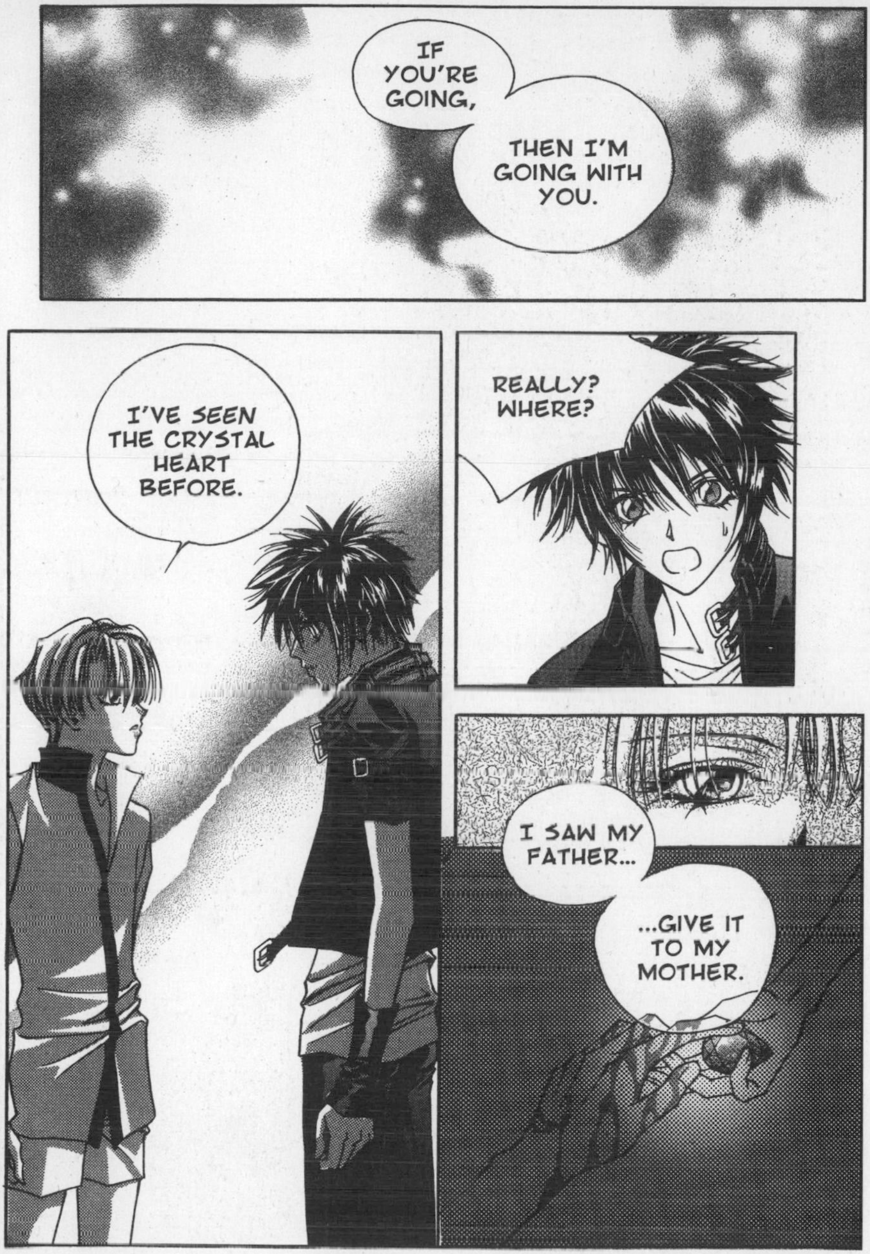
IF YOU'RE GOING,
THEN I'M GOING WITH YOU.
I'VE SEEN THE CRYSTAL HEART BEFORE.
REALLY? WHERE?
I SAW MY FATHER...
...GIVE IT TO MY MOTHER.

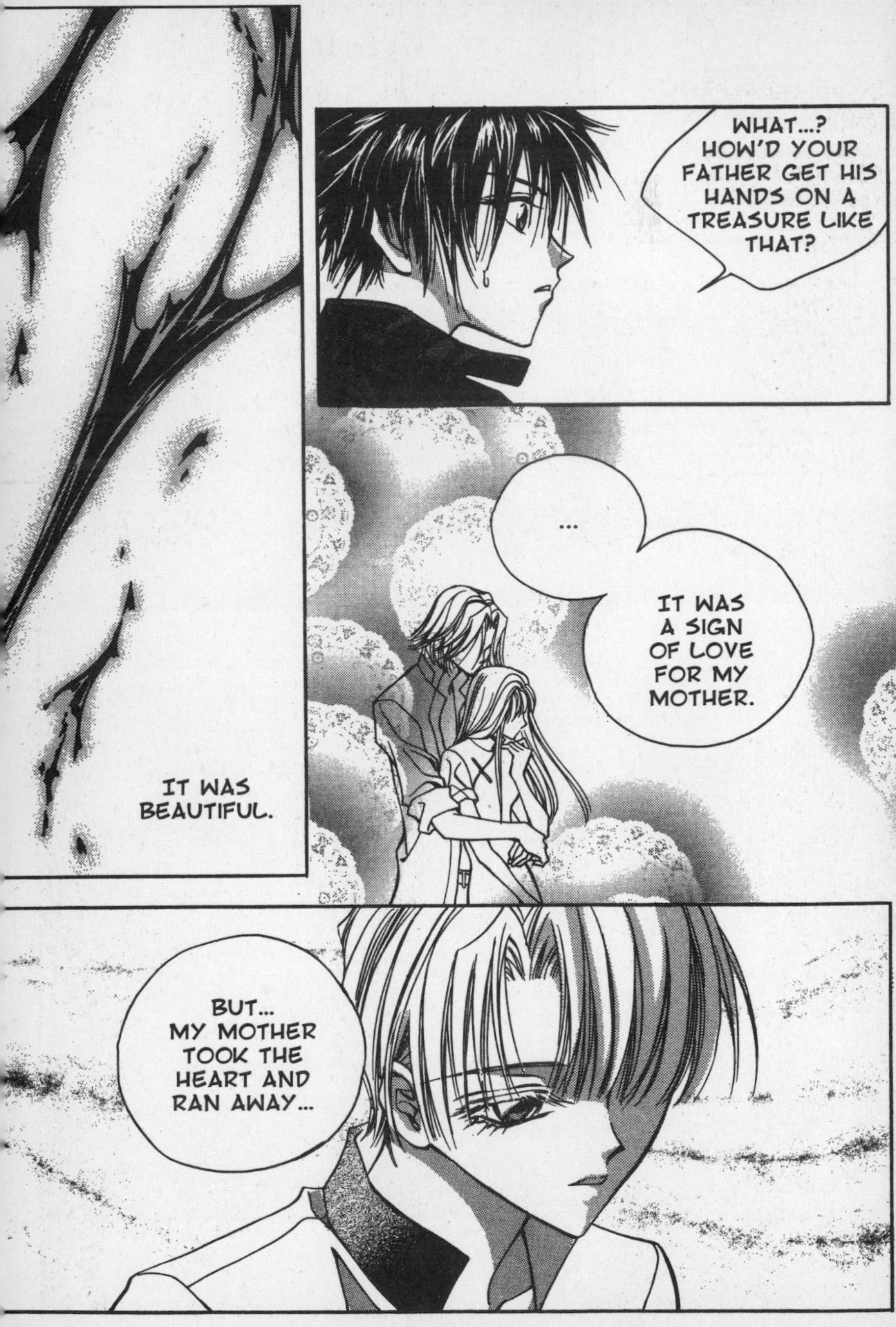
WHAT...? HOW'D YOUR FATHER GET HIS HANDS ON A TREASURE LIKE THAT?
...
IT WAS A SIGN OF LOVE FOR MY MOTHER.
IT WAS BEAUTIFUL.
BUT... MY MOTHER TOOK THE HEART AND RAN AWAY...

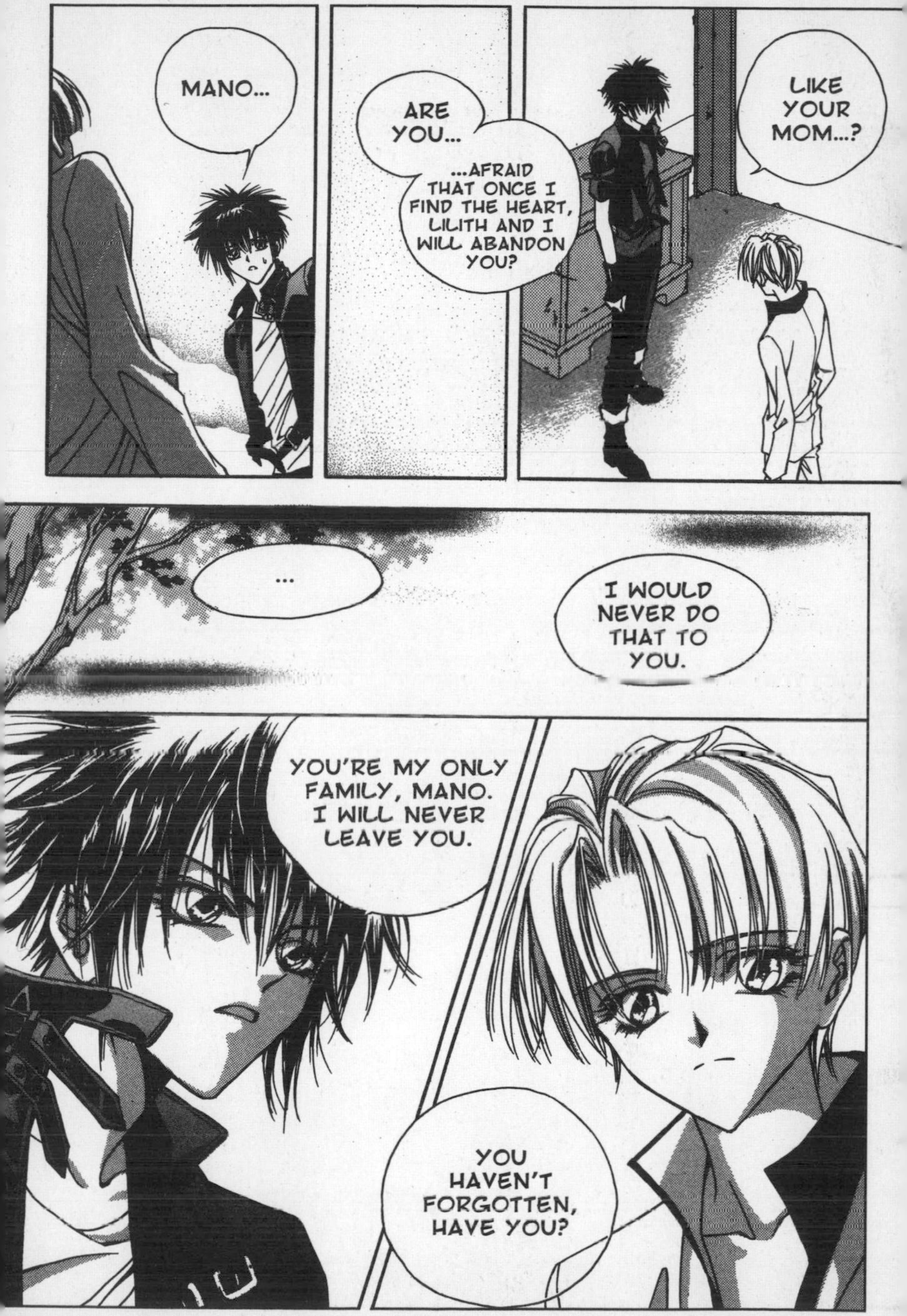
LIKE YOUR MOM...?
ARE YOU...
...AFRAID THAT ONCE I FIND THE HEART, LILITH AND I WILL ABANDON YOU?
MANO...
I WOULD NEVER DO THAT TO YOU.
...
YOU'RE MY ONLY FAMILY, MANO. I WILL NEVER LEAVE YOU.
YOU HAVEN'T FORGOTTEN, HAVE YOU?

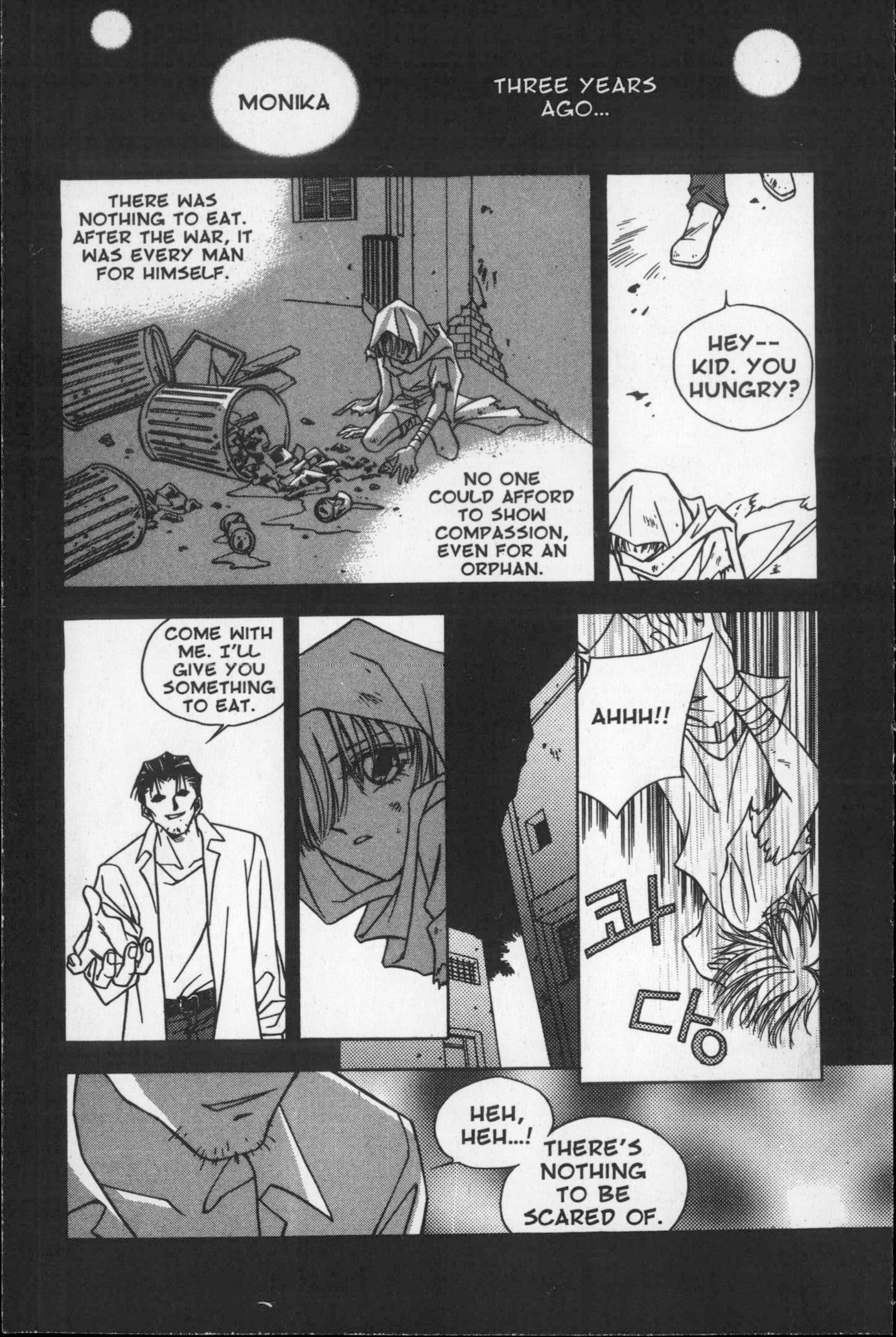
MONIKA
THREE YEARS AGO...
THERE WAS NOTHING TO EAT. AFTER THE WAR, IT WAS EVERY MAN FOR HIMSELF.
NO ONE COULD AFFORD TO SHOW COMPASSION, EVEN FOR AN ORPHAN.
HEY-- KID. YOU HUNGRY?
COME WITH ME. I'LL GIVE YOU SOMETHING TO EAT.
AHHH!!
콰당
HEH, HEH...!
THERE'S NOTHING TO BE SCARED OF.

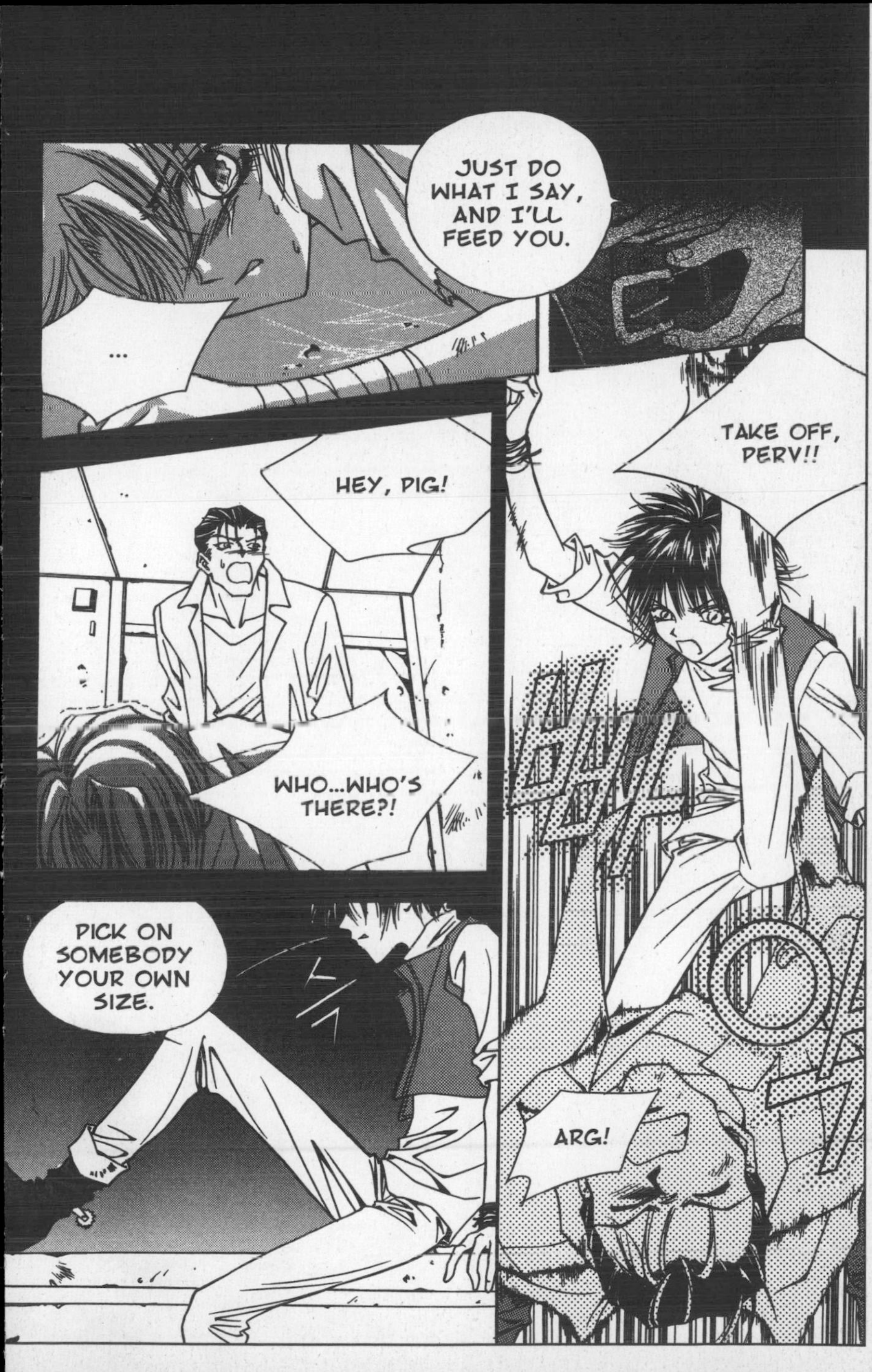
JUST DO WHAT I SAY, AND I'LL FEED YOU.
...
HEY, PIG!
WHO...WHO'S THERE?!
PICK ON SOMEBODY YOUR OWN SIZE.
TAKE OFF, PERV!!
ARG!

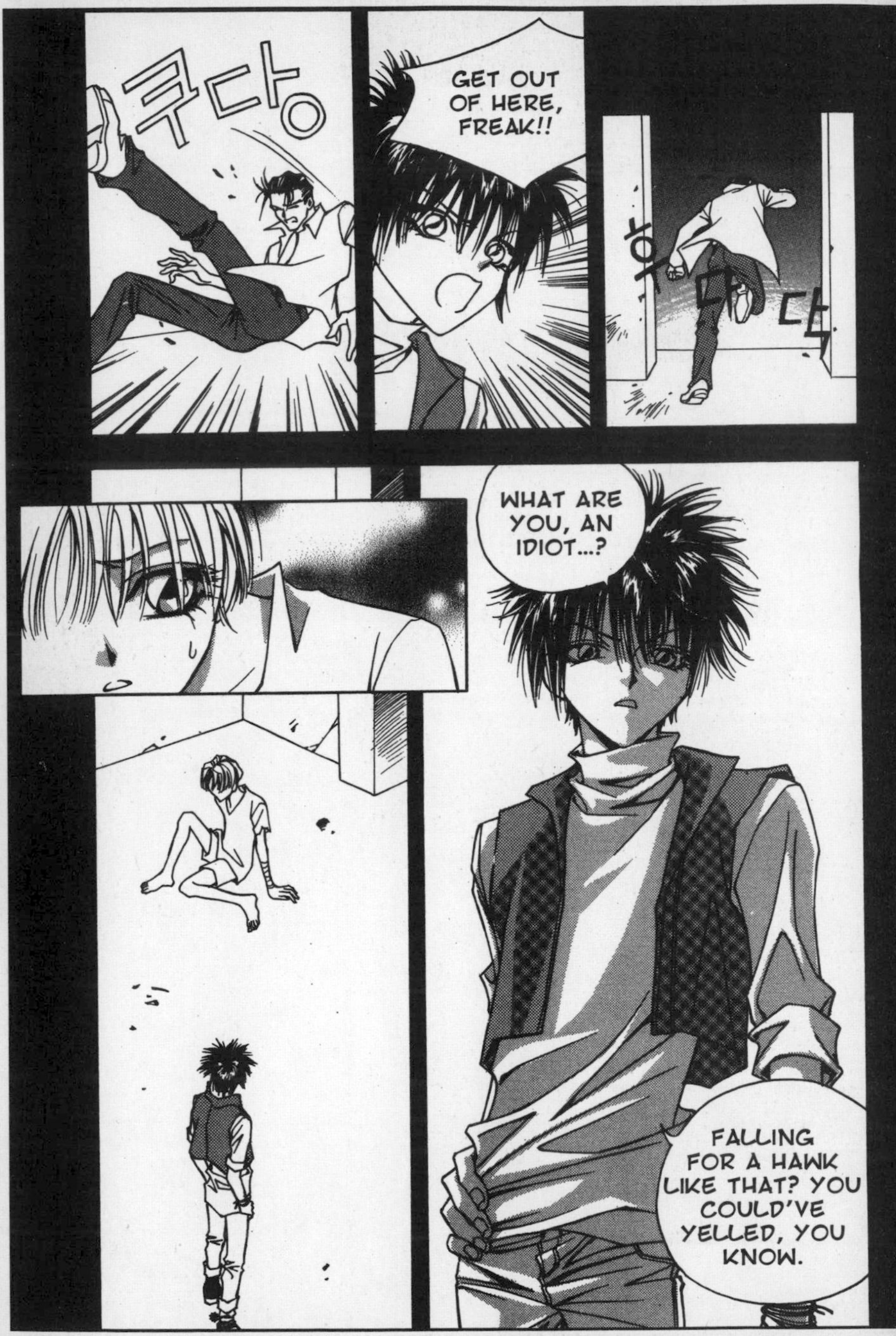
GET OUT OF HERE, FREAK!!
WHAT ARE YOU, AN IDIOT...?
FALLING FOR A HAWK LIKE THAT? YOU COULD'VE YELLED, YOU KNOW.

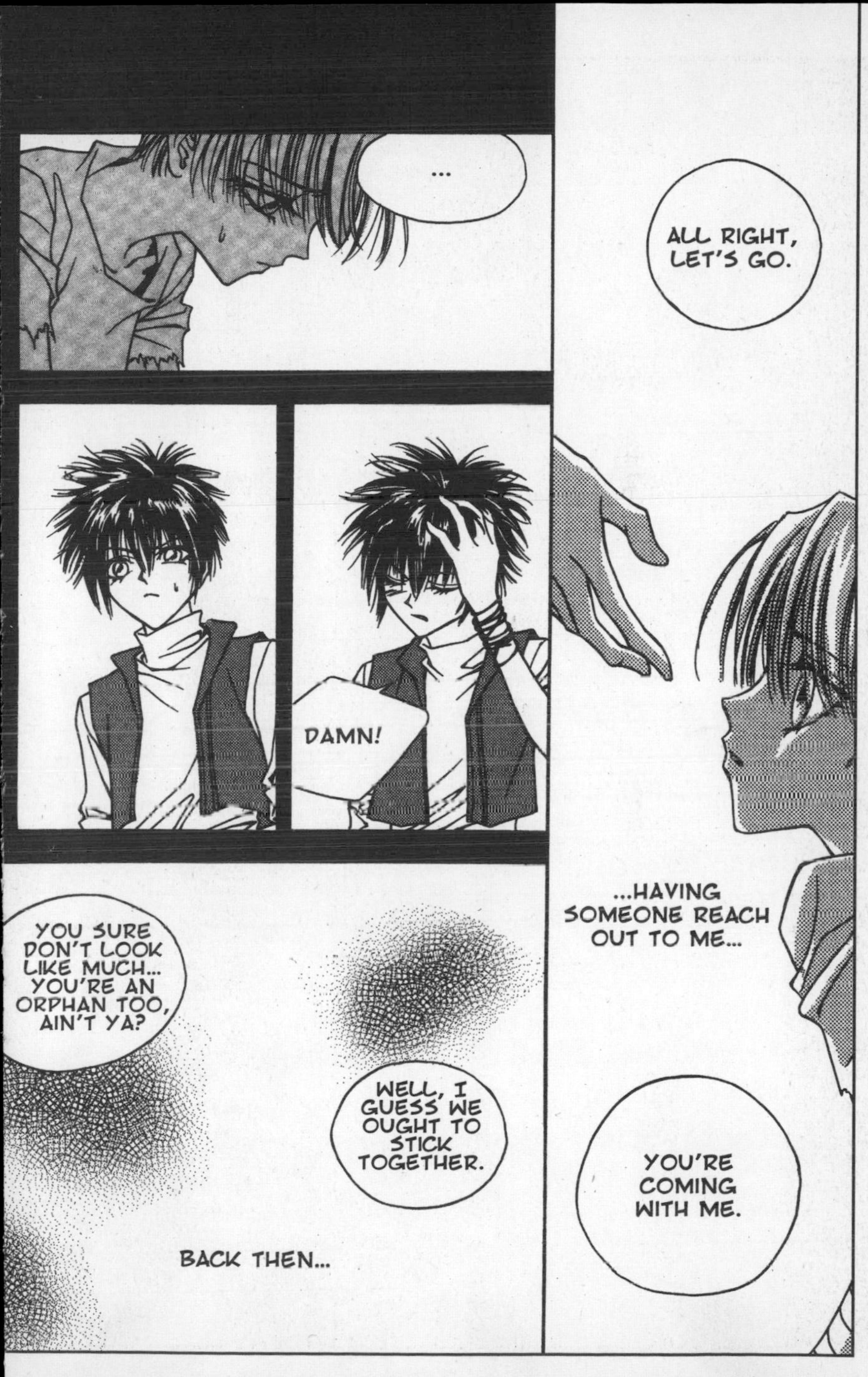
ALL RIGHT, LET'S GO.
...HAVING SOMEONE REACH OUT TO ME...
YOU'RE COMING WITH ME.
...
DAMN!
YOU SURE DON'T LOOK LIKE MUCH... YOU'RE AN ORPHAN TOO, AIN'T YA?
WELL, I GUESS WE OUGHT TO STICK TOGETHER.
BACK THEN...

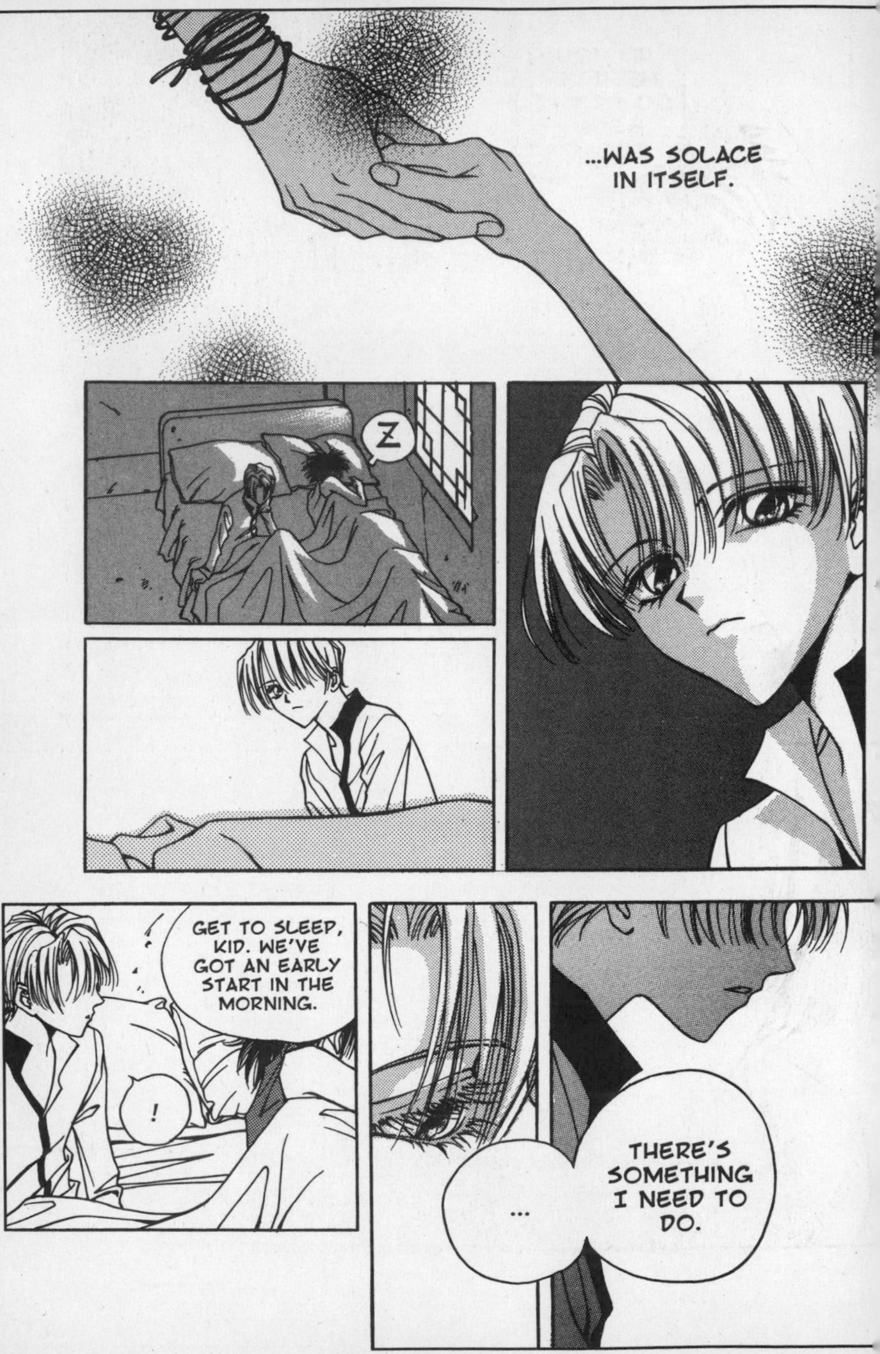
...WAS SOLACE IN ITSELF.
Z
GET TO SLEEP, KID. WE'VE GOT AN EARLY START IN THE MORNING.
!
THERE'S SOMETHING I NEED TO DO.
...

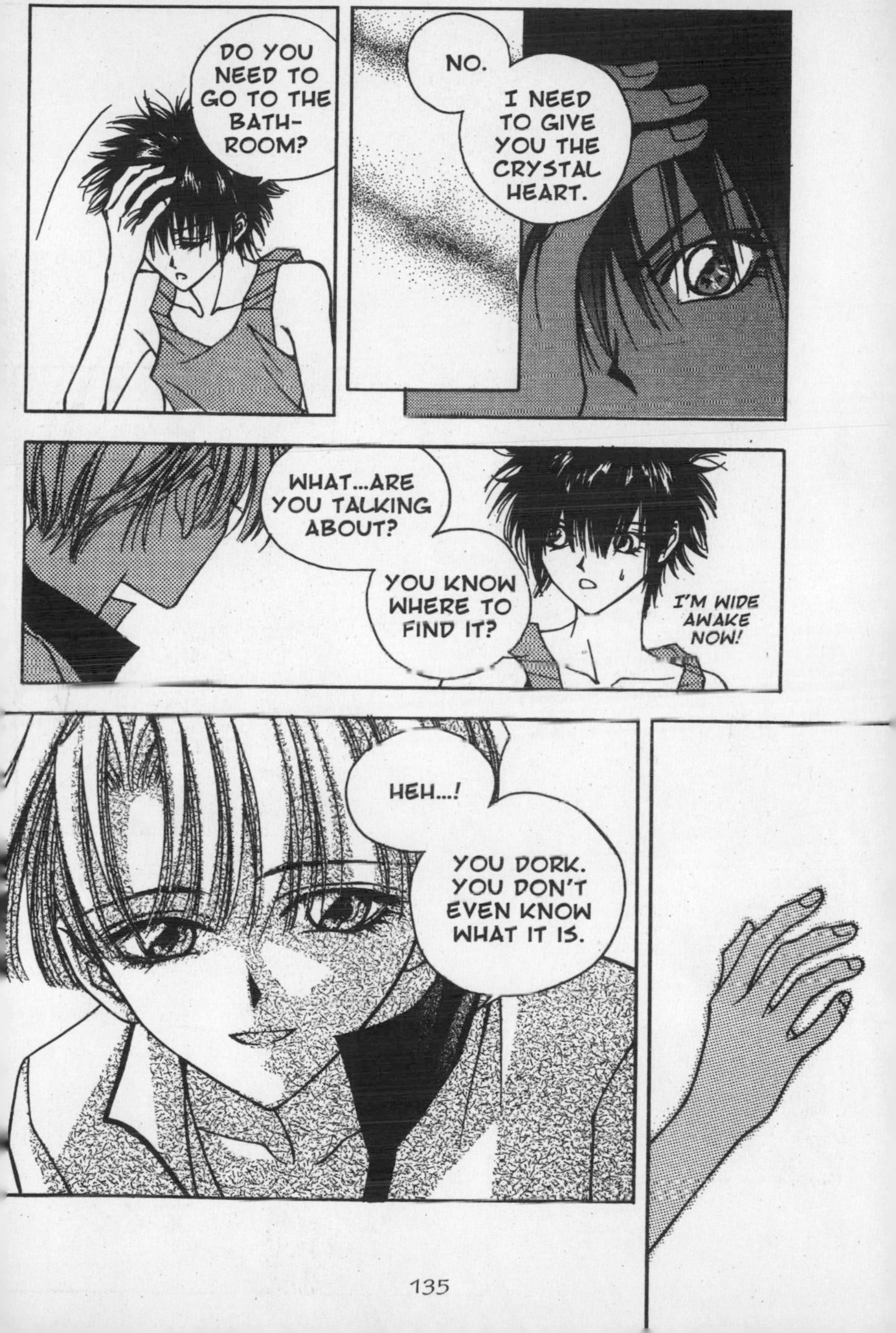
DO YOU NEED TO GO TO THE BATH-ROOM?
NO.
I NEED TO GIVE YOU THE CRYSTAL HEART.
WHAT...ARE YOU TALKING ABOUT?
YOU KNOW WHERE TO FIND IT?
I'M WIDE AWAKE NOW!
HEH...!
YOU DORK. YOU DON'T EVEN KNOW WHAT IT IS.

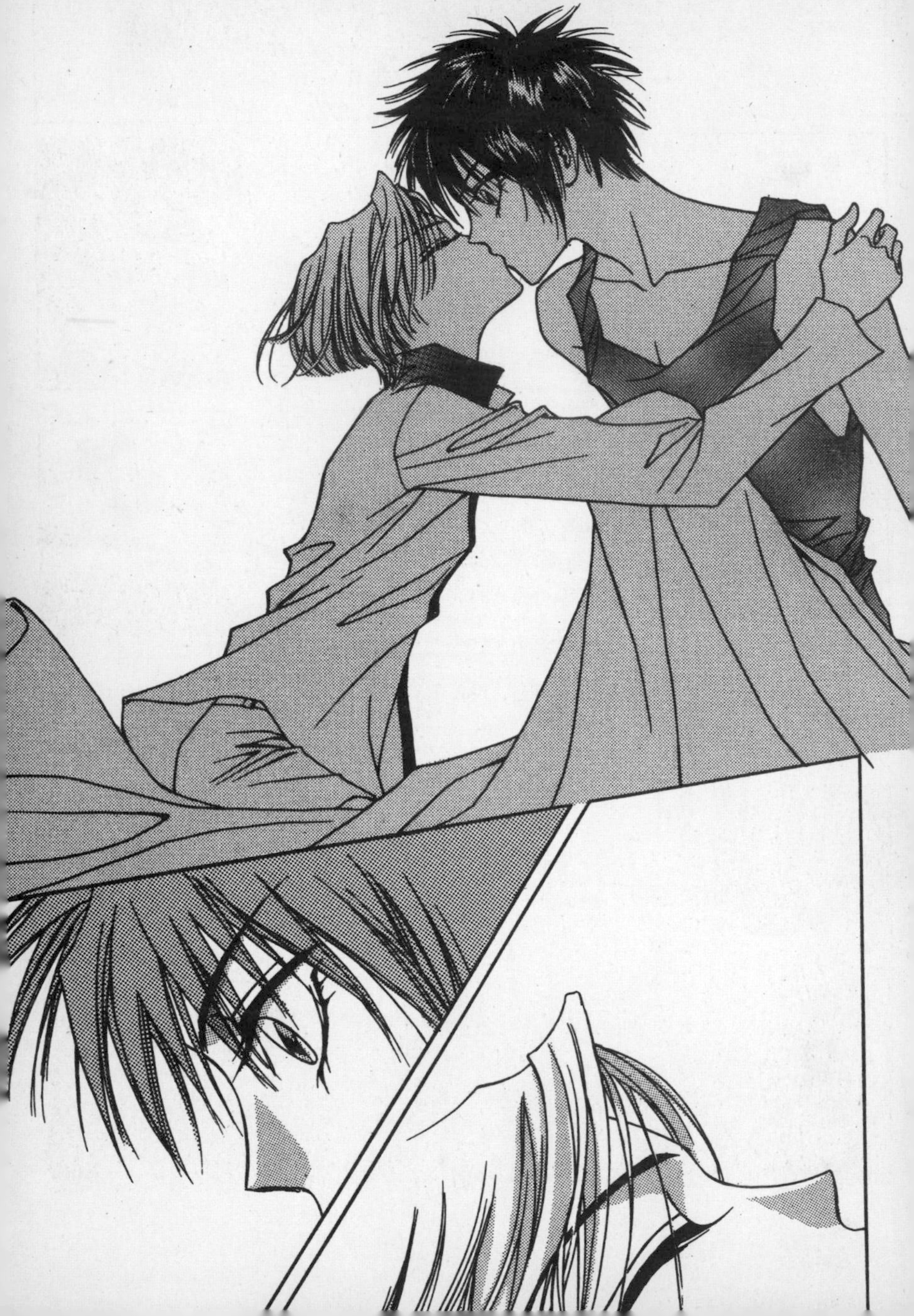

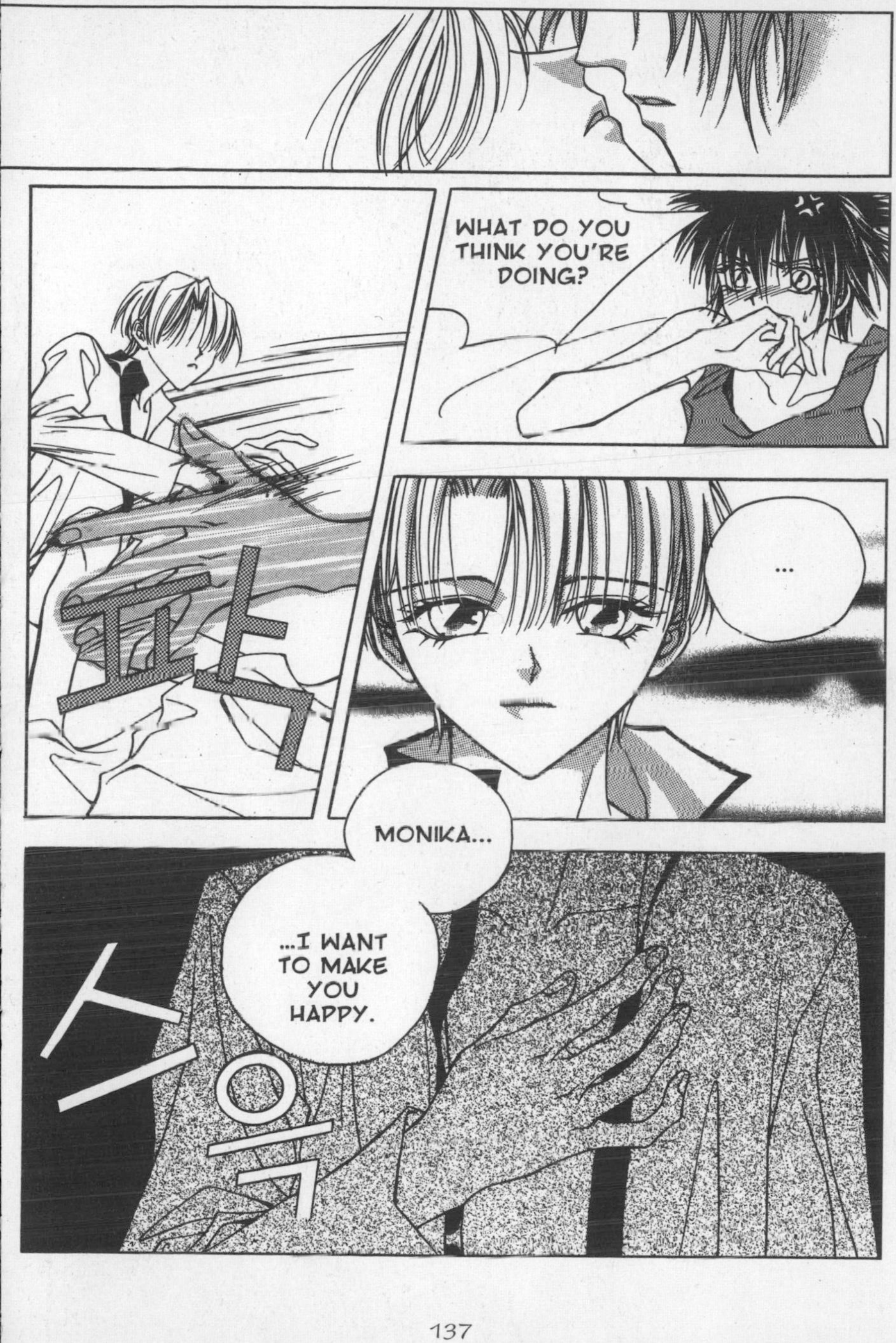
WHAT DO YOU THINK YOU'RE DOING?
...
MONIKA...
...I WANT TO MAKE YOU HAPPY.

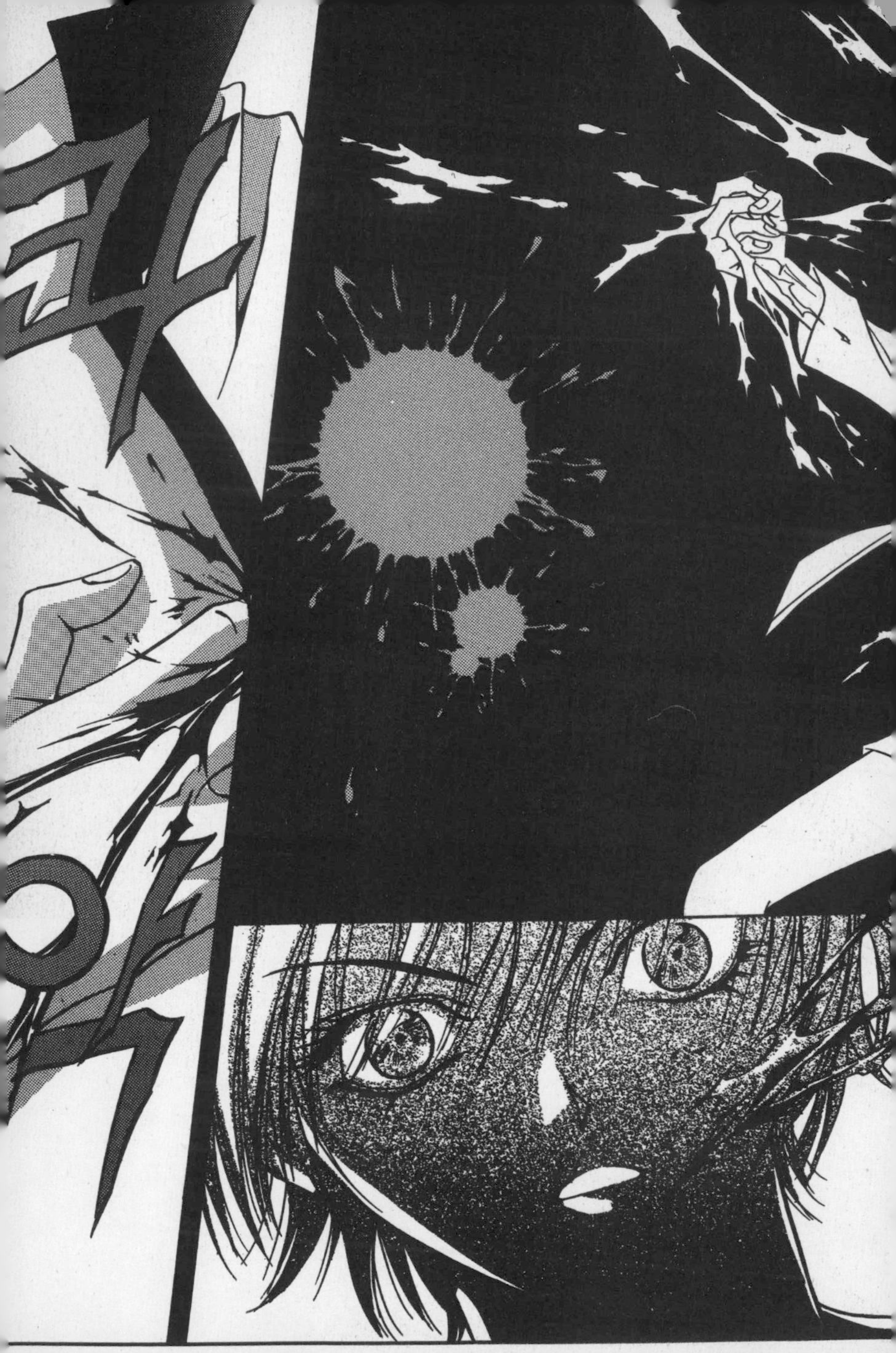

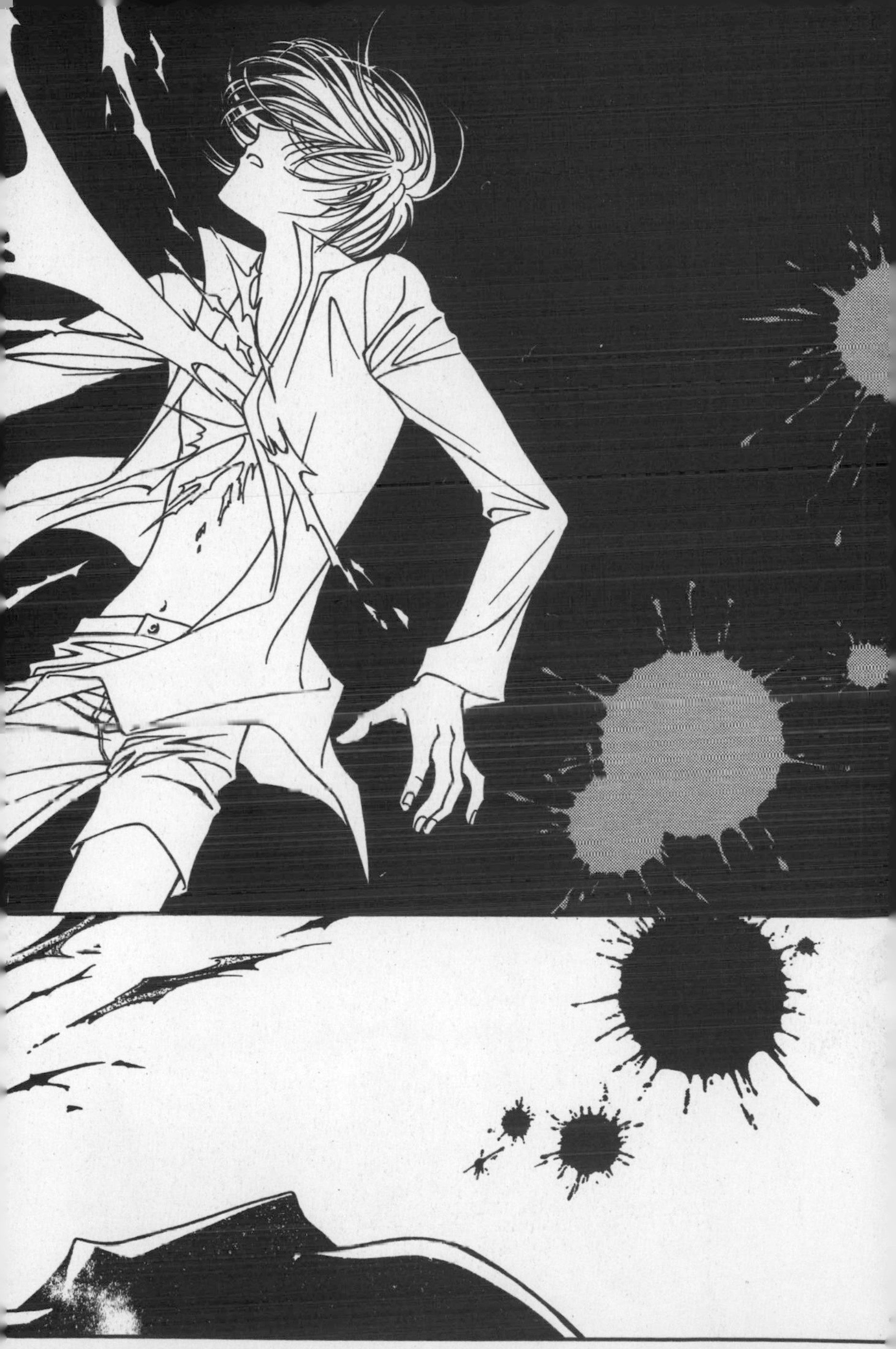

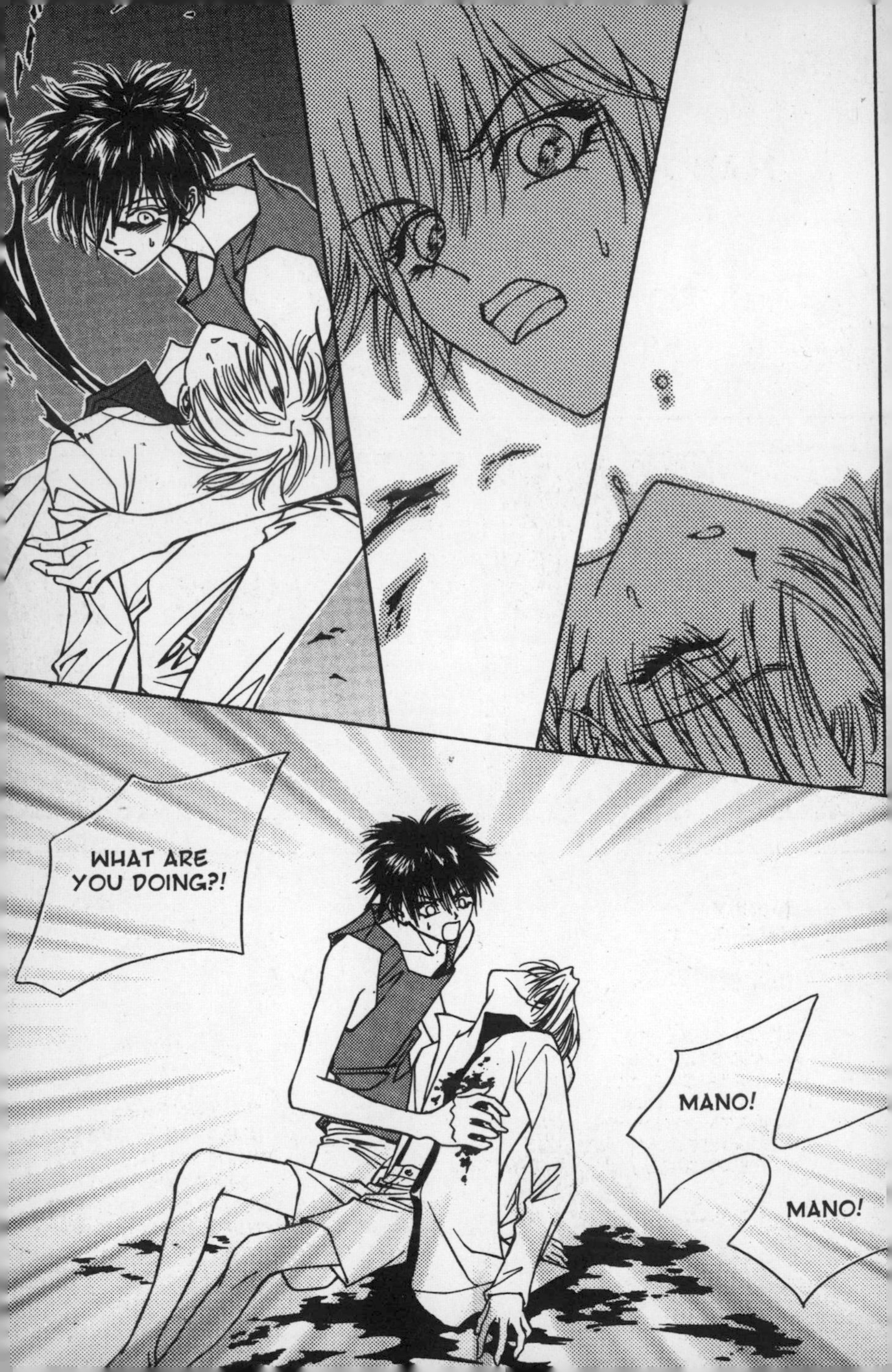
WHAT ARE YOU DOING?!
MANO!
MANO!

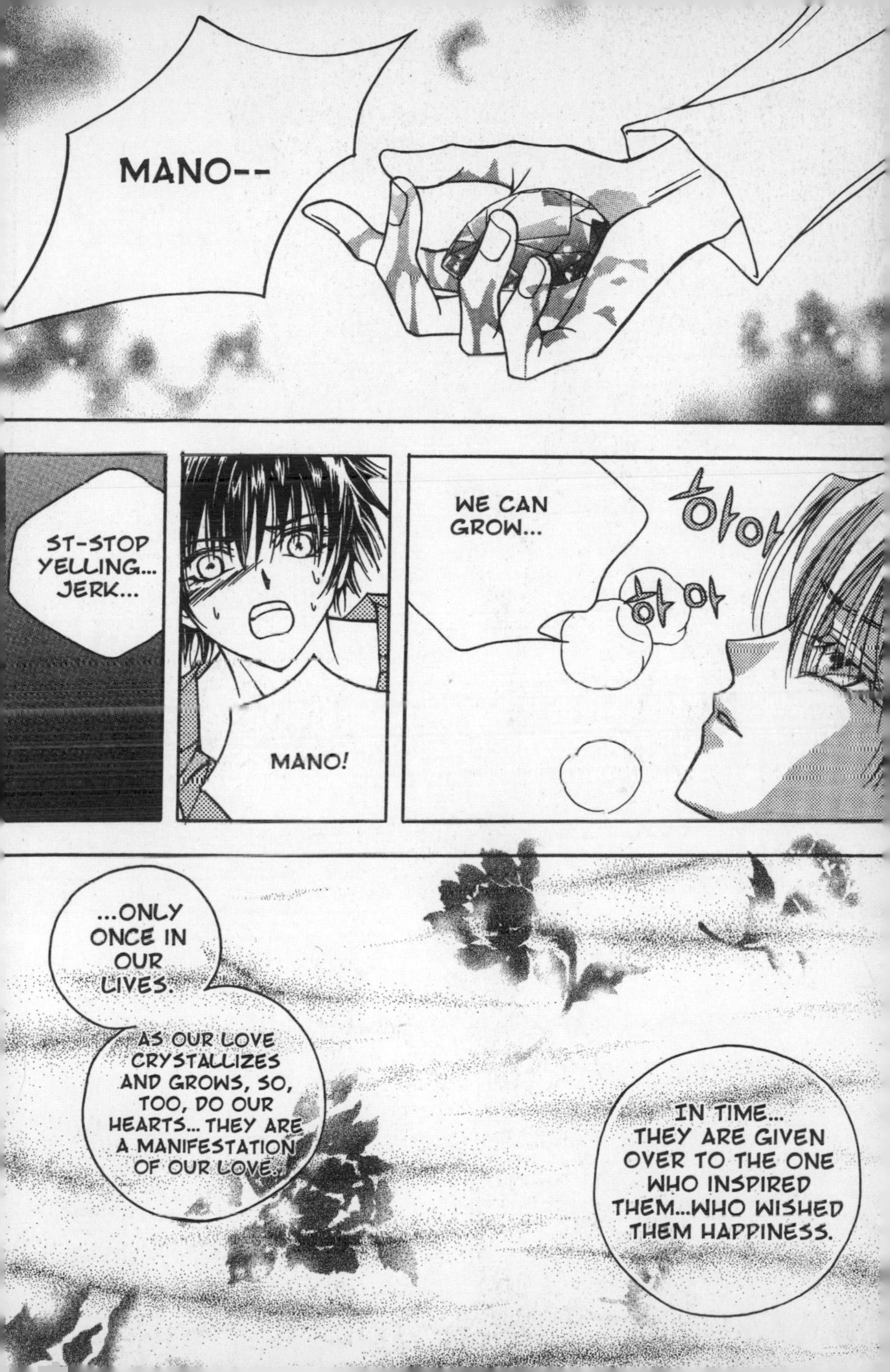
MANO--
WE CAN GROW...
MANO!
ST-STOP YELLING... JERK...
...ONLY ONCE IN OUR LIVES.
AS OUR LOVE CRYSTALLIZES AND GROWS, SO, TOO, DO OUR HEARTS... THEY ARE A MANIFESTATION OF OUR LOVE.
IN TIME... THEY ARE GIVEN OVER TO THE ONE WHO INSPIRED THEM...WHO WISHED THEM HAPPINESS.

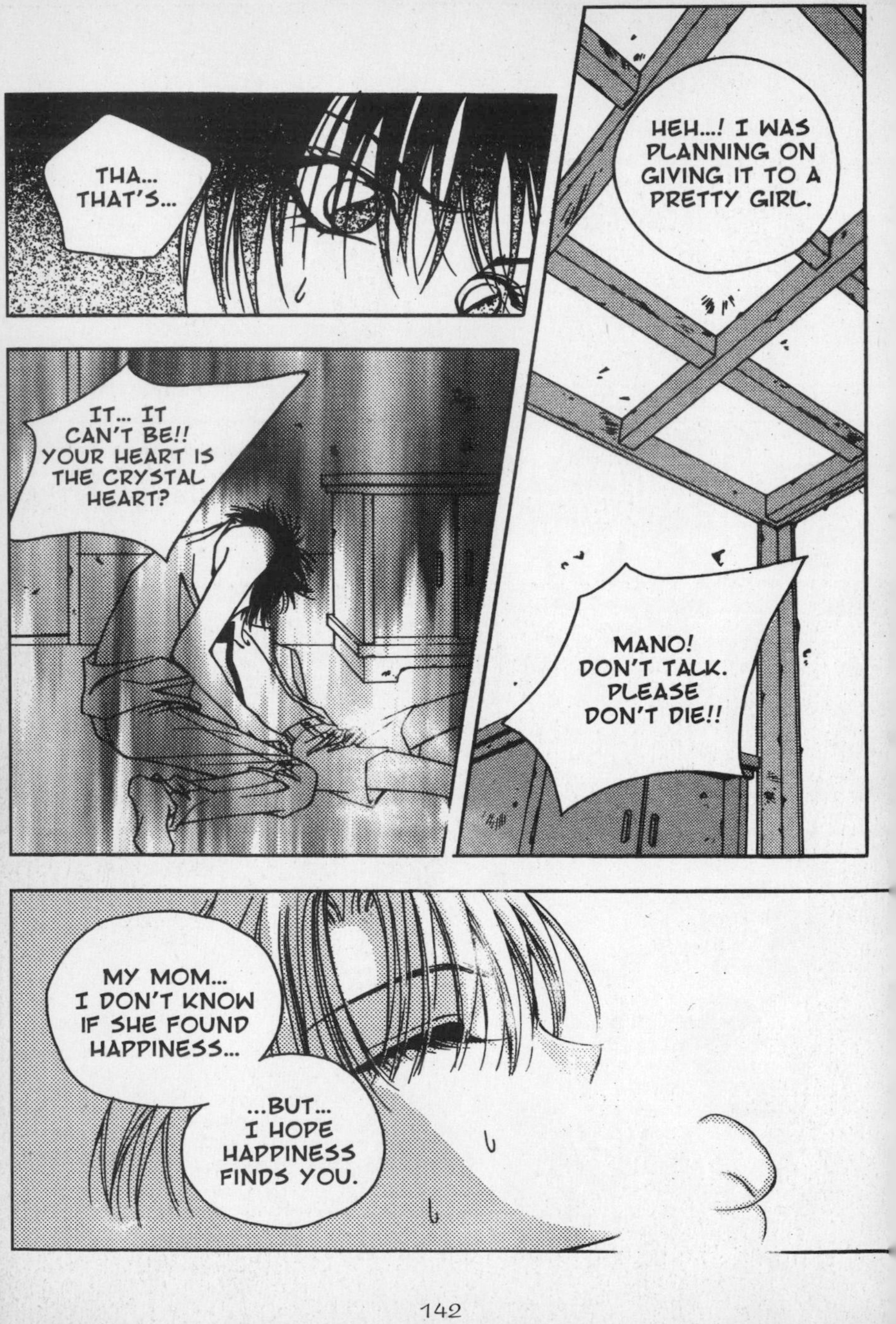
HEH...! I WAS PLANNING ON GIVING IT TO A PRETTY GIRL.
MANO! DON'T TALK. PLEASE DON'T DIE!!
THA... THAT'S...
IT... IT CAN'T BE!! YOUR HEART IS THE CRYSTAL HEART?
MY MOM... I DON'T KNOW IF SHE FOUND HAPPINESS...
...BUT... I HOPE HAPPINESS FINDS YOU.

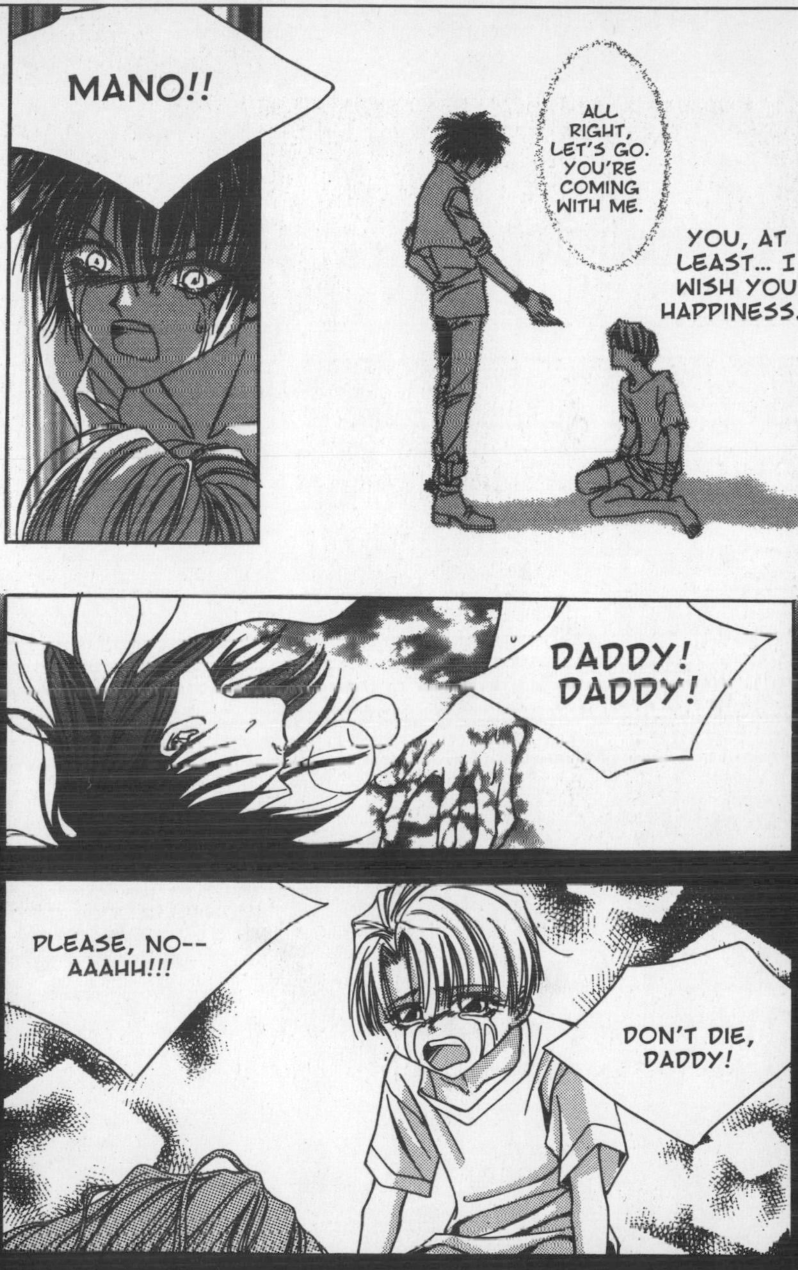
ALL RIGHT, LET'S GO. YOU'RE COMING WITH ME.
YOU, AT LEAST... I WISH YOU HAPPINESS...
MANO!!
DADDY! DADDY!
DON'T DIE, DADDY!
PLEASE, NO-- AAAHH!!!

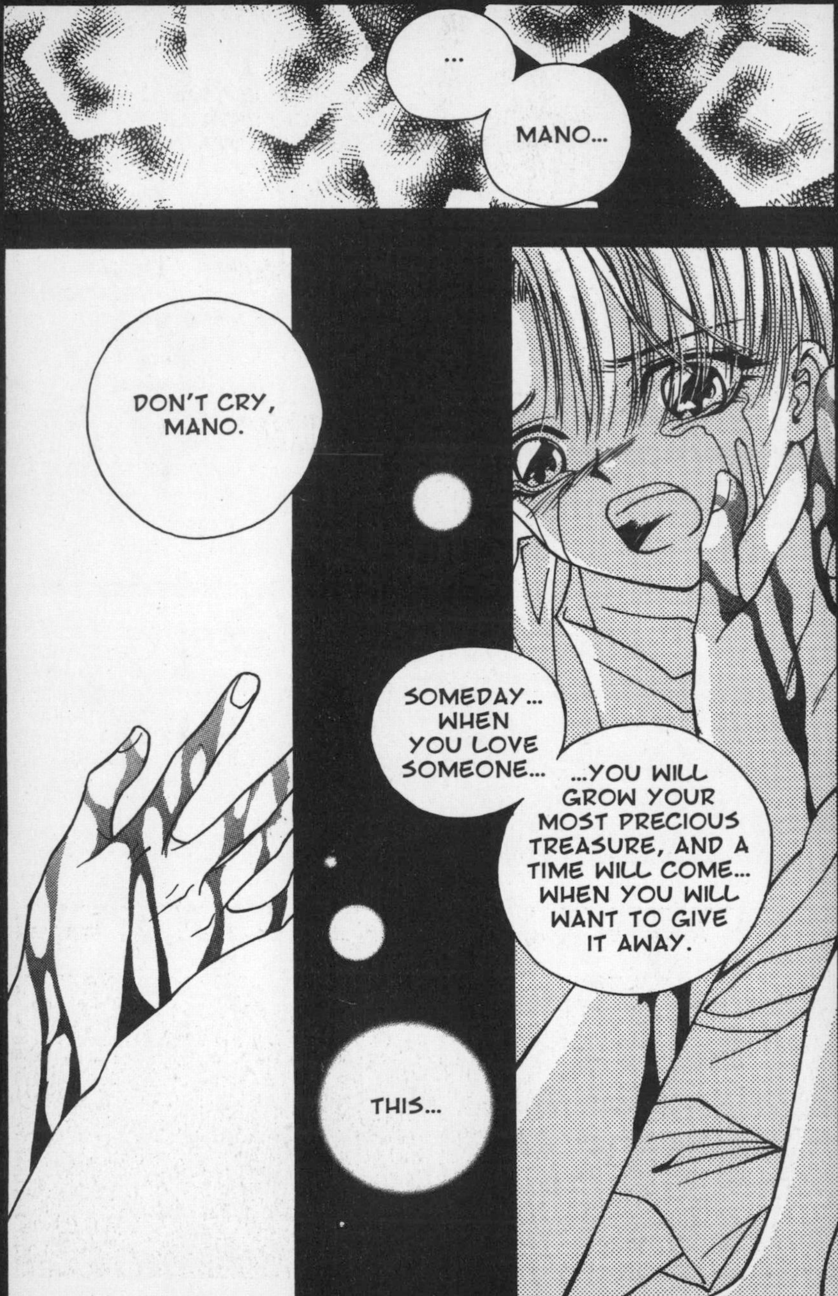
...
MANO...
DON'T CRY, MANO.
SOMEDAY... WHEN YOU LOVE SOMEONE...
...YOU WILL GROW YOUR MOST PRECIOUS TREASURE, AND A TIME WILL COME... WHEN YOU WILL WANT TO GIVE IT AWAY.
THIS...

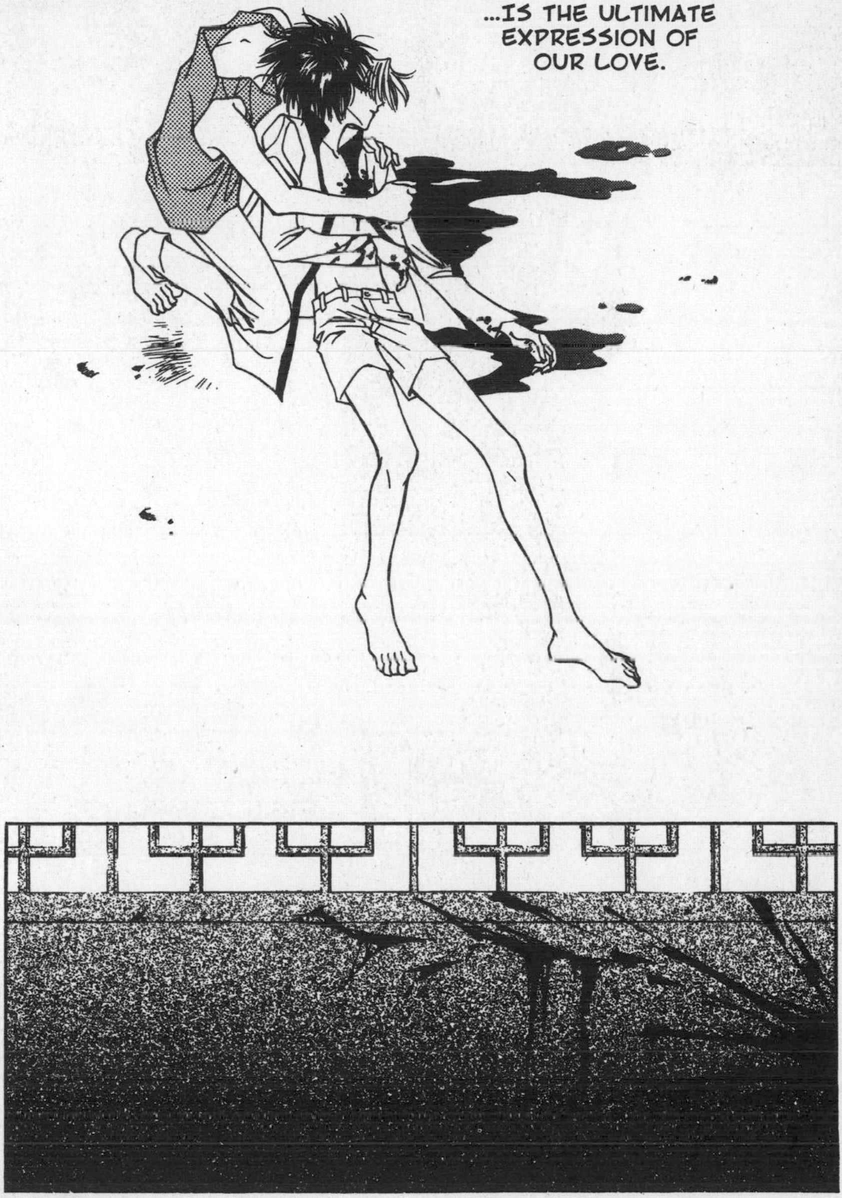
...IS THE ULTIMATE EXPRESSION OF OUR LOVE.

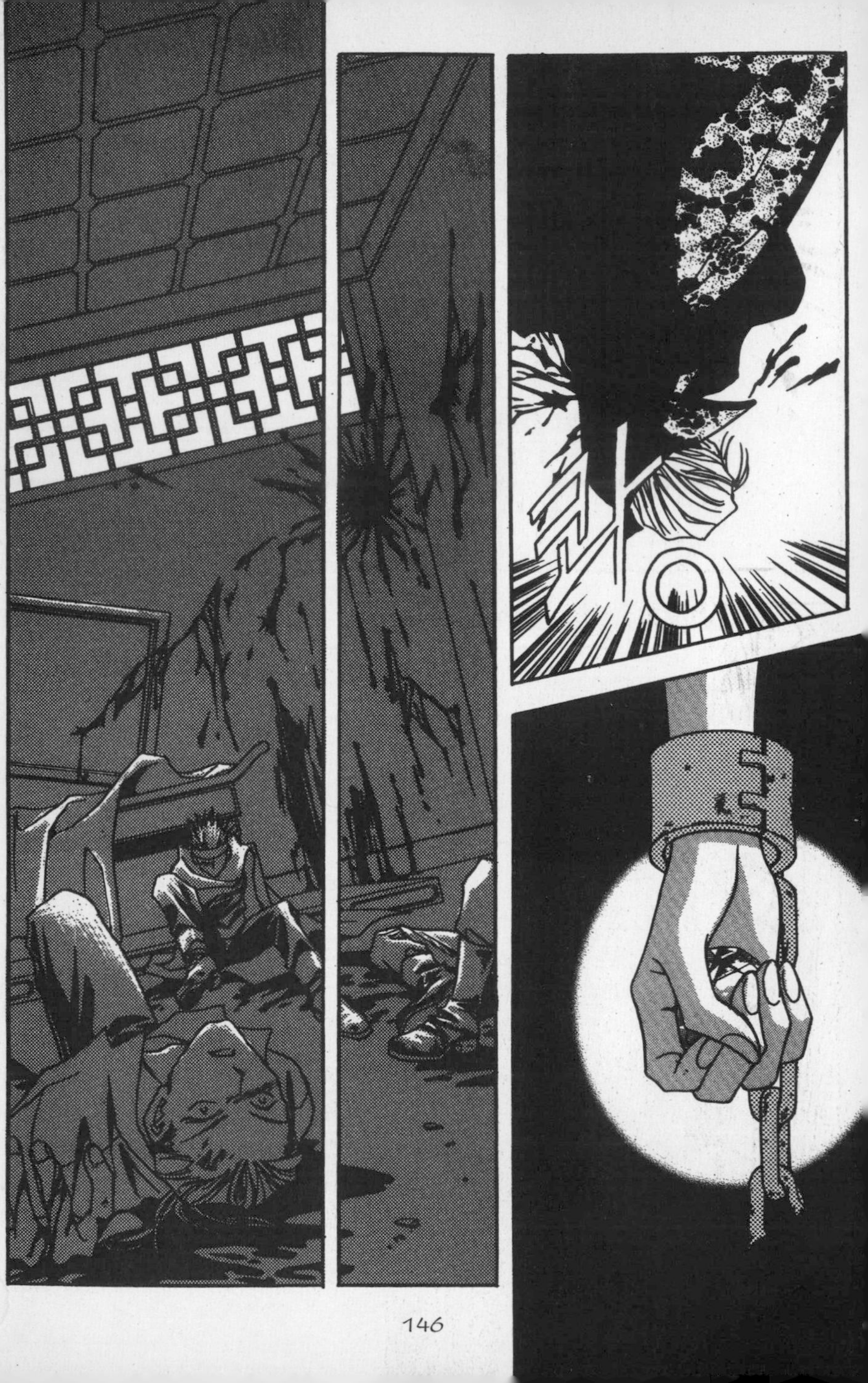

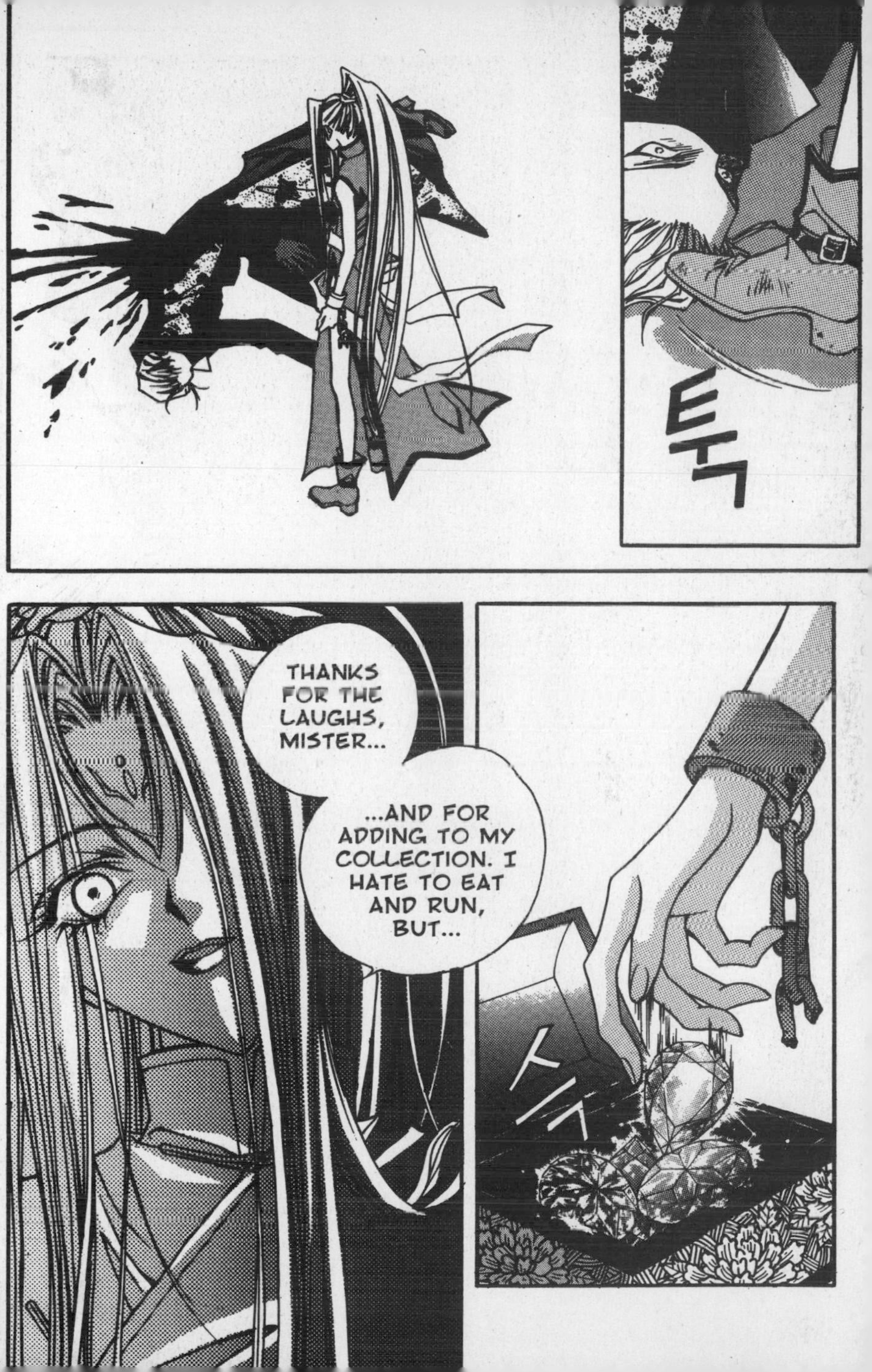
THANKS FOR THE LAUGHS, MISTER...
...AND FOR ADDING TO MY COLLECTION. I HATE TO EAT AND RUN, BUT...

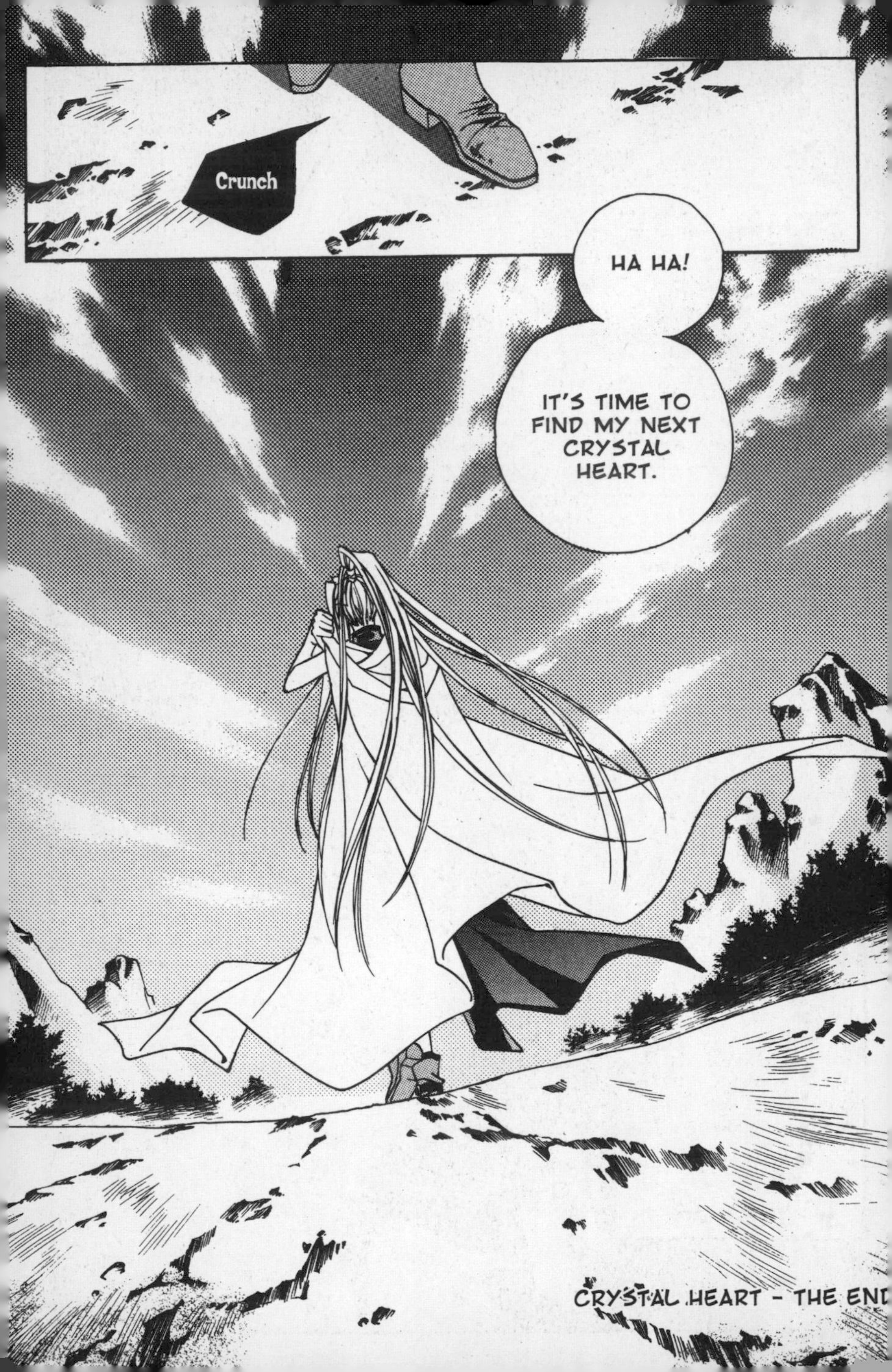
Crunch
HA HA!
IT'S TIME TO FIND MY NEXT CRYSTAL HEART.
CRYSTAL HEART - THE END

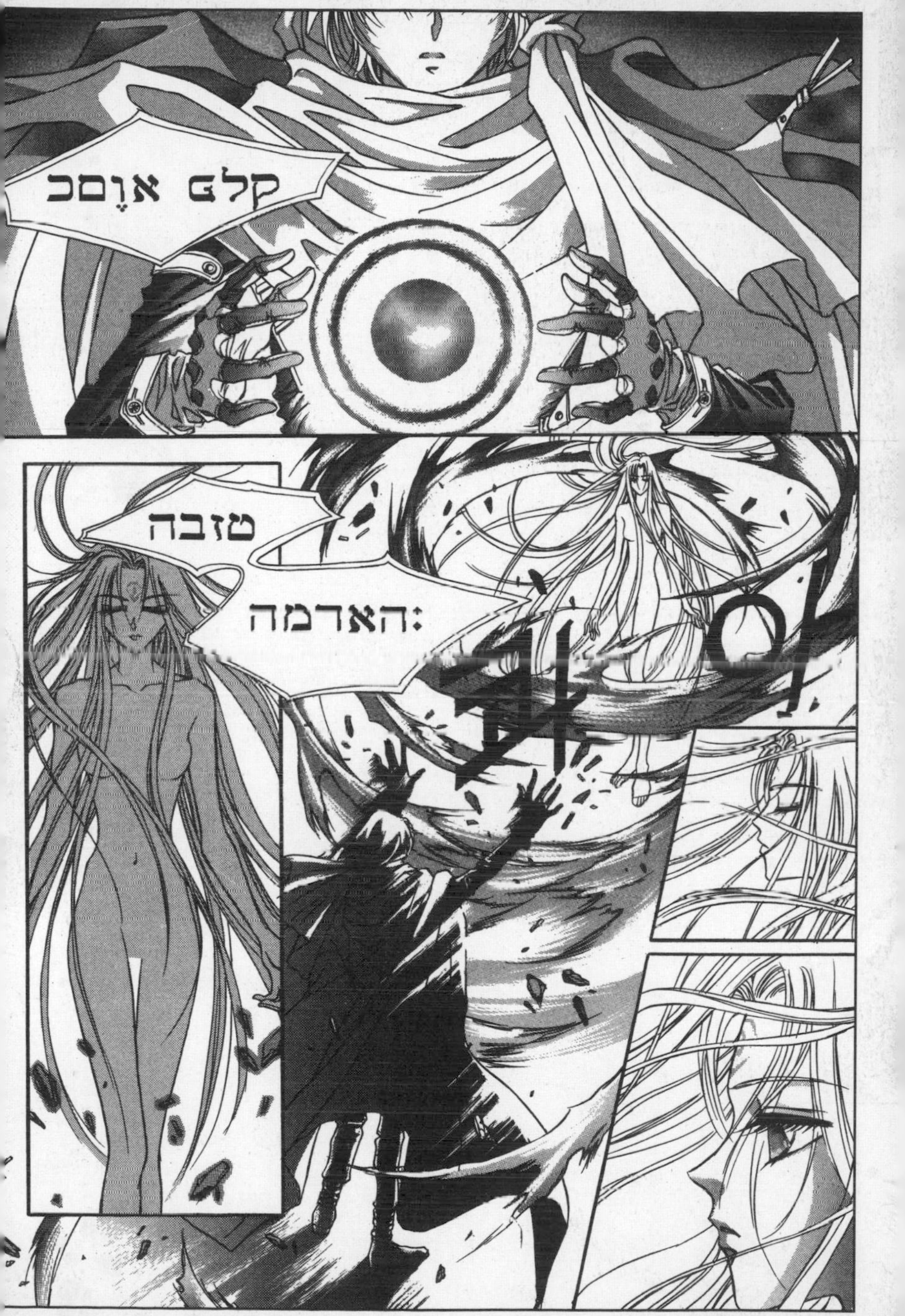

קלG אֶוםכ
טזבה
הארמה:

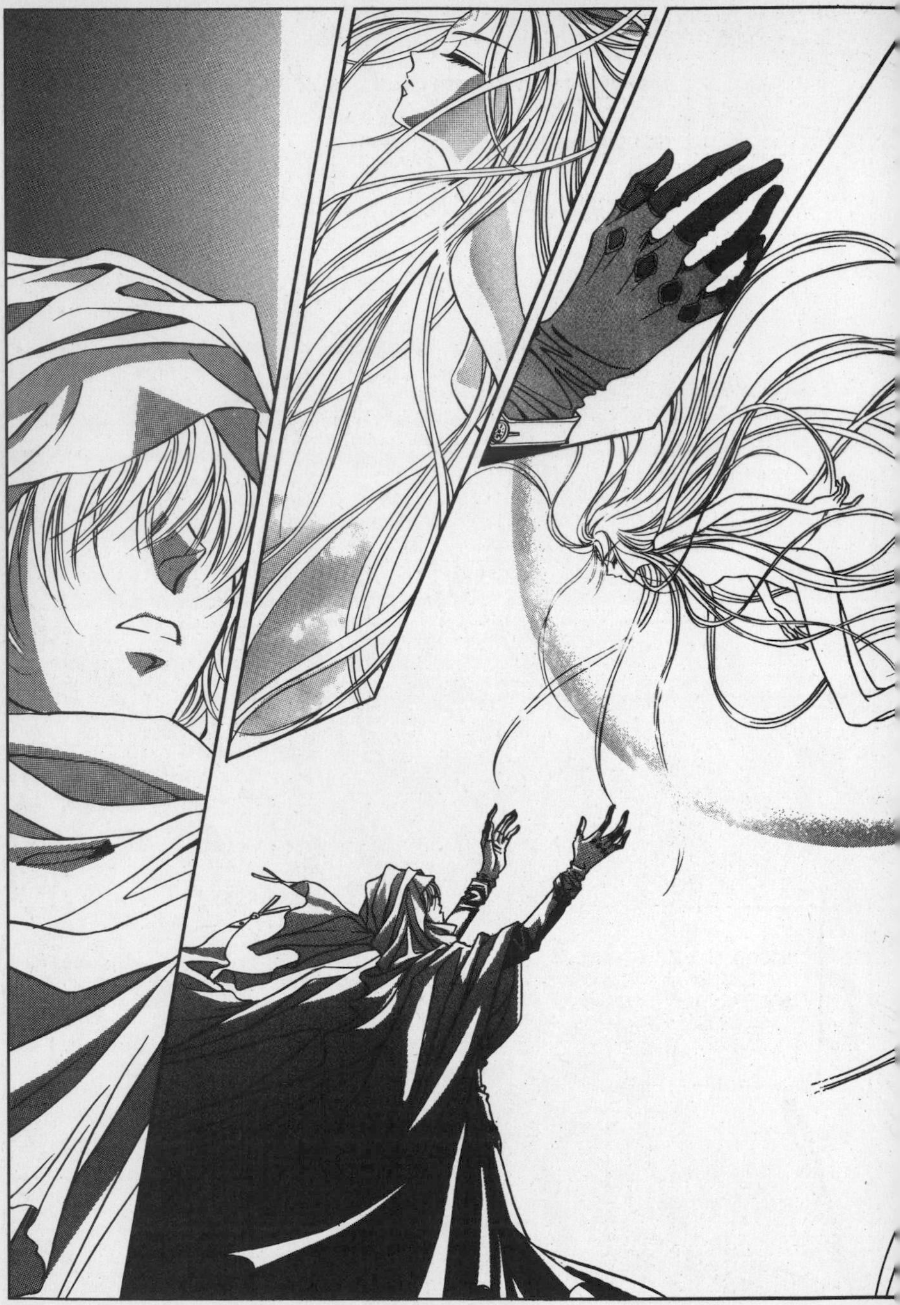

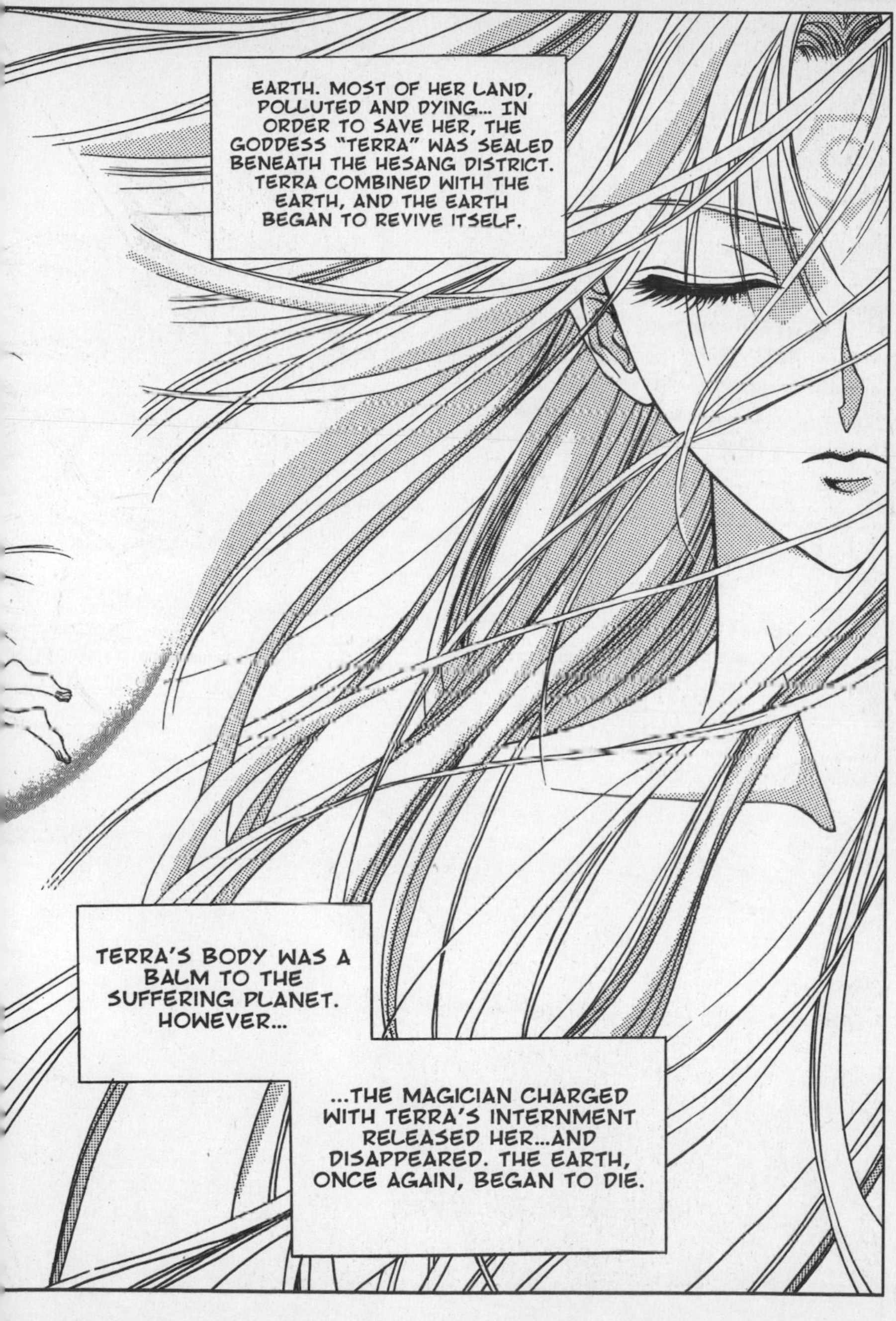
EARTH. MOST OF HER LAND, POLLUTED AND DYING... IN ORDER TO SAVE HER, THE GODDESS "TERRA" WAS SEALED BENEATH THE HESANG DISTRICT. TERRA COMBINED WITH THE EARTH, AND THE EARTH BEGAN TO REVIVE ITSELF.
TERRA'S BODY WAS A BALM TO THE SUFFERING PLANET. HOWEVER...
...THE MAGICIAN CHARGED WITH TERRA'S INTERNMENT RELEASED HER...AND DISAPPEARED. THE EARTH, ONCE AGAIN, BEGAN TO DIE.

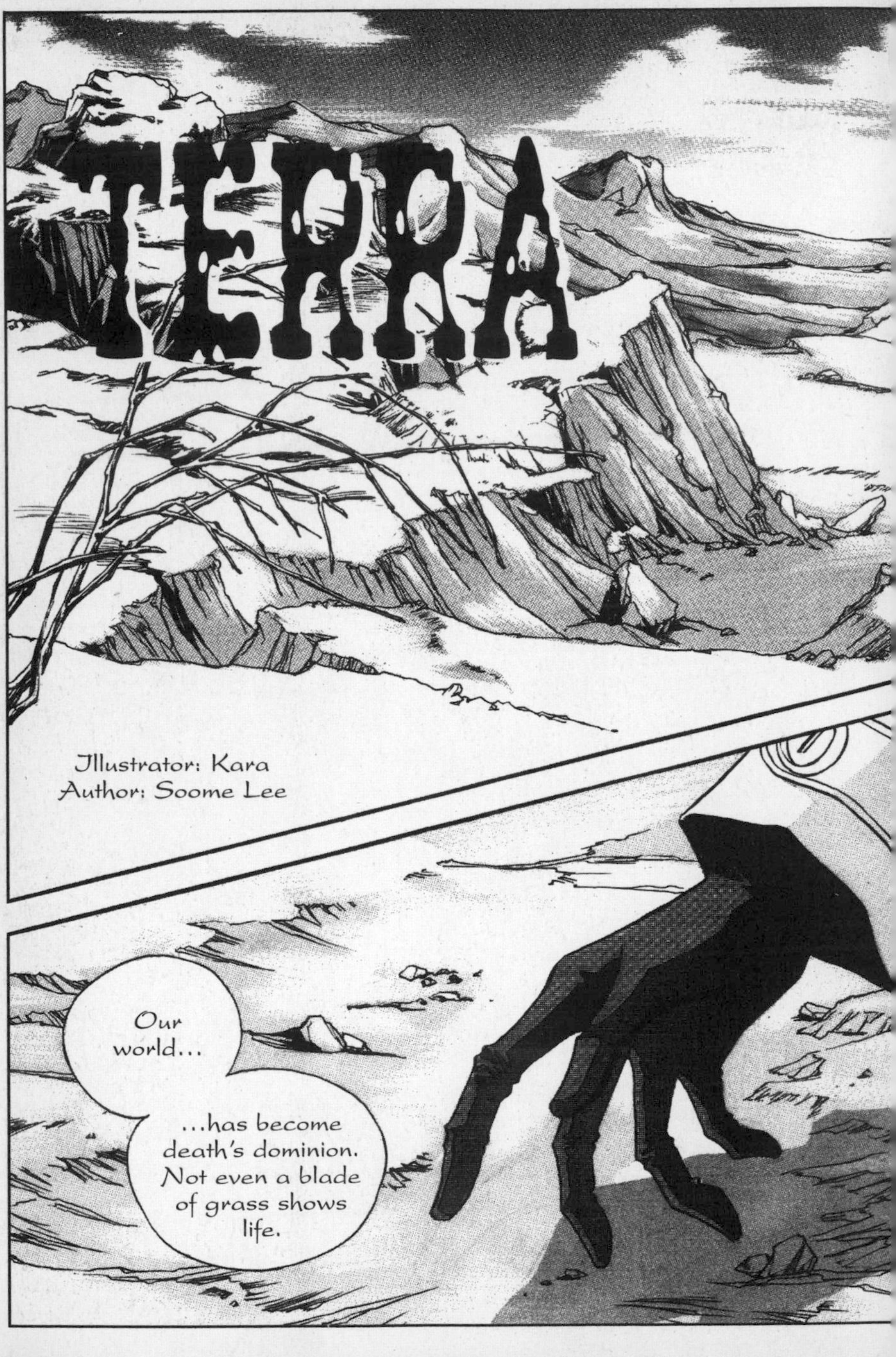
TERRA
Illustrator: Kara
Author: Soome Lee
Our world...
...has become death's dominion. Not even a blade of grass shows life.

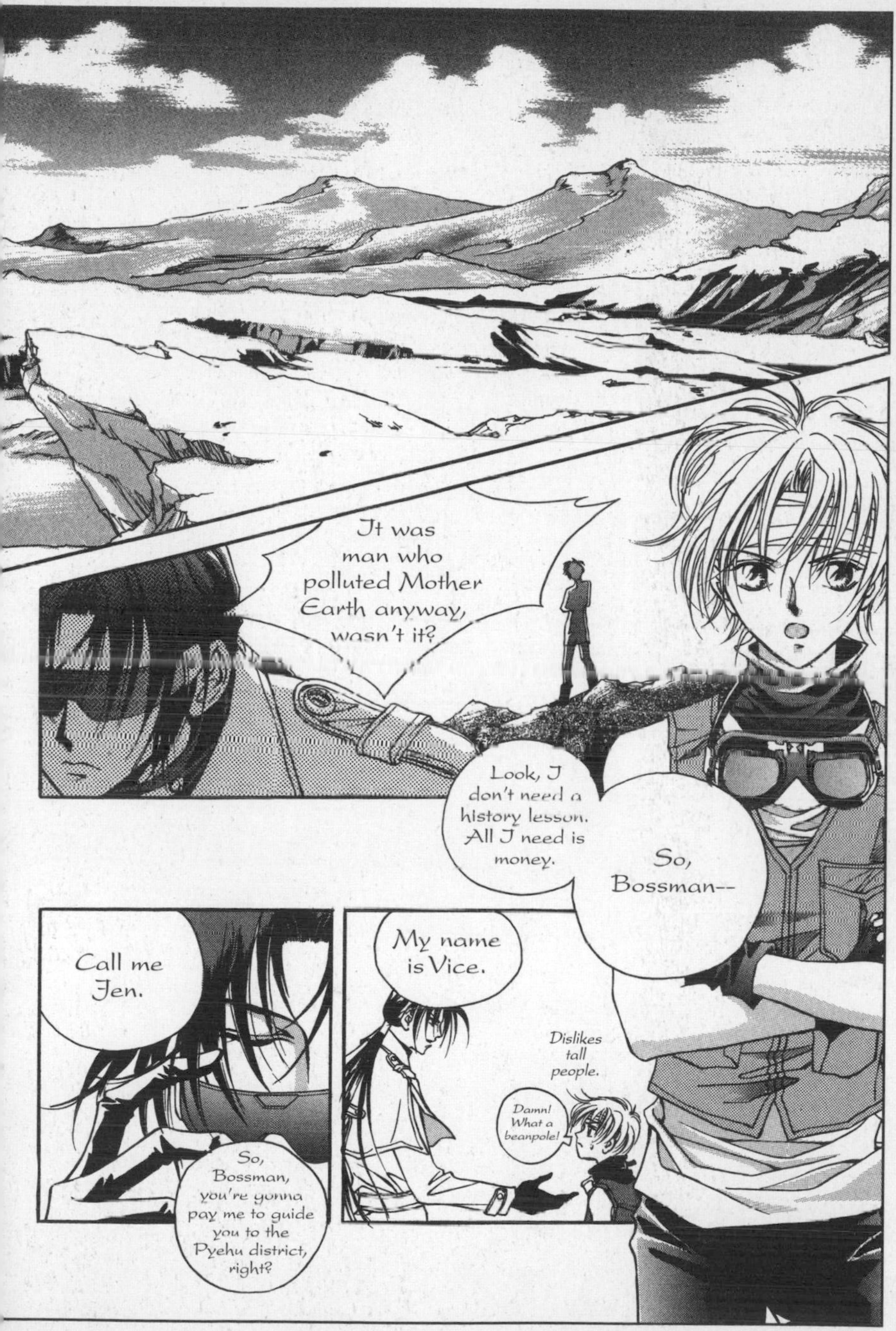
It was man who polluted Mother Earth anyway, wasn't it?
Look, I don't need a history lesson. All I need is money.
So, Bossman--
My name is Vice.
Dislikes tall people.
Damn! What a beanpole!
Call me Jen.
So, Bossman, you're gonna pay me to guide you to the Pyehu district, right?

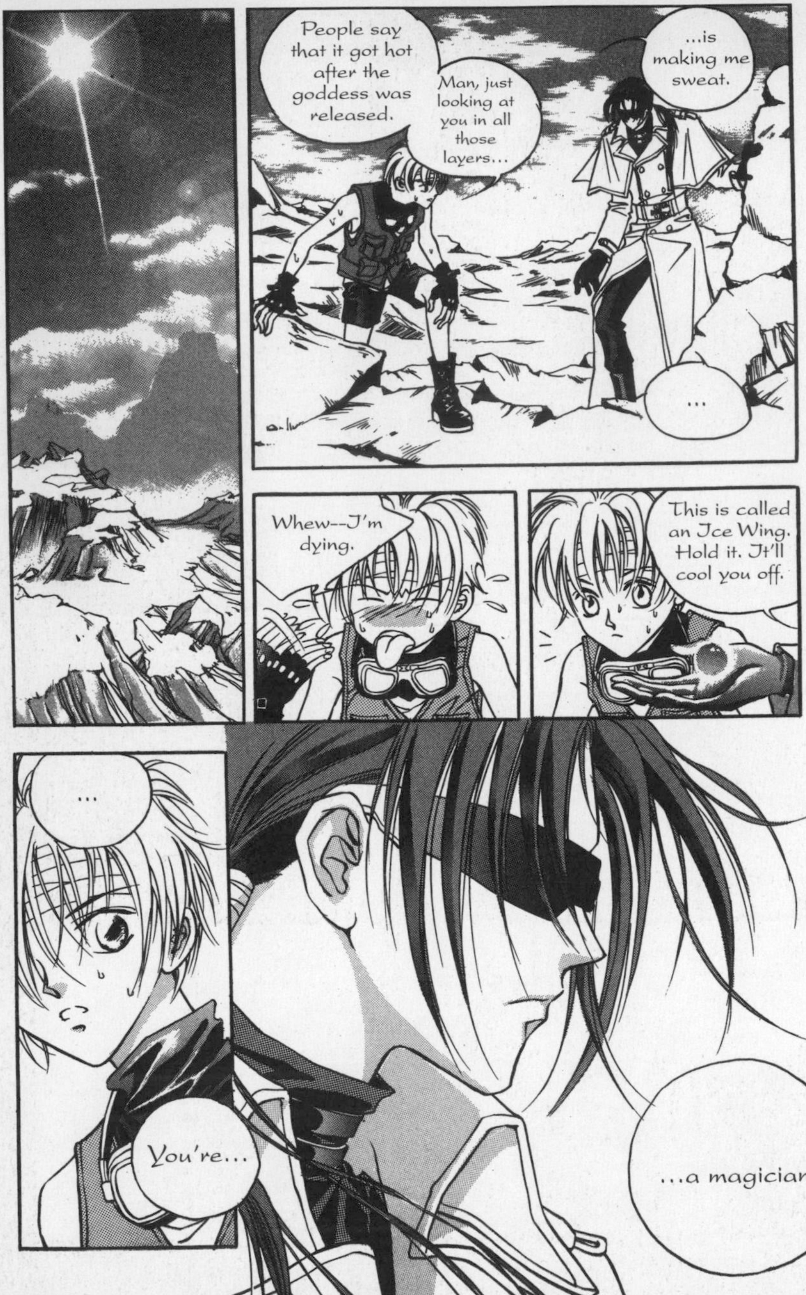
People say that it got hot after the goddess was released.
Man, just looking at you in all those layers...
...is making me sweat.
...
Whew--I'm dying.
This is called an Ice Wing. Hold it. It'll cool you off.
...
You're...
...a magician?

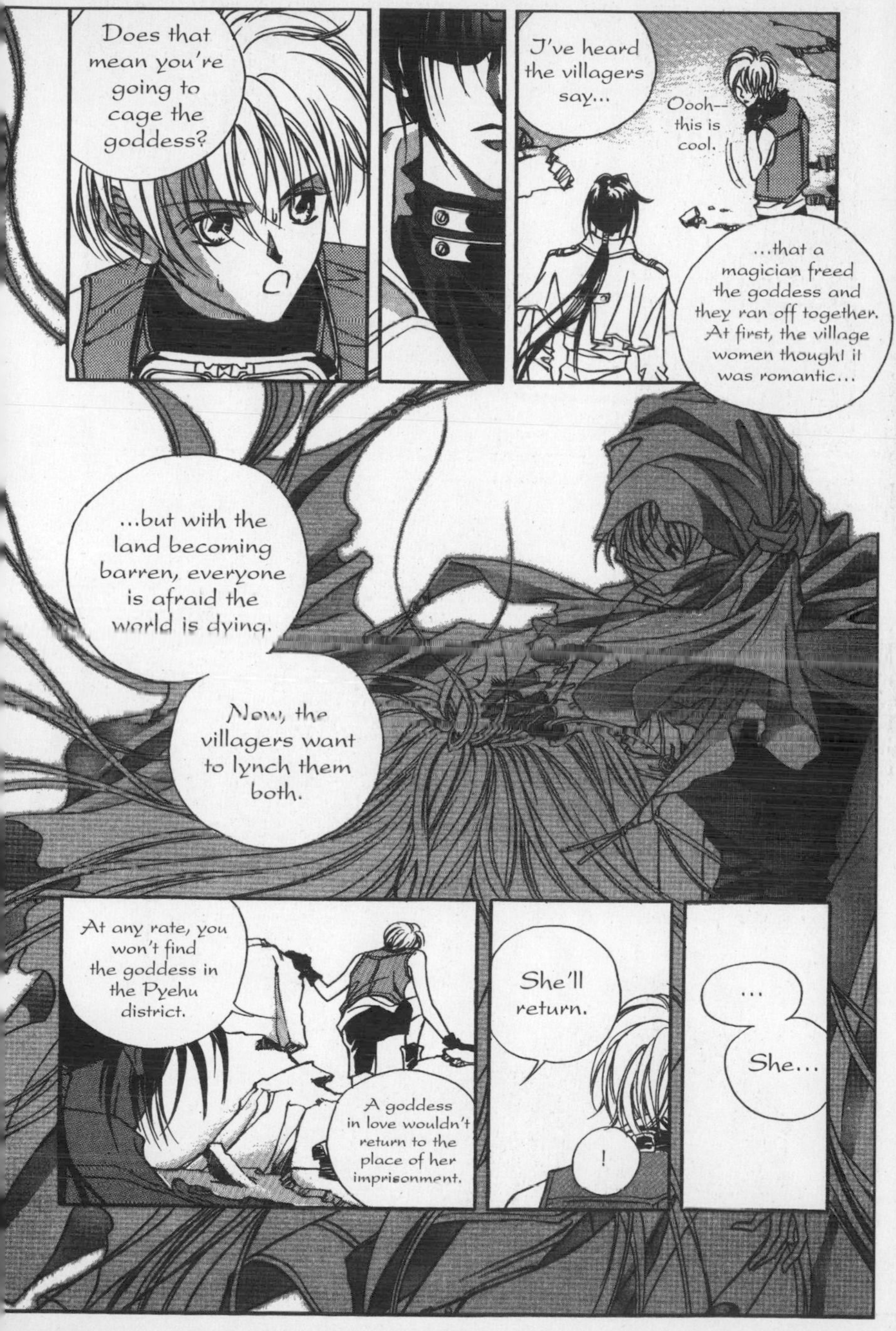
Does that mean you're going to cage the goddess?
I've heard the villagers say...
Oooh-- this is cool.
...that a magician freed the goddess and they ran off together. At first, the village women thought it was romantic...
...but with the land becoming barren, everyone is afraid the world is dying.
Now, the villagers want to lynch them both.
At any rate, you won't find the goddess in the Pyehu district.
A goddess in love wouldn't return to the place of her imprisonment.
She'll return.
!
...
She...

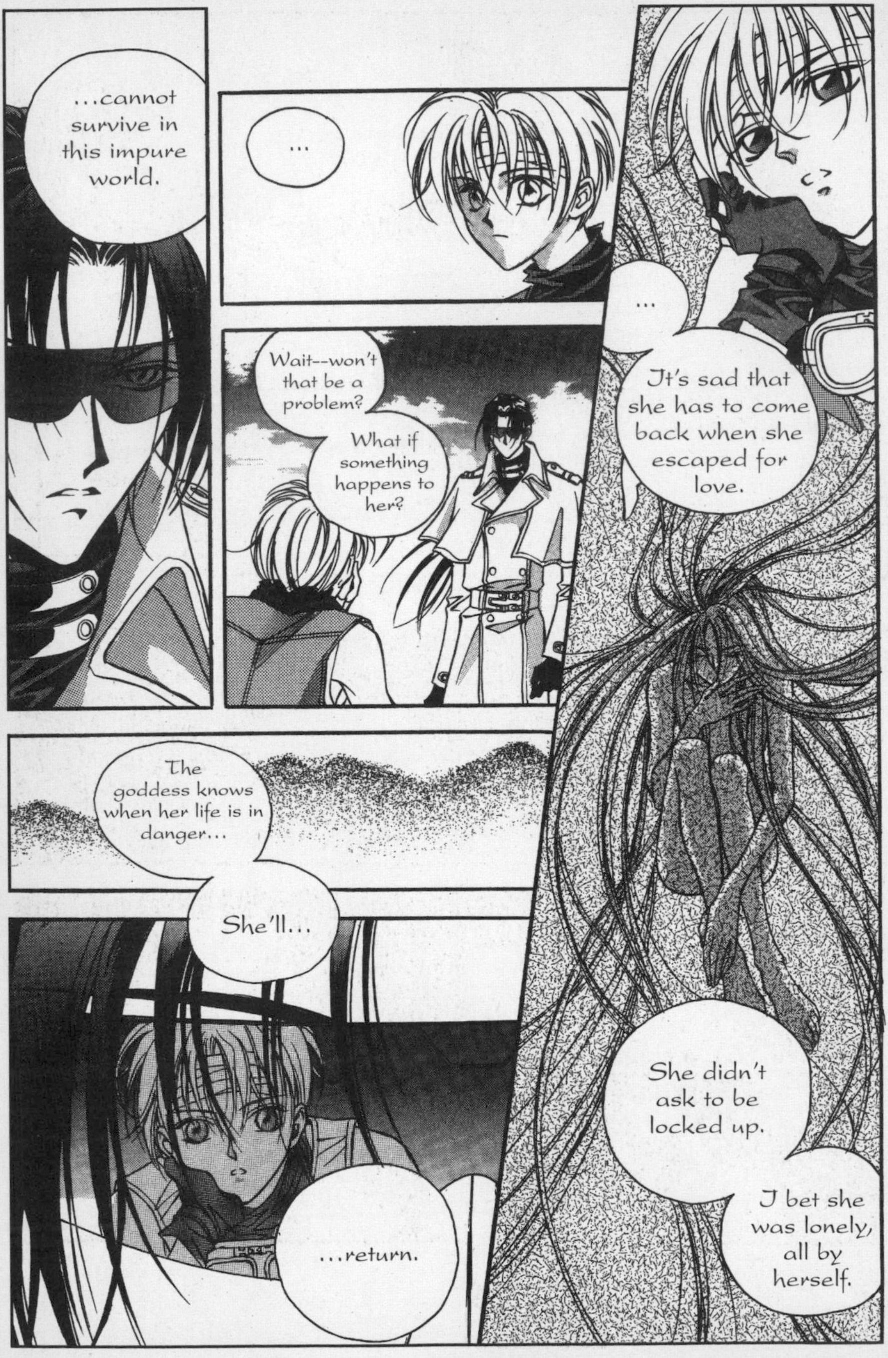
...cannot survive in this impure world.
...
Wait--won't that be a problem?
What if something happens to her?
The goddess knows when her life is in danger...
She'll...
...return.
...
It's sad that she has to come back when she escaped for love.
She didn't ask to be locked up.
I bet she was lonely, all by herself.

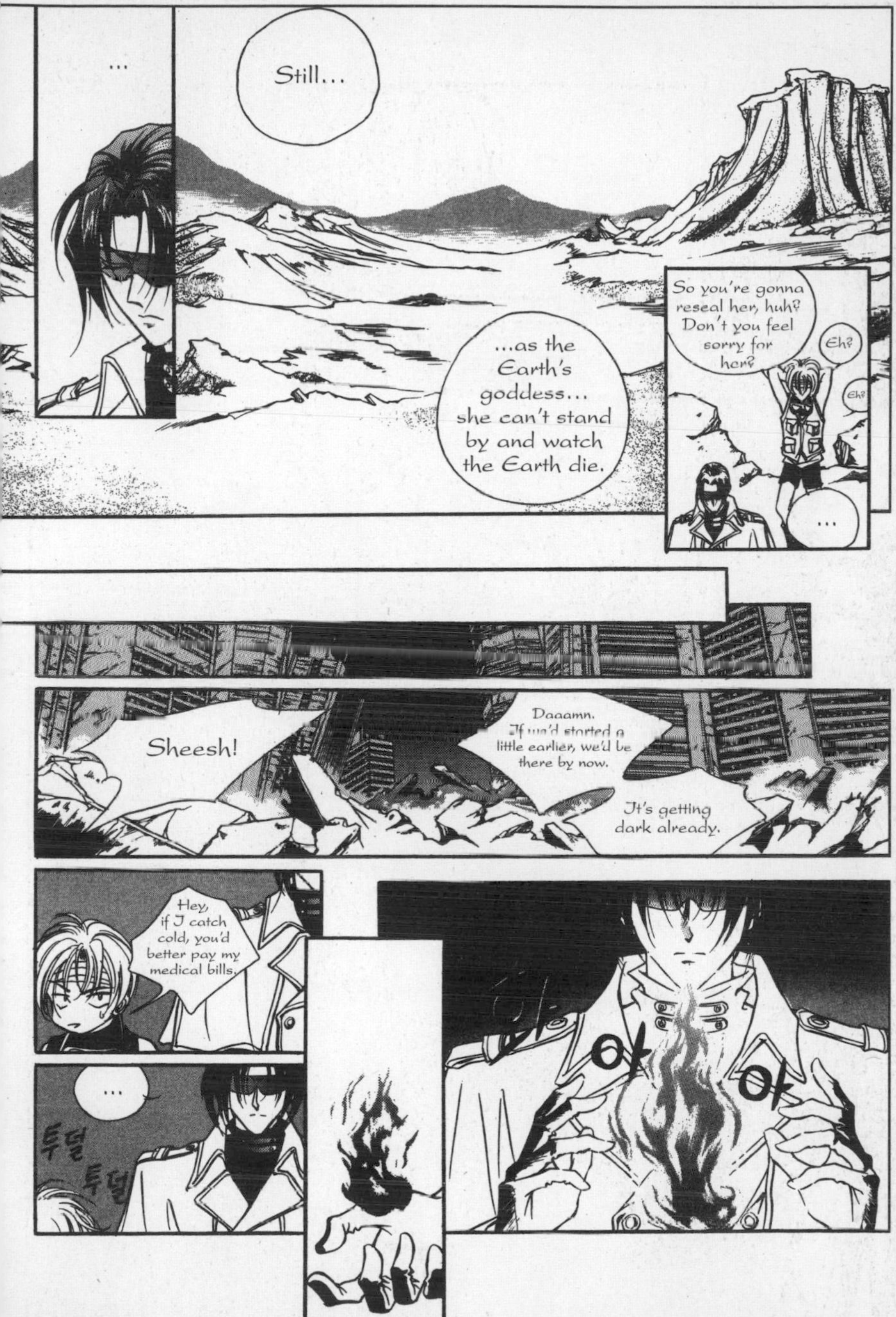
...
Still...
...as the Earth's goddess... she can't stand by and watch the Earth die.
So you're gonna reseal her, huh? Don't you feel sorry for her?
Eh?
Eh?
...
Sheesh!
Daaamn. If we'd started a little earlier, we'd be there by now.
It's getting dark already.
Hey, if I catch cold, you'd better pay my medical bills.
...
투덜 투덜

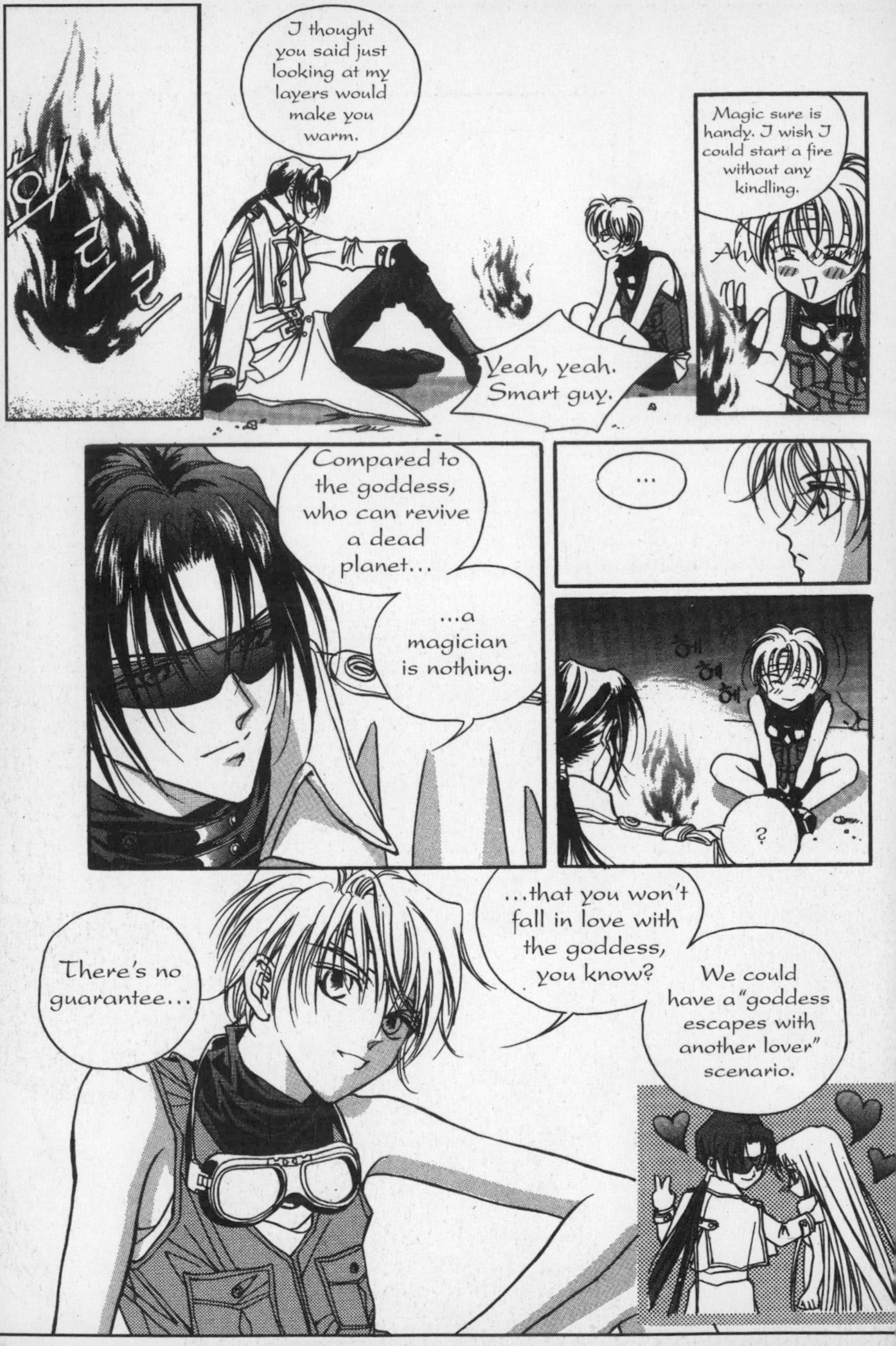

Magic sure is handy. I wish I could start a fire without any kindling.
Ah
I thought you said just looking at my layers would make you warm.
Yeah, yeah. Smart guy.
...
헤 헤 헤
?
Compared to the goddess, who can revive a dead planet...
...a magician is nothing.
There's no guarantee...
...that you won't fall in love with the goddess, you know?
We could have a "goddess escapes with another lover" scenario.

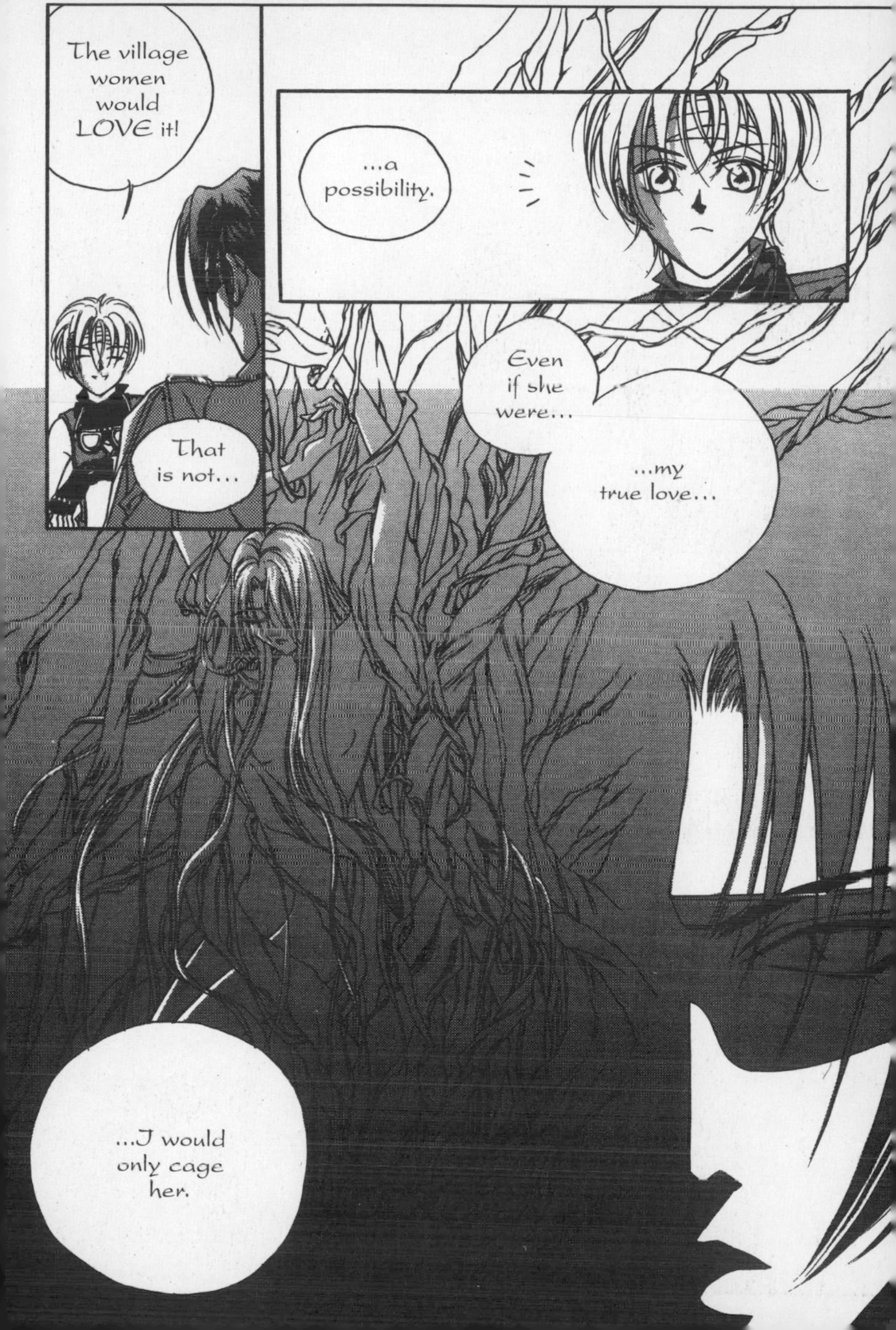

The village women would LOVE it!
That is not...
...a possibility.
Even if she were...
...my true love...
...I would only cage her.

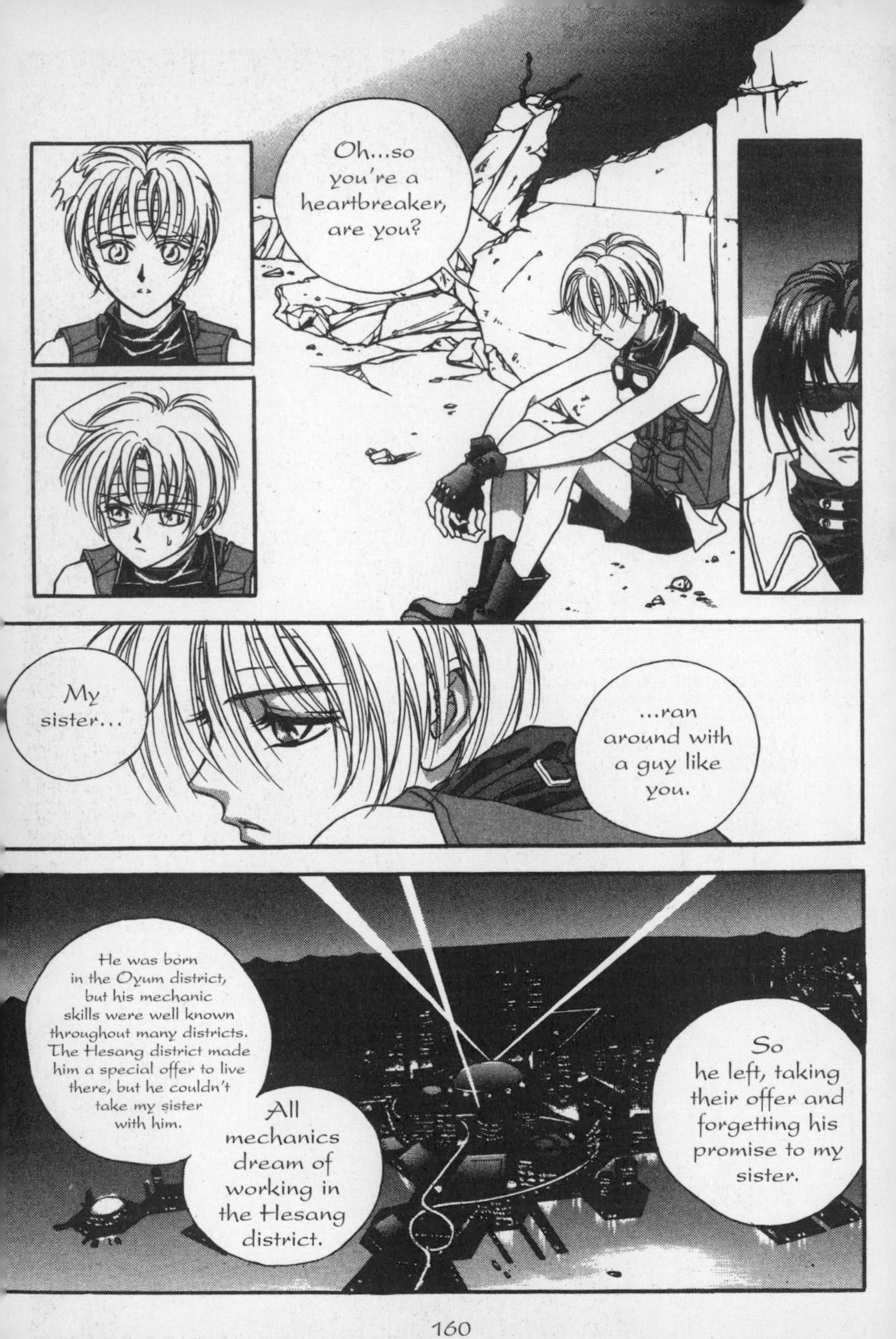
Oh...so you're a heartbreaker, are you?
My sister...
...ran around with a guy like you.
He was born in the Oyum district, but his mechanic skills were well known throughout many districts. The Hesang district made him a special offer to live there, but he couldn't take my sister with him.
All mechanics dream of working in the Hesang district.
So he left, taking their offer and forgetting his promise to my sister.

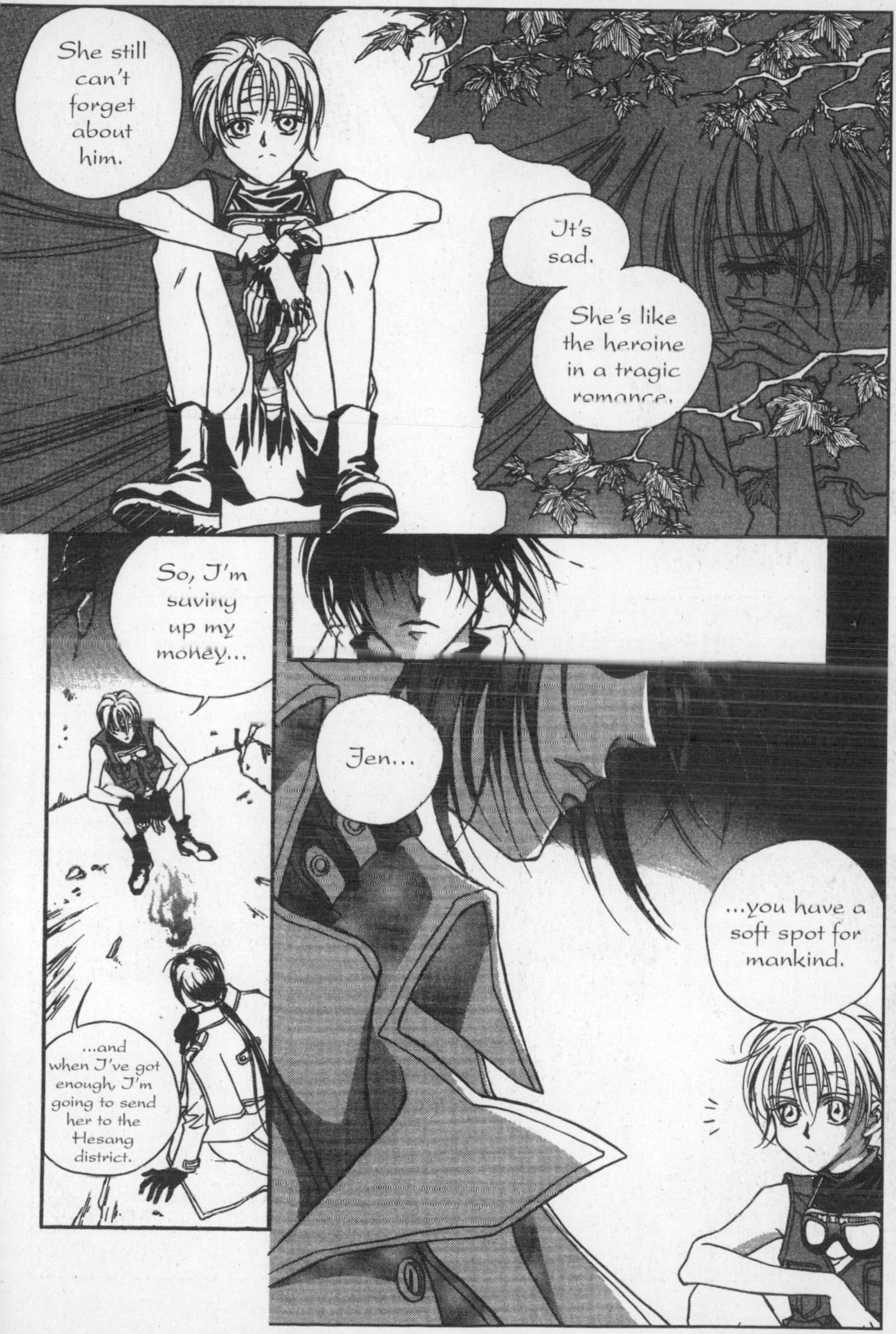
She still can't forget about him.
It's sad.
She's like the heroine in a tragic romance.
So, I'm saving up my money...
...and when I've got enough, I'm going to send her to the Hesang district.
Jen...
...you have a soft spot for mankind.

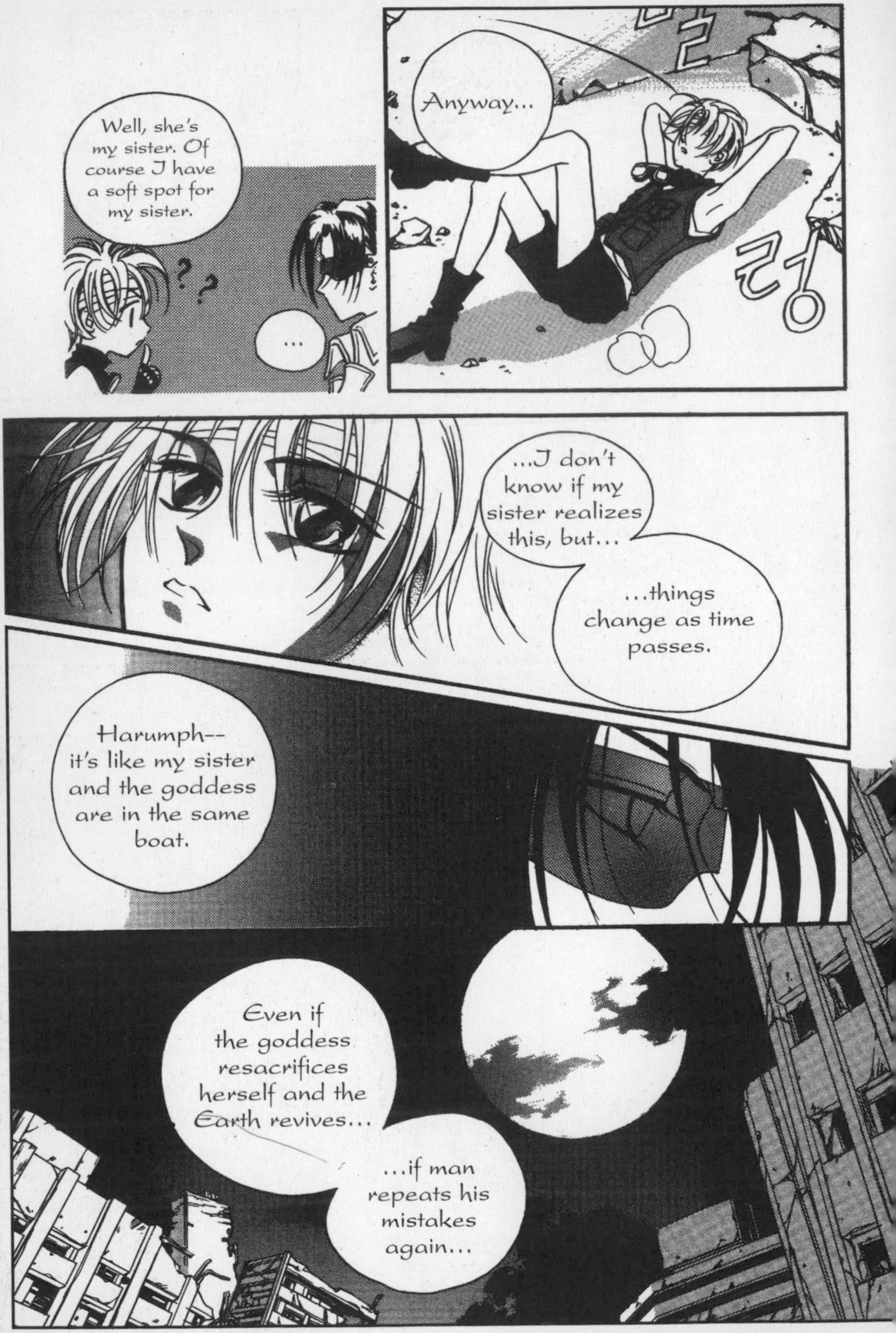
Anyway...
Well, she's my sister. Of course I have a soft spot for my sister.
...
...I don't know if my sister realizes this, but...
...things change as time passes.
Harumph-- it's like my sister and the goddess are in the same boat.
Even if the goddess resacrifices herself and the Earth revives...
...if man repeats his mistakes again...

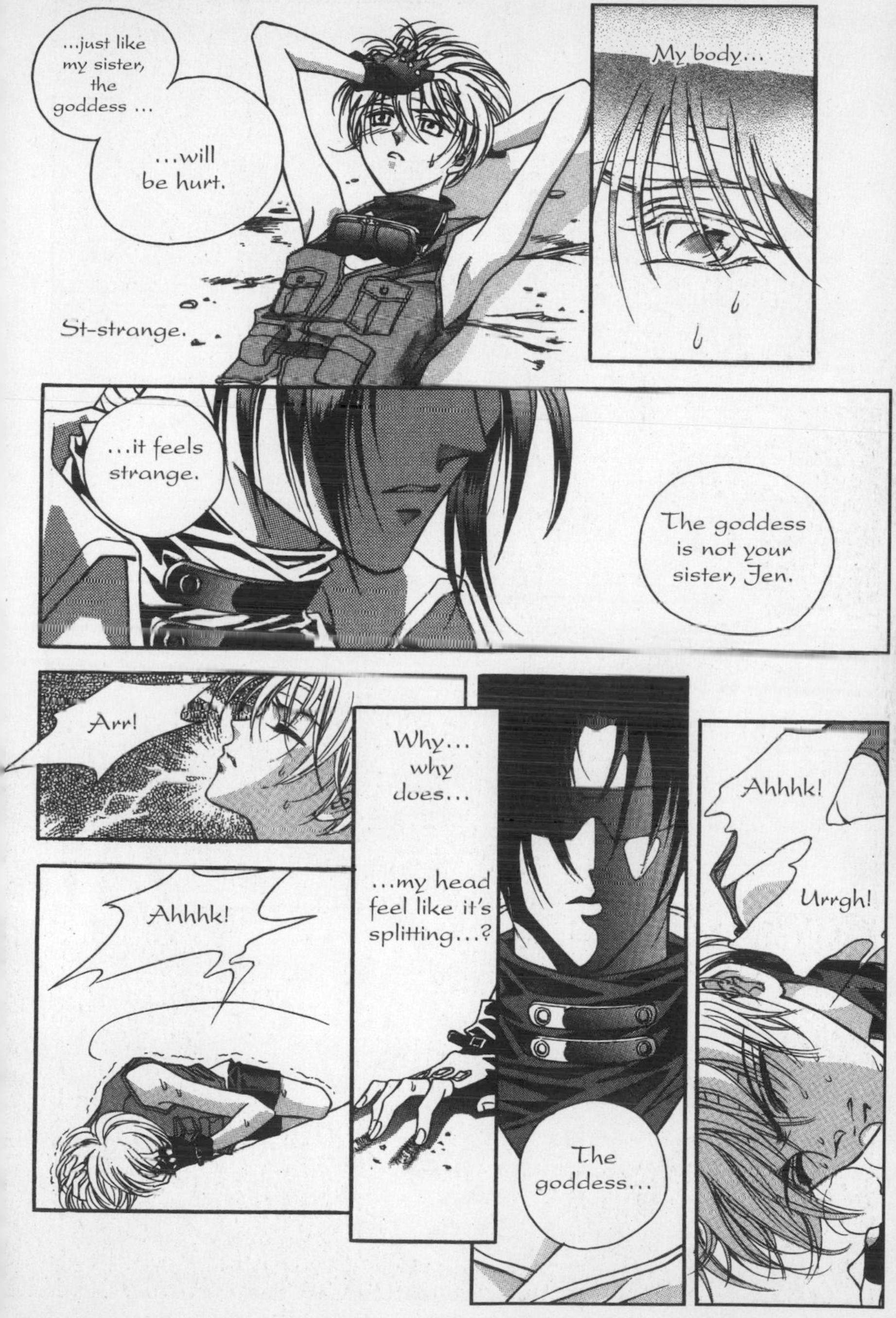

My body…
…just like my sister, the goddess …
…will be hurt.
St-strange.
The goddess is not your sister, Jen.
…it feels strange.
Ahhhk!
Urrgh!
The goddess…
Why… why does…
…my head feel like it's splitting…?
Arr!
Ahhhk!

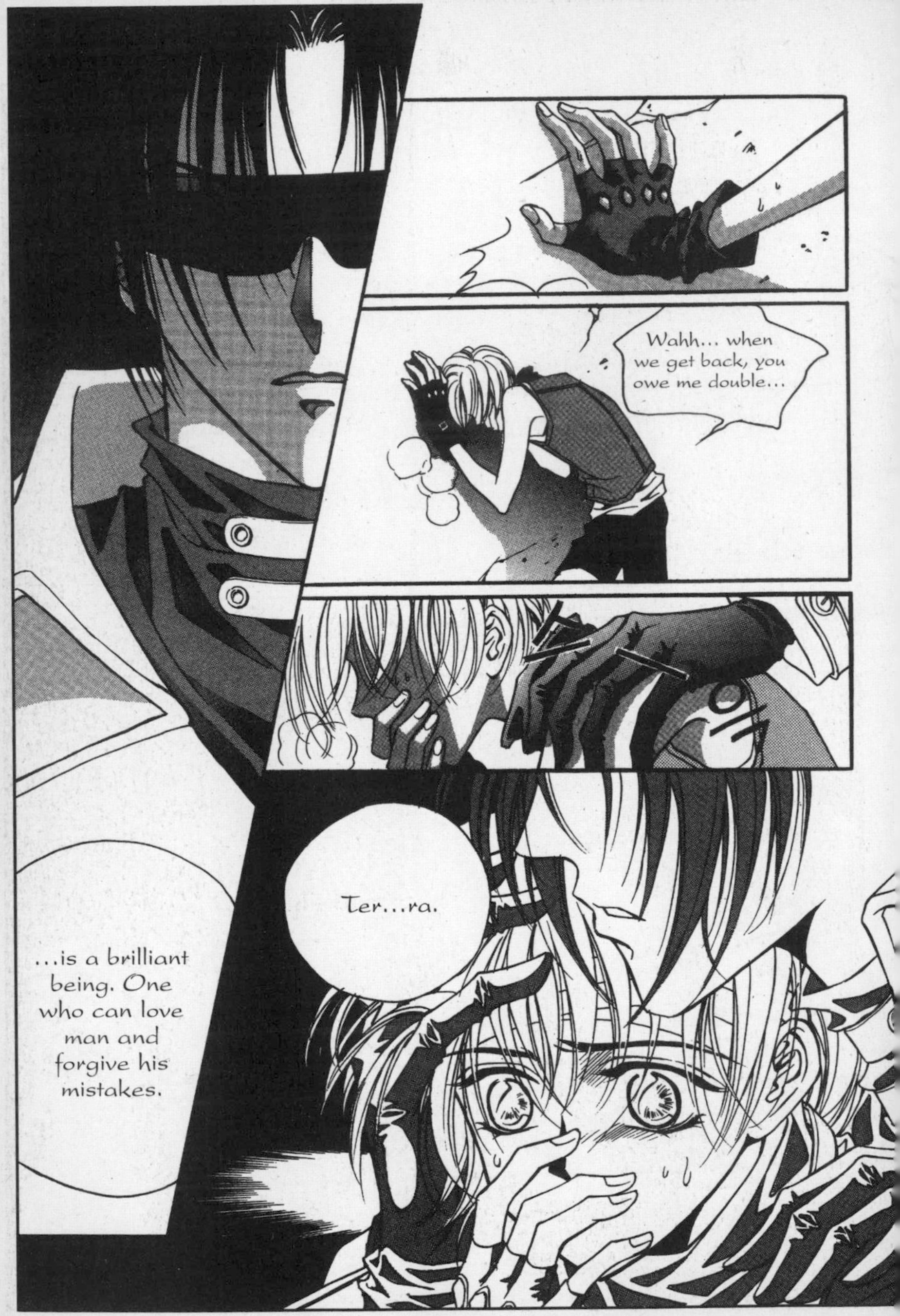
Wahh... when we get back, you owe me double...
Ter...ra.
...is a brilliant being. One who can love man and forgive his mistakes.

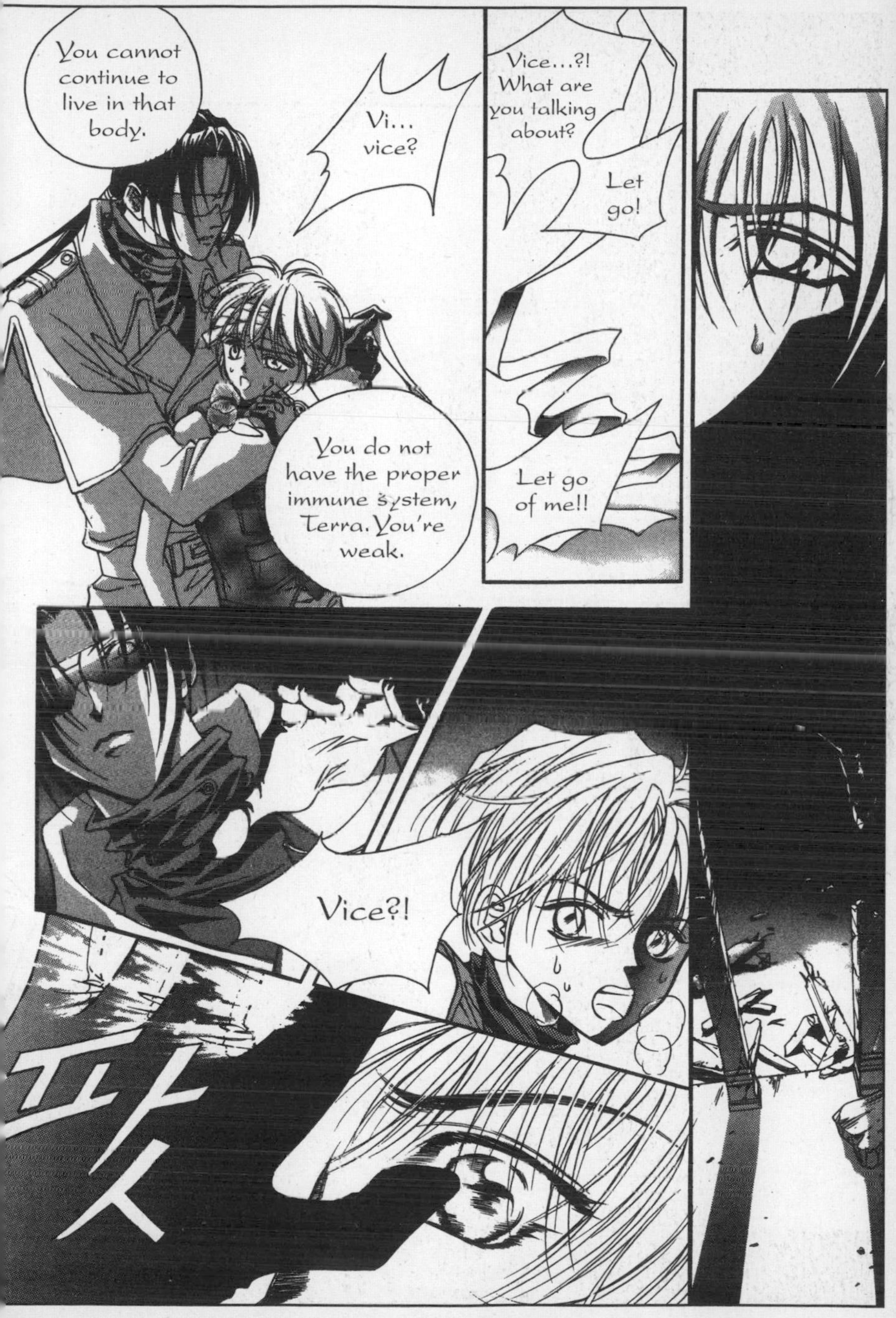
You cannot continue to live in that body.
Vi... vice?
You do not have the proper immune system, Terra. You're weak.
Vice...?! What are you talking about?
Let go!
Let go of me!!
Vice?!

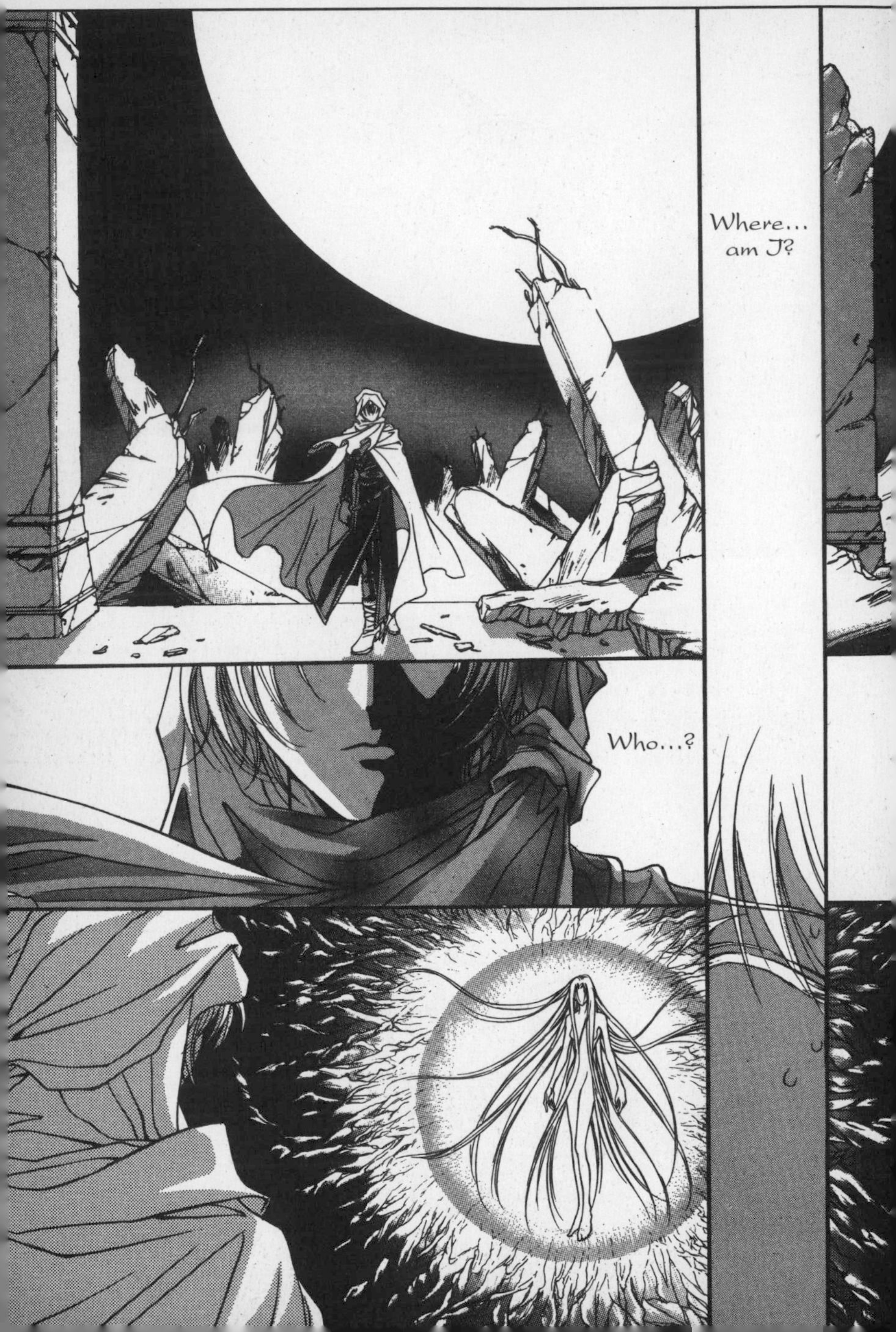
Where... am I?
Who...?

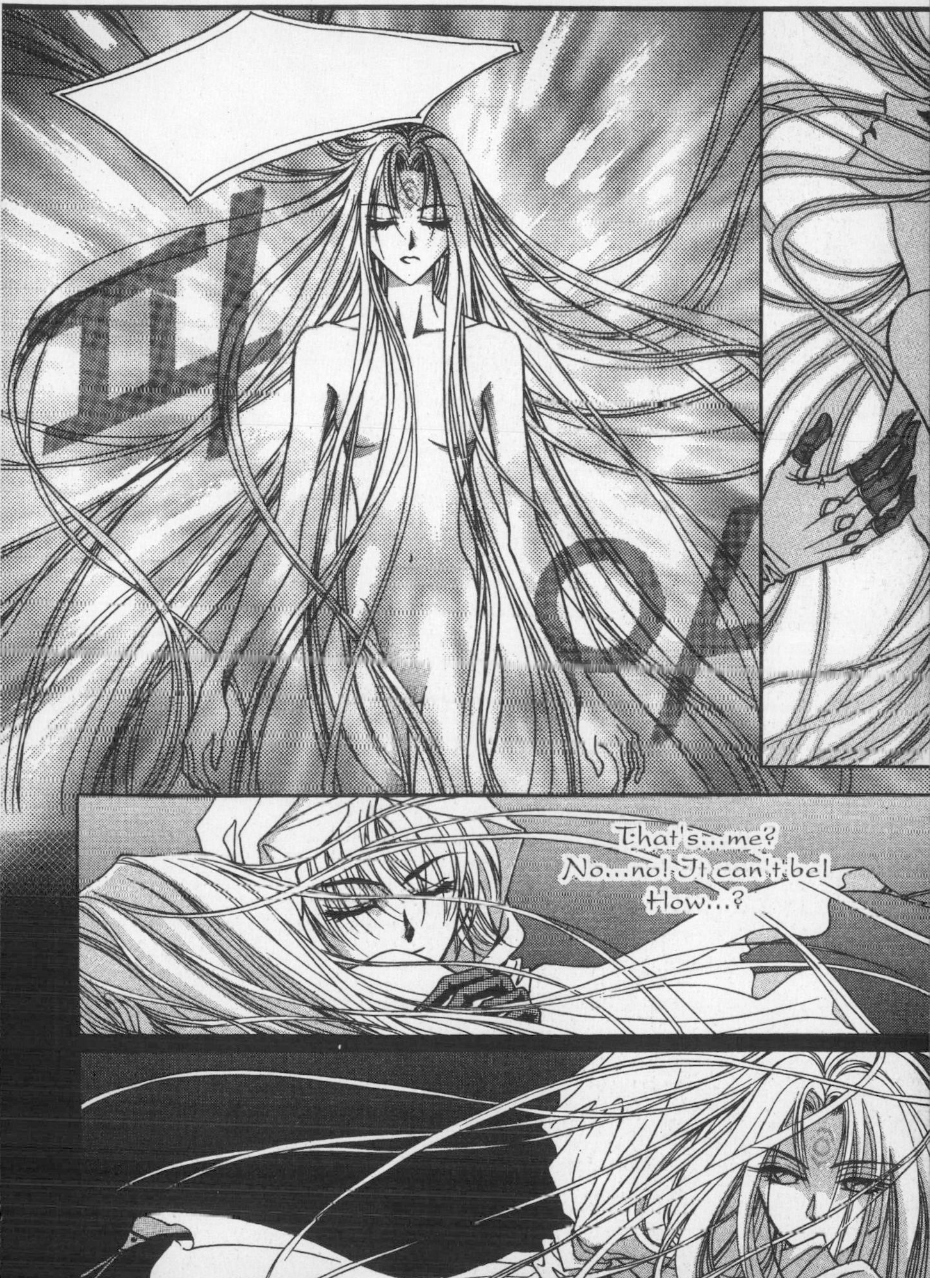
That's...me?
No...no! It can't be!
How...?

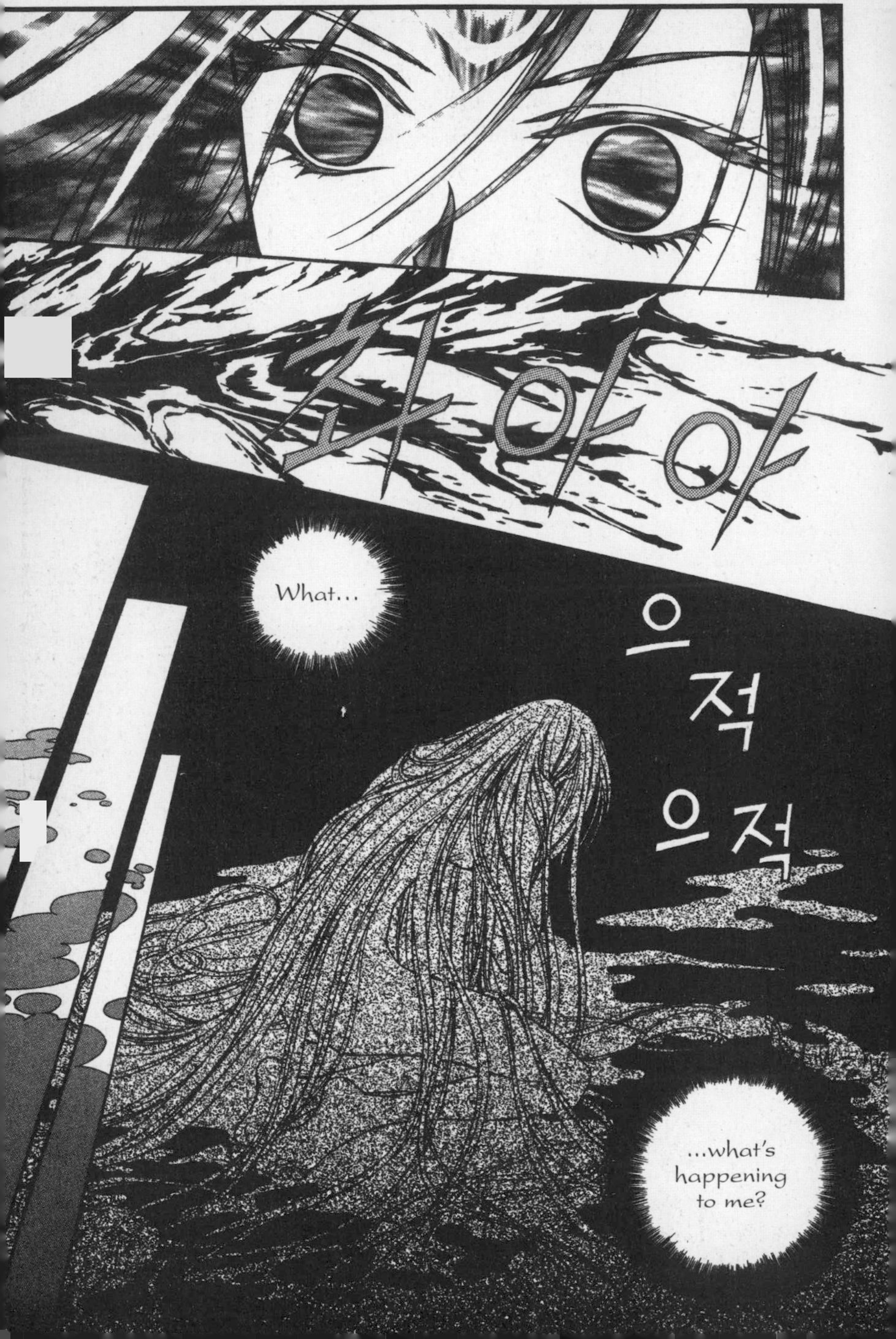
쏴아아
What...
으적 으적
...what's happening to me?

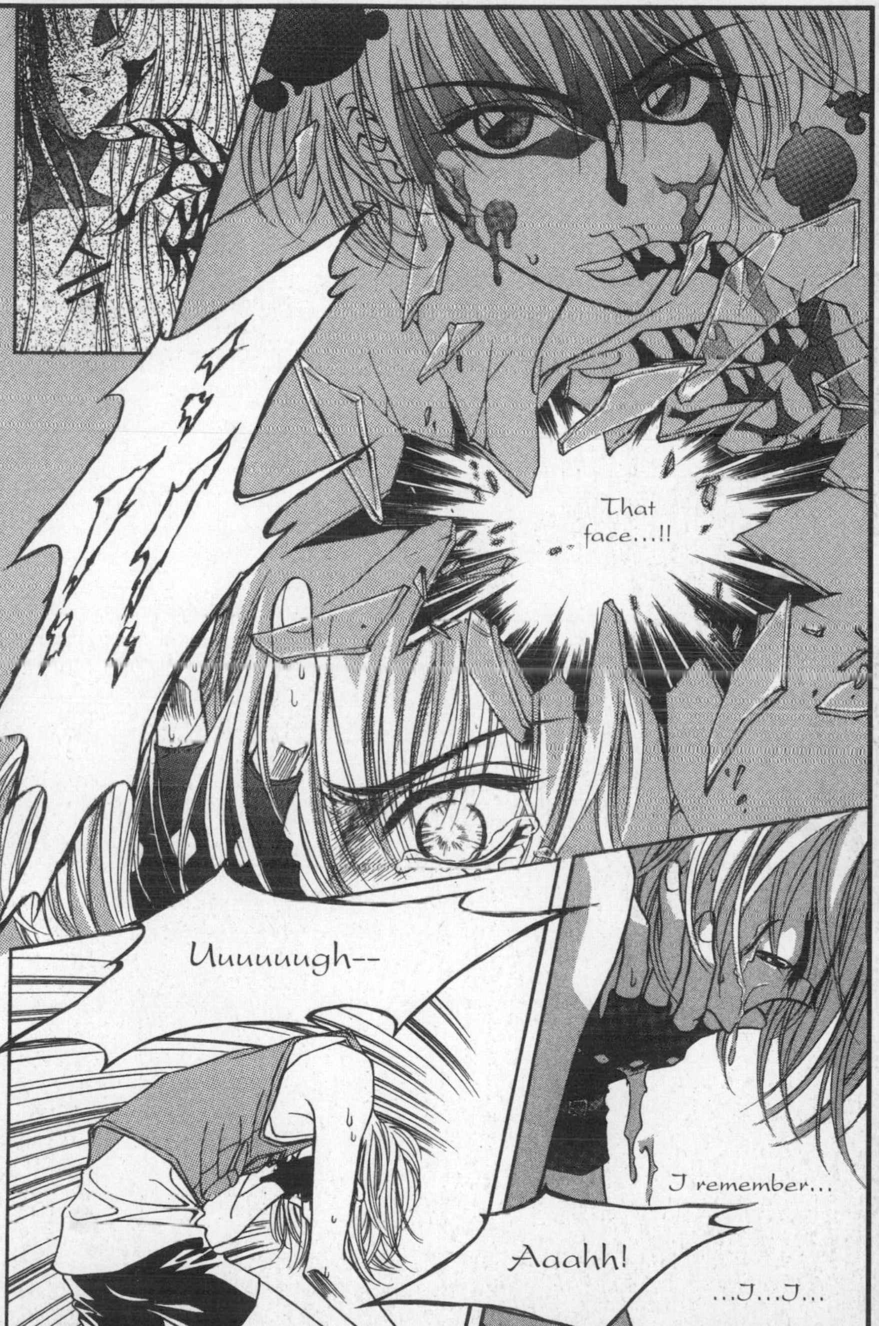
That face...!!
Uuuuuugh--
I remember...
...I...I...
Aaahh!

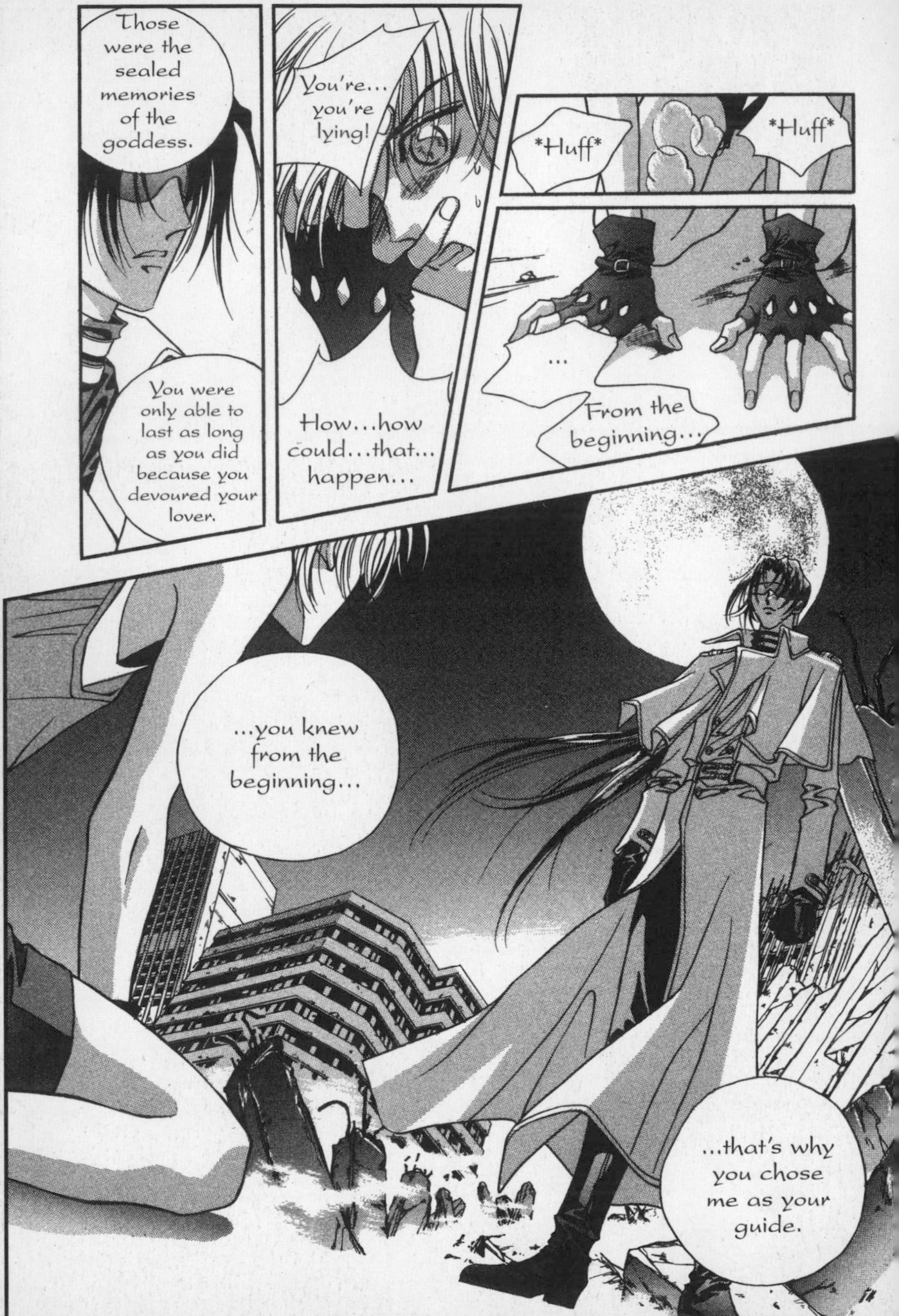
Those were the sealed memories of the goddess.
You were only able to last as long as you did because you devoured your lover.
You're... you're lying!
How...how could...that... happen...
Huff
Huff
...
From the beginning...
...you knew from the beginning...
...that's why you chose me as your guide.

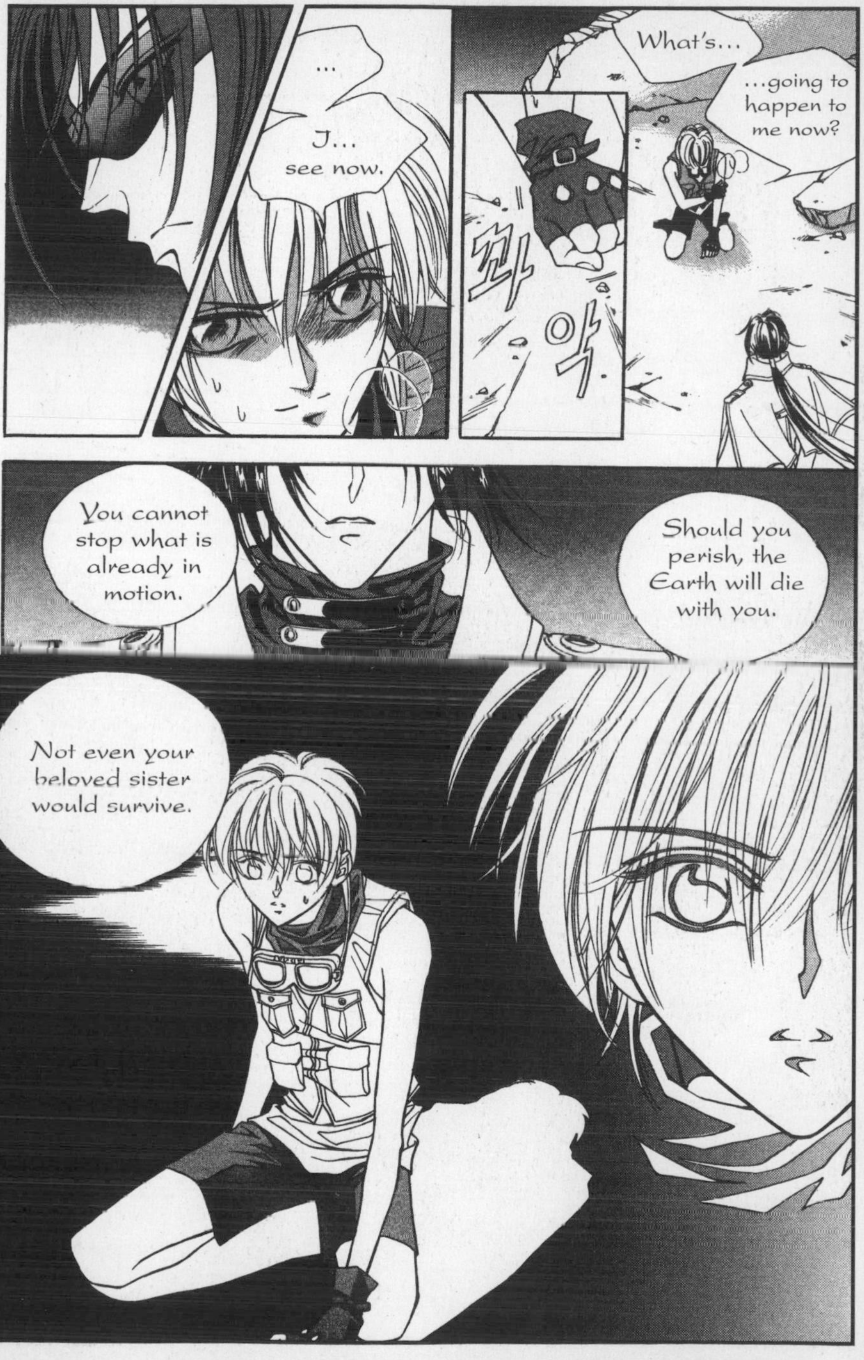
What's...
...going to happen to me now?
꽈
악
...
I... see now.
Should you perish, the Earth will die with you.
You cannot stop what is already in motion.
Not even your beloved sister would survive.

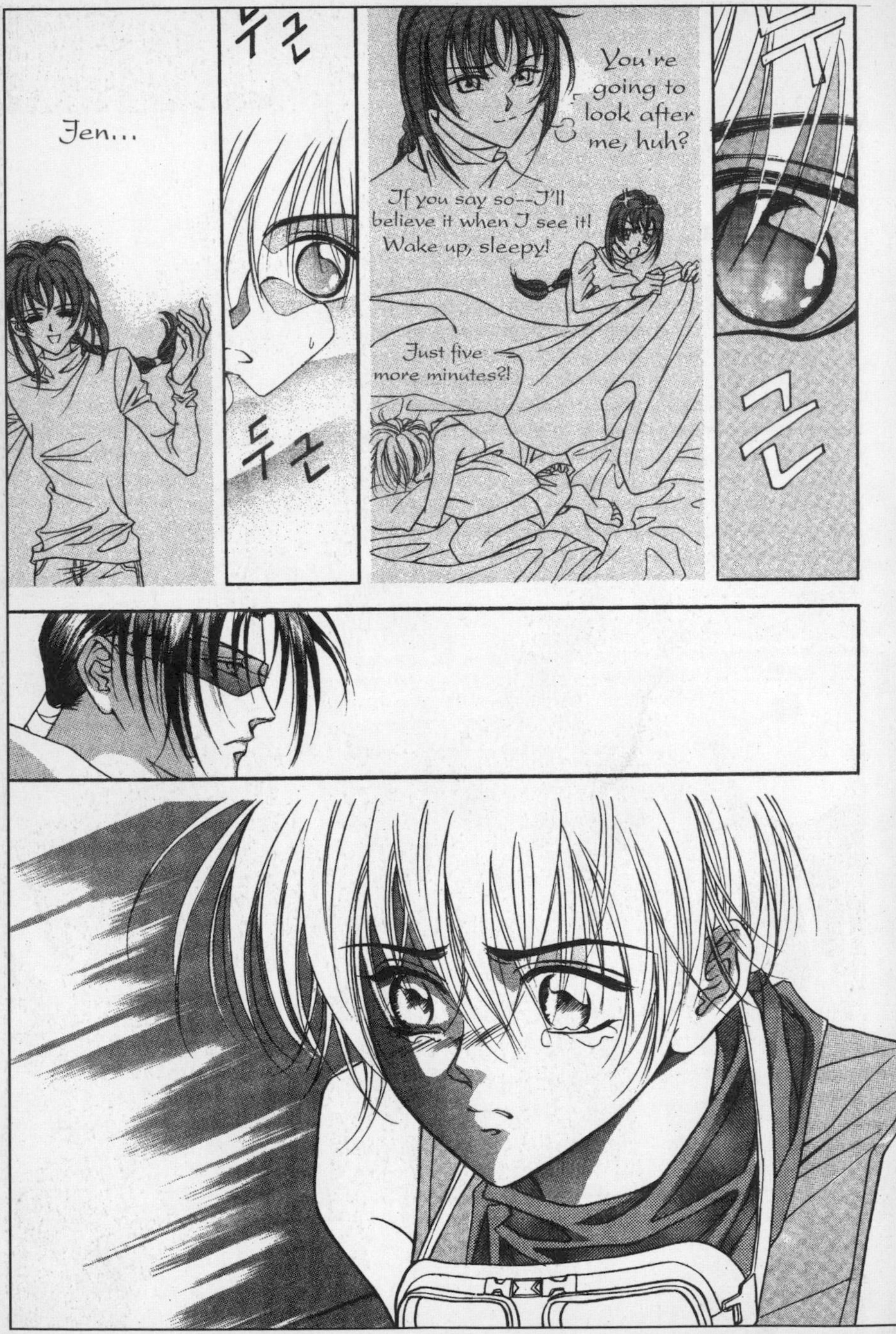

Jen...
두근
두근
You're going to look after me, huh?
If you say so--I'll believe it when I see it! Wake up, sleepy!
Just five more minutes?!
근

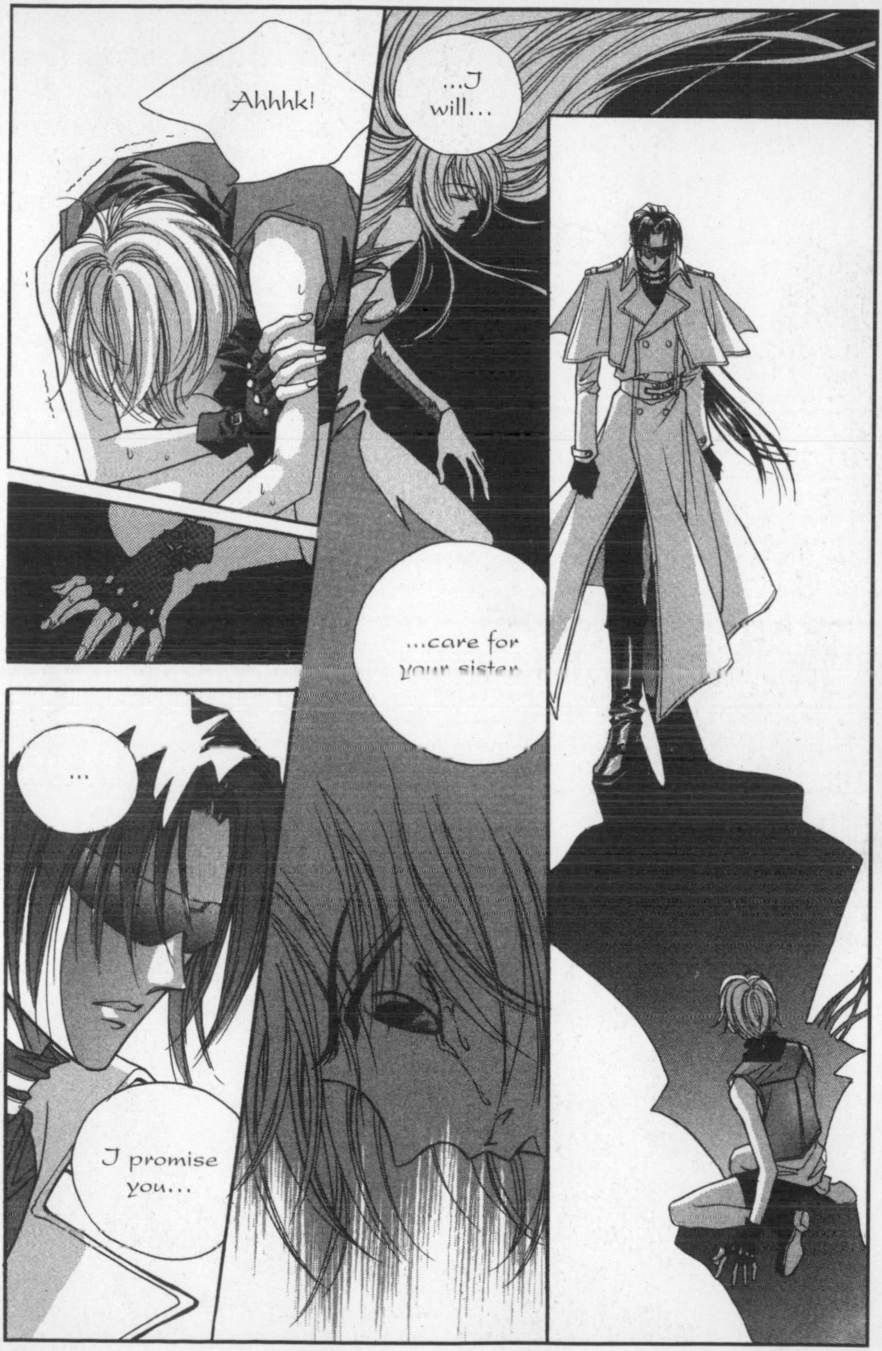

...I will...
...care for your sister
Ahhhk!
...
I promise you...

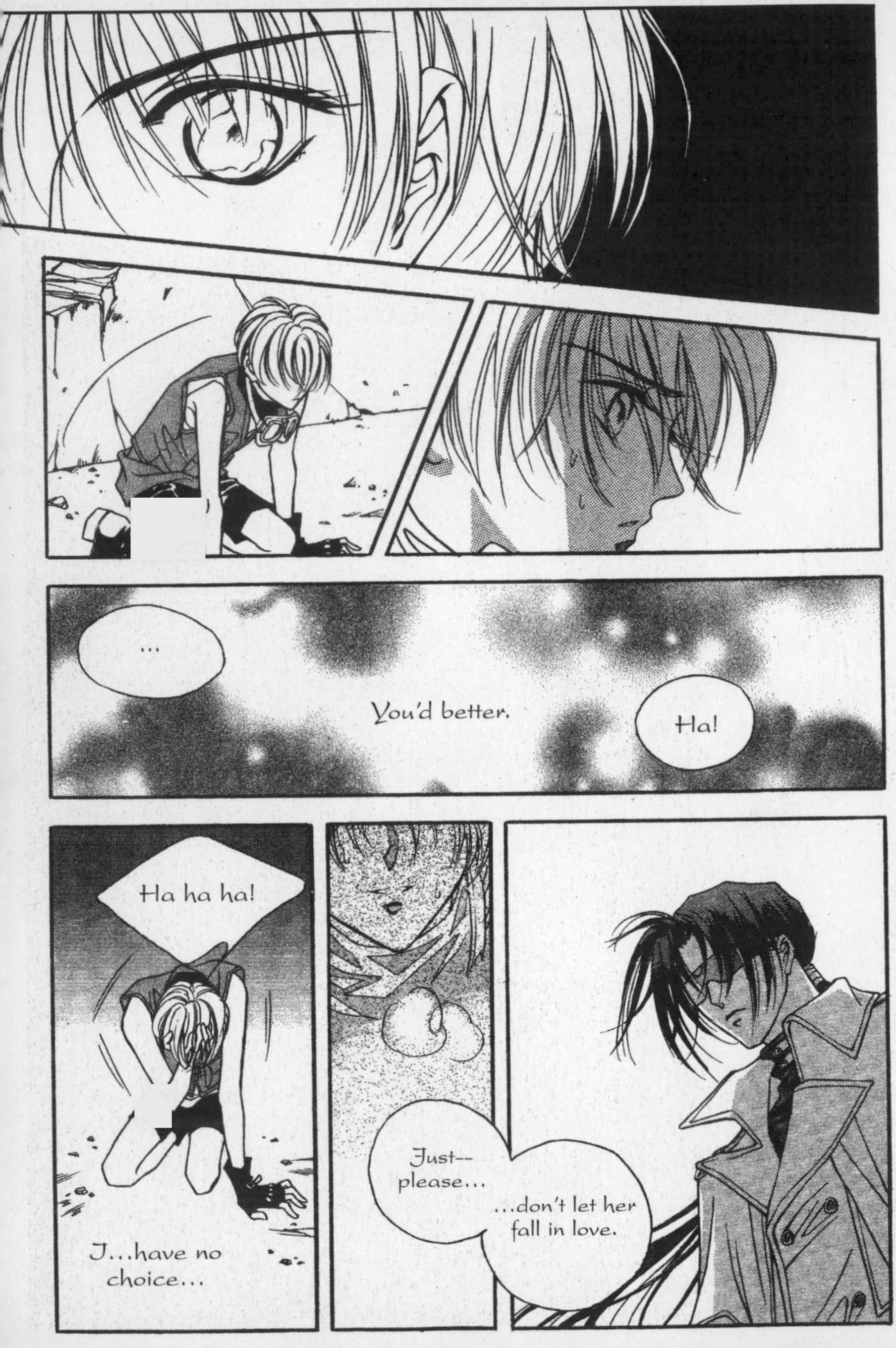
Ha!
You'd better.
...
Just-- please...
...don't let her fall in love.
Ha ha ha!
I...have no choice...

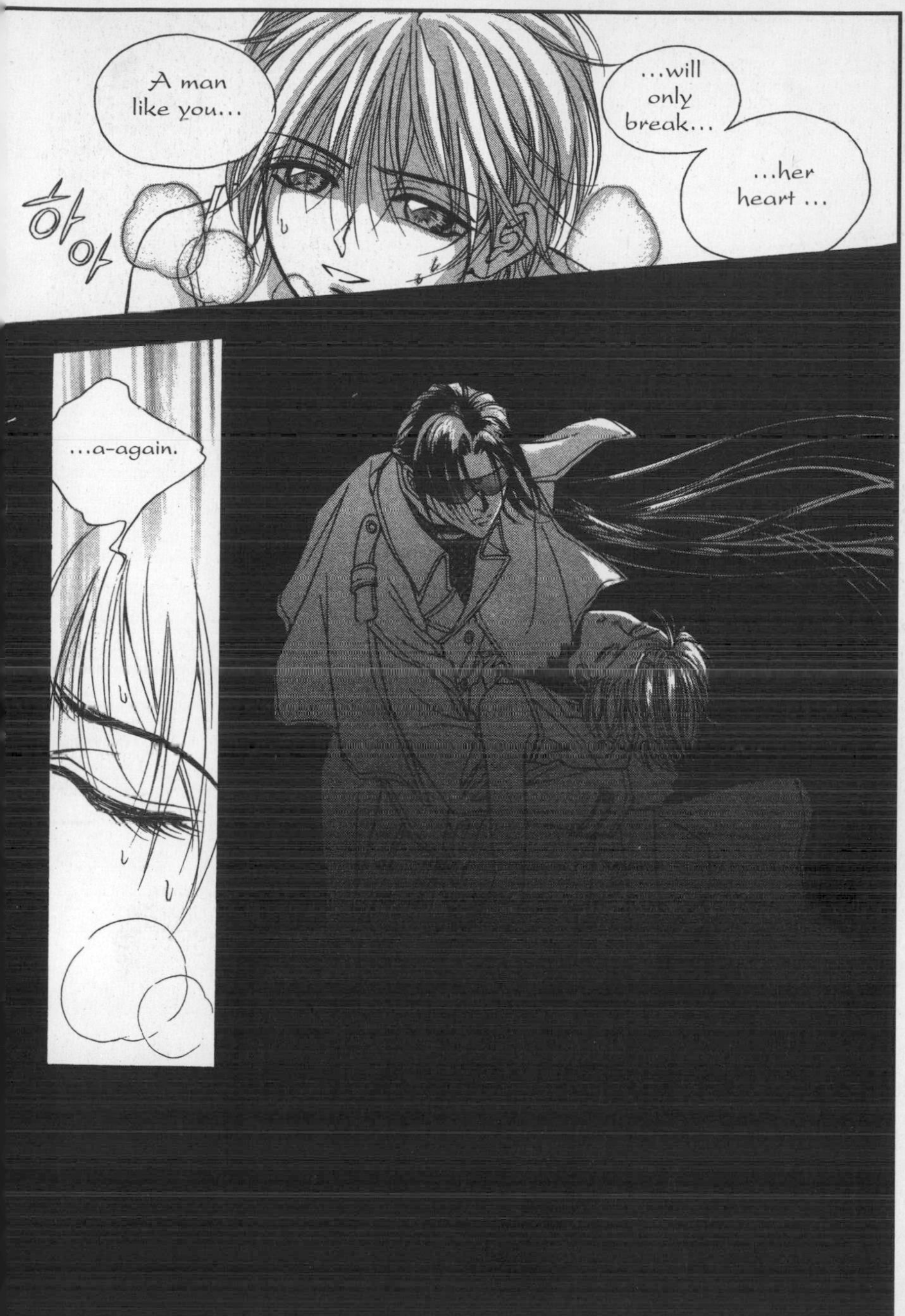
A man like you...
하아
...will only break...
...her heart ...
...a-again.

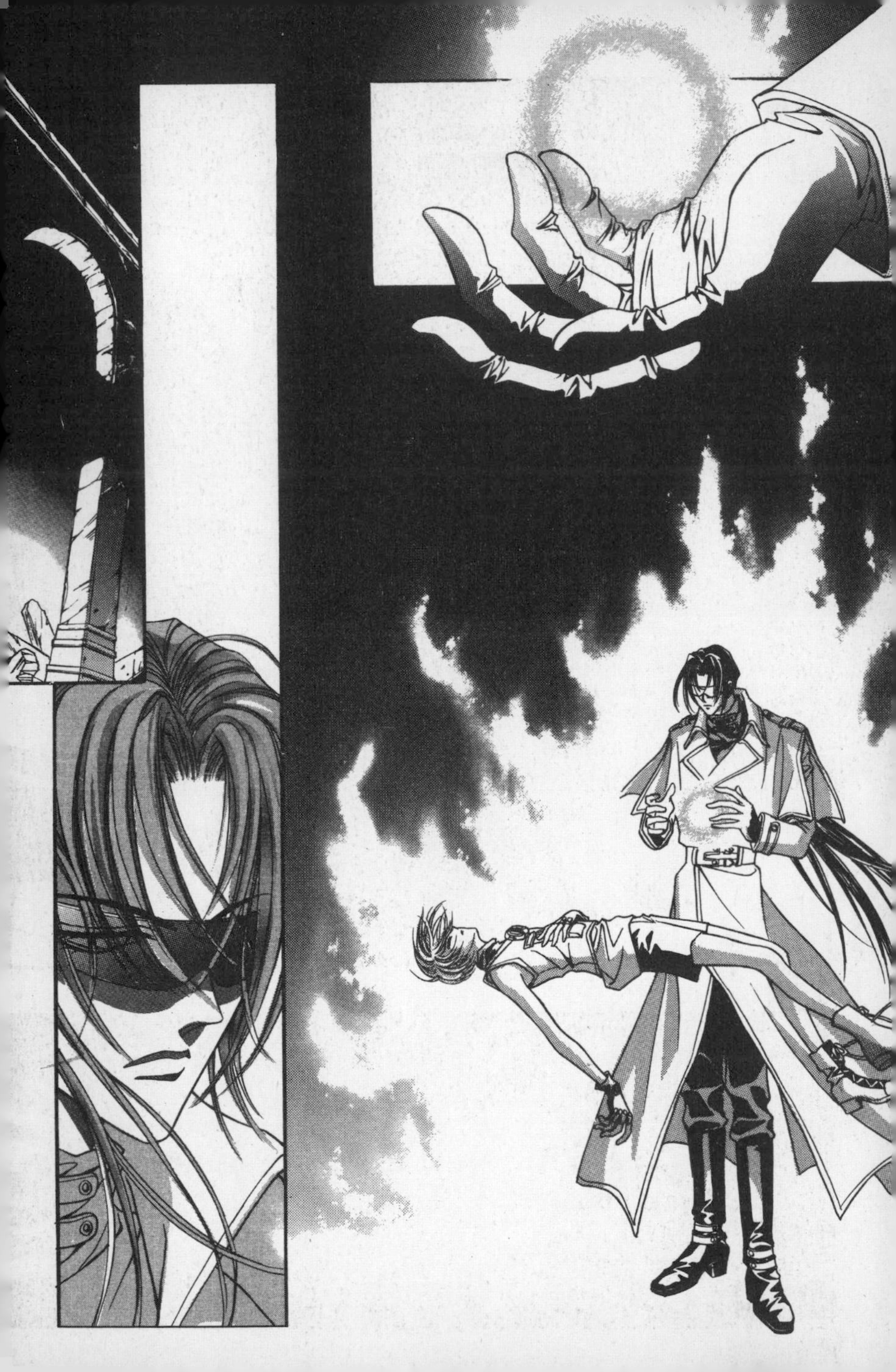

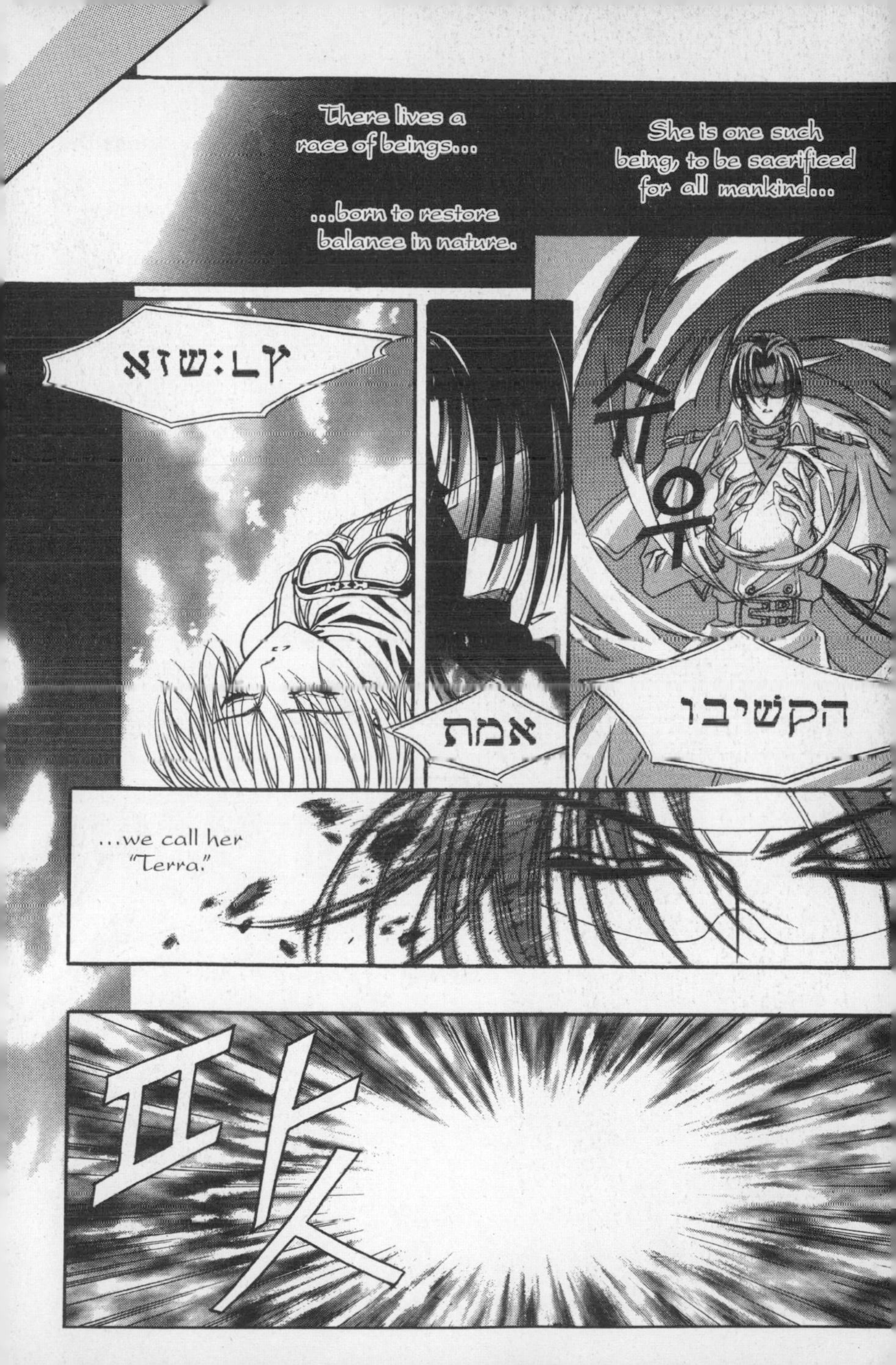
There lives a race of beings...
...born to restore balance in nature.
She is one such being, to be sacrificed for all mankind...
הקשיבו
אמת
...we call her "Terra."

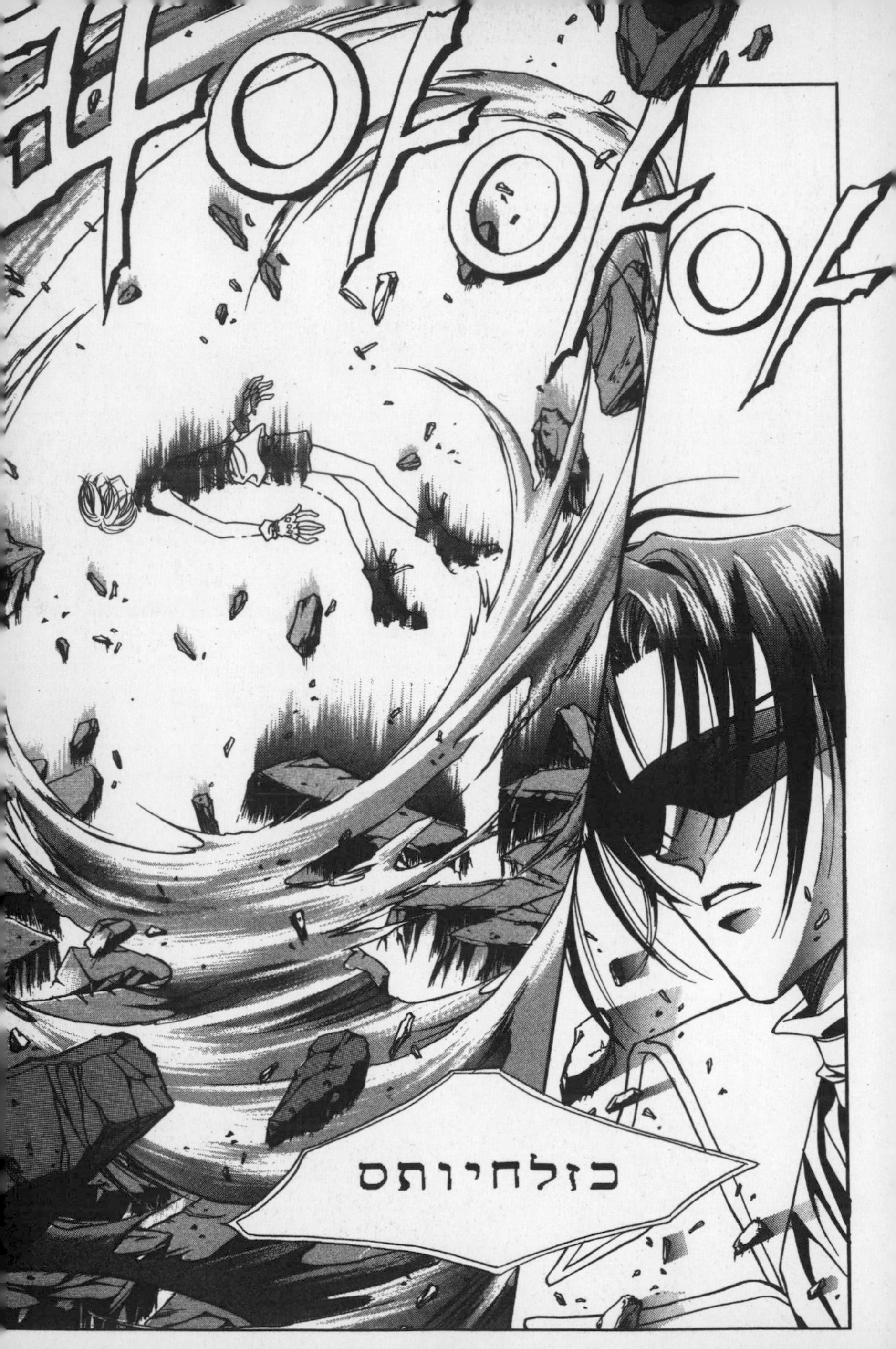

כזלחיותס

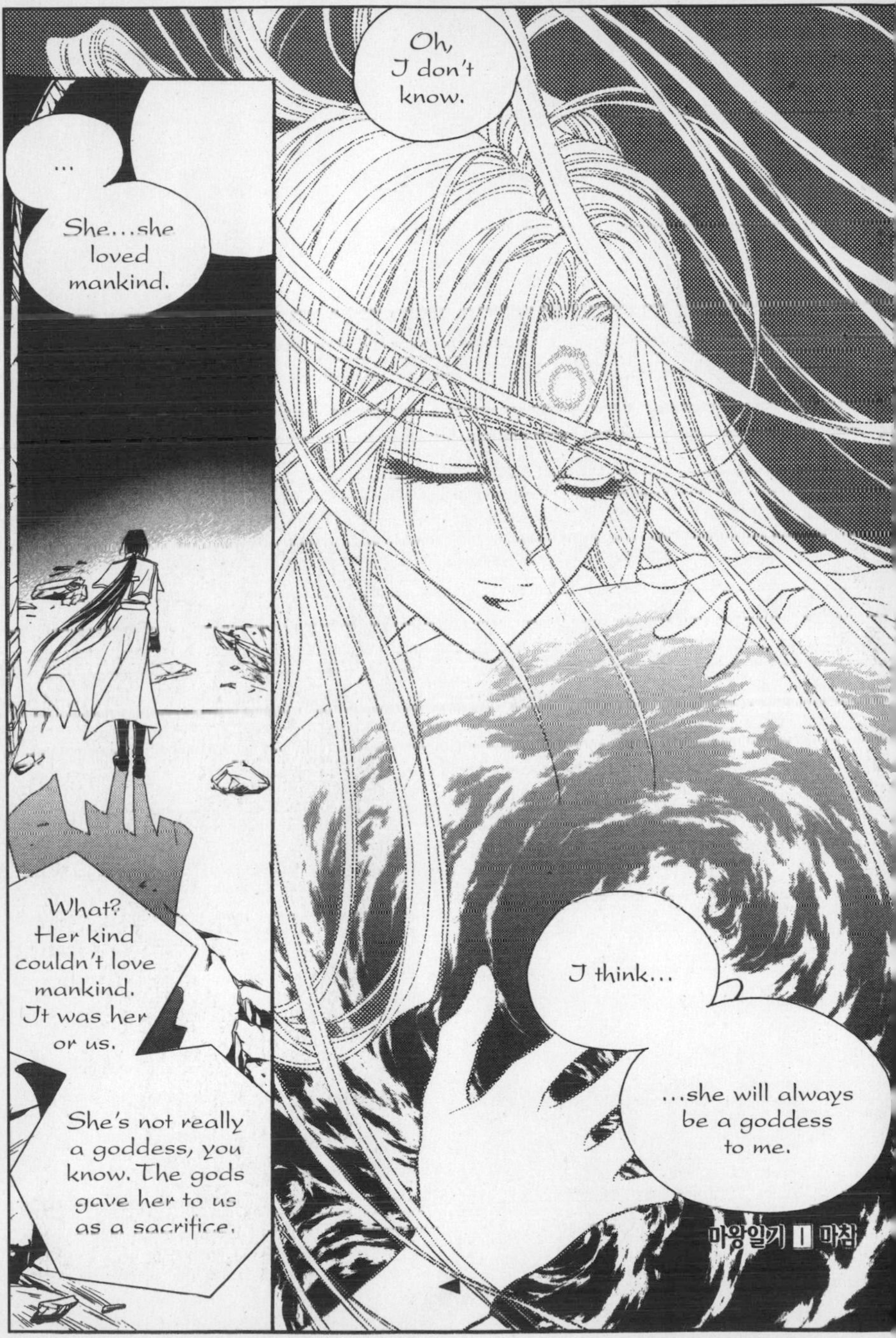
Oh, I don't know.
...
She...she loved mankind.
What? Her kind couldn't love mankind. It was her or us.
She's not really a goddess, you know. The gods gave her to us as a sacrifice.
I think...
...she will always be a goddess to me.
마왕일기 1 마침

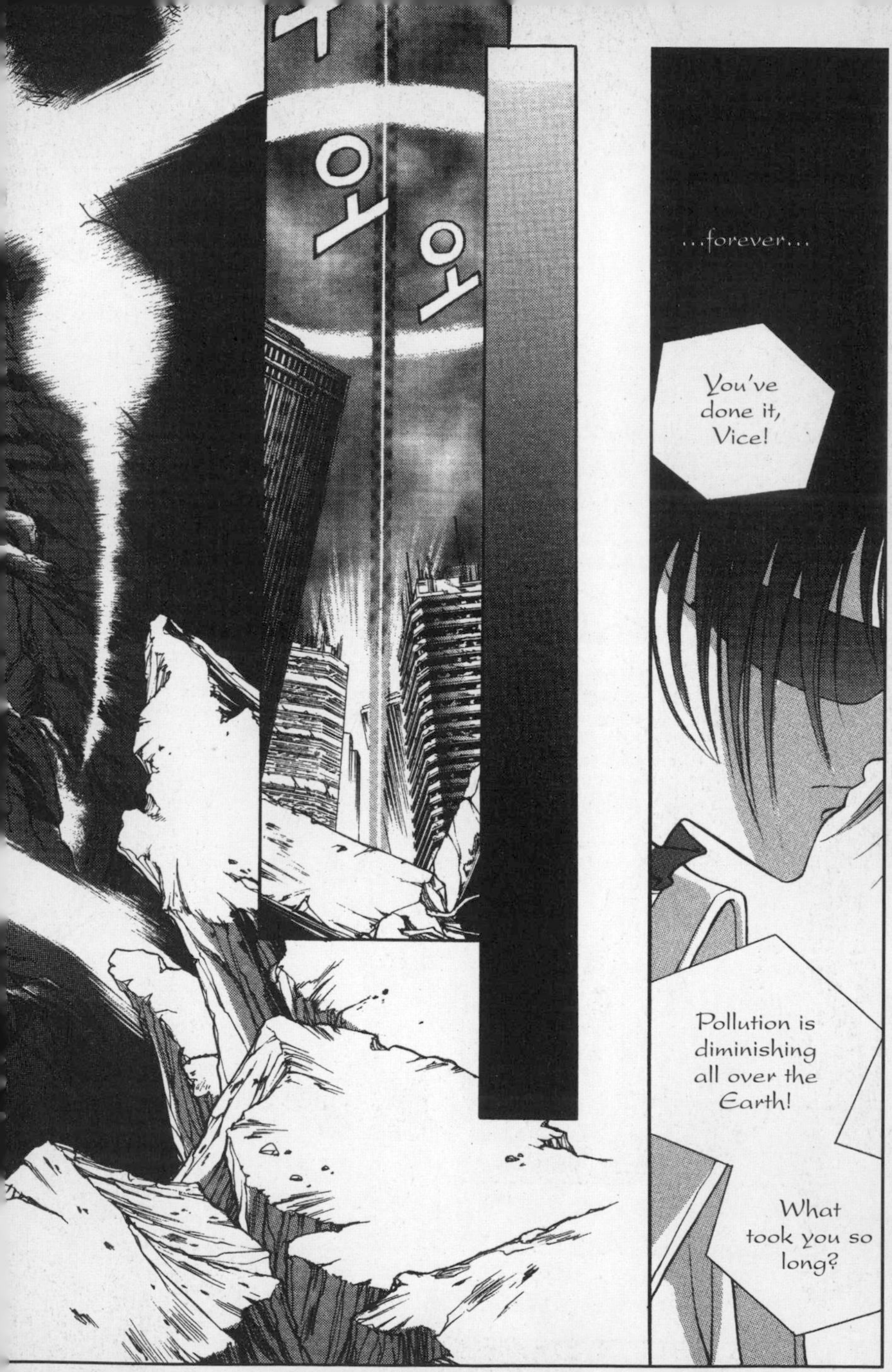

...forever...
You've done it, Vice!
Pollution is diminishing all over the Earth!
What took you so long?

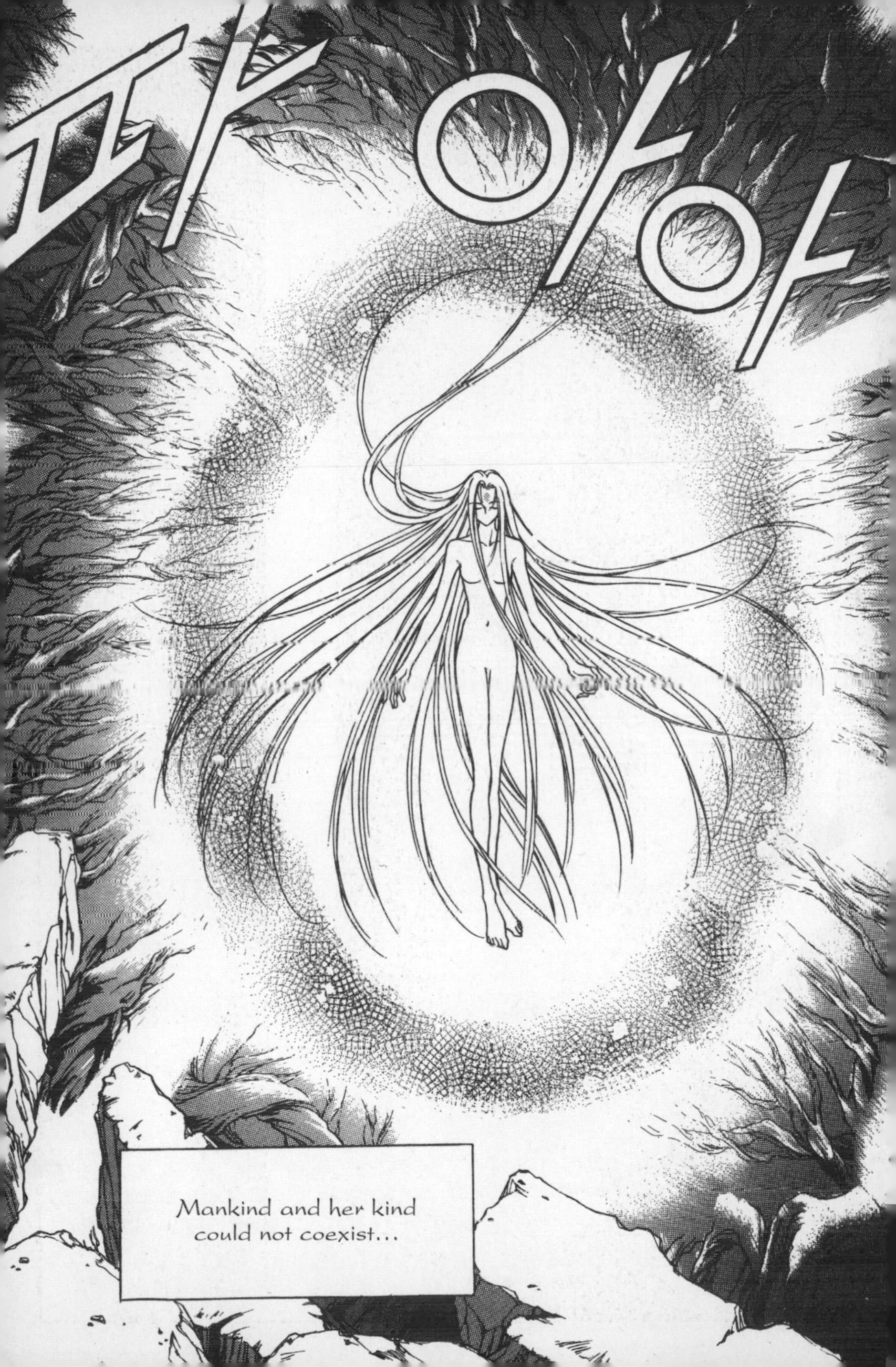
Mankind and her kind
could not coexist...

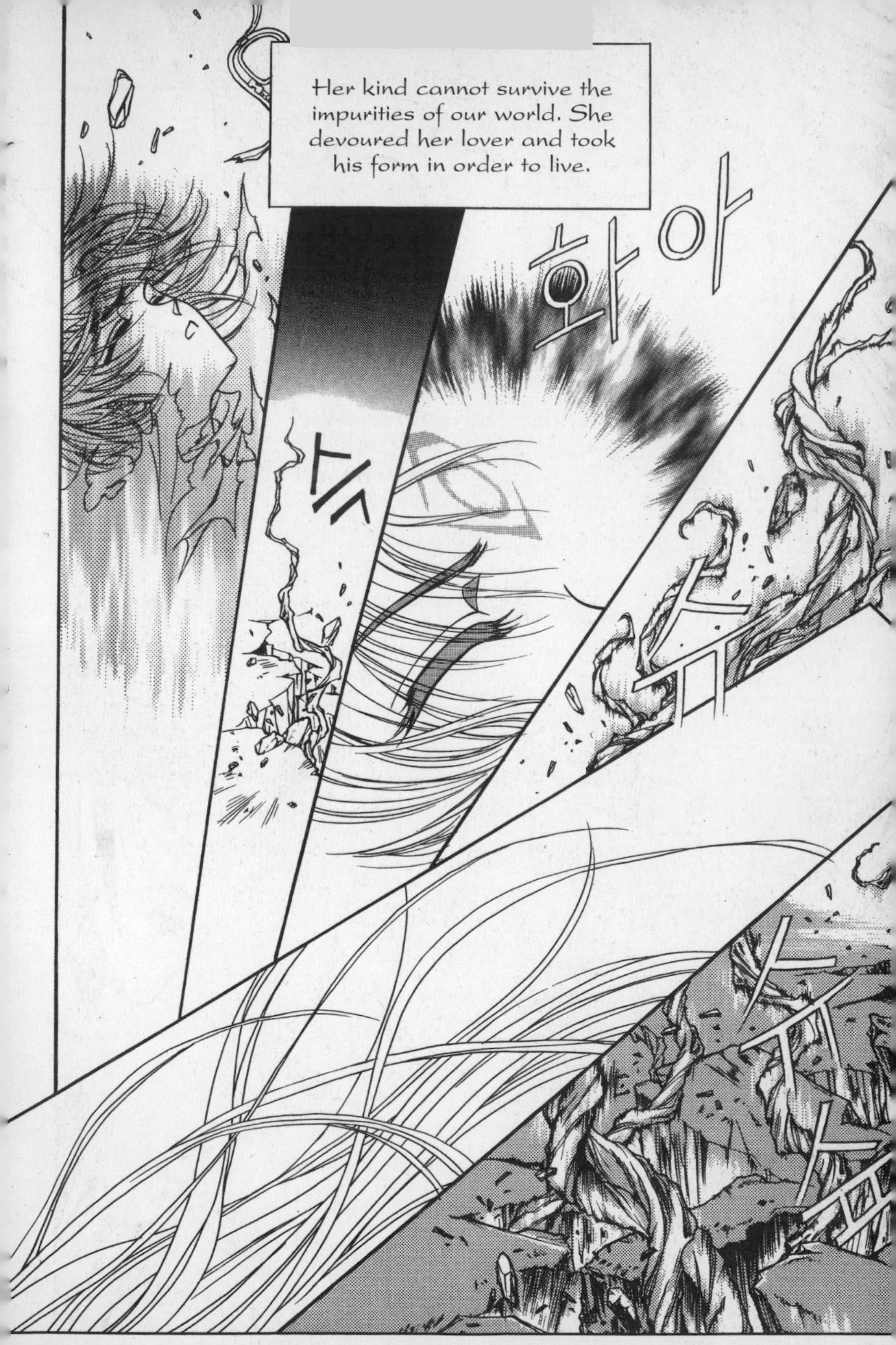
Her kind cannot survive the impurities of our world. She devoured her lover and took his form in order to live.
화아

Preview for Volume 2

After failing his tutor, Eclipse, and sparing the life of an enemy (very un-demonlike!), young Raenef decides to leave his homeland alone until he's become a demon lord. But life in the big world isn't easy for an unskilled demon. There are many who hate demons and would kill Raenef on sight. When Raenef stumbles into the temple of Rased, he meets someone who would love to do just that. Fortunately, Raenef isn't the only one still in training...

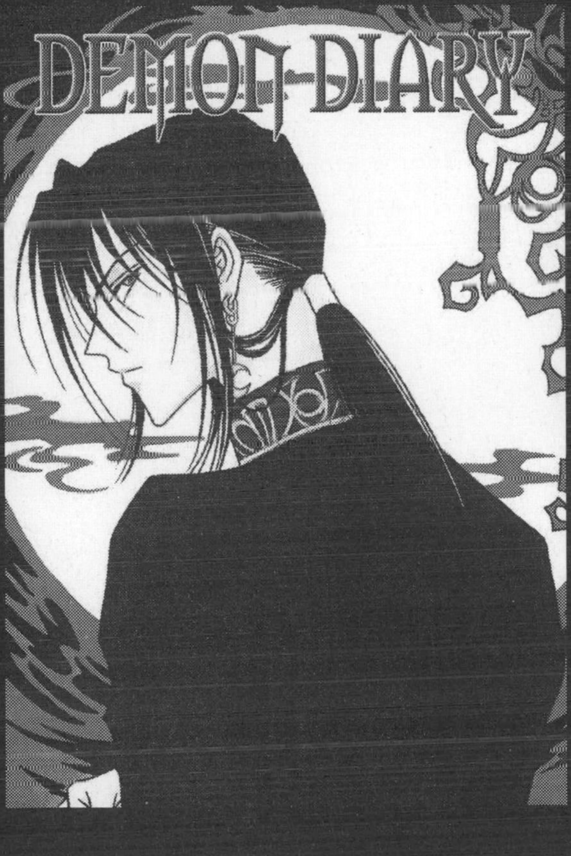
DEMON DIARY